The Perception and Evocation of Literature

Leland H. Roloff
NORTHWESTERN UNIVERSITY

The Perception

and Evocation of Literature

Scott, Foresman and Company

GLENVIEW, ILLINOIS   BRIGHTON, ENGLAND

Credits

page 10, Rene Magritte: "The Golden Legend," Collection of Harry Torczyner, New York. Photograph by Ronald Burkhardt;　page 19, Rene Magritte: "Natural Graces," P. Scheidweiler Collection, Brussels; page 157, Maurits Escher: "Drawing Hands," from the Collection of C. V. S. Roosevelt, Washington, D.C.; pages 172–173, Michael Snow: "Five Girl Panels," Collection Department of External Affairs, Ottawa, Courtesy The Isaacs Gallery, Toronto;　pages 246–247, Page from "Concert For Piano and Orchestra" by John Cage. Copyright © 1960 by Henmar Press, Inc., 373 Park Ave. South, New York, N.Y. 10016. Reprint permission granted by the publisher;　page 268, Robert Amft: "Portrait of Angela";　page 274, Roy Lichtenstein: "Varoom." Collection of Kimiko and John Powers, Aspen, Colorado.

IBSN: 0-673-07550-8
Library of Congress Catalog Card Number 72-89832

Regional offices of Scott, Foresman and Company are located in Dallas, Texas; Glenview, Illinois; Oakland, New Jersey; Palo Alto, California; Tucker, Georgia; and Brighton, England.

Acknowledgments

In the public act of personal thanks, I am in the debt of many persons in the development of this book: my editors at Scott, Foresman, numerous colleagues throughout the country, sympathetic friends. But in the cases of the following individuals, they have contributed to the manuscript in more elusive and less tangible ways. Tempted as I am to give to each a personal citation, I will only state that they are all teachers and personal friends, and that they have, in the truest sense of the word, fulfilled Horace Mann's trenchant observation, "A teacher affects eternity; there is no knowing where his influence stops." They are Wallace A. Bacon, Janet Bolton, Norman Freestone, Charlotte Lee, William B. McCoard, Frances McCurdy, Francine Merritt, Robert Overstreet, Omar Paxson, June Singer, Edwina Snyder, and Beverly Whitaker.

There is one colleague and friend, however, whose perceptions have shaped every sentence (except this one). She is Joan G. Roloff, my wife, and it is to her that this book is dedicated. We share together a longing that C. G. Jung has expressed so well: "The longing for light is the longing for consciousness."

Ultimately, there would have been no book, whatever my personal intentions might have been, had there not existed those teachers whose venture toward an understanding of literature was, in the final word, courage itself—my students.

Leland H. Roloff
Evanston, Illinois

Preface

The Perception and Evocation of Literature is an approach to the study of literature through the performing self. It draws the student to an understanding of the fact that his body "thinks," that his physiological and psychological processes are inextricably bound in all acts of understanding. When the body thinks, all of these processes are united: bodily sensations that see, hear, touch, smell, and taste; feelings that spring from within the individual and attach values to what is perceived; intuitions that non-rationally perceive alternatives and possibilities; and thinking that compares, defines, differentiates. The senses encounter; the feelings shape reactions; the intuitions expand the senses into possible but unseen meanings; and thinking defines experience. Obviously, all of us have not developed all functions equally, nor will we ever be likely to. But through study we can cultivate and affirm the variety of processes by which the body thinks.

When a student performs literature, when he extends all those physiological and psychological dimensions that he senses in a piece of literature, he discovers what can seldom be explicated: "the seamless web" of literature's implicative reaches.[1] Such an approach is not an attempt to supplant intellectual and cognitive studies of literature, or to arrogate the study of literature to solely a performing base. It is, rather, an alternative to the traditional critical approach to literature which is the academic experience of most students. Many instructors have felt that studying literature exclusively through intellectual analyses and definitions is something of an incomplete approach. Alternatives, however, have not always been clear. This book defines and explores behavioral alternatives and stresses the shared performance of literature as well as acts of perception and certain of the more elusive aspects of apperception. The overriding intent of the book is to enlarge the instructional parameters of literary study.

Pedagogically, the book is arranged to promote incremental understanding and growth in the complementary processes of perception and evocation. The first seven chapters describe what happens in literature from the silent performance of reading to its public utterance. The bodily states and behaviors in literature that must be performed are identified. The various kinds of time which literature occupies within its internal contexts are explored. The particular demands of figurative thought and language are examined. And the form, style, and personae that literary genres create are studied. From the indisputable premise that literature is art, the text encourages the student to conceive the performance of it as a process no less compelling and provocative than the literature itself. Because of the implications in Chapter 1 concerning the performance of literature, that chapter should be considered the base upon which succeeding chapters build. Indeed, a student might be asked

---

1. Stanley Burnshaw's *The Seamless Web* (New York: George Braziller, 1970) is a sustained essay of concentrated attention to the physiological and psychological bases of literature. It is strongly recommended reading.

to read Chapter 1 with a certain degree of tentativeness at the beginning of the term, returning to it at the end for additional probing and discussion. The chapter is conceived not only as an introduction but as a summation, and should be so used.

For instructors who are, perhaps, unfamiliar with the vagaries of performance, it is urged that *criticisms* of performances be replaced with *evaluation processes* that are primarily constructive and that facilitate student growth. Students in the delicate domain of artistic growth profit more from positive reinforcements than from any other single influence. Not all students experience immediate success or polish in performance (indeed, many are quite intimidated by it), and their differing abilities require the most sensitive nurturing. A student can hardly be penalized for what he cannot do; that special care be taken to insure individual growth cannot be stressed enough. To facilitate this growth, a Performance Evaluation Form has been developed to assist incremental growth in terms of the behavioral objectives of each chapter. This chart appears at the end of the first seven chapters. With the study of each chapter, the student advances another step on the chart until, at the end of Chapter 7, he should be prepared to respond meaningfully to questions on all aspects of a performance.

For those instructors who wish to develop analytical attitudes and skills in their students, a Checklist for Analysis also appears at the end of each chapter. It, too, stresses a cumulative growth in perception. The Checklist, increasing by one question for each chapter, consists of seven general questions covering literature in performance. While the content of each chapter stands by itself, the Checklist provides a continuity of intellectual purview and conceptual interrelatedness. The instructor has the freedom to give each chapter its special emphasis while at the same time the Checklist is a reminder of the larger context in which material should be considered for performance.

The Exercises and Assignments accompanying each chapter are obviously to be used for directed student work. They can, as well, serve as models for projects that students and instructors may wish to develop together.

A fresh variety of poetry, fiction, and drama has been included, some of it analyzed closely within the text to demonstrate a point and some of it for student presentation. Materials have been selected for each chapter on the basis of their direct bearing on the chapter's purposes, but students and instructors should feel free to draw from literature throughout the text at any time and also from other sources.

The photographs are intended as nonverbal probes of each chapter's emphasis and can be used to stimulate discussion in their own right.

This book's purpose, more than any other, is to lead the student to respond with all of his being to the "touch of art"—to that which is most expressive of man, and in so doing, by that touch, to be changed.

Art touches things and, as by a touch of magic, changes them. Eventually it changes the world and man along with it so that what is outside man should show itself as being own to man and man as own to it. An indifferent nature touched by art turns into a genuinely human world and man becomes an authentic dweller within it.[2]

2. Albert Hofstadter, *Agony and Epitaph* (New York: George Braziller, 1970), p. 55.

Contents

Literature as a Presentational Act   6

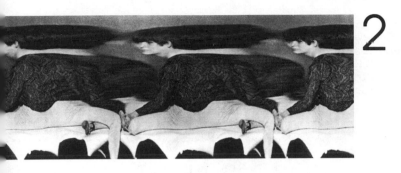

2

Behavior in Performance　60

3

Time in the Performance of Literature

4

The Perception and Evocation of Figurative Language   154

Language as Symbolism   156

The Performer as Icon   156
    Symbolic Processes Inherent in Presentation   157

Figurative Language   159
    Symbols and Sensory Perception   159
    Animism   160
    Figurative Meaning Versus Literal Meaning   160

5

The Perception and Evocation of Form   182

Form Defined in Poetry and Prose   185

Form as Experience   187

Form as Structure   189
    The Auditory Form   189
    The Printed Form   190
    Set Patterns and Free Patterns   192

6

The Perception and Evocation of Style 264

7

The Perception and Evocation of Personae 302

8

Multiforms: Experimental Approaches   344

The Perception and Evocation of Literature

Introduction

André Kertész

This book is a small act of participation in a tradition so old its origins are speculative. Literature, born in the oral tradition, is emerging from its long association with print into its original acoustical and spatial dimensions. A new generation knows this feelingfully and instinctively. What once motivated a man to write a poem can now prompt the creation of a film, or a vast orchestration of electronically manipulated sound, or a mixed-media environment that entirely envelops the participants. This sense of envelopment is the restoration of the oral tradition; but it is, at the same time, the creation of a new one. The study of the oral presentation of literature, as approached in this book, links these traditions of the old and the new.

What is the oral study of literature? It is, at its most fundamental, *somatic thinking*—that is, thinking, intuiting, and feeling about literature with the body. Somatic thinking transmutes intellectual, critical responses to literature into intuitive and "knowing" responses of all the body: the voice, the musculature, the senses. But performances of literature originating somatically are not mere performances nor acts of self-indulgent posturings imposed upon unwary audiences by "elocutionists," "actors," and "readers"—terms stamped as pejorative by those who opt for silent reading and cool reflection. Rather, the oral and bodily study of literature is a profound engagement with a vulnerable self. It is an act of being nakedly human, publicly. It is a presentational act of literature that is a "showing" and a "telling" simultaneously. *To show* and *to tell:* what better substantive verbs can describe literature's effects?

This book leads the student to understand that thinking about literature and revealing literature in a presentational act are not two separate and discrete acts. They never can be truly separate. Our bodies reveal our minds. Two hundred years of silent reading have advanced the illusion of the separation of mind and body, intellect and emotion, reflective thought and generative behavior. Thinking and feeling about literature can be accomplished by means other than literary and rhetorical criticism. Literature is an art form, and so may be the performance of it. The two mutually include each other. How this mutuality might be better understood has shaped the approaches in the text that follows.

It is not easy to restore the wisdom of the body and of the feeling-filled soul, or to trust in the judgments of the body. The soul has been out of fashion in education, and its neglect has wreaked an inestimable toll. However, the holistic position of the nature of man is being argued once again by psychiatrists, psychologists, anthropologists, sociologists, humane men of letters, and—most persuasively—by a fresh breed of students challenging every assumption of learning and education. Man cannot help but benefit, if he will but heed the urgings.

Literature, the act of *poesis* or of giving language over for observation, is one of the many art forms comprising that intangible epoxy uniting man with himself. No critic or student of literature denies this. Literature can also be a thing in itself, an act of personal outrage, an argument, a philosophy of life. Literature is a thing of fashion, responding to currents and sensibilities of a time and a people. It is protean in its shapes, in its forms, in its styles, in its diction; and because it is forever *un*stable, it is often taught from a prescriptive bias. It is evaluated: the poor, the fair, the good, the best, and—eventually—the classic, the monument, the ultimate. Thus, we are taught a priori to understand what makes literature, or a piece of literature, work. The approach of this book, through the study of presentational form, begins not with canons or critical guidelines but with perception of form and effect, of utterance, behavior, and knowing. It is *sensibly* oriented, restoring to that word a confidence in the sensorium of experience.

Also, the intent in the oral study of literature is to integrate the *wholeness* of space-time-sound. This approach urges, ultimately, a trust in the simultaneity of multiple perceptions of what the human organism sees, hears, feels; and in so doing, it establishes an appreciation for the wholeness of literature that emerges from the integration of parts.

The print culture of the past four hundred years has produced works of literature *for print* and for print alone; however, these works often yield to the transformation of space-time-sound, and in the transformation of presentation can yield values unrecognized in silent reading. Our willingness to hear poets read their works aloud, to enjoy the art forms of film and television which consistently transform one medium into another, and—most significantly—the indestructability of interest in the oral interpretation of literature from the time of Homer or even earlier, attest to our natural response to space-time-sound experiences. The best case for the oral study of literature is usually made by the students who have studied it well, in depth, and with the courage it ultimately takes to confront others in a presentation.

This book asks the student to approach this study in the following ways: (1) to sense, to observe, to participate in the *totality* of a literary act before knowing, perhaps, how the literary act was put together; (2) to understand his body as a performing vehicle; (3) to renew awareness of how time is experienced; (4) to enter the imaginative domains that language creates; (5) to appreciate the elements of form and style; and (6) to listen to dialogue (and its implications) of dramatized persons. These six goals constitute what can be called the essentials—the irreducible elements—of literature in performance. There is no text that can inform anyone *how* to perform; there is an approach, the one taken in this text, that asks two questions: (1) What happens in literature? and (2) What happens in performance? How the student achieves his leap of understanding from his knowledge of literary perceptions to the performing evocations is, ultimately, his own ''mystery.'' It is his mystery in the medieval sense of the word as it applied to the learning of a craft—as in learning the "mystery" of carpentry, of baking, of silversmithing. Thus, the mystery plays, the stories of the Bible presented by common folk and tradesmen in medieval England, were not "mysterious plays" but, rather, plays given by craftsmen who knew the mystery of their work. The students who willingly apprentice themselves to the perception and evocation of literature may be assured that life given poetic utterance places the perceiver and evocator on the edge of the *mysterium tremendum*, and that they will return to the daily affairs of life in a body and being transformed.

Objectives for Performance Growth

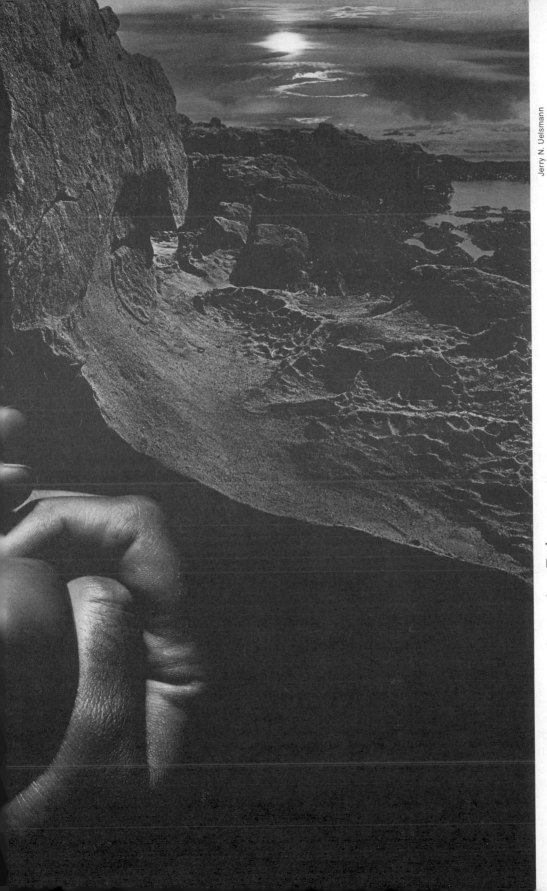

Jerry N. Uelsmann

TO PERCEIVE AND EVOKE THE METAWORLDS OF LITERATURE

—by developing a creative
disposition

—by responding to the
presentative values of the
literature

—by evoking the wholeness of
the literary experience

—by allowing language to
energize a genuine sense
of performance

CHAPTER ONE

Literature as a Presentational Act

The performer of literature translates language into a behaviorial act, into a moment that is pure transformation for him and his listener. He begins by studying the special nature of literature and the literary act. And he then seeks to learn the processes that can most effectively assist him in the translation and transformation of literature into performance.

THE UNIQUENESS OF LITERATURE

From the stance of the performing artist, the unique characteristics of literary material are these: (1) Literature depends upon—is, in fact, inseparable from—*performance;* (2) Literature creates *metaworlds*—worlds within worlds whose reality is primarily in the mind; and (3) Literature is oriented essentially to *acoustic space.*

LITERATURE AND PERFORMANCE ARE INSEPARABLE

With only a little thought we can recognize the inherently performing nature of all literature. It offers or presents itself to our sensory awareness as a performance. There is no such thing as literature without a performance, and this truth unites all men who value the use of language and symbol in creating, re-creating, and interpreting human experience.

When we read to ourselves or others, silently or aloud, we are engaged in a performance. What is read is pictured, is felt, is thought about. Actually, we give to the act of reading a *series* of performances. With the eye, we perform acts of scanning, of perceiving, of sending to the brain a succession of coded, symbolized messages.

Consider the first line from Robert Frost's "Stopping by Woods on a Snowy Evening":

Whose woods these are I think I know . . .

This is a relatively simple message, easily symbolized: it is performed almost effortlessly. Because the thought is expressed in a common language, the reader's understanding is not impeded or impaired by any sense of the unfamiliar, the strange, or the rare.

Now read:

'Twas brillig, and the slithy toves
Did gyre and gimble in the wabe . . .

These lines from Lewis Carroll's "Jabberwocky" are familiar, but in a rather unexpected way that is subtle and innovative. If it were "brillig," and if indeed "the slithy toves did gyre and gimble in the wabe," then understanding the passage is suddenly complicated by a factor which one was not forced to think about when reading the Robert Frost line: *the structure of the language.* Only grammatically are the lines from "Jabberwocky" familiar. Abruptly, the mental-performance world of the reader is arrested. He knows that there is no *wabe,* and he knows that he has never seen a *tove.* There may be something familiar in the verb *gyre,* but what of the word *gimble?* The structure of the English language and the performance of the words in relationship to each other present Carroll's marvelous nonsense to the reader in a way calculated to create in him the sense of a world never before seen or heard, a world instantly created by the power and alchemy of language.

Thus, whether the individual reads silently, or whether he listens to or watches a performance of literature by another individual or group of individuals, language creates new and inner worlds which are real to the perceiver, worlds in which he believes, worlds to which he reacts, and worlds which—when conveyed with a touch of genius—live with him always. We call them *metaworlds,* and their importance to the oral interpreter of literature will be discussed in some detail.

LITERATURE CREATES METAWORLDS

Despite the fact that a metaworld is a reality only within the mind, the existence of such a world is readily accepted. Regardless of how strange or remote it may be, we say that it "really" exists: we *believe* in it. We suspend our disbelief. The reader be-

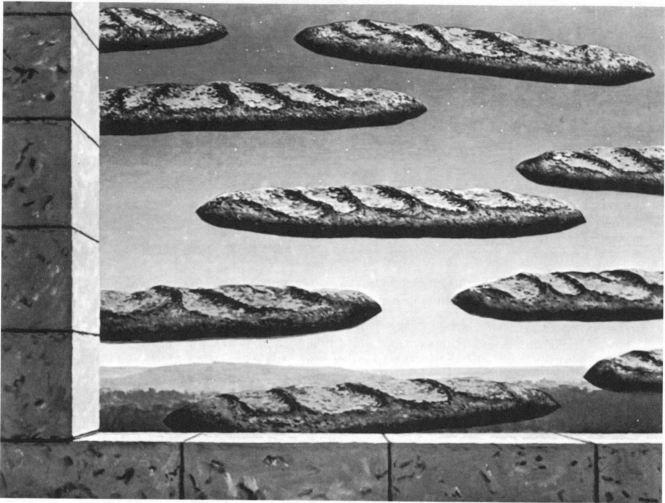

lieves in the world of Homer, and he relives the mortal battle between Hector and Achilles. Fictively, the reader believes in Beowulf and in the struggle with Grendel under the sea. Familiar to us all are the metaworlds of Shakespeare — worlds within worlds of errant kings, lovesick courtiers, dallying maids, a suicidal prince. For many of us the metaworld of Romeo and Juliet or of Antony and Cleopatra is *the* world of all doomed lovers.

Finally, we should remember that since metaworlds are created both by silent reading and by oral performances of literature, the metaworld of silent creation may be jarred or enhanced by the metaworld voiced in performance. In our time much of this conflict may be traced to the fact that we are oriented to the printed page rather than to what we will refer to as *acoustic space*.

LITERATURE IS ORIENTED TO ACOUSTIC SPACE

For the greater part of man's history, literature was not printed; literature was uttered. Literature was created and transmitted *orally* as myth, story, fable, song, poem, chant, rite, ritual, and play. In earlier times (and in some primitive cultures today), literature was communicated to the young by tribal ceremonies, rituals, and other presentational forms. Before print, before the abundance of books printed and produced faster than the human capacity to read and absorb them, this tradition of the spoken performance of literature prevailed. Sometimes this presentation in acoustic space has been called the *oral tradition,* sometimes the *bardic tradition.* And it is from this tradition that the folk epic, the folktale, the fable, the ballad, the lyric, and the myth have come to us.

The notion of literature as print, as book available to all men, began with the invention of movable type by Johann Gutenberg in the middle of the fifteenth century. As one result, from the seventeenth to the twentieth century the acoustic-space world of literature was temporarily replaced by the one-dimensional world of the printing press. Necessarily, in most cultures great emphasis was, and continues to be, placed upon literacy. The education of the young has been concentrated on the ability of the child to read the printed page, and through this medium he is introduced very early to the metaworlds of story and poem. The acoustic world and space of early man, to a very large extent replaced by the printing press, have thus been almost lost to modern man.

Fortunately, during the past few decades—due largely to the advent of the motion picture, the radio, and television—the oral tradition is experiencing a rebirth. In today's electronic world many individuals are introduced to metaworlds of literature through visual and auditory presentations *before* they learn how to read. Here, in the twentieth century, with the development and expansion of such media as recordings, tapes, film cameras and projectors, television tubes, and videotapes, acoustic space has been redeveloped and expanded. Now in milliseconds electrical transmission can unite men all over the earth in a single acoustic event. This use of sound for the presentation of literature—as well as sight and some of the other senses—has been hailed as *return* to acoustic space. In fact, Marshall McLuhan uses the phrase to describe a world which is sound oriented, which is dependent upon sound for the meaningful learning of culture, and which is filled with machines and devices for instantaneous "hearing" and "seeing."

The performer should keep in mind that acoustic space, in all the history of human kind, has been used to confront man with his apparently insatiable need: to give form to experience and in literature—more precisely—*to give voice to experience.* Literature is, then, life released in language. *Literature is language performed by life.*

PERCEPTION, EVOCATION, AND CREATIVITY

There is no reason why a student should stand helpless before a piece of literature. Nor is there any reason why a performance of literature should be a paralyzing and deadly experience for an audience. Within the oral tradition of storytelling, of singing of love and death, and of giving flesh and voice to dramatic characters, a sense of excitement and expectancy exists. Philosophers and critics continue ever to be fascinated by the *effect* of literature; that it does indeed *affect* is beyond question.

The performer's perceptions of literature and the potential evocations radiating from the literature constitute the two irreducible factors in the performance of the literature: *perception* and *creativity*.

PERCEPTION

Any truly coherent performance of literature is an amalgam of many discrete perceptions. Though these perceptions may vary in complexity and difficulty, they are essential, indeed basic, to any sensitive appreciation of the literary act of creation. In the silent performance of reading, the reader perceives the metaworld created by the literature; that is, he evokes or calls forth certain sensory awarenesses *within himself*, and the sum of these awarenesses or perceptions makes up the metaworld for him. Thus, the reader's acts of perception yield an evocation. When the performance of the literature is an *oral* act—an act intended to evoke perceptions *in others*—that which is evoked becomes more complex. In such situations, where interaction with the literature and with others is intended, the responsibility of the performer to be sensitive to and perceptive of the evocative elements within the literature is of crucial importance. When literature is being performed in acoustic space, the audience is dependent upon the performer for its perception of the evocative elements. In other words, oral performance requires "creative" evocation; and in order better to understand this idea, we need to look closely at one concept of creativity.

CREATIVITY

Contemporary studies in creativity suggest that the act of creation is an attempt to express the uncommunicable.[1] For many this is no doubt an extremely bewildering

---

1. While it would be impossible to cite the literature in so brief a space, there are two works of interest to students: Arthur Koestler, *The Act of Creation* (New York: Macmillan Co., 1964), and Anton Ehrenzweig, *The Hidden Order of Art* (Berkeley: University of California Press, 1967).

notion to accept. Yet, when we consider the effect of the literary artist upon a sensitive reader, the idea comes more sharply into focus: the writer, the original artist, has taken an experience which most people find "inexpressible" and has given it expression. By creating, he has expressed the inexpressible, the uncommunicable. In the actual performance of literature, the interpretive artist imbues the event with this sense of wonder at the accuracy with which the original creator has put into words an idea, an experience, a feeling which had generally been considered inexpressible. The interpreter communicates this wonder, restoring it and creating it anew.

To appreciate more fully the impact of performance, let us examine briefly how research explains this phenomenon of accepting the expression of the creative artist. When men share a common language, they also share many common ways of thinking about the world, its events, the nature of life, the inevitability of death, and so on. Most people experience these commonalities rather early as they coexist in the families in which they are reared. The individual learns to think the way his family thinks, at least for a while. When many families are put together, communities are created; and collected communities add up to nations and national cultures. Ordinarily, the resultant collective manner of thinking is taken for granted. The popular literature —popular magazines, popular novels, popular music, popular motion pictures— expresses these collective modes of thought. These "popular" modes of expression reflect "popular" ways of thinking.

Seldom are there serious artists of popular expression. An artist's original expression may, in time, become popular; or he may choose a popular form of expression, but what he does with it is likely to be quite innovative or at least arresting. A creative mind refuses to accept, or veers away from accepting, the collective manner of thinking. Creative thinking forces us to reclassify our thoughts, to perceive a world of experience by a use of language not tried before, or through a use of language we have not previously considered possible for expression.

A fresh voice in poetry, for example, almost always experiences an unfavorable reaction from readers oriented to collective thinking. On initial appearance, the works of T. S. Eliot, James Joyce, Dylan Thomas, and other greats of twentieth-century expression did not receive immediate acceptance. Even educated sensibilities can be offended by unfamiliar modes of expression, by new and daring forms. John Keats, whose work is usually regarded as the finest example of Romantic expression, raised the ire of a critic who, upon reading Keats for the first time, penned a now-immortal line of criticism about a poet and his poetry: "This will never do." Fortunately, in large part because the creative mind refuses to abide conventional boundaries, culture is blessed with the gift of a literature that grows and is not static. Literate members of a society—some soon, some later—learn how to respond to the metaworlds perceived and evoked by its more creative artists.

LITERATURE IS DEPENDENT UPON MANY PERFORMANCES:

It is dependent upon the capacity to conceive and perceive.

It is dependent upon the capacity to understand the language and its structure, although they may vary significantly from what is familiar.

It is dependent upon an inner capacity to create imaginatively the world of the literature within the human psyche, to conceive of metaworlds.

It is dependent upon artists who give voice to experience, who do so through symbols and language, and whose language energizes a genuine sense of performance.

In understanding creativity we need to remember, too, that *a creative expression is not so much informative as it is evocative.* By this we mean that the creative expression may tell us very little about what took place in the mind and body of the artist. Moreover, the expression itself does not exist as a copy of the experience. What happens when we experience literature is that the artist's statement triggers a series of responses within the reader and/or the hearer. *These responses, in turn, awaken and evoke reactions not hitherto thought about; each new response stimulates new perceptual relationships between events.* As a result, we have not one but many possible performances in the interpretation of literature.

CREATIVE DISPOSITION VERSUS CREATIVE ACT

Every student of literature, and most particularly the performer who is seriously concerned with its perception and evocation, is involved in the affective domain. The performer's obligation is to cast a spell, to evoke magic, to achieve an alchemy of language. To do this, the beginning student of performance needs to understand the difference between the concepts of *creative disposition* and *creative (or re-creative) act.*

THE CREATIVE DISPOSITION

At first glance, the relationship between most audiences and the performing artist appears to be essentially this: the audience is creatively disposed toward the literary event whereas the artist is performing a creative act. A creative disposition, which can characterize both an actively engaged performer and a passively receptive audience, is a willingness to respond to the language of the original artist. *Both* the audience and the performing artist, then, may be creatively disposed toward the literary event and, in fact, *must* be for successful interaction. While most people, it is true, do not profess to be creative artists, they do have the capacity to recognize what they felt but did not say themselves when they encounter it in literature; that is, they have a creative *disposition* toward it.

Of course, no two people will have identical creative dispositions toward a piece of literature. This may explain in part why writers often are reluctant to permit public performances of their work: they mistrust the nature of the creative disposition within the performer, and in particular they fear the performer may bend the literature to exaggerated extremes.

Most studies of literature, taught as they are through critical approaches, are based on the assumption that what is gained from the study is a creative disposition toward literature as an art form. Or, more simply, students are taught to read or to listen to the creative acts of a writer by consenting to participate in the dispositions of that writer. When a student complains, "I cannot understand what that author is saying," what he may really be saying is, "I do not have any disposition to read that writer." Or a puzzled student may mutter, "This writer says everything in an *unfamiliar language!*" That, precisely, is the writer's intention: What makes a writer a writer is that he writes "his language."

THE CREATIVE ACT

Whereas within an audience, ideally, creative dispositions facilitate receptivity and reaction, the oral interpreter *acts* upon his creative dispositions, as well as those of his hearers. As Jaroslav Havelka points out, a creative disposition in an artist ends in an act of creative expression.[2] To a degree, this may explain why we have audiences for creative acts: it is the creative artist who follows through on his disposition to listen to himself.

One of the values in studying the performance of literature is that the student, in being challenged to give an evocation, breaks down his own provinciality. Literature forces him—when he chooses to let it do so—to seek new levels of creative dispositions, to evolve new creative willingnesses which can function within himself. And, further, in the creative act of a performance, the student explores and experiences, profoundly, the sense of participation.

The interaction of creative disposition and creative act assures that every literary act is fresh and novel. The performing artist, in having a creative disposition for and in moving toward a creative act, sets up within himself and his auditor a sense of

2. Jaroslav Havelka, *The Nature of the Creative Process in Art, a Psychological Study* (The Hague: Martinus Nijhoff, 1968), p. 50.

resonance—an empathic echo—whether this resonance emanates from hearing an old tale told anew and freshly, or whether it is a new story expressed in a strange and different mode. *The affect of art is resonance.* This resonance creates a tension, a kind of cognitive dissonance, and a compelling center of interest within both the interpretive artist and his hearers. Metaworlds are energized into being; evocations generate forms of energy between the literary work of art and those who receive it; and creativity flows swiftly in a two-way stream between audience and artist.

Arthur Tress

LITERATURE AS PROCESS

Many people, if they stop to think about art at all, tend to think of art as an *art object:* a painting they can recall, a piece of sculpture they admire, an object which exists in substantive and literal form, a tangible object confronting them in space. In our print-oriented world, it is natural to conceive first of a poem as something existing in print, as a perceptual object which can be seen on a page. Even a novel is thought of as an entity contained in a book. For the interpretive artist, however, literature cannot be viewed as a fixed and static art object. While a poem or novel may indeed be an art work, the performer will more accurately view it as an "art working." Literature, for him, is *art in process.* Literature, he knows, is something that must be revealed or disclosed to the perceiver unit by unit, piece by piece, element by element, image by image. It is incremental. It can never be fixed and finished in our minds because it is always in the process of becoming. Like a piece of music, it can only be disclosed in time. In disclosing the content of literature, the performer is creating a process situation that subtly but surely requires his auditors to forget about literature as an object. In the hands of a skilled performer, the literature seems to be creating its *own* existence, forming itself from the words, lines, stanzas, or other elements of the piece.

The performer of literature attempts to reveal the "workings" of a literary experience. He tries to give a *presentational form* to literature, to create a metaworld so impinging, so alive, so real to the inner senses that the external world of the receiver is forgotten. In the effective performance of literature, there is a sense of something being revealed; through the unique impact of sound and physical presence emanating from a performer, the perceiver senses an art form working upon and within him. What he sees and hears happening before him is *both the literature and the performer attaining a state of being.*

This is no accident, no mystical occurrence. The performer of literature, as he participates in this transformational process, must recognize the necessity of maintaining certain attitudes crucial to the attaining of his goal: the artful presentation of the ideas and experiences of the original artist. To begin with, the power of will is involved. If the interpretive artist chooses to perform a particular piece of literature created by another, he cannot impose his own tastes, prejudices, or preferences; he must subordinate his own will and the biases of his own perceptions. This is no small task. Whereas sharing common ways of thinking with many people is relatively easy and frequently pleasurable, giving ourselves over to uncommon ways is difficult, often painful. Moreover, as we have pointed out, the performer must develop an attitude of willing participation, of matching his creative disposition to the creative process of the literature. This means that the performing artist must come to rely heavily upon his intuition. Paradoxically, many students who come to the performing arts from academic backgrounds have been cautioned not always to trust their intuitive inclinations. Yet, in the performance of literature, it is of paramount importance that the artist develop his intuition and learn to act confidently upon it.

To reiterate, then, a piece of literature is not an art object; a performance of literature is not an art object. Both are art works: they cannot be perceived as a totality and all at once. Literature reveals itself incrementally, unit by unit. Performance, too, is incremental; and by gradually disclosing human experiences, it works itself into the consciousness of those who hear and perceive it.

THE PERFORMER OF LITERATURE AS AUXILIARY ARTIST

In literature the *primary* act of creation lies with the writer, the man of poesis who uses language as an artist might use paint, a sculptor plastic media, a composer sound. In certain of the art forms—notably music, drama, and literature—the satisfactory fulfillment of the form requires one additional and final creative intuition: that of the performer. The musician, the actor, and the interpreter, then, can be designated appropriately as *auxiliary artists*.

THE ROLE AND FUNCTIONS OF THE AUXILIARY ARTIST

How might the auxiliary artist of literature, the interpreter, best think of himself and his role? His answer must be influenced by these considerations:

Although he does not, as a general rule, create his own literature, he informs himself
 as completely as possible as to the nature of the literary selection.
His media are "timeless" *time*, acoustic *space*, and oral *sound*.
He exists in a unique relationship to his receivers; and because he is involved in an
 interactive situation with them, he explores presentational values in and with
 audience relationships.

How, then, might the performer of literature be defined? Within the framework of the foregoing discussion, we can say *the performer of literature is an expressive artist who utilizes the media of time, space, and sound to communicate intuitive insights of literature and, in so doing, generates a sense of the inevitability of experience from the symbols of feeling inherent in the printed word.*

The performer of literature as a creative auxiliary artist is an effective translator, communicating his intuited and sensed emotional life of the literature to an audience. In his presentation he establishes a sense of experience, externalizing and emphasizing the nature of the internal reactions that the literature creates in him. In this presentation he takes an attitudinal stance which involves (1) an appreciation of the literary act; (2) an appreciation of the expressive elements within the literature; and (3) a willing participation in a behavioral, performative creation of literature.

Rene Magritte: "Natural Graces"

Having entered into the literary experience sympathetically and intuitively, the creative performer now approaches the act of *translation* and should do so in ways that seem both spontaneous and inevitable. In responding to the metaworlds created by the literary artist, the performer comes to know that his task is translating and transforming the stimuli of written symbology into language discernible in audible and visible behavior. In this translation and transformation, the performing artist is reflecting and redefining the function of all art: "An art involves doing something (a process) to and with something (a medium) in order to make or do something else (a product or a performance)."[3] The oral interpreter's capacity to make his mind and imagination freely available to the stimuli of the literature—to allow them to flow within the flexible confines of the literary experience—creates what the audience experiences as *spontaneity* in the performance. This is the performer's creation of a sense of *inevitability;* it is his artistry.

3. Thomas Munro, *The Arts and Their Interrelations* (New York: Liberal Arts Press, 1956), p. 438.

The eminent Italian philosopher of the arts Benedetto Croce once stated that poetry was the presentation of "tissues of imagery."[4] These "tissues" are what the poet perceives and what he produces, and they spring from the artist's mental life, a life committed to observation of the world about him. When the intuitive life is a significant part of living, what is felt is a sense of buoyancy, a wash of feeling that unites the sensory life and the mental life. Small wonder, then, that a performance of literature is seldom intellectual; rather, it is an obvious performing of what the emotional life of man is. When a performer translates a knowledge of emotion into some form of sound and movement, he externalizes his intuition in art.

PERFORMANCE: EXPRESSIVE ACT IN EXPRESSIVE LANGUAGE

Literature performed is an expressive act in expressive language. At one and the same time it is *imaginative creation* and *living speech.* In the moment of performance, the atmosphere is charged with sight, sound, gesture, and the subtle interrelationships among the three. It follows that the techniques of this performing art cannot be isolated because expression and technique exist simultaneously.

When we stated earlier that the performer creates a sense of inevitable experience, we meant that the performer creates an excitement in the present moment; it is in the *present tense* that art is being created. The performer has the power to change the quality of an auditor's life, to create within that auditor a never-ending memory of what a piece of literature is. In this sense art is a celebration of a human experience, whatever that experience may be; and the performance is the act of making that celebration *observable.* The act of expression should emerge as an inevitable experience, suggesting that it could not have happened in any other way.

Words, the irreducible elements of literature, act as the counterpart of the thing they denote: feeling. This denoting is not the feeling itself, but a conception of what a feeling is. Art reveals what a feeling is *like;* it is a transformation of inner worlds as they can be expressed only in the language chosen by the writer. What the performer does is to reveal features of human feelings; he offers a mirror of experience. In showing, for instance, what a tantrum is like, he does not have one.

UNDERSTANDING PRESENTATIVE ART IN LITERATURE

Because the purpose of the performer is to bring to life the literature and the experiencing of it, we may properly call his art "presentative." This kind of presentative act places the literature and the performer into a precise relationship, a relationship

4. Gian N. G. Orsini, *Benedetto Croce; Philosopher of Art and Literary Critic* (Carbondale: Southern Illinois University Press, 1961), p. 25.

which—initially at least—demands that he ask, "What aesthetic *directions* does the literature demand?" To answer this question, the performing artist must ask himself a number of analytical questions:

Is this literature characterized by subtle detail and close observation?
Is this literature an expression of an age, a time, a sensitivity to the pressures of life?
Is this literature an intense vision of a private world of the original artist, a personal
      vision, an intimate discovery of self?
Is this literature primarily an expressive release on the part of the writer?

UNDERSTANDING THE ORIGINAL ARTIST'S INTENTIONS

Once the performer, as auxiliary artist, has begun to ask himself directional questions of this kind, he must become concerned with how the original artist has presented the literature. The performer must ask himself whether the writer has attempted an imitation of an external and outer world or the revelation of an intensely private and inner world. The performer looks at the style of the language and attempts to determine if it is conventional or highly individualized. The term *conventional* suggests the external world and quite probably provides clues as to what we would do or experience in that kind of world; the term *individualized* suggests idiosyncracies of diction, style, and personal vision unique to the original artist. Understandably, a writer may—in a given piece of literature—be more concerned with a replication of an external environment than with a personal view of it; or, conversely, he may be more concerned with evoking a world which he alone has experienced, thus endowing it with his own highly individualistic expression of life. The performer, in order to ascertain the view that he will take of the original artist's creation, will have to concern himself with four types of direction: (1) conventionalized, (2) individualized, (3) imitative, and (4) expressive. By placing these pairs of directions on two intersecting axes, thus:

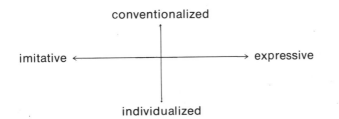

he can begin to determine the structure of presentative art. By adding details and pertinent examples, as suggested in the diagram which follows, he can elaborate upon his assessments of the literature he will eventually perform.

STRUCTURE OF PRESENTATIVE ART [5]

CONVENTIONALIZED

REALISM • NATURALISM • CLASSICISM Discloses the familiar world of our acquaintance in fine detail and great comprehensiveness. **Robert Frost** **Henry James**	EXPRESSIONISTS • ART AND SPIRIT OF THE TIME Reflects the response of a more or less generalized human sensitivity to the pressures of life. **Lord Byron** **Charles Dickens** **William Faulkner**
IMPRESSIONISM • SURREALISM Discovers for us, in the private vision of the artist, aspects of the world that are novel and unsuspected. **Dylan Thomas** **Franz Kafka**	ROMANTICISM • ART AS RELEASE Reflects the personal impact of life and the world upon the individual artist. **William Blake** **Thomas Wolfe** **James Joyce**

IMITATIVE (left axis) — **EXPRESSIVE** (right axis)

INDIVIDUALIZED

ESTABLISHING THE PRESENTATIVE FOCUS

A close study of this diagram will enable the performer-in-training to determine what it is in a literary creation that *asks* to be presented. Clearly, to present a piece written in conventionalized style requires a concentration on quite different presentational values from those he would expect to encounter in, say, material exuberantly written with an individualized style abounding in imitative sounds and words, all brimming with release and expressiveness. The conventionalized style of a writer such as Henry James, for instance, places different demands upon the performer than does the individualized style of Dylan Thomas. How, for example, is the performer to give presentative values to William Blake? *To establish the proper presentative focus is the performer's first task.* This is his primary act of evocation, and all other problems of performance hinge upon and derive from this.

5. Chart adapted from Iredell Jenkins, *Art and the Human Enterprise.* Cambridge, Mass.: Harvard University Press, © 1958. Reprinted by permission.

As the student begins his study of the literature, he must recognize that, whatever the form of expression or the kind of style involved, his function as a performer is to permit the literary selection "to be itself." It is not the performer's function to comment on or editorialize about Robert Frost or Thomas Wolfe or Franz Kafka. As the auxiliary artist, the performer demonstrates what a writer's literary act *is,* doing what *it* does. An art work does not comment upon itself, reflexively stating what it is about; it *acts* and, in the full sense of the present tense, it *is.* It is not "self" conscious; it is a vitalized presence. The performer is the catalyst by which a literary presence is energized and fulfilled.

By the term *presence* in art we mean that strong impression or feeling that the work of art as such has no beginning or end. If it is an act at all, it is an act of continuance: a *process.* In the smile of the Mona Lisa, for example, a sense of timeless and curious presence continues and will continue as long as the painting exists; and even if the painting were to be destroyed, the smile would continue to haunt the minds of those who had seen it. Literature, in the act of being presented, is like this. It is haunted with many presences. It is filled with possibilities for meaning, for enjoyment, for the arrestment of the senses; and these possibilities grow from the moment of confrontation, from the act of presentation.

THE PRESENTATIONAL MODE AS CREATIVE PROBLEM-SOLVING

From what we have said, the performer of literature must now be aware that his performance will require not quantitative but qualitative problem-solving. Every aspect of his study is focused upon acts of judgment, meditation, and direct confrontation with materials which were themselves acts of creation, which were, in effect, acts of qualitative problem-solving.

STEPS IN THE QUALITATIVE PROBLEM-SOLVING PROCESS

The qualitative problem-solving process incorporates six distinct steps:
1. *Confrontation.* Reading the literature for the first time, experiencing it freely and receptively.
2. *Meditation.* Asking "What happened to me in this initial experience? What is this piece of literature all about?"
3. *Control.* Asking "How is this experience kept in directional control? expressively? imitatively? conventionally? by means of a highly individualistic style of expression?"
4. *Recognition of structural dynamics.* Asking "What formal elements make this literature 'work'? What is its structure?"

5. *Exploration.* Putting the selection into performance: exploring the sounds, the gestural realm of the language, the literature as "whole" experience.
6. *Completion.* The actual performance of the literary work.[6]

The qualitative problem-solving sequence is helpful to the degree that it establishes, on the one hand, the idea that the elements for artistic production are qualitative and remain so throughout the creative discovery. On the other hand, it is useful in that the steps promote a pattern of analysis/performance: insight, meditation, a study of artistic elements, a search for control, the emergence of the qualitative mode, the continuing sense of discovery, and the significance—however transitory—of completion.

EXPANDING A CAPACITY FOR SUSTAINED ATTENTION

Finally, these steps toward artistic creation or re-creation emphasize what is a paramount factor in all artistic and aesthetic disciplines: *the capacity for sustained attention.* For this reason alone the first assignments or exercises in this chapter are those which ask the student to attend carefully and with sustained interest to a series of problems. And because it is the literary artist's sustained attention to the world within and the world without which creates acts of literary worth, this is a very natural assignment for the performer to give himself over to. The task of the interpretive artist is, of course, different in degree. As the auxiliary artist, he must direct his attention to the original artist's preoccupation as it is revealed only through the literary work itself.

The challenge, then, for the performer of literature is to offer for observation a presentative act of literature, disclosing the necessary particulars of feeling. How the performer's intuition can be trained, how the performer can concentrate his efforts so as to create an act of what appears to be an inevitable experience, and how he can, in short, move from the perception of literature to its artistically satisfying evocation is the purpose of the remainder of this book.

6. For a complete discussion of the qualitative problem-solving method, consult David W. Ecker, "The Artistic Process as Qualitative Problem Solving," *The Journal of Aesthetics and Art Criticism* 21 (Spring, 1962), p. 283.

Stopping by Woods
on a Snowy Evening[7]

Robert Frost

Whose woods these are I think I know.
His house is in the village, though;
He will not see me stopping here
To watch his woods fill up with snow.

My little horse must think it queer
To stop without a farmhouse near
Between the woods and frozen lake
The darkest evening of the year.

He gives his harness bells a shake
To ask if there is some mistake.
The only other sound's the sweep
Of easy wind and downy flake.

The woods are lovely, dark, and deep,
But I have promises to keep,
And miles to go before I sleep,
And miles to go before I sleep.

The Beast in the Jungle[8]
PART 6

Henry James

[Section 6 is the last and concluding part of Henry James' long short story of fated love. Meeting by chance through mutual friends many years prior to this excerpt, May Bartram and John Marcher spent those years in the propriety of a relationship rather than in its passion. The relationship, tortured and labyrinthine, existed because "something" and "nothing" took place at one and the same time: the love of May Bartram for John Marcher was its own thing for her, a clearly *felt* and *perceived* thing of her consciousness; but his love for her remained closed from his feeling

7. "Stopping by Woods on a Snowy Evening" from *The Poetry of Robert Frost,* edited by Edward Connery Lathem. Copyright 1923, 1930, 1939, © 1969 by Holt, Rinehart and Winston, Inc. Copyright 1951, © 1958 by Robert Frost. Copyright © 1967 by Lesley Frost Ballantine. Reprinted by permission of Holt, Rinehart and Winston, Inc.
8. "The Beast in the Jungle" by Henry James from *The Better Short Stories* by Henry James. Published by Charles Scribner's Sons.

self, sealed off from its acting out. A psychological lifetime of inaction is conveyed in the story, and May Bartram's death in Section 5 is the inevitable end of her "affair of the heart." Her warning to Marcher that he would, eventually, meet the Beast in the Jungle seems far from a reality for him, though his vague disquietude belies that, even to himself. After May's death, Marcher quits England to travel, ostensibly to search out what values he can regarding his life. Yet his fate dictates that he return to England, the locale of his suffering, to face her and the Beast. This is his destiny in Part 6.]

He stayed away, after this, for a year; he visited the depths of Asia, spending himself on scenes of romantic interest, of superlative sanctity; but what was present to him everywhere was that for a man who had known what *he* had known the world was vulgar and vain. The state of mind in which he had lived for so many years shone out to him, in reflexion, as a light that coloured and refined, a light beside which the glow of the East was garish and cheap and thin. The terrible truth was that he had lost—with everything else—a distinction as well; the things he saw couldn't help being common when he had become common to look at them. He was simply now one of them himself—he was in the dust, without a peg for the sense of difference; and there were hours when, before the temples of gods and the sepulchres of kings, his spirit turned for nobleness of association to the barely discriminated slab in the London suburb. That had become for him, and more intensely with time and distance, his one witness of a past glory. It was all that was left to him for proof or pride, yet the past glories of Pharaohs were nothing to him as he thought of it. Small wonder then that he came back to it on the morrow of his return. He was drawn there this time as irresistibly as the other, yet with a confidence, almost, that was doubtless the effect of the many months that had elapsed. He had lived, in spite of himself, into his change of feeling, and in wandering over the earth had wandered, as might be said, from the circumference to the centre of his desert. He had settled to his safety and accepted perforce his extinction; figuring to himself, with some colour, in the likeness of certain little old men he remembered to have seen, of whom, all meagre and wizened as they might look, it was related that they had in their time fought twenty duels or been loved by ten princesses. They indeed had been wondrous for others while he was but wondrous for himself; which, however, was exactly the cause of his haste to renew the wonder by getting back, as he might put it, into his own presence. That had quickened his steps and checked his delay. If his visit was prompt it was because he had been separated so long from the part of himself that alone he now valued.

It's accordingly not false to say that he reached his goal with a certain elation and stood there again with a certain assurance. The creature beneath the sod *knew* of his rare experience, so that, strangely now, the place had lost for him its mere blankness of expression. It met him in mildness—not, as before, in mockery; it wore for him the air of conscious greeting that we find, after absence, in things that have closely belonged to us and which seem to confess of themselves to the connexion. The plot of ground, the graven tablet, the tended flowers affected him so as belonging to him that he resembled for the hour a contented landlord reviewing a piece of property. Whatever had happened—well, had happened. He had not come back this time with the vanity of that question, his former worrying "what, *what?*" now practically so spent. Yet he would none the less never again so cut himself off from the spot; he would come back to it every month, for if he did nothing else by its aid he at least held up his head. It thus grew for him, in the oddest way, a positive resource; he carried out his idea of periodical returns, which took their place at last among the most inveterate of his habits. What it all amounted to, oddly enough, was that in his finally so simplified world this garden of death gave him the few square feet of earth on which he could still most live. It was as if, being nothing anywhere else for anyone, nothing even for himself, he were just everything here, and if not for a crowd of witnesses or indeed for any witness but John Marcher, then by clear right of the register that he could scan like an open page. The open page was the tomb of his friend, and *there* were the facts of the past, there the truth of his life, there the backward reaches in which he could lose himself. He did this from time to time with such effect that he seemed to wander through the old years with his hand in the arm of a companion who was, in the most extraordinary manner, his other, his younger self; and to wander, which was more extraordinary yet, round and round a third presence—not wandering she, but stationary, still, whose eyes, turning with his revolution, never ceased to follow him, and whose seat was his point, so to speak, of orientation. Thus in short he settled to live—feeding all on the sense that he once *had* lived, and dependent on it not alone for a support but for an identity.

It sufficed him in its way for months and the year elapsed; it would doubtless even have carried him further but for an accident, superficially slight, which moved him, quite in another direction, with a force beyond any of his impressions of Egypt or of India. It was a thing of the merest chance—the turn, as he afterwards felt, of a hair, though he was indeed to live to believe that if light hadn't come to him in this particular fashion it would still have come in another. He was to live to believe this, I say, though he was not to live, I may not less definitely mention, to do much else. We allow him at any rate the benefit of the conviction, struggling up for him at the end, that, whatever might have happened or not happened, he would have come round of himself to the light. The incident of an autumn day had put the match to the train laid from of old by his misery. With the light before him he knew that even of late his ache had only been smothered. It was strangely drugged, but it throbbed; at the touch it began to bleed. And the touch, in the event, was the face of a fellow mortal. This face, one grey afternoon when the leaves were thick in the alleys, looked into Marcher's own, at the cemetery, with an expression like the cut of a blade. He felt it, that is, so deep down that he winced at the steady thrust. The person who so mutely assaulted him was a figure he had noticed, on reaching his own goal, absorbed by a grave a short distance away, a grave apparently fresh, so that the emotion of the visitor would probably match it for frankness. This face alone forbade further attention, though during the time he stayed he remained vaguely conscious of his neighbour, a middle-aged man apparently, in mourning, whose bowed back, among the clustered monuments and mortuary yews, was constantly presented. Marcher's theory that these were elements in contact with which he himself revived, had suffered, on this occasion, it may be granted, a marked, an excessive check. The autumn day was dire for him as none had recently been, and he rested with a heaviness he had not yet known on the low stone table that bore May Bartram's name. He rested without power to move as if some spring in him, some spell vouchsafed, had suddenly been broken for ever. If he could have done that moment as he wanted he would simply have stretched himself on the slab that was ready to take him, treating it as a place prepared to receive his last sleep. What in all the wide world had he now to keep awake for? He stared before him with the question, and it was then that, as one of the cemetery walks passed near him, he caught the shock of the face.

His neighbour at the other grave had withdrawn, as he himself, with force enough in him, would have done by now, and was advancing along the path on his way to one of the gates. This brought him close, and his pace was slow, so that — and all the more as there was a kind of hunger in his look — the two men were for a minute directly confronted. Marcher knew him at once for one of the deeply stricken — a perception so sharp that nothing else in the picture comparatively lived, neither his dress, his age, nor his presumable character and class; nothing lived but the deep ravage of the features he showed. He *showed* them — that was the point; he was moved, as he passed, by some impulse that was either a signal for sympathy or, more possibly, a challenge to an opposed sorrow. He might already have been aware of our friend, might at some previous hour have noticed in him the smooth habit of the scene, with which the state of his own senses so scantly consorted, and might thereby have been stirred as by an overt discord. What Marcher was at all events conscious of was in the first place that the image of scarred passion presented to him was conscious too — of something that profaned the air; and in the second that, roused, startled, shocked, he was yet the next moment looking after it, as it went, with envy. The most extraordinary thing that had happened to him — though he had given that name to other matters as well — took place, after his immediate vague stare, as a consequence of this impression. The stranger passed, but the raw glare of his grief remained, making our friend wonder in pity what wrong, what wound it expressed, what injury not to be healed. What had the man *had*, to make him by the loss of it so bleed and yet live?

Something—and this reached him with a pang—that *he*, John Marcher, hadn't; the proof of which was precisely John Marcher's arid end. No passion had ever touched him, for this was what passion meant; he had survived and maundered and pined, but where had been *his* deep ravage? The extraordinary thing we speak of was the sudden rush of the result of this question. The sight that had just met his eyes named to him, as in letters of quick flame, something he had utterly, insanely missed, and what he had missed made these things a train of fire, made them mark themselves in an anguish of inward throbs. He had seen *outside* of his life, not learned it within, the way a woman was mourned when she had been loved for herself: such was the force of his conviction of the meaning of the stranger's face, which still flared for him as a smoky torch. It hadn't come to him, the knowledge, on the wings of experience; it had brushed him, jostled him, upset him, with the disrespect of chance, the insolence of accident. Now that the illumination had begun, however, it blazed to the zenith, and what he presently stood there gazing at was the sounded void of his life. He gazed, he drew breath, in pain; he turned in his dismay, and, turning, he had before him in sharper incision than ever the open page of his story. The name on the table smote him as the passage of his neighbour had done, and what it said to him, full in the face, was that *she* was what he had missed. This was the awful thought, the answer to all the past, the vision at the dread clearness of which he grew as cold as the stone beneath him. Everything fell together, confessed, explained, overwhelmed; leaving him most of all stupefied at the blindness he had cherished. The fate he had been marked for he had met with a vengeance—he had emptied the cup to the lees; he had been the man of his time, *the* man to whom nothing on earth was to have happened. That was the rare stroke—that was his visitation. So he saw it, as we say, in pale horror, while the pieces fitted and fitted. So *she* had seen it while he didn't, and so she served at this hour to drive the truth home. It was the truth, vivid and monstrous, that all the while he had waited the wait was itself his portion. This the companion of his vigil had at a given moment made out, and she had then offered him the chance to baffle his doom. One's doom, however, was never baffled, and on the day she told him his own had come down she had seen him but stupidly stare at the escape she offered him.

The escape would have been to love her; then, *then* he would have lived. *She* had lived—who could say now with what passion?—since she had loved him for himself; whereas he had never thought of her (ah how it hugely glared at him!) but in the chill of his egotism and the light of her use. Her spoken words came back to him—the chain stretched and stretched. The Beast had lurked indeed, and the Beast, at its hour, had sprung it; it had sprung in that twilight of the cold April when, pale, ill, wasted, but all beautiful, and perhaps even then recoverable, she had risen from her chair to stand before him and let him imaginably guess. It had sprung as he didn't guess; it had sprung as she hopelessly turned from him, and the mark, by the time he left her, had fallen where it *was* to fall. He had justified his fear and achieved his fate; he had failed, with the last exactitude, of all he was to fail of; and a moan now rose to his lips as he remembered she had prayed he mightn't know. This horror of waking—*this* was knowledge, knowledge under the breath of which the very tears in his eyes seemed to freeze. Through them, none the less, he tried to fix it and hold it; he kept it there before him so that he might feel the pain. That at least, belated and bitter, had something of the taste of life. But the bitterness suddenly sickened him, and it was as if, horribly, he saw, in the truth, in the cruelty of his image, what had been appointed and done. He saw the Jungle of his life and saw the lurking Beast; then, while he looked, perceived it, as by a stir of the air, rise, huge and hideous, for the leap that was to settle him. His eyes darkened—it was close; and, instinctively turning, in his hallucination, to avoid it, he flung himself, face down, on the tomb.

Jerry N. Uelsmann

Literature as a Presentational Act

She Walks in Beauty

George Noel Gordon, Lord Byron

She walks in beauty, like the night
    Of cloudless climes and starry skies;
And all that's best of dark and bright
    Meet in her aspect and her eyes:
Thus mellowed to that tender light
    Which heaven to gaudy day denies.

One shade the more, one ray the less,
    Had half impaired the nameless grace
Which waves in every raven tress,
    Or softly lightens o'er her face;
Where thoughts serenely sweet express
    How pure, how dear their dwelling-place.

And on that cheek, and o'er that brow,
    So soft, so calm, so eloquent,
The smiles that win, the tints that glow,
    But tell of days in goodness spent,
A mind at peace with all below,
    A heart whose love is innocent!

from **Little Dorrit**

Charles Dickens

The Circumlocution Office was (as everybody knows without being told) the most important Department under Government. No public business of any kind could possibly be done at any time, without the acquiescence of the Circumlocution Office. Its finger was in the largest public pie, and in the smallest public tart. It was equally impossible to do the plainest right and to undo the plainest wrong, without the express authority of the Circumlocution Office. If another Gunpowder Plot had been discovered half an hour before the lighting of the match, nobody would have been justified in saving the parliament until there had been half a score of boards, half a bushel of minutes, several sacks of official memoranda, and a family-vault full of ungrammatical correspondence, on the part of the Circumlocution Office.

Literature for Presentation and Study   31

This glorious establishment had been early in the field, when the one sublime principle involving the difficult art of governing a country, was first distinctly revealed to statesmen. It had been foremost to study that bright revelation, and to carry its shining influence through the whole of the official proceedings. Whatever was required to be done, the Circumlocution Office was beforehand with all the public departments in the art of perceiving — HOW NOT TO DO IT.

Through this delicate perception, through the tact with which it invariably seized it, and through the genius with which it always acted on it, the Circumlocution Office had risen to over-top all the public departments; and the public condition had risen to be — what it was.

It is true that How not to do it was the great study and object of all public departments and professional politicians all round the Circumlocution Office. It is true that every new premier and every new government, coming in because they had upheld a certain thing as necessary to be done, were no sooner come in than they applied their utmost faculties to discovering How not to do it. It is true that from the moment when a general election was over, every returned man who had been raving on hustings because it hadn't been done, and who had been asking the friends of the honourable gentleman in the opposite interest on pain of impeachment to tell him why it hadn't been done, and who had been asserting that it must be done, and who had been pledging himself that it should be done, began to devise, How it was not to be done. It is true that the debates of both Houses of Parliament the whole session through, uniformly tended to the protracted deliberation, How not to do it. It is true that the royal speech at the opening of such session virtually said, My lords and gentlemen, you have a considerable stroke of work to do, and you will please to retire to your respective chambers, and discuss, How not to do it. It is true that the royal speech, at the close of such session, virtually said, My lords and gentlemen, you have through several laborious months been considering with great loyalty and patriotism, How not to do it, and you have found out; and with the blessing of Providence upon the harvest (natural, not political), I now dismiss you. All this is true, but the Circumlocution Office went beyond it.

Because the Circumlocution Office went on mechanically, every day, keeping this wonderful, all-sufficient wheel of statesmanship, How not to do it, in motion. Because the Circumlocution Office was down upon any ill-advised public servant who was going to do it, or who appeared to be by any surprising accident in remote danger of doing it, with a minute, and a memorandum, and a letter of instructions, that extinguished him. It was this spirit of national efficiency in the Circumlocution Office that had gradually led to its having something to do with everything. Mechanicians, natural philosophers, soldiers, sailors, petitioners, memorialists, people with grievances, people who wanted to prevent grievances, people who wanted to redress grievances, jobbing people, jobbed people, people who couldn't get rewarded for merit, and people who couldn't get punished for demerit, were all indiscriminately tucked up under the foolscap paper of the Circumlocution Office.

Numbers of people were lost in the Circumlocution Office. Unfortunates with wrongs, or with projects for the general welfare (and they had better have had wrongs at first, than have taken that bitter English recipe for certainly getting them), who in slow lapse of time and agony had passed safely through other public departments; who, according to rule, had been bullied in this, over-reached by that, and evaded by the other; got referred at last to the Circumlocution Office, and never reappeared in the light of day. Boards sat upon them, secretaries minuted upon them, commissioners gabbled about them, clerks registered, entered, checked, and ticked them off, and they melted away. In short, all the business of the country went through the Circumlocution Office, except the business that never came out of it; and *its* name was Legion.

Sometimes, angry spirits attacked the Circumlocution Office. Sometimes, parliamentary questions were asked about it, and even parliamentary motions made or threatened about it, by demagogues so low and ignorant as to hold that the real recipe of government was, How to do it. Then would the noble lord, or right honourable gentleman, in whose department it was to defend the Circumlocution Office, put an orange in his pocket, and make a regular field-day of the occasion. Then would he come down to that house with a slap upon the table, and meet the honourable gentleman foot to foot. Then would he be there to tell that honourable gentleman that the Circumlocution Office not only was blameless in this matter, but was commendable in this matter, was extollable to the skies in this matter. Then would he be there to tell that honourable gentleman, that, although the Circumlocution Office was invariably right and wholly right, it never was so right as in this matter. Then would he be there to tell that honourable gentleman that it would have been more to his honour, more to his credit, more to his good taste, more to his good sense, more to half the dictionary of commonplaces, if he had left the Circumlocution Office alone, and never approached this matter. Then would he keep one eye upon a coach or crammer from the Circumlocution Office sitting below the bar, and smash the honourable gentleman with the Circumlocution Office account of this matter. And although one of two things always happened; namely, either that the Circumlocution Office had nothing to say and said it, or that it had something to say of which the noble lord, or right honourable gentleman, blundered one half and forgot the other; the Circumlocution Office was always voted immaculate, by an accommodating majority.

Wash[9]

William Faulkner

Sutpen stood above the pallet bed on which the mother and child lay. Between the shrunken planking of the wall the early sunlight fell in long pencil strokes, breaking upon his straddled legs and upon the riding whip in his hand, and lay across the still shape of the mother, who lay looking up at him from still, inscrutable, sullen eyes, the child at her side wrapped in a piece of dingy though clean cloth. Behind them an old Negro woman squatted beside the rough hearth where a meager fire smoldered.

"Well, Milly," Sutpen said, "too bad you're not a mare. Then I could give you a decent stall in the stable."

Still the girl on the pallet did not move. She merely continued to look up at him without expression, with a young, sullen, inscrutable face still pale from recent travail. Sutpen moved, bringing into the splintered pencils of sunlight the face of a man of sixty. He said quietly to the squatting Negress, "Griselda foaled this morning."

"Horse or mare?" the Negress said.

"A horse. A damned fine colt. . . . What's this?" He indicated the pallet with the hand which held the whip.

"That un's a mare, I reckon."

"Hah," Sutpen said. "A damned fine colt. Going to be the spit and image of old Rob Roy when I rode him North in '61. Do you remember?"

"Yes, Marster."

"Hah." He glanced back towards the pallet. None could have said if the girl still watched him or not. Again his whip hand indicated the pallet. "Do whatever they need with whatever we've got to do it with." He went out, passing out the crazy doorway and stepping down into the rank weeds (there yet leaned rusting against the corner of the porch the scythe which Wash had borrowed from him three months ago to cut them with) where his horse waited, where Wash stood holding the reins.

When Colonel Sutpen rode away to fight the Yankees, Wash did not go. "I'm looking after the Kernel's place and niggers," he would tell all who asked him and some who had not asked—a gaunt malaria-ridden man with pale, questioning eyes, who looked about thirty-five, though it was known that he had not only a daughter but an eight-year-old granddaughter as well. This was a lie, as most of them—the few remaining men between eighteen and fifty—to whom he told it, knew, though

9. "Wash" Copyright 1934 and renewed 1962 by William Faulkner. Reprinted from *The Faulkner Reader*, by William Faulkner, by permission of Random House, Inc.

there were some who believed that he himself really believed it, though even these believed that he had better sense than to put it to the test with Mrs. Sutpen or the Sutpen slaves. Knew better or was just too lazy and shiftless to try it, they said, knowing that his sole connection with the Sutpen plantation lay in the fact that for years now Colonel Sutpen had allowed him to squat in a crazy shack on a slough in the river bottom on the Sutpen place, which Sutpen had built for a fishing lodge in his bachelor days and which had since fallen in dilapidation from disuse, so that now it looked like an aged or sick wild beast crawled terrifically there to drink in the act of dying.

The Sutpen slaves themselves heard of his statement. They laughed. It was not the first time they had laughed at him, calling him white trash behind his back. They began to ask him themselves, in groups, meeting him in the faint road which led up from the slough and the old fish camp, "Why ain't you at de war, white man?"

Pausing, he would look about the ring of black faces and white eyes and teeth behind which derision lurked. "Because I got a daughter and family to keep," he said. "Git out of my road, niggers."

"Niggers?" they repeated; "niggers?" laughing now. "Who him, calling us niggers?"

"Yes," he said. "I ain't got no niggers to look after my folks if I was gone."

"Nor nothing else but dat shack down yon dat Cunnel wouldn't *let* none of us live in."

Now he cursed them; sometimes he rushed at them, snatching up a stick from the ground while they scattered before him, yet seeming to surround him still with that black laughing, derisive, evasive, inescapable, leaving him panting and impotent and raging. Once it happened in the very back yard of the big house itself. This was after bitter news had come down from the Tennessee mountains and from Vicksburg, and Sherman had passed through the plantation, and most of the Negroes had followed him. Almost everything else had gone with the Federal troops, and Mrs. Sutpen had sent word to Wash that he could have the scuppernongs ripening in the arbor in the back yard. This time it was a house servant, one of the few Negroes who remained; this time the Negress had to retreat up the kitchen steps, where she turned. "Stop right dar, white man. Stop right whar you is. You ain't never crossed dese steps whilst Cunnel here, and you ain't ghy' do hit now."

This was true. But there was this of a kind of pride: he had never tried to enter the big house, even though he believed that if he had, Sutpen would have received him, permitted him. "But I ain't going to give no black nigger the chance to tell me I can't go nowhere," he said to himself. "I ain't even going to give Kernel the chance to have to cuss a nigger on my account." This, though he and Sutpen had spent more than one afternoon together on those rare Sundays when there would be no company in the house. Perhaps his mind knew that it was because Sutpen had nothing else to do, being man who could not bear his own company. Yet the fact remained that the two of them would spend whole afternoons in the scuppernong arbor, Sutpen in the hammock and Wash squatting against a post, a pail of cistern water between them, taking drink for drink from the same demijohn. Meanwhile on weekdays he would see the fine figure of the man—they were the same age almost to a day, though neither of them (perhaps because Wash had a grandchild while Sutpen's son was a youth in school) ever thought of himself as being so—on the fine figure of the black stallion, galloping about the plantation. For that moment his heart would be quiet and proud. It would seem to him that that world in which Negroes, whom the Bible told him had been created and cursed by God to be brute and vassal to all men of white skin, were better found and housed and even clothed than he and his; that world in which he sensed always about him mocking echoes of black laughter was but a dream and an illusion, and that the actual world was this one across which his own lonely apotheosis seemed to gallop on the black thoroughbred, thinking how the Book said also that all men were created in the image of God and hence all men made the same image in God's eyes at least; so that he could say, as though speaking of himself, "A fine proud man. If God Himself was to come down and ride the natural earth, that's what He would aim to look like."

Sutpen returned in 1865, on the black stallion. He seemed to have aged ten years. His son had been killed in action the same winter in which his wife had died. He returned with his citation for gallantry from the hand of General Lee to a ruined plantation, where for a year now his daughter had subsisted partially on the meager bounty of the man to whom fifteen years ago he had granted permission to live in that tumbledown fishing camp whose very existence he had at the time forgotten. Wash was there to meet him, unchanged: still gaunt, still ageless, with his pale, questioning gaze, his air diffident, a little servile, a little familiar, "Well, Kernel," Wash said, "they kilt us but they ain't whupped us yit, air they?"

That was the tenor of their conversation for the next five years. It was inferior whisky which they drank now together from a stoneware jug, and it was not in the scuppernong arbor. It was in the rear of the little store which Sutpen managed to set up on the highroad: a frame shelved room where, with Wash for clerk and porter, he dispensed kerosene and staple foodstuffs and stale gaudy candy and cheap beads and ribbons to Negroes or poor whites of Wash's own kind, who came afoot or on gaunt mules to haggle tediously for dimes and quarters with a man who at one time could gallop (the black stallion was still alive; the stable in which his jealous get lived was in better repair than the house where the master himself lived) for ten miles across his own fertile land and who had led troops gallantly in battle; until Sutpen in fury would empty the store, close and lock the doors from the inside. Then he and Wash would repair to the rear and the jug. But the talk would not be quiet now, as when Sutpen lay in the hammock, delivering an arrogant monologue while

Wash squatted guffawing against his post. They both sat now, though Sutpen had the single chair while Wash used whatever box or keg was handy, and even this for just a little while, because soon Sutpen would reach that stage of impotent and furious undefeat in which he would rise, swaying and plunging, and declare again that he would take his pistol and the black stallion and ride single-handed into Washington and kill Lincoln, dead now, and Sherman, now a private citizen. "Kill them!" he would shout. "Shoot them down like the dogs they are—"

"Sho, Kernel; sho, Kernel," Wash would say, catching Sutpen as he fell. Then he would commandeer the first passing wagon or, lacking that, he would walk the mile to the nearest neighbor and borrow one and return and carry Sutpen home. He entered the house now. He had been doing so for a long time, taking Sutpen home in whatever borrowed wagon might be, talking him into locomotion with cajoling murmurs as though he were a horse, a stallion himself. The daughter would meet them and hold open the door without a word. He would carry his burden through the once white formal entrance, surmounted by a fanlight imported piece by piece from Europe and with a board now nailed over a missing pane, across a velvet carpet from which all nap was now gone, and up a formal stairs, now but a fading ghost of bare boards between two strips of fading paint, and into the bedroom. It would be dusk by now, and he would let his burden sprawl onto the bed and undress it and then he would sit quietly in a chair beside. After a time the daughter would come to the door. "We're all right now," he would tell her. "Don't you worry none, Miss Judith."

Then it would become dark, and after a while he would lie down on the floor beside the bed, though not to sleep, because after a time—sometimes before midnight—the man on the bed would stir and groan and then speak. "Wash?"

"Hyer I am, Kernel. You go back to sleep. We ain't whupped yit, air we? Me and you kin do hit."

Even then he had already seen the ribbon about his granddaughter's waist. She was now fifteen, already mature, after the early way of her kind. He knew where the ribbon came from; he had been seeing it and its kind daily for three years, even if she had lied about where she got it, which she did not, at once bold, sullen, and fearful. "Sho now," he said. "Ef Kernel wants to give hit to you, I hope you minded to thank him."

His heart was quiet, even when he saw the dress, watching her secret, defiant, frightened face when she told him that Miss Judith, the daughter, had helped her to make it. But he was quite grave when he approached Sutpen after they closed the store that afternoon, following the other to the rear.

"Get the jug," Sutpen directed.

"Wait," Wash said. "Not yit for a minute."

Neither did Sutpen deny the dress. "What about it?" he said.

But Wash met his arrogant stare; he spoke quietly. "I've knowed you for going on twenty years. I ain't never yit denied to do what you told me to do. And I'm a man nigh sixty. And she ain't nothing but a fifteen-year-old gal."

"Meaning that I'd harm a girl? I, a man as old as you are?"

"If you was ara other man, I'd say you was as old as me. And old or no old, I wouldn't let her keep that dress nor nothing else that come from your hand. But you are different."

"How different?" But Wash merely looked at him with his pale, questioning, sober eyes. "So that's why you are afraid of me?"

Now Wash's gaze no longer questioned. It was tranquil, serene. "I ain't afraid. Because you air brave. It ain't that you were a brave man at one minute or day of your life and got a paper to show hit from General Lee. But you air brave, the same as you air alive and breathing. That's where hit's different. Hit don't need no ticket from nobody to tell me that. And I know that whatever you handle or tech, whether hit's a regiment of men or a ignorant gal or just a hound dog, that you will make hit right."

Now it was Sutpen who looked away, turning suddenly, brusquely. "Get the jug," he said sharply.

"Sho, Kernel," Wash said.

So on that Sunday dawn two years later, having watched the Negro midwife, which he had walked three miles to fetch, enter the crazy door beyond which his granddaughter lay wailing, his heart was still quiet though concerned. He knew what they had been saying—the Negroes in cabins about the land, the white men who loafed all day long about the store, watching quietly the three of them: Sutpen, himself, his granddaughter with her air of brazen and shrinking defiance as her condition became daily more and more obvious, like three actors that came and went upon a stage. "I know what they say to one another," he thought. "I can almost hyear them: *Wash Jones has fixed old Sutpen at last. Hit taken him twenty years, but he has done hit at last.*"

It would be dawn after a while, though not yet. From the house, where the lamp shone dim beyond the warped doorframe, his granddaughter's voice came steadily as though run by a clock, while thinking went slowly and terrifically, fumbling, involved somehow with a sound of galloping hooves, until there broke suddenly free in mid-gallop the fine proud figure of the man on the fine proud stallion, galloping; and then that at which thinking fumbled, broke free too and quite clear, not in justification nor even explanation, but as the apotheosis, lonely, explicable, beyond all fouling by human touch: "He is bigger than all them Yankees that kilt his son and his wife and taken his niggers and ruined his land, bigger than this hyer durn country that he fit for and that has denied him into keeping a little country store; bigger than the denial which hit helt to his lips like the bitter cup in the Book. And how could I have lived this nigh to him for twenty years without being teched and changed by him? Maybe I ain't as big as him and maybe I ain't done none of the galloping. But at least I done been drug along. Me and him kin do hit, if so be he will show me what he aims for me to do."

Then it was dawn. Suddenly he could see the house, and the old Negress in the door looking at him. Then he realized that his granddaughter's voice had ceased. "It's a girl," the Negress said. "You can go tell him if you want to." She reëntered the house.

"A girl," he repeated; "a girl"; in astonishment, hearing the galloping hooves, seeing the proud galloping figure emerge again. He seemed to watch it pass, galloping through avatars which marked the accumulation of years, time, to the climax where it galloped beneath a brandished saber and a shot-torn flag rushing down a sky in color like thunderous sulphur, thinking for the first time in his life that perhaps Sutpen was an old man like himself. "Gittin a gal," he thought in that astonishment; then he thought with the pleased surprise of a child: "Yes, sir. Be dawg if I ain't lived to be a great-grandpaw after all."

He entered the house. He moved clumsily, on tiptoe, as if he no longer lived there, as if the infant which had just drawn breath and cried in light had dispossessed him, be it of his own blood too though it might. But even above the pallet he could see little save the blur of his granddaughter's exhausted face. Then the Negress squatting at the hearth spoke, "You better gawn tell him if you going to. Hit's daylight now."

But this was not necessary. He had no more than turned the corner of the porch where the scythe leaned which he had borrowed three months ago to clear away the weeds through which he walked, when Sutpen himself rode up on the old stallion. He did not wonder how Sutpen had got the word. He took it for granted that this was what had brought the other out at this hour on Sunday morning, and he stood while the other dismounted, and he took the reins from Sutpen's hand, an expression on his gaunt face almost imbecile with a kind of weary triumph, saying, "Hit's a gal, Kernel. I be dawg if you ain't as old as I am—" until Sutpen passed him and entered the house. He stood there with the reins in his hand and heard Sutpen cross the floor to the pallet. He heard what Sutpen said, and something seemed to stop dead in him before going on.

The sun was now up, the swift sun of Mississippi latitudes, and it seemed to him that he stood beneath a strange sky, in a strange scene, familiar only as things are familiar in dreams, like the dreams of falling to one who has never climbed. "I kain't have heard what I thought I heard," he thought quietly. "I know I kain't." Yet the voice, the familiar voice which had said the words was still speaking, talking now to the old Negress about a colt foaled that morning. "That's why he was up so early," he thought. "That was hit. Hit ain't me and mine. Hit ain't even hisn that got him outen bed."

Sutpen emerged. He descended into the weeds, moving with that heavy deliberation which would have been haste when he was younger. He had not yet looked full at Wash. He said, "Dicey will stay and tend to her. You better—" Then he seemed to see Wash facing him and paused. "What?" he said.

"You said—" To his own ears Wash's voice sounded flat and ducklike, like a deaf man's. "You said if she was a mare, you could give her a good stall in the stable."

"Well?" Sutpen said. His eyes widened and narrowed, almost like a man's fists flexing and shutting, as Wash began to advance towards him, stooping a little. Very astonishment kept Sutpen still for the moment, watching that man whom in twenty years he had no more known to make any motion save at command than he had the horse which he rode. Again his eyes narrowed and widened; without moving he seemed to rear suddenly upright. "Stand back," he said suddenly and sharply. "Don't you touch me."

"I'm going to tech you, Kernel," Wash said in that flat, quiet, almost soft voice, advancing.

Sutpen raised the hand which held the riding whip; the old Negress peered around the crazy door with her black gargoyle face of a worn gnome. "Stand back, Wash," Sutpen said. Then he struck. The old Negress leaped down into the weeds with the agility of a goat and fled. Sutpen slashed Wash again across the face with the whip, striking him to his knees. When Wash rose and advanced once more he held in his hands the scythe which he had borrowed from Sutpen three months ago and which Sutpen would never need again.

When he reëntered the house his granddaughter stirred on the pallet bed and called his name fretfully. "What was that?" she said.

"What was what, honey?"

"That ere racket out there."

"'Twarn't nothing," he said gently. He knelt and touched her hot forehead clumsily. "Do you want ara thing?"

"I want a sup of water," she said querulously. "I been laying here wanting a sup of water a long time, but don't nobody care enough to pay me no mind."

"Sho now," he said soothingly. He rose stiffly and fetched the dipper of water and raised her head to drink and laid her back and watched her turn to the child with an absolutely stonelike face. But a moment later he saw that she was crying quietly. "Now, now," he said, "I wouldn't do that. Old Dicey says hit's right fine gal. Hit's all right now. Hit's all over now. Hit ain't no need to cry now."

But she continued to cry quietly, almost sullenly, and he rose again and stood uncomfortably above the pallet for a time, thinking as he had thought when his own wife lay so and then his daughter in turn: "Women. Hit's a mystry to me. They seem to want em, and yit when they git em they cry about hit. Hit's a mystry to me. To ara man." Then he moved away and drew a chair up to the window and sat down.

Through all that long, bright, sunny forenoon he sat at the window, waiting. Now and then he rose and tiptoed to the pallet. But his granddaughter slept now, her face sullen and calm and weary, the child in the crook of her arm. Then he returned to the chair and sat again, waiting, wondering why it took them so long, until he remembered that it was Sunday. He was sitting there at midafternoon when a half-grown white boy came around the corner of the house upon the body and gave a choked cry and looked up and glared for a mesmerized instant at Wash in the window before he turned and fled. Then Wash rose and tiptoed again to the pallet.

The granddaughter was awake now, wakened perhaps by the boy's cry without hearing it. "Milly," he said, "air you hungry?" She didn't answer, turning her face away. He built up the fire on the hearth and cooked the food which he had brought home the day before: fatback it was, and cold corn pone; he poured water into the stale coffee pot and heated it. But she would not eat when he carried the plate to her, so he ate himself, quietly, alone, and left the dishes as they were and returned to the window.

Now he seemed to sense, feel, the men who would be gathering with horses and guns and dogs—the curious, and the vengeful: men of Sutpen's own kind, who had made the company about Sutpen's table in the time when Wash himself had yet to approach nearer to the house than the scuppernong arbor—men who had also shown the lesser ones how to fight in battle, who maybe also had signed papers from the generals saying that they were among the first of the brave; who had also galloped in the old days arrogant and proud on the fine horses across the fine plantations—symbols also of admiration and hope; instruments too of despair and grief.

That was whom they would expect him to run from. It seemed to him that he had no more to run from than he had to run to. If he ran, he would merely be fleeing one set of bragging and evil shadows for another just like them, since they were all of a kind throughout all the earth which he knew, and he was old, too old to flee far even if he were to flee. He could never escape them, no matter how much or how far he ran: a man going on sixty could not run that far. Not far enough to escape beyond the boundaries of earth where such men lived, set the order and the rule of living. It seemed to him that he now saw for the first time, after five years, how it was that Yankees or any other living armies had managed to whip them: the gallant, the proud, the brave; the acknowledged and chosen best among them all to carry courage and honor and pride. Maybe if he had gone to the war with them he would have discovered them sooner. But if he had discovered them sooner, what would he have done with his life since? How could he have borne to remember for five years what his life had been before?

Now it was getting toward sunset. The child had been crying; when he went to the pallet he saw his granddaughter nursing it, her face still bemused, sullen, inscrutable. "Air you hungry yit?" he said.

"I don't want nothing."

"You ought to eat."

This time she did not answer at all, looking down at the child. He returned to his chair and found that the sun had set. "Hit kain't be much longer," he thought. He could feel them quite near now, the curious and the vengeful. He could even seem to hear what they were saying about him, the undercurrent of believing beyond the immediate fury: *Old Wash Jones he come a tumble at last. He thought he had Sutpen, but Sutpen fooled him. He thought he had Kernel where he would have to marry the gal or pay up. And Kernel refused.* "But I never expected that, Kernel!" he cried aloud, catching himself at the sound of his own voice, glancing quickly back to find his granddaughter watching him.

"Who you talking to now?" she said.

"Hit ain't nothing. I was just thinking and talked out before I knowed hit."

Her face was becoming indistinct again, again a sullen blur in the twilight. "I reckon so. I reckon you'll have to holler louder than that before he'll hear you, up yonder at that house. And I reckon you'll need to do more than holler before you get him down here too."

"Sho now," he said. "Don't you worry none." But already thinking was going smoothly on: "You know I never. You know how I ain't never expected or asked nothing from ara living man but what I expected from you. And I never asked that. I didn't think hit would need. I said, *I don't need to. What need has a fellow like Wash Jones to question or doubt the man that General Lee himself says in a handwrote ticket that he was brave?* Brave," he thought. "Better if nara one of them had never rid back home in '65"; thinking *Better if his kind and mine too had never drawn the breath of life on this earth. Better that all who remain of us be blasted from the face of earth than that another Wash Jones should see his whole life shredded from him and shrivel away like a dried shuck thrown onto the fire.*

He ceased, became still. He heard the horses, suddenly and plainly; presently he saw the lantern and the movement of men, the glint of gun barrels, in its moving light. Yet he did not stir. It was quite dark now, and he listened to the voices and the sounds of underbrush as they surrounded the house. The lantern itself came on; its light fell upon the quiet body in the weeds and stopped, the horses tall and shadowy. A man descended and stooped in the lantern light, above the body. He held a pistol; he rose and faced the house. "Jones," he said.

"I'm here," Wash said quietly from the window. "That you, Major?"

"Come out."

"Sho," he said quietly. "I just want to see to my granddaughter."

"We'll see to her. Come on out."

"Sho, Major. Just a minute."

"Show a light. Light your lamp."

"Sho. In just a minute." They could hear his voice retreat into the house, though they could not see him as he went swiftly to the crack in the chimney where he kept the butcher knife: the one thing in his slovenly life and house in which he took pride, since it was razor sharp. He approached the pallet, his granddaughter's voice:

"Who is it? Light the lamp, Grandpaw."

"Hit won't need no light, honey. Hit won't take but a minute," he said, kneeling, fumbling toward her voice, whispering now. "Where air you?"

"Right here," she said fretfully. "Where would I be? What is . . ." His hand touched her face. "What is . . . Grandpaw! Grand. . . ."

"Jones!" the sheriff said. "Come out of there!"

"In just a minute, Major," he said. Now he rose and moved swiftly. He knew where in the dark the can of kerosene was, just as he knew that it was full, since it was not two days ago that he had filled it at the store and held it there until he got a ride home with it, since the five gallons were heavy. There were still coals on the hearth; besides, the crazy building itself was like tinder: the coals, the hearth, the walls exploding in a single blue glare. Against it the waiting men saw him in a wild instant springing toward them with the lifted scythe before the horses reared and whirled. They checked the horses and turned them back toward the glare, yet still in wild relief against it the gaunt figure ran toward them with the lifted scythe.

"Jones!" the sheriff shouted; "stop! Stop, or I'll shoot. Jones! *Jones!*" Yet still the gaunt, furious figure came on against the glare and roar of the flames. With the scythe lifted, it bore down upon them, upon the wild glaring eyes of the horses and the swinging glints of gun barrels, without any cry, any sound.

Love's Secret

William Blake

Never seek to tell thy love,
    Love that never told can be;
For the gentle wind doth move
    Silently, invisibly.

I told my love, I told my love,
    I told her all my heart,
Trembling, cold in ghastly fears.
    Ah! she did depart!

Soon after she was gone from me,
    A traveller came by,
Silently, invisibly:
    He took her with a sigh.

The Meadows of Sensation[10]

Thomas Wolfe

Eugene was loose now in the limitless meadows of sensation: his sensory equipment was so complete that at the moment of perception of a single thing, the whole background of color, warmth, odor, sound, taste established itself, so that later, the breath of hot dandelion brought back the grass-warm banks of Spring, a day, a place, the rustling of young leaves, or the page of a book, the thin exotic smell of tangerine, the wintry bite of great apples; or, as with *Gulliver's Travels,* a bright windy day in March, the spurting moments of warmth, the drip and reek of the earth-thaw, the feel of the fire.

    He had won his first release from the fences of home—he was not quite six, when, of his own insistence, he went to school. Eliza did not want him to go, but his only close companion, Max Isaacs, a year his senior, was going, and there was in his heart a constricting terror that he would be left alone again. She told him he could not go: she felt, somehow, that school began the slow, the final loosening of the cords that held them together, but as she saw him slide craftily out the gate one morning in September and run at top speed to the corner where the other little boy was waiting, she did nothing to bring him back. Something taut snapped in her; she remembered his furtive backward glance, and she wept. And she did not weep for herself, but for him: the hour after his birth she had looked in his dark eyes and had seen something that would brood there eternally, she knew, unfathomable wells of remote and intangible loneliness: she knew that in her dark and sorrowful womb a stranger had come to life, fed by the lost communications of eternity, his own ghost, haunter of his own house, lonely to himself and to the world. O lost.

    Busy with the ache of their own growing pains, his brothers and sisters had little time for him: he was almost six years younger than Luke, the youngest of them, but they exerted over him the occasional small cruelties, petty tormentings by elder children of a younger, interested and excited by the brief screaming insanity of his temper when, goaded and taunted from some deep dream, he would seize a carving knife and pursue them, or batter his head against the walls.

10. "The Meadows of Sensation" is reprinted by permission of Charles Scribner's Sons from *Look Homeward, Angel* by Thomas Wolfe. Copyright 1929 Charles Scribner's Sons, renewal copyright © 1957 Edward G. Aswell, Administrator, C.T.A. and/or Fred W. Wolfe.

They felt that he was "queer"—the other boys preached the smug cowardice of the child-herd, defending themselves, when their persecutions were discovered, by saying they would make a "real boy" of him. But there grew up in him a deep affection for Ben who stalked occasionally and softly through the house, guarding even then with scowling eyes, and surly speech, the secret life. Ben was a stranger: some deep instinct drew him to his child-brother, a portion of his small earnings as a paper-carrier he spent in gifts and amusement for Eugene, admonishing him sullenly, cuffing him occasionally, but defending him before the others.

Gant, as he watched his brooding face set for hours before a firelit book of pictures, concluded that the boy liked books, more vaguely, that he would make a lawyer of him, send him into politics, see him elected to the governorship, the Senate, the presidency. And he unfolded to him time after time all the rude American legendry of the country boys who became great men because they were country boys, poor boys, and hard-working farm boys. But Eliza thought of him as a scholar, a learned man, a professor, and with that convenient afterthought that annoyed Gant so deeply, but by which she firmly convinced herself, she saw in this book-brooder the fruit of her own deliberate design.

"I read every moment I could get the chance the summer before he was born," she said. And then, with a complacent and confidential smile which, Gant knew, always preceded some reference to her family, she said: "I tell you what: it may all come out in the Third Generation."

"The Third Generation be Goddamned!" answered Gant furiously.

"Now, I want to tell you," she went on thoughtfully, speaking with her forefinger, "folks have always said that his grandfather would have made a fine scholar if—"

"Merciful God!" said Gant, getting up suddenly and striding about the room with an ironical laugh. "I might have known that it would come to this! You may be sure," he exclaimed in high excitement, wetting his thumb briefly on his tongue, "that if there's any credit to be given I won't get it. Not from you! You'd rather die than admit it! No, but I'll tell you what you will do! You'll brag about that miserable old freak who never did a hard day's work in his life."

"Now, I wouldn't be so sure of that if I were you," Eliza began, her lips working rapidly.

"Jesus God!" he cried, flinging about the room with his customary indifference to reasoned debate. "Jesus God! What a travesty! A travesty on Nature! Hell hath no fury like a woman scorned!" he exclaimed, indefinitely but violently, and then as he strode about he gave way to loud, bitter, forced laughter.

Thus, pent in his dark soul, Eugene sat brooding on a firelit book, a stranger in a noisy inn. The gates of his life were closing him in from their knowledge, a vast aerial world of fantasy was erecting its fuming and insubstantial fabric. He steeped his soul in streaming imagery, rifling the book-shelves for pictures and finding there such treasures as *With Stanley in Africa*, rich in the mystery of the jungle, alive with combat, black battle, the hurled spear, vast snake-rooted forests, thatched villages, gold and ivory; or Stoddard's *Lectures,* on whose slick heavy pages were stamped the most-visited scenes of Europe and Asia; a Book of Wonder, with enchanting drawings of all the marvels of the age—Santos Dumont in his balloon, liquid air poured from a kettle, all the navies of the earth lifted two feet from the water by an ounce of radium (Sir William Crookes), the building of the Eiffel Tower, the Flatiron Building, the stick-steered automobile, the submarine. After the earthquake in San Francisco there was a book describing it, its cheap green cover lurid with crumbling towers, shaken spires, toppling many-storied houses plunging into the splitting flame-jawed earth. And there was another called *Palaces of Sin,* or *The Devil in Society,* purporting to be the work of a pious millionaire, who had drained his vast fortune in exposing the painted sores that blemish the spotless-seeming hide of great position, and there were enticing pictures showing the author walking in a silk hat down a street full of magnificent palaces of sin.

Out of this strange jumbled gallery of pictures the pieced-out world was expanding under the brooding power of his imagination; the lost dark angels of the Doré "Milton" swooped into cavernous Hell beyond this upper earth of soaring or toppling spires, machine wonder, maced and mailed romance. And, as he thought of his future liberation into this epic world, where all the color of life blazed brightest far away from home, his heart flooded his face with lakes of blood.

He had heard already the ringing of remote church bells over a countryside on Sunday night; had listened to the earth steeped in the brooding of dark, and the million-noted little night things; and he had heard thus the far retreating wail of a whistle in a distant valley, and faint thunder on the rails; and he felt the infinite depth and width of the golden world in the brief seductions of a thousand multiplex and mixed mysterious odors and sensations, weaving, with a blinding interplay and aural explosions, one into the other.

He remembered yet the East India Tea House at the Fair, the sandalwood, the turbans, and the robes, the cool interior and the smell of India tea; and he had felt now the nostalgic thrill of dew-wet mornings in Spring, the cherry scent, the cool clarion earth, the wet loaminess of the garden, the pungent breakfast smells and the floating snow of blossoms. He knew the inchoate sharp excitement of hot dandelions in young Spring grass at noon; the smell of cellars, cobwebs, and built-on secret earth; in July, of watermelons bedded in sweet hay, inside a farmer's covered wagon; of cantaloupe and crated peaches; and the scent of orange rind, bitter-sweet, before a fire of coals. He knew the good male smell of his father's sitting-room; of the smooth worn leather sofa, with the gaping horse-hair rent; of the blistered varnished wood upon the hearth; of the heated calf-skin bindings; of the flat moist plug of apple tobacco, stuck with a red flag; of wood-smoke and burnt leaves in October; of the brown tired autumn earth; of honey-suckle at night; of warm nasturtiums; of a clean ruddy farmer who comes weekly with printed butter, eggs and milk; of fat limp underdone bacon and of coffee; of a bakery-oven in the wind; of large deep-hued stringbeans smoking-hot and seasoned well with salt and butter; of a room of old pine boards in which books and carpets have been stored, long closed; of Concord grapes in their long white baskets.

Yes, and the exciting smell of chalk and varnished desks; the smell of heavy bread-sandwiches of cold fried meat and butter; the smell of new leather in a saddler's shop, or of a warm leather chair; of honey and of unground coffee; of barrelled sweet-pickles and cheese and all the fragrant compost of the grocer's; the smell of stored apples in the cellar, and of orchard-apple smells, of pressed cider pulp; of pears ripening on a sunny shelf, and of ripe cherries stewing with sugar on hot stoves before preserving; the smell of whittled wood, of all young lumber, of sawdust and shavings; of peaches stuck with cloves and pickled in brandy; of pine-sap, and green pine-needles; of a horse's pared hoof; of chestnuts roasting, of bowls of nuts and raisins; of hot cracklin, and of young roast pork; of butter and cinnamon melting on hot candied yams.

Yes, and of the rank slow river, and of tomatoes rotten on the vine; the smell of rain-wet plums and boiling quinces; of rotten lily-pads; and of foul weeds rotting in green marsh scum; and the exquisite smell of the South, clean but funky, like a big woman; of soaking trees and the earth after heavy rain.

Yes, and the smell of hot daisy-fields in the morning; of melted puddling-iron in a foundry; the winter smell of horse-warm stables and smoking dung; of old oak and walnut; and the butcher's smell of meat, of strong slaughtered lamb, plump gouty liver, ground pasty sausages, and red beef; and of brown sugar melted with slivered bitter chocolate; and of crushed mint leaves, and of a wet lilac bush; of magnolia beneath the heavy moon, of dogwood and laurel; of an old caked pipe and Bourbon rye, aged in kegs of charred oak; the sharp smell of tobacco; of carbolic and nitric acids; the coarse true smell of a dog; of old imprisoned books; and the cool fern-smell near springs; of vanilla in cake-dough; and of cloven ponderous cheeses.

Yes, and of a hardware store, but mostly the good smell of nails; of the developing chemicals in a photographer's dark-room; and the young-life smell of paint and turpentine; of buckwheat batter and black sorghum; and of a Negro and his horse, together; of boiling fudge; the brine smell of pickling vats; and the lush undergrowth smell of southern hills; of a slimy oyster-can, of chilled gutted fish; of a hot kitchen Negress; of kerosene and linoleum; of sarsaparilla and guavas; and of ripe autumn persimmons; and the smell of the wind and the rain; and of the acrid thunder; of cold starlight, and the brittle-bladed frozen grass; of fog and the misted winter sun; of seed-time, bloom, and mellow dropping harvest.

And now, whetted intemperately by what he had felt, he began, at school, in that fecund romance, the geography, to breathe the mixed odors of the earth, sensing in every squat keg piled on a pier-head a treasure of golden rum, rich port, fat Burgundy; smelling the jungle growth of the tropics, the heavy odor of plantations, the salt-fish smell of harbors, voyaging in the vast, enchanting, but unperplexing world.

Now the innumerable archipelago had been threaded, and he stood, firm-planted, upon the unknown but waiting continent.

He learned to read almost at once, printing the shapes of words immediately with his strong visual memory; but it was weeks later before he learned to write, or even to copy, words. The ragged spume and wrack of fantasy and the lost world still floated from time to time through his clear schoolday morning brain, and although he followed accurately all the other instruction of his teacher, he was walled in his ancient unknowing world when they made letters. The children made their sprawling alphabets below a line of models, but all he accomplished was a line of jagged wavering spear-points on his sheet, which he repeated endlessly and rapturously, unable to see or understand the difference.

"I have learned to write," he thought.

Then, one day, Max Isaacs looked suddenly, from his exercise, on Eugene's sheet, and saw the jagged line.

"That ain't writin'," said he. And clubbing his pencil in his warted grimy hand, he scrawled a copy of the exercise across the page.

The line of life, the beautiful developing structure of language that he saw flowing from his comrade's pencil, cut the knot in him that all instruction failed to do, and instantly he seized the pencil, and wrote the words in letters fairer and finer than his friend's. And he turned, with a cry in his throat, to the next page, and copied it without hesitation, and the next, the next. They looked at each other a moment with that clear wonder by which children accept miracles, and they never spoke of it again.

"That's writin' now," said Max. But they kept the mystery caged between them.

Eugene thought of this event later; always he could feel the opening gates in him, the plunge of the tide, the escape; but it happened like this one day at once. Still midget-near the live pelt of the earth, he saw many things that he kept in fearful secret, knowing that revelation would be punished with ridicule. One Saturday in Spring, he stopped with Max Isaacs above a deep pit in Central Avenue where city workmen were patching a broken watermain. The clay walls of their pit were much higher than their heads; behind their huddled backs there was a wide fissure, a window in the earth which opened on some dark subterranean passage. And as the boys looked, they gripped each other suddenly, for past the fissure slid the flat head of an enormous serpent; passed, and was followed by a scaled body as thick as a man's; the monster slid endlessly on into the deep earth and vanished behind the working and unwitting men. Shaken with fear they went away, they talked about it then and later in hushed voices, but they never revealed it.

The Force That Through the Green Fuse Drives the Flower[11]

Dylan Thomas

The force that through the green fuse drives the flower
Drives my green age; that blasts the roots of trees
Is my destroyer.
And I am dumb to tell the crooked rose
My youth is bent by the same wintry fever.

The force that drives the water through the rocks
Drives my red blood; that dries the mouthing streams
Turns mine to wax.
And I am dumb to mouth unto my veins
How at the mountain spring the same mouth sucks.

The hand that whirls the water in the pool
Stirs the quicksand; that ropes the blowing wind
Hands my shroud sail.
And I am dumb to tell the hanging man
How of my clay is made the hangman's lime.

The lips of time leech to the fountain head;
Love drips and gathers, but the fallen blood
Shall calm her sores.
And I am dumb to tell a weather's wind
How time has ticked a heaven round the stars.

And I am dumb to tell the lover's tomb
How at my sheet goes the same crooked worm.

from A Portrait of the Artist as a Young Man[12]

James Joyce

He went up to his room after dinner in order to be alone with his soul: and at every
step his soul seemed to sigh: at every step his soul mounted with his feet, sighing in

the ascent, through a region of viscid gloom.

He halted on the landing before the door and then, grasping the porcelain knob, opened the door quickly. He waited in fear, his soul pining within him, praying silently that death might not touch his brow as he passed over the threshold, that the fiends that inhabit darkness might not be given power over him. He waited still at the threshold as at the entrance to some dark cave. Faces were there; eyes: they waited and watched.

—We knew perfectly well of course that although it was bound to come to the light he would find considerable difficulty in endeavouring to try to induce himself to try to endeavour to ascertain the spiritual plenipotentiary and so we knew of course perfectly well—

Murmuring faces waited and watched; murmurous voices filled the dark shell of the cave. He feared intensely in spirit and in flesh but, raising his head bravely, he strode into the room firmly. A doorway, a room, the same room, same window. He told himself calmly that those words had absolutely no sense which had seemed to rise murmurously from the dark. He told himself that it was simply his room with the door open.

He closed the door and, walking swiftly to the bed, knelt beside it and covered his face with his hands. His hands were cold and damp and his limbs ached with chill. Bodily unrest and chill and weariness beset him, routing his thoughts. Why was he kneeling there like a child saying his evening prayers? To be alone with his soul, to examine his conscience, to meet his sins face to face, to recall their times and manners and circumstances, to weep over them. He could not weep. He could not summon them to his memory. He felt only an ache of soul and body, his whole being, memory, will, understanding, flesh, benumbed and weary.

That was the work of devils, to scatter his thoughts and overcloud his conscience, assailing him at the gates of the cowardly and sincorrupted flesh: and, praying God timidly to forgive him his weakness, he crawled up on to the bed and, wrapping the blankets closely about him, covered his face again with his hands. He had sinned. He had sinned so deeply against heaven and before God that he was not worthy to be called God's child.

Could it be that he, Stephen Dedalus, had done those things? His conscience sighed in answer. Yes, he had done them, secretly, filthily, time after time, and, hardened in sinful impenitence, he had dared to wear the mask of holiness before the tabernacle itself while his soul within was a living mass of corruption. How came it that God had not struck him dead? The leprous company of his sins closed about him, breathing upon him, bending over him from all sides. He strove to forget them in an act of prayer, huddling his limbs closer together and binding down his eyelids: but the senses of his soul would not be bound and, though his eyes were shut fast, he saw the places where he had sinned and, though his ears were tightly covered, he heard. He desired with all his will not to hear or see. He desired till his frame shook under the strain of his desire and until the senses of his soul closed. They closed for an instant and then opened. He saw.

A field of stiff weeds and thistles and tufted nettlebunches. Thick among the tufts of rank stiff growth lay battered canisters and clots and coils of solid excrement. A faint marshlight struggled upwards from all the ordure through the bristling greygreen weeds. An evil smell, faint and foul as the light, curled upwards sluggishly out of the canisters and from the stale crusted dung.

Creatures were in the field; one, three, six: creatures were moving in the field, hither and thither. Goatish creatures with human faces, hornybrowed, lightly bearded and grey as india-rubber. The malice of evil glittered in their hard eyes, as they moved hither and thither, trailing their long tails behind them. A rictus of cruel malignity lit up greyly their old bony faces. One was clasping about his ribs a torn flannel waistcoat, another complained monotonously as his beard stuck in the tufted weeds. Soft language issued from their spittleless lips as they swished in slow circles round and round the field, winding hither and thither through the weeds, dragging their long tails amid the rattling canisters. They moved in slow circles, circling closer and closer to enclose, to enclose, soft language issuing from their lips, their long swishing tails besmeared with stale shite, thrusting upwards their terrific faces . . .

Help!

He flung the blankets from him madly to free his face and neck. That was his hell. God had allowed him to see the hell reserved for his sins: stinking, bestial, malignant, a hell of lecherous goatish fiends. For him! For him!

He sprang from the bed, the reeking odour pouring down his throat, clogging and revolting his entrails. Air! The air of heaven! He stumbled towards the window, groaning and almost fainting with sickness. At the washstand a convulsion seized him within; and, clasping his cold forehead wildly, he vomited profusely in agony.

When the fit had spent itself he walked weakly to the window and, lifting the sash, sat in a corner of the embrasure and leaned his elbow upon the sill. The rain had drawn off; and amid the moving vapours from point to point of light the city was spinning about herself a soft cocoon of yellowish haze. Heaven was still and faintly luminous and the air sweet to breathe, as in a thicket drenched with showers: and amid peace and shimmering lights and quiet fragrance he made a covenant with his heart.

He prayed:

—He once had meant to come on earth in heavenly glory but we sinned: and then He could not safely visit us but with a shrouded majesty and a bedimmed radiance for He was God. So He came Himself in weakness not in power and He sent thee, a creature in His stead, with a creature's comeliness and lustre suited to our state.

And now thy very face and form, dear mother, speak to us of the Eternal; not like earthly beauty, dangerous to look upon, but like the morning star which is thy emblem, bright and musical, breathing purity, telling of heaven and infusing peace. O harbinger of day! O light of the pilgrim! Lead us still as thou hast led. In the dark night, across the bleak wilderness guide us on to our Lord Jesus, guide us home.

His eyes were dimmed with tears and, looking humbly up to heaven, he wept for the innocence he had lost.

Jackals and Arabs[13]

Franz Kafka

We were camping in the oasis. My companions were asleep. The tall, white figure of an Arab passed by; he had been seeing to the camels and was on his way to his own sleeping place.

I threw myself on my back in the grass; I tried to fall asleep; I could not; a jackal howled in the distance; I sat up again. And what had been so far away was all at once quite near. Jackals were swarming round me, eyes gleaming dull gold and vanishing again, lithe bodies moving nimbly and rhythmically, as if at the crack of a whip.

One jackal came from behind me, nudging right under my arm, pressing against me, as if he needed my warmth, and then stood before me and spoke to me almost eye to eye.

"I am the oldest jackal far and wide. I am delighted to have met you here at last. I had almost given up hope, since we have been waiting endless years for you; my mother waited for you, and her mother, and all our fore-mothers right back to the first mother of all the jackals. It is true, believe me!"

"That is surprising," said I, forgetting to kindle the pile of firewood which lay ready to smoke away jackals, "that is very surprising for me to hear. It is by pure chance that I have come here from the far North, and I am making only a short tour of your country. What do you jackals want, then?"

As if emboldened by this perhaps too friendly inquiry the ring of jackals closed in on me; all were panting and openmouthed.

"We know," began the eldest, "that you have come from the North; that is just what we base our hopes on. You Northerners have the kind of intelligence that is not

13. "Jackals and Arabs" from *The Penal Colony* by Franz Kafka. Copyright 1948 by Schocken Books Inc. Reprinted by permission.

to be found among Arabs. Not a spark of intelligence, let me tell you, can be struck from their cold arrogance. They kill animals for food, and carrion they despise."

"Not so loud," said I, "there are Arabs sleeping near by."

"You are indeed a stranger here," said the jackal, "or you would know that never in the history of the world has any jackal been afraid of an Arab. Why should we fear them? Is it not misfortune enough for us to be exiled among such creatures?"

"Maybe, maybe," said I, "matters so far outside my province I am not competent to judge; it seems to me a very old quarrel; I suppose it's in the blood, and perhaps will only end with it."

"You are very clever," said the old jackal; and they all began to pant more quickly; the air pumped out of their lungs although they were standing still; a rank smell which at times I had to set my teeth to endure streamed from their open jaws, "you are very clever; what you have just said agrees with our old tradition. So we shall draw blood from them and the quarrel will be over."

"Oh!" said I, more vehemently than I intended, "they'll defend themselves; they'll shoot you down in dozens with their muskets."

"You misunderstand us," said he, "a human failing which persists apparently even in the far North. We're not proposing to kill them. All the water in the Nile couldn't cleanse us of that. Why, the mere sight of their living flesh makes us turn tail and flee into cleaner air, into the desert, which for that very reason is our home."

And all the jackals around, including many new-comers from farther away, dropped their muzzles between their forelegs and wiped them with their paws; it was as if they were trying to conceal a disgust so overpowering that I felt like leaping over their heads to get away.

"Then what are you proposing to do?" I asked, trying to rise to my feet; but I could not get up; two young beasts behind me had locked their teeth through my coat and shirt; I had to go on sitting. "These are your trainbearers," explained the old jackal, quite seriously, "a mark of honor." "They must let go!" I cried, turning now to the old jackal, now to the youngsters. "They will, of course," said the old one, "if that is your wish. But it will take a little time, for they have got their teeth well in, as is our custom, and must first loosen their jaws bit by bit. Meanwhile, give ear to our petition." "Your conduct hasn't exactly inclined me to grant it," said I. "Don't hold it against us that we are clumsy," said he, and now for the first time had recourse to the natural plaintiveness of his voice, "we are poor creatures, we have nothing but our teeth; whatever we want to do, good or bad, we can tackle it only with our teeth." "Well, what do you want?" I asked, not much mollified.

"Sir," he cried, and all the jackals howled together; very remotely it seemed to resemble a melody. "Sir, we want you to end this quarrel that divides the world. You are exactly the man whom our ancestors foretold as born to do it. We want to be troubled no more by Arabs; room to breathe; a skyline cleansed of them; no more bleating of sheep knifed by an Arab; every beast to die a natural death; no interference till we have drained the carcass empty and picked its bones clean. Cleanliness, nothing but cleanliness is what we want"—and now they were all lamenting and sobbing—"how can you bear to live in such a world, O noble heart and kindly bowels? Filth is their white; filth is their black; their beards are a horror; the very sight of their eye sockets makes one want to spit; and when they lift an arm, the murk of hell yawns in the armpit. And so, sir, and so, dear sir, by means of your all-powerful hands slit their throats through with these scissors!" And in answer to a jerk of his head a jackal came trotting up with a small pair of sewing scissors, covered with ancient rust, dangling from an eyetooth.

"Well, here's the scissors at last, and high time to stop!" cried the Arab leader of our caravan who had crept upwind towards us and now cracked his great whip.

The jackals fled in haste, but at some little distance rallied in a close huddle, all the brutes so tightly packed and rigid that they looked as if penned in a small fold girt by flickering will-o'-the-wisps.

"So you've been treated to their entertainment too, sir," said the Arab, laughing as gaily as the reserve of his race permitted. "You know, then, what the brutes are after?" I asked. "Of course," said he, "it's common knowledge; so long as Arabs exist, that pair of scissors goes wandering through the desert and will wander with us to the end of our days. Every European is offered it for the great work; every European is just the man that Fate has chosen for them. They have the most lunatic hopes, these beasts; they're just fools, utter fools. That's why we like them; they are our dogs; finer dogs than any of yours. Watch this, now, a camel died last night and I have had it brought here."

Four men came up with the heavy carcass and threw it down before us. It had hardly touched the ground before the jackals lifted up their voices. As if irresistibly drawn by cords each of them began to waver forward, crawling on his belly. They had forgotten the Arabs, fogotten their hatred, the all-obliterating immediate presence of the stinking carrion bewitched them. One was already at the camel's throat, sinking his teeth straight into an artery. Like a vehement small pump endeavoring with as much determination as hopefulness to extinguish some raging fire, every muscle in his body twitched and labored at the task. In a trice they were all on top of the carcass, laboring in common, piled mountain-high.

And now the caravan leader lashed his cutting whip crisscross over their backs. They lifted their heads; half swooning in ectasy; saw the Arabs standing before them; felt the sting of the whip on their muzzles; leaped and ran backwards a stretch. But the camel's blood was already lying in pools, reeking to heaven, the carcass was torn wide open in many places. They could not resist it; they were back again; once more the leader lifted his whip; I stayed his arm.

"You are right, sir," said he, "we'll leave them to their business; besides, it's time to break camp. Well, you've seen them. Marvelous creatures, aren't they? And how they hate us!"

Jabberwocky

Charles Lutwidge Dodgson (Lewis Carroll)

'Twas brillig, and the slithy toves
    Did gyre and gimble in the wabe;
All mimsy were the borogoves,
    And the mome raths outgrabe.

"Beware the Jabberwock, my son!
    The jaws that bite, the claws that catch!
Beware the Jubjub bird, and shun
    The frumious Bandersnatch!"

He took his vorpal sword in hand;
    Long time the manxome foe he sought—
So rested he by the Tumtum tree,
    And stood awhile in thought.

And, as in uffish thought he stood,
    The Jabberwock, with eyes of flame,
Came whiffling through the tulgey wood,
    And burbled as it came!

One, two! One, two! And through and through
    The vorpal blade went snicker-snack!
He left it dead, and with its head
    He went galumphing back.

"And hast thou slain the Jabberwock?
    Come to my arms, my beamish boy!
O frabjous day! Callooh! Callay!"
    He chortled in his joy.

'Twas brillig, and the slithy toves
　　Did gyre and gimble in the wabe;
All mimsy were the borogoves,
　　And the mome raths outgrabe.

CHECKLIST FOR ANALYSIS

1. How would the metaworld of the literature be described? What is the "state of being" in the selection? What is the principal presentational value of the selection? (See chart on page 22.)

EXERCISES AND ASSIGNMENTS

1. Consult the dictionary for the meanings of the following:
　　meta-
　　world
　　perception
　　evocation
Compare the dictionary definitions with the meaning of these words as used in Chapter 1. How do *you* define these terms?

2. Why can it be said that a performance of anything is a *metaworld?*

3. Compare the effects upon you from experiencing the metaworld of (a) a film, (b) a novel, (c) a film based on this novel.

4. Explain how the metaworlds vary in the following presentational forms of *Alice's Adventures in Wonderland:* (a) a silent reading, (b) a retelling of the story, (c) a single interpreter's performing of the story, (d) a staged version of the tale, and (e) an animated-film version of the tale.

5. Elaborate upon the statement: "Any piece of literature is dependent upon many performances."

6. Can you perform an evocative statement informatively? an informative statement evocatively? Describe what happens in these processes.

7. Must a performer-in-training be able to create poetry as well as perform it? Must you be capable of the creative act of literature in order to give a creative act of performance? Why, do you suppose, do so many people not follow through from a creative disposition to a creative act? Is there anything in your background which would suggest difficulty in summoning up a creative disposition? in performing a creative act?

8. How does criticism affect a creative disposition? a creative act? What kinds of criticism do you feel are helpful in a performing art? If your teacher has one set of criteria for an effective, creative performance and you have another, what are some of the effects that such a conflict might possibly have upon you and your work as an interpretive artist?

9. What problems does an auxiliary artist have that would be different from those of the primary artist? Are the problems different *in kind* or *in degree?*

10. A definition of auxiliary artist appears on page 18 of this book. Put this definition into your own words.

11. Consult an encyclopedia of the arts for definitions of the following:
>   realism
>   naturalism
>   classicism
>   expressionism
>   romanticism
>   impressionism
>   surrealism

How would you describe a performance of one of these art "isms"?

12. Select a work from one of the writers listed on the chart, "Structure of Presentative Art" (page 22), and perform it for yourself or for the class. What happens to the literature when you attempt to "lean" in the direction of the expression? What happens if you perform all selections in the same style? How does performance change the experience of literature from the silent reading of the literature?

13. As you begin your work with the perception and evocation of literature, keep a journal for several days, writing your reactions to one of the selections in the Literature for Presentation and Study as you attempt to come to grips with the material through creative problem-solving. Although you may as yet lack skill and background for thorough explorations (as in the case of formal elements), nevertheless, this record will be an important attitude-reference as you proceed on through the course.

Objectives for Performance Growth

	1 Exciting	2 Enjoyable	3 Adequate	4 Need for Development

To Evoke the Metaworlds

_____ a sense of inner resonance
_____ a sense of attaining a state of being
_____ a responsiveness to presentational values
_____ IMPRESSION

To Relate the Performing Body to Literary Experience

_____ behavior congruent to mode
_____ language of gesture natural to literary space
_____ sound of language natural to literary space
_____ appropriate behavioral presses
_____ appropriate use of total bodily energy
_____ IMPRESSION

To Share Awareness of Literary Time

_____ sense of performing time appropriate to literary time
_____ literary time understood and evocated
_____ silences understood and evocated
_____ metrical time understood and evocated
_____ IMPRESSION

To Evoke Figurative Thought and Language

_____ appropriate exemplification of language
_____ a sense of symbolic intent
_____ a sharing of paradox and irony—where appropriate
_____ IMPRESSION

To Evoke Form

_____ form of experience immediate and compelling
_____ form of literary structure appreciated and evocated
_____ IMPRESSION

To Present Style as New Information

_____ expectations in performance congruent to language
_____ performer and style linked / fused
_____ stylistic elements perceived and evocated
_____ narrator attachment or detachment appropriate
_____ IMPRESSION

To Evoke the Presence of Personae

_____ interactional and / or transactional dialogue evocated
_____ significant gesture of characters evocated
_____ structure of dialogue evocated
_____ IMPRESSION

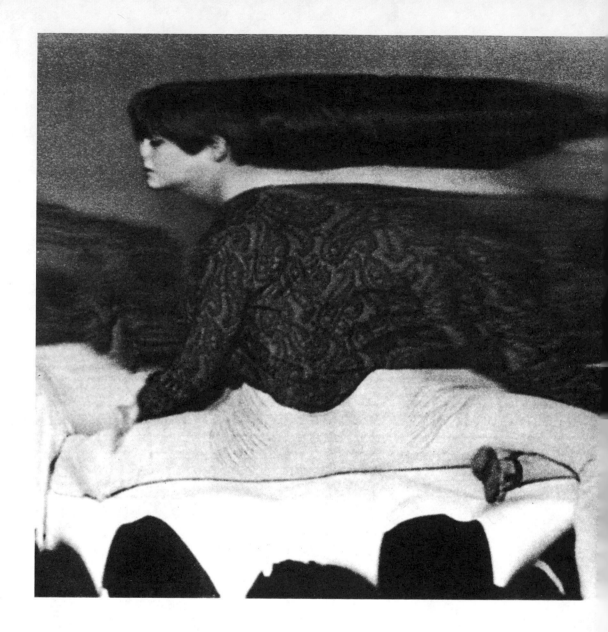

2

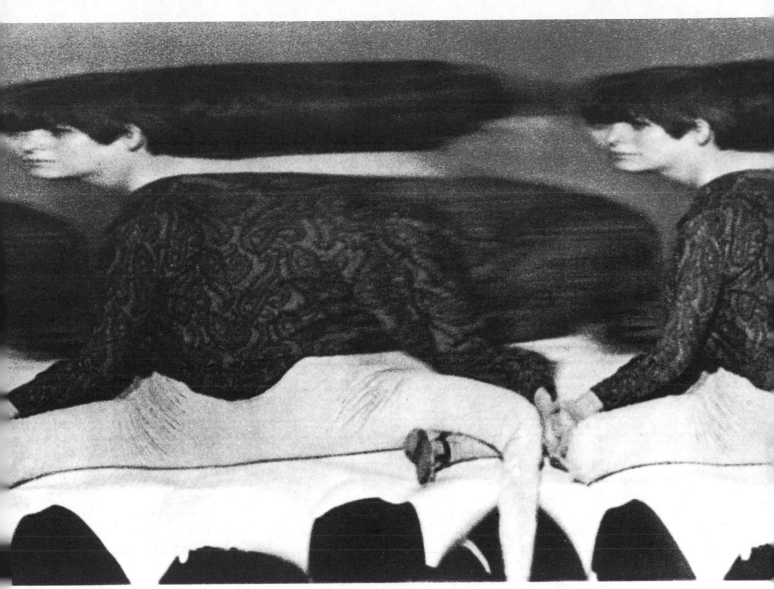

TO RELATE THE BODY IN PERFORMANCE TO THE LITERARY EXPERIENCE

—through behavior that is natural and congruent to the literary mode
—through behavior that is natural to the inherent gestures in the language
—through empathic or sympathetic participation in the literature
—through vocal responsiveness to the tonal elements in the literature
—through the suggestion of general bodily states that reveal the presses in the
  literature
—through appropriate use of presentational energy

CHAPTER TWO

Behavior in Performance

BEHAVIORAL PATTERNING

The artful performance of literature is a unified behavioral patterning. It is behavioral because all of the resources of the body are employed; it is a patterning because all behavior is dependent upon patterns within the literature. A performance of literature is a behavioral revelation in language and gesture.

BEHAVIOR VERSUS DELIVERY

The term *behavior* should be distinguished from another word closely allied to and often confused with it: that term is *delivery*. Delivery is a useful word to describe a conscious control of voice and body, a manifestation of poise and confidence, and a relationship of mutual recognition between performer and audience. Delivery may be said to include also the performer's communicative capacities to relate to an audience, to seize its attention, to recognize its presence. Important as these qualifications are to all forms of social intercourse—including public speaking, interpersonal communication, and the like—they are not sufficient to distinguish *all* that happens to the body in the performance of literature. This is not to say that more happens or that less happens; rather, the performance of literature is different *in kind* from other so-called platform activities.

Georges Gusdorf has written ". . . man speaks the world, but he does not speak to the world."[1] What Gusdorf is suggesting is that the phenomenon of *man giving voice to life* can be distinguished from his seeking communication with other people. He is also suggesting that all of us, whoever we are, speak only from the world inside us. That is, as we perceive the world, feel it, think about it, utter it, we are speaking only our experience of it. The gift of speaking, the capacity to express the essences of life's experiences in language, is the act of *poesis:* the creative use of language for artful observation and contemplation—in short, literature.

---

1. Georges Gusdorf, *Speaking,* trans. Paul T. Brockelman (Evanston, Ill.: Northwestern University Press, 1965), p. 47.

The distinction may be clearer if we say that literature is man speaking; public address (rhetoric) is man speaking *to* the world: i. e., it is man communicating. Because in ordinary usage the two words *speaking* and *communicating* are often used synonymously, the distinction between them can be troublesome. If *speaking* and *communicating* can be perceived, for uses in this course of study, as suggesting two different human activities, the following discussion of behavior in performance can be more easily grasped.

INTERPRETIVE STANCES

The performance of literature—springing as it does from the oral mode, from the bardic tradition—begins with the assumption that the performer is endowed with a certain special power: *a power to summon forth experience.* In "speaking the worlds

Harry Callahan

of experience" within literature, he has the capacity to hold audiences in rapt attention, to cast spells of enchantment, to generate prolonged involvement on the part of his listeners. In "speaking worlds of experience" to his audience, the performer will be speaking from one of three possible stances or viewpoints. First, he may suggest that the experience within the language is coming *from his own personal condition,* his own inner life. Second, he may suggest that the experience is being told *through him,* that he knows elements of the situation well enough to tell what happened to "them." Third, he may assume the personalities of the individuals of the story as totally as he can, eliminating a sense of being the "teller," and *dramatizing events* solely through the characters in the story.

LITERARY MODES AND PERFORMATIVE BEHAVIORS

The following three stances or viewpoints from which to "speak the world" form the basis of what can be called the literary modes.[2] That is, they represent what might be called the vantage positions from which the teller of the tale or the singer of the song or the actor of the drama is performing and behaving.

THE LYRICAL MODE

In the first mode or vantage position, in which the artist is employing *language as inner life,* the point of view is usually first person singular ("When I have fears that I may cease to be . . ."). This mode is infused with the tension of a single voice speaking the world of love and death, time and circumstance, youth and age. It is, by literary genre, the *lyrical mode.*[3]

THE EPIC MODE

In the second mode, in which *language of another is voiced through a speaker,* the artist conveys a sense of story, of tale, of narrative. It is the evocation of a "time" placed "upon" a "onceness" of an experience ("Once upon a time . . ."). This, by literary genre, is the *epic mode.*[4]

---

2. For a discussion of literary modes from another perspective, see Wallace A. Bacon, *The Art of Interpretation,* 2nd ed. (New York: Holt, Rinehart & Winston, 1972), pp. 218-219.

3. For examples of the lyrical mode, see Sonnet 141 ("In faith, I do not love thee with mine eyes") by William Shakespeare (p. 207) and "If You Love the Body" by Richard Tillinghast (p. 215).

4. For examples of the epic mode, see "Eben Sayles" by Arthur Davison Ficke (p 209); "Wash" by William Faulkner (p. 34); the excerpt from *Invisible Man* by Ralph Ellison (p. 95); and the excerpt from *Cane* by Jean Toomer (p. 296).

THE DRAMATIC MODE

The third mode, using *the sense of dramatization,* permits experience to speak only through characters in confrontation and interaction. This is, by literary genre, the *dramatic mode.*[5]

LITERARY MODES AND PERFORMATIVE BEHAVIORS

Lyrical Mode

Introspective.

Personal.

Mulling.

Personal sense of loss, gain, insight.

Audience observes process of excitement, depression, etc., *without* a sense of being the one addressed.

Detached from the audience.

Attached to unseen listener.

Audience senses and experiences the overhearing of a world being spoken.

Often an impelling sense of "present tenseness": *it is happening now.*

Intensity of utterance.

High sense of imagery participation: a world seen, felt, touched, heard, etc.

Sense of self revealed.

First person, as a rule.

Epic Mode

Direct confrontation with audience: "I have a story to tell you."

In a lyrical passage, the performer slips out of direct confrontation into behavior appropriate to the lyrical mode.

Past-tense orientation—yet compelling: *it happened, but . . .*

Vivid sense of eye and memory for detail.

Strong sense of rapport between the performer and the audience.

Character revealed by expository passages and descriptive elements.

Third person, as a rule.

Dramatic Mode

Involvement with audience only when inherent in dramatic material (chorus in Greek drama, Elizabethan play, etc.)

Strong elements of characterization suggested.

Strong sense of mimesis, particularly in terms of voice, general attitudes, posture, etc.

Language is related only to the psychological condition of the character.

Present-tense involvement: *it is happening now.*

When lyrical passages are present, they are uttered in terms of the essence of the fictive character speaking.

Self revealed solely through interaction, dialogue, etc.

---

5. For an example of the dramatic mode, see *The Lady from Larkspur Lotion* by Tennessee Williams (p. 336).

These modes, which exist in both prose and poetry, reflect the specific and unique points of view from which the literary artist summons forth the experience upon which he wants his reader or listener to focus. Since *the mode determines the primary behavior in performance,* the importance of the performer's responding accurately and appropriately to the mode cannot be stated emphatically enough.

To make each of these three modes completely discrete is impossible, of course, but the performer must keep constantly in mind the fact that each mode has its own set of performing behaviors, highly identifiable in their impact and significantly suggestive in their interpretation. When, for instance, the performer makes the error of translating lyrical poetry into an act of rhetorical communication, he is doing a great disservice to the poetry and, at the same time, depriving his auditors of important nonverbal behaviors that should complement and add dimension to the language. If the interpretive artist can keep foremost in his mind that it is the *poet* who rediscovers speech and gives to speech a compelling sense of experience through "speaking the world," then the performer is much more likely to give to the poet's mode of expression congruent performing values. By studying and analyzing the chart of "Literary Modes and Performative Behaviors," the student can more easily determine what these congruencies are.

SPACE AND SOUND DIMENSIONS IN PERFORMANCE

While there are generalized modes of behavior for the modes of literature, the *dimensions* in which these behaviors take place must be identified and analyzed quite specifically. These dimensions are: (1) *time,* (2) *space,* and (3) *sound.* The dimension of time in literature and performance will be treated separately in Chapter 3. In the remainder of this chapter we will examine the dimensions of space and sound as they relate to performative behavior.

The auditor of literature, we should remember, is not reading the literature; he is *experiencing* it as it is being performed. The function of the performer, as we have seen, is to share those important behaviors inherent within the literature, to participate with his audience in a shared space as he presents identifiable elements of the literature, and to do so as oral/aural or "sounding" behaviors encompass both performer and auditor in the dimension of time.

THE DUALITY OF SPACE

The interpretive artist must deal not with one kind of space, but with two: *physical space* and the special *space implied by or inherent in the literature.* This duality, while posing an ever-present challenge to the performer, affords opportunities for artistic and flexible re-creation.

Physical space.　　The performer must always have a certain degree of physical relationship to an auditor or group of auditors in a room, auditorium, or other physically bounded space. Traditionally, he stands before, sits in front of, or is encircled by his hearers.

Space in literature.　　At the same time, the performer attempts to re-create, establish, or suggest places or environments in which the events and/or feelings of the literature are happening or being enacted. It is this sense of inner space which is the metaworld of the literary experience.

How shall the performer cope with this duality of performing space and literary space? He will find at least part of the answer in a reexamination of the literary/performative modes; for it is the modes which largely determine how a performer will occupy space and how he will perform in it. He must develop and maintain a style of performance which adjusts easily and smoothly and appropriately to the various modes of the literature, for quite often the original artist will have employed a variety of modes, often shifting from one to another with surprising suddennesses and unexpected turnings. The performer must not impose a rigid, inflexible style of performance upon the literature which, in essence, produces merely a conversational communication between speaker and audience.

THE BEHAVIORS INHERENT IN LANGUAGE

We have noted that the performance of literature is a literary act in a medium other than print. While print shows language, a performance reveals *behavior* in the language. Behavior is revealed and shown in space; behavior itself is a full-dimensional presentation of self to others.[6]

Gestural response to language.　　Words affect us, and the effects are visible. The insistence of language as gesture can be noticed in the growth and development of language within us. In our first attempts to name a world, we point, and our gestures may precede, coincide with, or follow our words. As we give action to our named world through the utterance of verbs, the compelling gesture of verbs is apparent. In fact, to a greater or lesser degree, the process of gesture applies to the voicing of *all* parts of speech. An analysis of this statement can be seen in the chart, "Gestural Behaviors in the Parts of Speech"; and the student is urged to test these relationships for himself as he experiments with the gestural components of language.

6. Students wishing to explore this concept more fully are referred to Erving Goffman, *The Presentation of Self in Everyday Life* (New York: Doubleday & Co., 1959).

GESTURAL BEHAVIORS IN THE PARTS OF SPEECH

Function and Part	Inherent Gesture

1. NAMING THE WORLD OF EXPERIENCE:
noun
noun phrase
noun clause

POINTING, INDICATING, SHOWING, REVEALING:
chair, ceiling, cloud, bird, noise, etc.
"*to see a world in autumn* (was) . . ."
"*that I was afraid* (astonished even me)"

2. SHAPING AND MODIFYING THE WORLD OF EXPERIENCE:
adjective
adjective phrase
adjective clause

SHOWING THROUGH MOTIONS OF HANDS, FACE, ARMS, BODY:
smooth, rough, round, weak, strong, etc.
"*running carelessly and wild,* (I came upon . . .)"
(The fear) *that I may die before I sing . . .*"

3. MOVING THE WORLD OF EXPERIENCE; EXPRESSING ITS STATE OF BEING:
verb

MIMESIS AND BY SHOWING STATE OF BEING:
kicked, sauntered, flitted, drifted, etc.
was tormented, am bereft, have been thinking

4. SHAPING THE ACTION AND THE STATE OF BEING:
adverbs
adverbial phrases
adverbial clauses

SHOWING THROUGH ACTIONS OF HANDS, FACE, ARMS, BODY:
slowly, mincingly, inevitably, suddenly, etc.
"(I came) *upon a stone,* (I looked) *into a pond,*"
"*When I have fears that I may cease to be . . .*"

5. SHOWING RELATIONSHIPS, PROXIMITIES:
prepositions (which function as adverbs and adjectives in single words and phrases

SHOWING THROUGH MOTIONS OF HANDS, FACE, AND BODILY INDICATIONS:
about, through, against, over, under, into, etc.
(Thoughts) *in winter*

6. CONNECTING ANYTHING AND EVERYTHING:
conjunctions

ATTITUDE, FACIAL EXPRESSION, GESTURES:
and, yet, but, and then, so, etc.

7. SUDDEN EXPLOSION OF LIFE IN LANGUAGE:
interjections

TOTAL BODILY RESPONSE:
Aye! Holy, Holy! O! O! O!

8. SUBSTITUTIONS:
pronouns

POINTING, INDICATING, ESTABLISHING BY BODILY ACTION:
he, she, it, them, mine, us, yours, etc.

There is no gesture in language that is not tied to the emotional circumstance of a situation or the character of a personality, but the degree to which gesture should be used in performance is not a matter that can be determined adequately or satisfactorily here. If the student will think of gesture as the total capacity to respond, considering gesture in its largest sense, then he may begin to free himself of a prevalent notion that gesture is some exaggerated action of the arms or the eyes. With only a little thought, any student of language will recognize gesture as a cultural phenomenon arising from tradition and language. It is psychological in origin, related to social position and personality, disposition and inner emotional state.

Interestingly, gestures can set up tensions that express the opposite of what is said: the bodily gesture of "yes" made while the voice says "no"; the voice that says "I will," but the eyes which declare "I will not"; the voice which says "I will try," and the body which insists "I cannot." Thus, whether there is a congruence or lack of it between word and behavior, the presence of language as gesture is of particular spatial importance in the behavioral interpretation of literature. We speak of the spatial importance of gesture because gesture occupies space.

There is a posture in literature, and this posture is restated and reaffirmed in performance. Just as the performer does not impose his personal, judgmental values upon the literature, neither does he impose his own posture, his physical stance, his physical attitude in performance. What he does suggest is the stance, posture, and physical attitude inherent in the literature. In this sense performance is a form of bodily tone; and the achievement of this body tonality is dependent in a large measure upon the performer's sensitivity and sensibility to language. This capacity to "lean into" the literature, to grasp the elusiveness of the position taken in the experience contained in print is called *empathy.*

Empathy and sympathy. Feeling with, feeling into, identifying with, and similar terms attempt to describe what *empathy* is. In its simplest sense, empathy is impossible without two or more people having a like or similar experience. A case can be made that it is impossible for one to feel empathy with that which has not been experienced. Obviously, on the other hand, a performer cannot be expected to possess empathy for every experience he wishes to present in performance. Empathically, then, how does the performing artist adjust his goals, his performance? How can he give to his interpretation the emotional validity and depth that could cause an auditor to think, "He performed so convincingly that he must have had this very same experience himself!"

The answers to such questions can be found in large part in the *cultivation of a sympathetic nature.* While we cannot empathize with every situation and circumstance, we can know *of* terror, *of* horror, *of* sorrow, *of* joy, just as we may well know tenderness, love, loss, regret, and frustration. Both literature and art reveal *the nature*

Photos: Floris Michael Neusüss

of, just as they create *the essence of,* what *is.* Thus, while no performer can give an empathic performance of what he has not experienced, he can be attuned sensitively to what life and its pleasures and vicissitudes are. That to which the performer can give empathy, he must; that to which he can give sympathy, he will. Both postures or attitudes have palpable presences. We know empathy and we know sympathy when they are demonstrated. Both occur in space; both are manifested by behavior.

Popular literature, popular song, popular theater, and popular entertainment characteristically capitalize upon what a great many people can empathize with. Conversely, genuinely great literature characteristically poses the *potentialities* of life most profoundly, if not always most sublimely. Popular literature, by its very nature, must have immediacy of impact, of accessibility—an easy accessibility that soon makes it grow pale and tiresome. Great literature, on the other hand, is richly evocative of growing life, of an unfolding life; its reaches are never fully plumbed or exhausted. For this reason great performances of great literature almost invariably restore the ambiguity of literature. The performances ask as many questions as does the literature itself. As the auditor/perceiver watches interpretive behavior in space, he may at first be puzzled or bewildered, then excited, and finally involved.

A definitive performance, in addition to being bountifully evocative of the source material, often provides a behavioral parallel. A student at the age of eighteen, for example, who approaches Hamlet or Ophelia may—depending upon the range of his or her life experiences—inform these characters skillfully, sometimes beautifully. Ten years later these same students will approach these characters with insights and experiences undreamed of earlier; and as performers they will, in all probability, demonstrate in their physical presences penetrative intuitions which will ambiguate their performances and which will almost surely add more mature behavioral dimensions. Of course, a definitive performance is always a mature act, regardless of the age of the performer.

A sympathetic approach to a piece of literature, we emphasize, does not make for a less artistic experience than an empathic one. In both, the evocation of attitude is important. While one may be formed by experience, the other will be informed by sympathy. What the performer must be honest about is in the distinctions he will make in his basic stance toward the literature. Performance, as we have defined it, is the giving of form and voice to the literature. The interpreter's body is, at one level, the chief resource for this informing: it is the supple response to the language of literature; it is empathic or sympathetic to the physical reactions to experience. The performer occupies space—in the most literal sense of the term—while performing, and he is absolutely obligated to occupy that space in terms suggested by the literature. It is imperative that his bodily tone be congruent to the mode, that the suppleness of his gesture be congruent to the language.

THE PRIMACY OF THE AUDITORY IMAGE

If physical presence were not important, if the gestural responses to language were not crucial, if the sense of empathy or of sympathy were not identifiable, there would be little justification for the performance of literature before an audience; a sound recording would be sufficient. It is the enhancing addition of physical presence to sound that distinguishes the nature of the performance itself and that necessitates the presence of an auditor-perceiver (rather than a mere auditor) in the performing situation. Exercises for testing this thesis can be found at the conclusion of this chapter.

Orality, as we have stressed, is the bardic tradition. In its origins literature was centered in sound, in the surrounding of an individual with vocal creations of imagination, the mythic deeds of ancient heroes. This idea of seizing sound and making of it the moment to remember, to recollect, has never been completely forgotten by any culture. Admittedly, what a culture *values* in sound may change. Our present world, for instance, is engaged in making a vast and challenging transition from one area of "sounding space" into another, a transition abetted and indeed made inescapable by the most sophisticated and complex systems of sound and entertainment ever devised. But in a culture that has been oriented to print as the source of the literary experience, the performer must take great care to ensure a behavioral literary experience.

Put another way, *the performance of literature restores to the culture the primacy of the auditory image*. The literary mind over hundreds of years has grown accustomed to the silent, inner sound of the imagination. As we have observed, silent reading—or, perhaps, as it should have been called, the silent performance of literature—relies upon the individual's inner capacity to establish and evoke imaginatively the auditory space within the literature. Now, however, in this electronic age, the performance of literature demands a relearning of the significance of acoustic space.

Acoustic space, as we have discussed it, is the entire world of experience. It is the hum of a city. It is the stereophonic reproduction of music and literature. Try as he may, the individual can never escape the environment of sound; for even were he to be placed within a soundproof chamber, he would hear the pulsing of his own heartbeat. Acoustic space is the sound of life as it is happening.

Historically, especially since Gutenberg, the process of learning has been often a process of learning to eliminate the world of acoustic space. To be quiet, to be silent while studying, to sit in silence while being taught, to read masterpieces of literature in silence—all these are familiar situations. In the study of the evocation and performance of literature, the student is suddenly asked to reverse his accustomed habits: he is asked to make visible the performance of literature in space, to create the experience of literature in both durational and literary time; and he is asked to make audible the sound of literature in an acoustic space which he himself has created. The shift is a profound one. What attitudes, if any, can help the performer in making this shift? It may help him to remember:

All languages are *tone* languages.
In the performance of literature, all sounds are heard.

In the performance of literature, only the sounds related to the experience of the literature are important.

All sound is framed by silence or by the presence of other sounds.

In the performance of literature, the performer must make important decisions regarding the patterning of sound: the sound of sentence patterns, the sound of
rhythmic patterns, and the sounding value of words.

All patternings of sound establish some kind of distance to the auditor-perceiver.

The auxiliary artist will find it helpful to examine each of the foregoing assertions
critically, not only to perceive their relationship to the behaviors inherent in literature, but to note how subtly they relate to everyday life as well. A number of these
assertions will be treated in subsequent chapters of this book, but they merit initial
and thoughtful analysis here.

GESTURE AND SOUND DERIVED FROM THE "PRESSES" OF LITERATURE

Recent research has suggested that specific emotions (love, hate, sexual desire, anger, reverence, etc.) produce distinct and rather precise muscular states within the
body. In experiments individuals have been asked to press a key when words like *love,
anger, reverence* are indicated. One researcher concludes, "When one perceives an
emotional expression, the nervous system recognizes the form, and decodes it into a
corresponding emotional idiolog. As the receiver of such messages, the nervous system is programmed to interpret the shape of movements, and there is little we can do
to change this program."[7] But moreover, "effective emotional communication depends on (1) a clear idea of the emotion one wants to express and (2) a precise execution of the muscular acts involved — finger movements, gestures, tone of voice, etc."[8]
The intimate interrelatedness of the voice and body to the emotional states is obvious.
The shift is a profound one. What attitudes, if any, can help the performer in making
this shift? It may help him to remember:

Literature creates its own "pulses" in many forms — in the rhythms of the language, in the emotive power of a single word, and, in the largest sense, by the *general
bodily state* it leaves the perceiver. These generalized bodily states create, in turn,
what might be called moods, tones of feeling that the entirety of a work achieves. The
performer of literature attempts to sense these tones of feeling and to demonstrate
the kinds of bodily states the literature signals within his sympathetic nervous system
and emotional being. Because the literature is exerting its influence through these

---

7. Manfred Clynes, "Sentic Cycles: The Seven Passions at Your Fingertips," *Psychology Today* 5 (May 1972), p. 70.
8. Ibid.

states, exerting the *pressure* of its own life, these tones of feeling can be identified as "presses." These distinct and identifiable presses manifest themselves in the body and thus in performance:

1. Expression
2. Impression
3. Depression
4. Compression
5. Suppression
6. Repression
7. Oppression

Rarely, if ever, do these presses exist independently or in isolation. However, for purposes of identification and analysis, they will be examined as separate entities.

EXPRESSION

In the broadest sense expression is performance—performance, first, on the part of the original artist, and second, on the part of the auxiliary artist. In the sense in which we are using expression here, we are analytically viewing evidences of the literary artist's state of mind while he is creating the literature. Moreover, in the following discussion of the various presses, we will use the term *speaker* to mean the "speaker" or "persona" of the literature.

Often what we know of an individual is revealed by the manner and mode in which he expresses himself. Is he articulate? Are his voice and body imbued with vitality? Is there a sharpness to his voice? a mildness?

The student can best begin his study of the components of expression by asking of the literary selection some crucial questions: What kind of language does the speaker use? Is the speaker direct and open? Or does he choose innuendo and indirect language? In order to keep expression distinct from the other presses of literature, we suggest that the student arbitrarily limit his analysis of expressiveness to the following qualities: *openness, exuberance, linguistic precision, candor, a sense of pouring out openly and freely the inner state of the character's being.*

The key to this approach lies in the prefix *ex-,* that is, the character's capacity to press *out* from his inner being what is necessary in any given situation. In selections from *Spoon River Anthology,* for instance, we find that the characters speak more freely and more openly than often they were allowed or permitted themselves to speak in life. In death the repressions are useless and unnecessary; and the power and interest generated by the literature springs from the freedom with which these characters can—at long last—*express* their lives. The impressions these characters made while living were clearly quite different from the expressions they make to the reader and perceiver as they speak—that is, express—their lives after they are dead.

Lucinda Matlock[9]

Edgar Lee Masters

I went to the dances at Chandlerville,
And played snap-out at Winchester.
One time we changed partners,
Driving home in the moonlight of middle June,
And then I found Davis.
We were married and lived together for seventy years,
Enjoying, working, raising the twelve children,
Eight of whom we lost
Ere I had reached the age of sixty.
I spun, I wove, I kept the house, I nursed the sick,
I made the garden, and for holiday
Rambled over the fields where sang the larks,
And by Spoon River gathering many a shell,
And many a flower and medicinal weed—
Shouting to the wooded hills, singing to the green valleys.
At ninety-six I had lived enough, that is all,
And passed to a sweet repose.
What is this I hear of sorrow and weariness,
Anger, discontent and drooping hopes?
Degenerate sons and daughters,
Life is too strong for you—
It takes life to love Life.

Expression, then, is release. Perceiving the quality of this release and determining how and under what conditions it is being accomplished is a significant part of the interpreter's performative task. The thoughts that Hamlet expresses in his soliloquies are quite different from his repressed speeches in the presence of others. For him the soliloquies become his releases, and "overhearing" them is essential for an auditor's understanding of his character.

9. "Lucinda Matlock" by Edgar Lee Masters from *Spoon River Anthology*. Copyright 1914, 1915, 1916, 1942, 1944 by Edgar Lee Masters. Reprinted with permission of Mrs. Ellen Masters.

IMPRESSION

All human beings, whether they or we wish it or not, make some kind of an impression upon us. Their body stance, the quality of their voice, the look of their eyes, their vocabulary range—these and many similar qualities contribute to our immediate and our lasting reactions. Another task of the performer of literature is to determine the general and specific impressions that his "voice" in the literature can and should make through implied and suggested behavior.

In Edwin Arlington Robinson's "Richard Cory" and in Edgar Lee Masters' "Lucinda Matlock"—to cite only two examples—the reader must be guided by, and indeed is made to feel, the strong impressions made by these title characters.

Richard Cory[10]

Edwin Arlington Robinson

Whenever Richard Cory went down town,
　　We people on the pavement looked at him:
He was a gentleman from sole to crown,
　　Clean favored, and imperially slim.

And he was always quietly arrayed,
　　And he was always human when he talked;
But still he fluttered pulses when he said,
　　"Good-morning," and he glittered when he walked.

And he was rich—yes, richer than a king,
　　And admirably schooled in every grace:
In fine, we thought that he was everything
　　To make us wish that we were in his place.

So on we worked, and waited for the light,
　　And went without the meat, and cursed the bread;
And Richard Cory, one calm summer night,
　　Went home and put a bullet through his head.

10. "Richard Cory" reprinted by permission of Charles Scribner's Sons from *The Children of the Night* by Edwin Arlington Robinson (1897).

Any performer who fails to achieve a sense of the "impressive" presence of both Richard Cory and Lucinda Matlock will fail in achieving a valid performance of them. In examining these poems, note especially where the key impressions occur and how they are made. An impression should be enduring, for to make an indelible imprint is to create an *image* to be remembered. The artist-performer has an obligation, first, to the voice and personage of the literature. If, instead, we are left with the impression of the performer and *his* personality, what we have experienced is not the impress of the characters in the literature, but, rather, the psychological makeup and behavioristic idiosyncracies of the performer. And that, however fascinating, is not interpretive art.

Impression is a behavioral metaphor. Among the common clichés in our culture are such phrases as "He is a tower of strength," "He is a worm," "He is a veritable bull in a china closet," "When she's around, it is a spring day." Obviously, impressions should tell us much about the behavior of another, and writers are deft in supplying the necessary clues to that behavior. Sometimes an individual creates impressions by what seem to be non-rational and totally inexplicable means, and we say that he has *charisma.* To identify and pin down the impressions made by such a character in literature makes the performer's task that much more difficult. Take the Beatitudes, for example. One man may read them aloud, and they will make little or no impression upon his listener. A second reader/interpreter, filled with a sense of conviction and purpose, may effect a deep and lasting impression upon a hearer, even to the extent of altering his behavior.

Since practically all criticism of the performance of literature hinges upon the impressions the performer makes upon his audience, impressions are among the first and most important presses to analyze in the literature to be performed.

DEPRESSION

A depression, as most of us are aware, is a mental state. Characteristically, the tone of the voice is flat and, significantly, lifeless. There is sluggish gesture and slack body tone. Almost always, a depression is a condition of feeling that life has crowded in and imposed itself too heavily, of failing to perceive alternatives or other choices. We can observe that the "expressive" tone of depression is identifiable. Note a paradox, however: the depressed voice in literature is articulate. In the depressed voice in "Stanzas Written in Dejection, Near Naples," the poet Shelley delineates well his depressed mental state.

Stanzas

WRITTEN IN DEJECTION, NEAR NAPLES

Percy Bysshe Shelley

> The sun is warm, the sky is clear,
>   The waves are dancing fast and bright,
> Blue isles and snowy mountains wear
>   The purple noon's transparent might,
>   The breath of the moist earth is light,
> Around its unexpanded buds;
>   Like many a voice of one delight,
> The winds, the birds, the ocean floods,
> The City's voice itself, is soft like Solitude's.
>
> I see the Deep's untrampled floor
>   With green and purple seaweeds strown;
> I see the waves upon the shore,
>   Like light dissolved in star-showers, thrown:
>   I sit upon the sands alone—
> The lightning of the noontide ocean
>   Is flashing round me, and a tone
> Arises from its measured motion,
> How sweet! did any heart now share in my emotion.
>
> Alas! I have nor hope nor health,
>   Nor peace within nor calm around,
> Nor that content surpassing wealth
>   The sage in meditation found,
>   And walked with inward glory crowned—
> Nor fame, nor power, nor love, nor leisure.
>   Others I see whom these surround—
> Smiling they live, and call life pleasure;—
> To me that cup has been dealt in another measure.
>
> Yet now despair itself is mild,
>   Even as the winds and waters are;
> I could lie down like a tired child,
>   And weep away the life of care
>   Which I have borne and yet must bear,
> Till death like sleep might steal on me,

And I might feel in the warm air
My cheek grow cold, and hear the sea
Breathe o'er my dying brain its last monotony.

Some might lament that I were cold,
    As I, when this sweet day is gone,
Which my lost heart, too soon grown old,
    Insults with this untimely moan;
    They might lament—for I am one
Whom men love not,—and yet regret,
    Unlike this day, which, when the sun
    Shall on its stainless glory set,
Will linger, though enjoyed, like joy in memory yet.

It is the *sense* of depression which comes first, the lifelessness and hopelessness which dictate the voice of depression. In T. S. Eliot's "The Hollow Men," even the capacity to express dejection fails, and we are left only with the depressive fragments of despair and hopelessness.

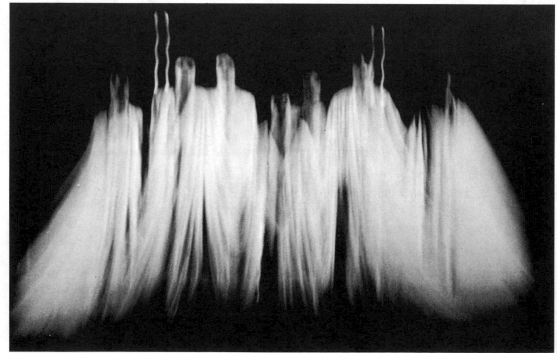

Edward Hartwig

The Hollow Men[11]

T. S. Eliot

A penny for the old guy

1
We are the hollow men
We are the stuffed men
Leaning together
Headpiece filled with straw. Alas!
Our dried voices, when
We whisper together
Are quiet and meaningless
As wind in dry grass
Or rats' feet over broken glass
In our dry cellar

Shape without form, shade without colour,
Paralysed force, gesture without motion;

Those who have crossed
With direct eyes, to death's other Kingdom
Remember us—if at all—not as lost
Violent souls, but only
As the hollow men
The stuffed men.

2
Eyes I dare not meet in dreams
In death's dream kingdom
These do not appear:
There, the eyes are
Sunlight on a broken column
There, is a tree swinging
And voices are
In the wind's singing
More distant and more solemn
Than a fading star.

Let me be no nearer
In death's dream kingdom
Let me also wear
Such deliberate disguises
Rat's coat, crowskin, crossed staves
In a field
Behaving as the wind behaves
No nearer—

Not that final meeting
In the twilight kingdom

3
This is the dead land
This is cactus land
Here the stone images
Are raised, here they receive
The supplication of a dead man's hand
Under the twinkle of a fading star.
Is it like this
In death's other kingdom
Waking alone
At the hour when we are
Trembling with tenderness
Lips that would kiss
Form prayers to broken stone.

4

The eyes are not here
There are no eyes here
In this valley of dying stars
In this hollow valley
This broken jaw of our lost kingdoms

In this last of meeting places
We grope together
And avoid speech
Gathered on this beach of the tumid river

Sightless, unless
The eyes reappear
As the perpetual star
Multifoliate rose
Of death's twilight kingdom
The hope only
Of empty men.

5

Here we go round the prickly pear
Prickly pear prickly pear
Here we go round the prickly pear
At five o'clock in the morning.

Between the idea
And the reality
Between the motion
And the act
Falls the Shadow
                    For Thine is the Kingdom

Between the conception
And the creation
Between the emotion
And the response
Falls the Shadow
                              Life is very long

Between the desire
And the spasm
Between the potency
And the existence
Between the essence
And the descent
Falls the Shadow
                    For Thine is the Kingdom

For Thine is
Life is
For Thine is the

This is the way the world ends
This is the way the world ends
This is the way the world ends
Not with a bang but a whimper.

Depression is tonality and physical state. It is the absence of meaning. It is life's negation. It is grayness . . . emptiness.

COMPRESSION

Compression is a distillation, a condensation of language and behavior from which nothing more can be taken and little added. At its tersest, it can be the interjection: the release in language of total frustration, total disgust, extreme elation, ultimate joy. Tennyson, in his "Flower in the Crannied Wall," uses compression of utterance for the purpose of distillation.

Flower in the Crannied Wall

Alfred, Lord Tennyson

Flower in the crannied wall,
I pluck you out of the crannies,
I hold you here, root and all, in my hand,
Little flower—but *if* I could understand
What you are, root and all, and all in all,
I should know what God and man is.

The performer's task in this short poem is to distill its compressed components.

In Adelaide Crapsey's "Cinquain: Triad" we experience total compression of event.

Cinquain: Triad[12]

Adelaide Crapsey

These be
Three silent things:
The falling snow . . . the hour
Before the dawn . . . the mouth of one
Just dead.

Nothing more, and nothing less, can be said or—more importantly for the performer—is said in the poem.

---

12. "Cinquain: Triad" by Adelaide Crapsey from *The New Poetry* by Harriet Monroe. Reprinted by permission of Marguerite F. Fetcher.

The problems of compression are so important to interpretive artistry that they will be treated again and in a somewhat different perspective in Chapters 4 and 7 where we discuss figurative language and persona. But we have touched upon the matter here because the student cannot begin too early to try to understand the profound effects of compression in delivery. Compression, for example, is clearly evident in the two stanzas of A. E. Housman's "When I Was One-and-Twenty," and it is overwhelming in the last four words of the poem.

When I Was One-and-Twenty[13]

A. E. Housman

When I was one-and-twenty,
    I heard a wise man say,
"Give crowns and pounds and guineas
    But not your heart away;
Give pearls away and rubies
    But keep your fancy free."
But I was one-and-twenty,
    No use to talk to me.

When I was one-and-twenty,
    I heard him say again,
"The heart out of the bosom
    Was never given in vain;
'Tis paid with sighs a plenty
    And sold for endless rue."
And I am two-and-twenty,
    And oh, 'tis true, 'tis true.

What is the performative behavior necessary to compress "And oh, 'tis true, 'tis true"?

Compression is tied to gesture: the shrug of the shoulder, the lowering of the eyes, the quick and blazing glance, the slowly exhaled breath, the admonition in word and look.

SUPPRESSION

Suppression is what cannot be uttered, cannot be stated, because of the risks that it would involve. Suppression is that which is willfully withheld. In stanza after stanza of the folk ballad "Edward," we experience suppression of real truth.

---

13. "When I Was One-and-Twenty" from "A Shropshire Lad"—Authorised Edition—from *The Complete Poems of A. E. Housman.* Copyright 1939, 1940, © 1965 by Holt, Rinehart and Winston, Inc. Copyright © 1967, 1968 by Robert E. Symons. Reprinted by permission of Holt, Rinehart and Winston, Inc., The Society of Authors as the literary representative of the Estate of A. E. Housman and Jonathan Cape Ltd., Publishers of A. E. Housman's *Collected Poems.*

Edward

Anonymous

"Why dois your brand sae drap wi bluid,
      Edward, Edward,
Why dois your brand sae drap wi bluid,
    And why sae sad gang yee O?"
"O I hae killed my hauke sae guid,
      Mither, mither,
O I hae killed my hauke sae guid,
    And I had nae mair bot hee O."

"Your haukis bluid was nevir sae reid,
      Edward, Edward,
Your haukis bluid was nevir sae reid,
    My deir son I tell thee O."
"O I hae killed my reid-roan steid,
      Mither, mither,
O I hae killed my reid-roan steid,
    That erst was sae fair and frie O."

"Your steid was auld, and ye hae gat mair,
      Edward, Edward,
Your steid was auld, and ye hae gat mair,
    Sum other dule ye drie O."
"O I hae killed my fadir deir,
      Mither, mither,
O I hae killed my fadir deir,
    Alas, and wae is mee O!"

"And whatten penance wul ye drie for that,
      Edward, Edward?
And whatten penance wul ye drie for that?
    My deir son, now tell me O."
"Ile set my feit in yonder boat,
      Mither, mither,
Ile set my feit in yonder boat,
    And Ile fare ovir the sea O."

"And what wul ye doe with your towirs and your ha,
     Edward, Edward?
And what wul ye doe wi your towirs and your ha,
    That were sae fair to se O?"
"Ile let thame stand tul they doun fa,
     Mither, mither,
Ile let thame stand tul they doun fa,
    For here nevir mair maun I bee O."

"And what wul ye leive to your bairns and your wife,
     Edward, Edward?
And what wul ye leive to your bairns and your wife,
    Whan ye gang ovir the sea O?"
"The warldis room, late them beg thrae life,
     Mither, mither,
The warldis room, late them beg thrae life,
    For thame nevir mair wul I see O."

"And what wul ye leive to your ain mither deir,
     Edward, Edward?
And what wul ye leive to your ain mither deir?
    My deir son, now tell me O."
"The curse of hell frae me sall ye beir,
     Mither, mither,
The curse of hell frae me sall ye beir,
    Sic counseils ye gave to me O."

In his anger and hostility, Edward suppresses the truth of his actions until finally he can no longer contain his anger and hatred for his mother. Until the performer comprehends the nature of Edward's boiling suppression, he cannot create the explosive atmosphere in which the audience awaits the information Edward is withholding.

Associated with and emerging from suppression is a behavior that must manifest itself in performance: tightness, wariness, withdrawal, a deliberate and anxious choosing of language, a sense of containing something within the mind that dare not be expressed. Suppression is the uneasy presence of unseen forces ready to erupt. The eruption or the struggle for control is often what makes literature intriguing and fascinating for the perceiver.

REPRESSION

Very closely allied to suppression is repression. We may describe repression as a psychological state of unconsciously holding in, of failing to recognize what is necessary to express. In "The Love Song of J. Alfred Prufrock," we encounter an aging man whose life has been, in effect, one of continual and habitual repression.

The Love Song of J. Alfred Prufrock[14]

T. S. Eliot

> *S'io credesse che mia risposta fosse*
> *A persona che mai tornasse al mondo,*
> *Questa fiamma staria senza piu scosse.*
> *Ma perciocche giammai di questo fondo*
> *Non torno vivo alcun, s'i'odo il vero,*
> *Senza tema d'infamia ti rispondo.*[15]

Let us go then, you and I,
When the evening is spread out against the sky
Like a patient etherised upon a table;
Let us go, through certain half-deserted streets,
The muttering retreats
Of restless nights in one-night cheap hotels
And sawdust restaurants with oyster-shells:
Streets that follow like a tedious argument
Of insidious intent
To lead you to an overwhelming question. . .
Oh, do not ask, "What is it?"
Let us go and make our visit.

In the room the women come and go
Talking of Michelangelo.

14. "The Love Song of J. Alfred Prufrock" from *Collected Poems 1909–1962* by T. S. Eliot, copyright, 1936, by Harcourt Brace Jovanovich, Inc.; copyright © 1963, 1964, by T. S. Eliot. Reprinted by permission of Harcourt Brace Jovanovich, Inc. and Faber and Faber Limited.

15. "If I could believe that my answer might be to a person who should ever return into the world, this flame would stand without more quiverings; but inasmuch as, if I hear the truth, never from this depth did any living man return, without fear of infamy I answer thee."—Dante, *Inferno,* XXVII, ll. 61–66.

The yellow fog that rubs its back upon the window-panes,
The yellow smoke that rubs its muzzle on the window-panes
Licked its tongue into the corners of the evening,
Lingered upon the pools that stand in drains,
Let fall upon its back the soot that falls from chimneys,
Slipped by the terrace, made a sudden leap,
And seeing that it was a soft October night,
Curled once about the house, and fell asleep.

And indeed there will be time
For the yellow smoke that slides along the street,
Rubbing its back upon the window-panes;
There will be time, there will be time
To prepare a face to meet the faces that you meet;
There will be time to murder and create,
And time for all the works and days of hands
That lift and drop a question on your plate;
Time for you and time for me,
And time yet for a hundred indecisions,
And for a hundred visions and revisions,
Before the taking of a toast and tea.

In the room the women come and go
Talking of Michelangelo.

And indeed there will be time
To wonder, "Do I dare?" and, "Do I dare?"
Time to turn back and descend the stair,
With a bald spot in the middle of my hair—
[They will say: "How his hair is growing thin!"]
My morning coat, my collar mounting firmly to the chin,
My necktie rich and modest, but asserted by a simple pin—
[They will say: "But how his arms and legs are thin!"]
Do I dare
Disturb the universe?
In a minute there is time
For decisions and revisions which a minute will reverse.

For I have known them all already, known them all:—
Have known the evenings, mornings, afternoons,

I have measured out my life with coffee spoons;
I know the voices dying with a dying fall
Beneath the music from a farther room.
　　　So how should I presume?

And I have known the eyes already, known them all—
The eyes that fix you in a formulated phrase,
And when I am formulated, sprawling on a pin,
When I am pinned and wriggling on the wall,
Then how should I begin
To spit out all the butt-ends of my days and ways?
　　　And how should I presume?

And I have known the arms already, known them all—
Arms that are braceleted and white and bare
[But in the lamplight, downed with light brown hair!]
Is it perfume from a dress
That makes me so digress?
Arms that lie along a table, or wrap about a shawl.
　　　And should I then presume?
　　　And how should I begin?

　　　　　.　　.　　.　　.　　.

Shall I say, I have gone at dusk through narrow streets
And watched the smoke that rises from the pipes
Of lonely men in shirt-sleeves, leaning out of windows? . . .

I should have been a pair of ragged claws
Scuttling across the floors of silent seas.

　　　　　.　　.　　.　　.　　.

And the afternoon, the evening, sleeps so peacefully!
Smoothed by long fingers,
Asleep . . . tired . . . or it malingers,
Stretched on the floor, here beside you and me.
Should I, after tea and cakes and ices,
Have the strength to force the moment to its crisis?
But though I have wept and fasted, wept and prayed,
Though I have seen my head [grown slightly bald] brought in upon a platter,
I am no prophet—and here's no great matter;

I have seen the moment of my greatness flicker,
And I have seen the eternal Footman hold my coat, and snicker,
And in short, I was afraid.

And would it have been worth it, after all,
After the cups, the marmalade, the tea,
Among the porcelain, among some talk of you and me,
Would it have been worth while,
To have bitten off the matter with a smile,
To have squeezed the universe into a ball
To roll it toward some overwhelming question,
To say: "I am Lazarus, come from the dead,
Come back to tell you all, I shall tell you all"—
If one, settling a pillow by her head,
      Should say: "That is not what I meant at all.
      That is not it, at all."

And would it have been worth it, after all,
Would it have been worth while,
After the sunsets and the dooryards and the sprinkled streets,
After the novels, after the teacups, after the skirts that trail along the floor—
And this, and so much more?—
It is impossible to say just what I mean!
But as if a magic lantern threw the nerves in patterns on a screen:
Would it have been worth while
If one, settling a pillow or throwing off a shawl,
And turning toward the window, should say:
      "That is not it at all,
      That is not what I meant, at all."

                    .   .   .   .   .   .

No! I am not Prince Hamlet, nor was meant to be;
Am an attendant lord, one that will do
To swell a progress, start a scene or two,
Advise the prince; no doubt, an easy tool,
Deferential, glad to be of use,
Politic, cautious, and meticulous;
Full of high sentence, but a bit obtuse;
At times, indeed, almost ridiculous—
Almost, at times, the Fool.

I grow old . . . I grow old . . .
I shall wear the bottoms of my trousers rolled.

Shall I part my hair behind? Do I dare to eat a peach?
I shall wear white flannel trousers, and walk upon the beach.
I have heard the mermaids singing, each to each.

I do not think that they will sing to me.

I have seen them riding seaward on the waves
Combing the white hair of the waves blown back
When the wind blows the water white and black.

We have lingered in the chambers of the sea
By sea-girls wreathed with seaweed red and brown
Till human voices wake us, and we drown.

Prufrock's incapacity to act, his dalliance with daring himself to do something — anything — is pathetic and strangely moving.

When a performer recognizes the experience of repression, he will want to ask
why the character he is encountering is repressed. Sometimes the sources of the repression will not be stated or made obvious; at other times, they are made explicit. In
either case the performer should *appear* as if he were withholding a key to the source
of the repression while, at the same time, subtly revealing important clues to the personality of the repressed one.

In the presentation of repression, certain intentional ambiguities haunt the performance. It could be argued that in Sylvia Plath's poem "Lady Lazarus" what is being
repressed is the will to live, to endure.

Lady Lazarus[16]

Sylvia Plath

I have done it again.
One year in every ten
I manage it—

A sort of walking miracle, my skin
Bright as a Nazi lampshade,
My right foot

A paperweight,
My face a featureless, fine
Jew linen.

Peel off the napkin
O my enemy.
Do I terrify?—

The nose, the eye pits, the full set of teeth?
The sour breath
Will vanish in a day.

Soon, soon the flesh
The grave cave ate will be
At home on me

And I a smiling woman.
I am only thirty.
And like the cat I have nine times to die.

This is Number Three.
What a trash
To annihilate each decade.

What a million filaments.
The peanut-crunching crowd
Shoves in to see

Them unwrap me hand and foot—
The big strip tease.
Gentleman, ladies,

These are my hands,
My knees.
I may be skin and bone,

Nevertheless, I am the same, identical woman.
The first time it happened I was ten.
It was an accident.

The second time I meant
To last it out and not come back at all.
I rocked shut

As a seashell.
They had to call and call
And pick the worms off me like sticky pearls.

Dying
Is an art, like everything else.
I do it exceptionally well.

I do it so it feels like hell.
I do it so it feels real.
I guess you could say I've a call.

It's easy enough to do it in a cell.
It's easy enough to do it and stay put.
It's the theatrical

Comeback in broad day
To the same place, the same face, the same brute
Amused shout:

"A miracle!"
That knocks me out.
There is a charge

For the eyeing of my scars, there is a charge
For the hearing of my heart—
It really goes.

And there is a charge, a very large charge,
For a word or a touch
Or a bit of blood

Or a piece of my hair or my clothes.
So, so, Herr Doktor.
So, Herr Enemy.

I am your opus,
I am your valuable,
The pure gold baby

That melts to a shriek.
I turn and burn.
Do not think I underestimate your great concern.

Ash, ash—
You poke and stir.
Flesh, bone, there is nothing there—

A cake of soap,
A wedding ring,
A gold filling.

Herr God, Herr Lucifer,
Beware
Beware.

Out of the ash
I rise with my red hair
And I eat men like air.

Paradoxically, what is being *expressed,* frankly and hauntingly, is the desire to die.
In a performance of ''Lady Lazarus,'' by what kind of specific behavior can the interpretive artist capture and project for his auditors the unseen and unstated repression?

94   Behavior in Performance

By reason of its subtleties, repression signals its presence by significant but often minute behavioral clues. A concomitant of the expressed statement "I am going to kill myself" is often the repressed plea "Save me!" The skillful performer has to make crucial decisions regarding the behavior he will employ to indicate the opposing life force. How, for instance, does a performer suggest Prufrock's need to be loved? When the interpretive artist moves toward the solution of such a dilemma, he must begin to make selective decisions regarding delivery and other performative behaviors.

OPPRESSION

Oppression is the insistence of an opposing force. As you may have noted in the ballad "Edward," it is Edward's mother who is the oppressor, the antagonist who presses in upon Edward and gives to his life anxiety and madness, but—at the same time—a will to endure. In literature the oppressive force or forces may exist *outside of* or external to the individual (oppressive social, moral, or political conditions); or they may exist *inside* his life or internally, an integral part of his existence (oppressive weights like the drag of time, the lack of energy, overwhelming doubts). In Ellison's *Invisible Man* how can the hero of the piece live in the oppressive white world?

from **Invisible Man**[17]

Ralph Ellison

[The speaker of this novel recounts his cruel and savage introduction to social bigotry and duplicity. Advised by a gentle, dying grandfather to "kill whites with kindness" ("undermine 'em with grins, agree 'em to death and destruction"), the narrator is left with guilt and confusion regarding his role and place in society. Upon his graduation from high school, he is selected to give the graduation oration, an oration that stresses "humility" as the essence of racial progress—a youthful and naive position as he later finds out. The speech is a success, and he is invited to give it at a gathering of the town's leading white citizens. When he arrives, however, he finds himself at something more than an evening of speaking: the whites are prepared for a "battle royal" between members of a black gang and the narrator. The battle itself is staged by blindfolding the participants and urging them to maul and hurt each other. The narrator is eventually pitched against Tatlock, one of the biggest mem-

17. From *Invisible Man*, by Ralph Ellison. Copyright 1952 by Ralph Ellison. Reprinted by permission of Random House, Inc.

bers of the gang. The two are frightened and moved to fight by a sheer instinct for survival, and the battle reaches a sadistic climax before it is eventually stopped. The boys are "paid" for their services by being asked to pick coins, old bills, and gold coins from an electrified rug. In the following excerpt it is after this ordeal that the narrator is brought back for his speech—an event almost overlooked by the socially prominent whites who had brought him there.]

When we had dressed the M.C. came in and gave us each five dollars, except Tatlock, who got ten for being last in the ring. Then he told us to leave. I was not to get a chance to deliver my speech, I thought. I was going out into the dim alley in despair when I was stopped and told to go back. I returned to the ballroom, where the men were pushing back their chairs and gathering in groups to talk.

The M.C. knocked on a table for quiet. "Gentlemen," he said, "we almost forgot an important part of the program. A most serious part, gentlemen. This boy was brought here to deliver a speech which he made at his graduation yesterday . . ."

"Bravo!"

"I'm told that he is the smartest boy we've got out there in Greenwood. I'm told that he knows more big words than a pocket-sized dictionary."

Much applause and laughter.

"So now, gentlemen, I want you to give him your attention."

There was still laughter as I faced them, my mouth dry, my eye throbbing. I began slowly, but evidently my throat was tense, because they began shouting, "Louder! Louder!"

"We of the younger generation extol the wisdom of that great leader and educator," I shouted, "who first spoke these flaming words of wisdom: 'A ship lost at sea for many days suddenly sighted a friendly vessel. From the mast of the unfortunate vessel was seen a signal: "Water, water; we die of thirst!" The answer from the friendly vessel came back: "Cast down your bucket where you are." The captain of the distressed vessel, at last heeding the injunction, cast down his bucket, and it came up full of fresh sparkling water from the mouth of the Amazon River.' And like him I say, and in his words, 'To those of my race who depend upon bettering their condition in a foreign land, or who underestimate the importance of cultivating friendly relations with the Southern white man, who is his next-door neighbor, I would say: "Cast down your bucket where you are"—cast it down in making friends in every manly way of the people of all races by whom we are surrounded . . .' "

I spoke automatically and with such fervor that I did not realize that the men were still talking and laughing until my dry mouth, filling up with the blood from the cut, almost strangled me. I coughed, wanting to stop and go to one of the tall brass, sand-filled spittoons to relieve myself, but a few of the men, especially the superintendent, were listening and I was afraid. So I gulped it down, blood, saliva and all, and continued. (What powers of endurance I had during those days! What enthusiasm! What a belief in the rightness of things!) I spoke even louder in spite of the pain. But still they talked and still they laughed, as though deaf with cotton in dirty ears. So I spoke with greater emotional emphasis. I closed my ears and swallowed blood until I was nauseated. The speech seemed a hundred times as long as before, but I could not leave out a single word. All had to be said, each memorized nuance considered, rendered. Nor was that all. Whenever I uttered a word of three or more syllables a group of voices would yell for me to repeat it. I used the phrase "social responsibility" and they yelled:

"What's that word you say, boy?"

"Social responsibility," I said.

"What?"

"Social . . ."

"Louder."

". . . responsibility."

"More!"

"Respon-"

"Repeat!"

"-sibility."

The room filled with the uproar of laughter until, no doubt, distracted by having to gulp down my blood, I made a mistake and yelled a phrase I had often seen denounced in newspaper editorials, heard debated in private.

"Social . . ."

"What?" they yelled.

". . . equality—"

The laughter hung smokelike in the sudden stillness. I opened my eyes, puzzled. Sounds of displeasure filled the room. The M.C. rushed forward. They shouted hostile phrases at me. But I did not understand.

A small dry mustached man in the front row blared out, "Say that slowly, son!"

"What, sir?"

"What you just said!"

"Social responsibility, sir," I said.

"You weren't being smart, were you, boy?" he said, not unkindly.

"No, sir!"

"You sure that about 'equality' was a mistake?"

"Oh, yes, sir," I said. "I was swallowing blood."

"Well, you had better speak more slowly so we can understand. We mean to do right by you, but you've got to know your place at all times. All right, now, go on with your speech."

I was afraid. I wanted to leave but I wanted also to speak and I was afraid they'd snatch me down.

"Thank you, sir," I said, beginning where I had left off, and having them ignore me as before.

Yet when I finished there was a thunderous applause. I was surprised to see the superintendent come forth with a package wrapped in white tissue paper, and, gesturing for quiet, address the men.

"Gentlemen, you see that I did not overpraise this boy. He makes a good speech and some day he'll lead his people in the proper paths. And I don't have to tell you that that is important in these days and times. This is a good, smart boy, and so to encourage him in the right direction, in the name of the Board of Education I wish to present him a prize in the form of this . . ."

He paused, removing the tissue paper and revealing a gleaming calfskin brief case.

". . . in the form of this first-class article from Shad Whitmore's shop."

"Boy," he said, addressing me, "take this prize and keep it well. Consider it a badge of office. Prize it. Keep developing as you are and some day it will be filled with important papers that will help shape the destiny of your people."

I was so moved that I could hardly express my thanks. A rope of bloody saliva forming a shape like an undiscovered continent drooled upon the leather and I wiped it quickly away. I felt an importance that I had never dreamed.

"Open it and see what's inside," I was told.

My fingers a-tremble, I complied, smelling the fresh leather and finding an official-looking document inside. It was a scholarship to the state college for Negroes. My eyes filled with tears and I ran awkwardly off the floor.

I was overjoyed; I did not even mind when I discovered that the gold pieces I had scrambled for were brass pocket tokens advertising a certain make of automobile.

When I reached home everyone was excited. Next day the neighbors came to congratulate me. I even felt safe from grandfather, whose deathbed curse usually spoiled my triumphs. I stood beneath his photograph with my brief case in hand and smiled triumphantly into his stolid black peasant's face. It was a face that fascinated me. The eyes seemed to follow everywhere I went.

That night I dreamed I was at a circus with him and that he refused to laugh at the clowns no matter what they did. Then later he told me to open my brief case and read what was inside and I did, finding an official envelope stamped with the state seal; and inside the envelope I found another and another, endlessly, and I thought I would fall of weariness. "Them's years," he said. "Now open that one." And I did and in it I found an engraved document containing a short message in letters of gold. "Read it," my grandfather said. "Out loud."

"To Whom It May Concern," I intoned. "Keep This Nigger-Boy Running."

I awoke with the old man's laughter ringing in my ears.

(It was a dream I was to remember and dream again for many years after. But at that time I had no insight into its meaning. First I had to attend college.)

In the interpretation of oppression, the performer must indicate by his behavior the existence and nature of the opposing force; he must make it manifest; he must clearly identify it and, often, its origins. Of course, he should be aware, too, that oppressive forces or conditions can lead to *de*pression, or *ex*pression, or *com*pression of statement, or *sup*pression of emotion. As auditors we know oppression by its presence.

THE INTERPLAY OF THE PRESSES

As we pointed out at the beginning of this discussion, the presses of literature seldom exist in isolation. Rather, as the preceding analysis would suggest, they come in combinations, often complex combinations. But however they may be present in the literature, they can only be made manifest by means of behavioral patterning. There is, for instance, a "voice" of depression just as surely as there is a "voice" of suppressed hostility. The interpreter's task is to make his physical organism and emotional sensitivities a suitable sounding board—a resonator—for these presses. He can do so only by beginning early in his training to identify, to isolate, and to experiment with them discriminatingly.

In analyzing a literary selection, the interpreter will need to make clear that a given press is working and how it is working; he will recognize that each press poses its own unique problems in delivery and performing behavior—always cognizant that a conscious awareness of the problems usually results in a richer and far more meaningful performance. In the analysis generally the more useful procedure is to concentrate on and describe the *overall* effect to be created, rather than to parcel the presses through the selection. An overall or totality of effect is almost always more significant and more involving than a mere elaboration of parts.

AESTHETIC DETERMINANTS OF PERFORMATIVE BEHAVIOR

Not only must the performing artist know what to *do;* he must also know what *not* to do. A major concern of the auxiliary artist is that he do nothing to detract from his listeners' enjoyment of the literature. He must eliminate personal mannerisms or behaviors that would by their nature call attention to themselves. To do otherwise can only result in a distracting conflict between his personal life style and his performing style. Although audience expectations may vary widely, and while tastes, being as diverse as they are, cannot be anticipated, the performer-in-training can be guided, nevertheless, by certain aesthetic principles fundamental to the presentation of literature.

DICTATES OF THE LITERATURE AND ITS STYLE

In all instances *the literature and its style dictate the general approaches and attitudes to be taken toward the audience.* As we pointed out earlier in this chapter, ascertaining the predominant mode determines in large part the kind of relationship the performer will have with his audience. If the student will review the chart outlining the broad differences in the three literary modes (page 65), he will see how behavior in performance can vary from a sense of intimate confrontation to a distance that is framed and ostensibly remote. While certain lyric poems, for instance, would be experienced by an auditor as an intimate overhearing of innermost exploration, an epic or narrative would be experienced through a storyteller who might vary widely his distance from or intimacy with an audience.

Most writers establish quite definitely the sense of distance between their creation and the reader-auditor-perceiver; the sensitive reader apprehends, or intuits, the distance the work requires, and the performing artist must be constantly aware of the precise *extent* of this distance. In the presentation of dramatic literature the interpretive artist often places an aesthetic distance between the characters he is embodying and the audience, being careful to avoid any direct confrontation. Distancing is not always advisable, however. Certain contemporary playwrights seem to strive for the ultimate in closeness, asking total involvement and no distancing at all between the audience and the presence of the literary characters. In this case the performer must achieve an imposing sense of presence.

The performer who, for any reason, distorts the distancing or non-distancing of the literature is placing himself or the preferences of his audience above the literature, thereby misrepresenting the intent of the original artist and the stylistic imperatives which are rightfully his. If a performer feels that an audience cannot "take" the outrages of the writer's passion, he may choose not to read the material for that audience; if he chooses to read it, his task is to be faithful to the candor of the writer's style. The behavior of the artist in performance must be congruent to the literature in performance if the whole is to be aesthetically satisfying.

THE PERFORMER AS SOURCE OF AESTHETIC ENJOYMENT

In the performance of a literary work, the performer becomes the source of enjoyment (aesthesis). In viewing a motion picture adapted from a play or novel, the viewer does not use the original play or novel as the basis for his reaction to the viewing experience. Rather, he uses the film-viewing experience. Should he want to compare this experience to the original play, that is his prerogative, of course. This would also be true in comparing the reading of the novel with the viewing of the film. The point is that the motion picture exists as motion picture, and it will be enjoyed or criticized or discussed from that perspective. Did it work? Did it move? Did it have distinctive style? Did it create satisfactory illusion? These and similar questions may be asked of the film.

There is a parallel here: in the performance of literature, it is the *performance* which is the source of enjoyment, not an abstract sense of literature-in-performance. The performer and the literature become as one; and in the truly successful interpretation, it should be as difficult to distinguish one from the other as to distinguish the dancer from the dance. In the successful performance of literature, the audience feels that the total behavior of the performer was appropriate to and congruent with the literature; in fact, the audience should perceive the *fusion.*

An example of this fusion would by Dylan Thomas, the Welsh poet, reading his own work. For those who were fortunate enough to see and hear him in concert, the only true performer of the literature of Dylan Thomas was *Dylan Thomas.* So complete is the fusion of sound, language, and behavior in the memory of his presentation that even today a performance of Thomas' poetry is inevitably compared to the recordings of the poet's own reading of his works. Earlier, American audiences felt the same way about Vachel Lindsay. No one, it was believed, could achieve a total realization of his writing as well as Lindsay himself. Audiences who heard Theodore Roethke no doubt retain a similarly strong sense of the fusion of the poetry and the poet-as-reader; any other performing artist would have to be exemplary to overcome the bias. In these cases memory fails to distinguish between the poet-performer and his poems; thus, the performer was the source of enjoyment.

THE ACCOUNTABILITY OF THE AUXILIARY ARTIST

The performer may be held accountable for his interpretation, his mastery, and his control of the literary work. Audiences in general become familiar with literary masterpieces, and students of literature come early to know literature's unique demands. Certain normative standards and concepts of behavior have come into existence through this knowledge and familiarity, and audiences are quick to note any deviations.

Body, voice, and personal projection. While the performing artist knows that the literature as such is his first and abiding concern, he also knows that it is through him that the experience of the literature is being perceived and felt; and for this reason he dedicates himself to the elimination of all personal mannerisms and stylistics of personal performance which might be intrusive. The questions in the behavioral-analysis checklist are offered as a point of departure for the beginning interpretive artist in exploring his potentialities and limitations.

A BEHAVIORAL-ANALYSIS CHECKLIST

1. Is my body a suitable instrument of expression?
    —Is it supple, free?
    —Is it responsive to rhythm and movement?
    —Does it capitalize upon nervous energy and use the energy for constructive purposes?
    —Does it move freely in space?
2. Is my voice a suitable instrument of expression?
    —Can I use my voice flexibly and project it effortlessly?
    —Am I using my voice at its natural pitch?
    —Do I have vocally responsive qualities that I may use at will?
    —Do I sustain tone by adequate breathing necessary for projection in performance?
    —Do I have the freedom to vary at will the rate (or speed) of my speaking?
3. Is my personality open and freely receptive to the varied ranges and experiences of literature?
    —Am I free of projecting my own feelings into everything I read?
    —Am I emotionally available to personalities other than my own?
    —Am I willing to take the risks that literary involvement demands?
    —Am I capable of not imposing my own morality upon literature, allowing writers to work freely and openly through me?
    —Am I open to and accepting of new and unusual experiences?

While the largest proportion of time and attention in this book will be directed to studying the aesthetics of literature, its form and its elements, it would be a serious omission to overlook the aesthetics of performance. Performance, as we have emphasized, is guided by three main considerations:

1. The aesthetic distance in performance is determined by the literature and not by the performer.
2. The performer is the source of the aesthetic enjoyment, and not the literature in the abstract sense of its being some kind of "object" existing between performer and audience.
3. The audience may—and usually does—hold the interpretive artist accountable for his interpretation, as well as for his mastery and control of the literary work.

With reference to aesthetic distance, the literature itself determines how intimately and integrally it shall be a part of an audience's experience; a performer's attempt to redistance the literature is an encroachment upon the writer's artistic individuality. In the case of the performer-as-source-of-aesthetic-satisfaction, the immediacy of performance and the unique role the auxiliary artist plays as intermediary between the creative artist and his literary work and between that work and the auditor/perceiver compel his recognition as the source of the literary experience. And finally, in the case of the performer's accountability, he is obligated to be free of idiosyncratic behaviors of all kinds and sensitively available to the material, modes, and moods of the literary artist.

Our consideration of behavior in performance would not be complete without an examination of what many consider to be one of the major non-aesthetic influences upon performative behavior: namely, stage fright. For our purposes we shall view this phenomenon in a more positive light and shall call it *presentational energy*.

PRESENTATIONAL ENERGY

The one fact of performance familiar to all students and artists is the phenomenon of inner turmoil, adrenalation, and possible physical discomfort—a condition commonly known as stage fright. There is no literature and no music that possesses stage fright in and of itself; it is human beings who impose upon performances the all-too-familiar manifestations of stage fright: muscular tension, a faltering voice, an excessively dry mouth, perspiration, an uncontrollable nervousness, and the like. Because stage fright immediately seizes the primary focus of the audience, it is detrimental to their aesthetic involvement with the literature being presented.

STAGE FRIGHT DEFINED

Psychologists and psychiatrists do not agree unreservedly on the proper definition and causes of the phenomenon, but certain helpful generalizations can be made. We may note, to begin with, that it is a natural phenomenon that occurs within the body when it is commanded to perform under conditions which the individual interprets as a stress situation. Athletes experience it; performers, of course, know it, as do lecturers and practically all others who are "set" for an important trial of talent. Stage fright, an adrenalation of the neurophysical system, occurs automatically upon the perception of that crucial moment. One can experience small waves of adrenalation long before the actual moment of performance; days before the event the thought of the impending presentation can trigger small amounts of inner turmoil.

There is no "cure" for stage fright, nor — if we view it as presentational energy — should there be. It is an entirely natural activity by which the body strives for alertness and maximization of its total resources. That it can become excessive and debilitating cannot be denied, but for most people this is fortunately rare. Wise individuals learn to use this energy for maximizing their particular talents.

How does stage fright come about? Part of its origin can be found in our reaction to a situation in which the opinion of a highly valued someone is held as being extremely important. For a performer this "someone" may be a critic, an audience in general, a group of special observers, anyone who, in a psychological sense, can reward or punish. Indeed, the someone may be the performer *himself.* (Note the expression, "He is his own severest critic.") Conversely, one experiences less stage fright when the stakes are low, when those in the audience are not perceived as crucial to one's functioning. In practice sessions or even with friends in genial competition, an athlete will not be excessively keyed up and will perform without anxiety. However, when the moment of crucial competition is at hand, he experiences the familiar signals of readiness and anxiety. It is important to the athlete to be judged a winner; so it is with the performer of literature. He wants the approval of an audience or a critic or a professor, perhaps; and his neurophysical system responds accordingly.

SOME DETRIMENTAL EFFECTS OF STAGE FRIGHT

Are there detrimental aspects of stage fright? Yes, most certainly there are. When the performer gives to the opinion of the critic a higher priority or value than he gives to a proper involvement with audience aesthesis, stage fright tends to be inordinate. If the performer confronts a crucial someone who he feels will be difficult to satisfy, anxiety will be high. In open and accepting situations, which the classroom should be, anxiety should be lower. One very important key to understanding stage fright is *approval:* from whom does the performer want it? to what degree or extent? when and how?

STAGE FRIGHT AS APPROVAL—SEEKING

From whom do you as a performer want approval? This question deserves careful thought because—consciously or subconsciously—you may aim your performance toward a particular person or a false standard, thereby distorting the actual values of the literature in favor of the values of the person or persons you are trying to impress. Most professional performers establish inner and outer approval patterns. They know what is adequate and professional for them, a standard of performance which is in all ways professional by their definition; and, at the same time, they remain receptive to the standards and evaluations of critics whom they value. Thus, they strike a balance between their own standards of performance and those being imposed from without. The development of any sensitive artist includes both.

To what degree and extent is approval necessary? Artists who are rather insecure often seem to ask that every aspect of their work be accepted in toto. This is, of course, an unreasonable request to make of any critic. A piece of true criticism is an act of sharing tastes. The performer need not feel it necessary to be approved by all critics unanimously. The artist's capacity to listen to criticism, to find worth and value in it—and to reject some of it—is an important aspect of growth and development.

When and how should criticism be given? The individual who is highly keyed up finds it almost impossible to be objectively receptive to criticism immediately after his performance. An athlete knows at the close of an event whether he has won or lost, but criticism of his performance is usually postponed, often as much as three or four days following the contest. However, the artistic performer will often seek criticism immediately, despite the fact that he is not really ready for it and despite the liklihood that he will not be able, actually, to benefit from it until he has had time to put his feelings about his performance into an objective frame.

Every performer should develop his own "when" for criticism. If criticism is to be valuable, it should be growth-oriented and not develop into debates. To listen and to evaluate is an important two-way process. Ideally, the critic has listened and has evaluated; and his performance of criticism—the perception and sensitivity with which he makes it—should be as respected as the performance of literature. Ideally, too, the critic has some sensibility about what is important criticism and what is not; but the performer should, in any case, hear him through or read him thoroughly and then decide which portions of the criticisms are useful and valid for him and which ones can be incorporated into his performative behavior.

PRESENTATIONAL ENERGY AS IMPETUS FOR GROWTH

We have noted that growth in the arts is incremental, but it is seldom an orderly and proportioned process. The artist experiences sudden spurts of creativity and capability, only to be confronted with ensuing fallow periods of no apparent change. The creative teacher and critic recognize that patterns of individual growth vary widely, and the performer should come to recognize and accept the rate and variations of his growth-progress. The study of his own growth and presentational energy should prompt the performer to ask himself two very important questions:

1. To whom am I directing my presentational energy?
    To myself? (−)
    To a specific person? (+/−)
    To a generalized audience? (+)
2. On what am I focusing my energy?
    On my distractive inadequacies? (−)
    On my attractive adequacies? (+)
    On the intricacies of the work at hand? (+)
    On the re-creation of an "event" in literature? (+)

Generally, the auxiliary performing artist may safely assume that if he is directing and focusing his presentational energies on the task at hand and if he has thoroughly and perceptively prepared the material he intends to perform, then—rather than anxiety, dread, or fright—he will experience a sense of competency and exhilaration. Under these circumstances, any criticism of his performance should not be interpreted as an attack upon his person or his integrity as an artist. Ego-strength, he should remember, is something which he must generate from within; it cannot be given to him by someone else. Unfortunately, he may from time to time encounter irresponsible critics who use the domain of criticism for making capricious and irresponsible attacks upon the personality of the artist and who do not honestly involve themselves with the task of evaluating the performance of the work and the fidelity of the performance to the demands of the literature. Such critics the artist must learn to recognize and to live with as best he can.

CHECKLIST FOR ANALYSIS

1. How would the metaworld of the literature be described? What is the "state of being" in the selection? What is the principal presentational value of the selection? (See chart on page 22.)

2. In what mode is the selection written? What are the central behavioral problems in the selection? in the "presses"?

EXERCISES AND ASSIGNMENTS

1. Select an example of the lyrical, narrative, and dramatic modes from the materials in this chapter. How does each seem to relate to an audience differently? How would performance of each require different attitudes toward an audience?

2. What are the specific bodily problems in the presentation of "Edward"? the selection from *Invisible Man?* What does a careful study of the parts of speech at any point reveal in these selections? What does the careful observation of verbs in each reveal?

3. What are examples of "language as gesture" in A. E. Housman's "When I Was One-and-Twenty"? How do the parts of speech function in this poem? What is the significance of tense in the poem?

4. What is the metaworld of T. S. Eliot's "The Hollow Men"? How does the world of the poem create gesture? What are the precise elements in the poem that point toward some particular press?

5. How would you describe the metaworld of Sylvia Plath's "Lady Lazarus"? What particular problems does it present for the performing body? In reading the poem aloud sympathetically, what is the message your own body tells you? How would you distinguish between this kind of "knowing" and a reflective, intellectual discussion of the poem?

6. How do the presses function through the body? What seems to be the key in allowing a particular press to work? How is the poem or prose transformed from print to body? Is there a change in the literature when a particular press is perceived and felt? How is perceiving not necessarily feeling?

7. Shelley's "Stanzas Written in Dejection, Near Naples" has a particular stanzaic structure. What are the "tonal" elements that give a particular pace to the language? (Use your everyday language to describe this; it is not necessary to know poetic terms to listen to the sound.) How is the pace of the poem akin to dejection itself?

8. What kind of love song does J. Alfred Prufrock sing? say? enact? What keys to Prufrock's bodily being are revealed by his language? How does the quotation from Dante's *Inferno* function in the poem? What behaviorial problems does it have for the performer?

9. Select any material from Chapter 1 and review it for its behaviorial problems in performance. Identify the modes of the material in Chapter 1.

10. In Thomas Wolfe's "Meadows of Sensation" (Chap. 1), what is the significance of the title for bodily involvements discussed in this chapter?

11. Why is stage fright a useful performing energy? How does it work to complement the energy of a poem or prose selection in performance? In the preparation of any material for class, how did the press of the literature seem more (or less) accessible in a private presentation? in a public presentation?

Objectives for Performance Growth

1 Exciting **2** Enjoyable **3** Adequate **4** Need for Development

To Evoke the Metaworlds

_____ a sense of inner resonance
_____ a sense of attaining a state of being
_____ a responsiveness to presentational values
_____ IMPRESSION

To Relate the Performing Body to Literary Experience

_____ behavior congruent to mode
_____ language of gesture natural to literary space
_____ sound of language natural to literary space
_____ appropriate behavioral presses
_____ appropriate use of total bodily energy
_____ IMPRESSION

To Share Awareness of Literary Time

_____ sense of performing time appropriate to literary time
_____ literary time understood and evocated
_____ silences understood and evocated
_____ metrical time understood and evocated
_____ IMPRESSION

To Evoke Figurative Thought and Language

_____ appropriate exemplification of language
_____ a sense of symbolic intent
_____ a sharing of paradox and irony—where appropriate
_____ IMPRESSION

To Evoke Form

_____ form of experience immediate and compelling
_____ form of literary structure appreciated and evocated
_____ IMPRESSION

To Present Style as New Information

_____ expectations in performance congruent to language
_____ performer and style linked / fused
_____ stylistic elements perceived and evocated
_____ narrator attachment or detachment appropriate
_____ IMPRESSION

To Evoke the Presence of Personae

_____ interactional and / or transactional dialogue evocated
_____ significant gesture of characters evocated
_____ structure of dialogue evocated
_____ IMPRESSION

3

Fredy Schnyder

TO SHARE AWARENESS OF LITERARY TIME

— through a sense of the function of time in literature
   — past, present, future
   — above (mythic time)
   — below
   — psychological time

— through an awareness of how language exists in time
   — its density
   — its sparsity

— through the perception and evocation of silences
   — characterological silence
   — situational silence
   — structural silence

— through metrical time perceived and evocated

CHAPTER THREE

Time in the Performance of Literature

TEMPORAL IMPLICATIONS IN LIFE AND LITERATURE

Literature has the peculiar and intriguing effect of providing us with perceptions *of* our lives at the same time it is being "performed" *in* the time of our lives. Just as there is a duality of space in literature, the metaworld that is created inside of us existing simultaneously with the world outside of us, so also is there a duality of time in literature, the time within and contained by the literature existing simultaneously with the time of our life.

As mortals, most of us — from the beginning — are reminded of and constantly confronted with the implications of temporality (yesterday, today, and tomorrow, forever and always) and contemporality (nowness, living, process, events, feelings). We celebrate birthdays and anniversaries; we eat and sleep; we start and conclude our workaday existence at specific times. Our lives all too often have a scheduled existence; we live by the clock, whether it be an inner mechanism or a ticking timepiece. Small wonder, then, that we try to analyze time, to categorize it, to control it. We may endeavor to speed it up, slow it down, race against it, momentarily suspend it, make it stand still. And writers seize time, mull on time, celebrate time, remember time, and even meld with time.

Why is time so very important to us? The answer, in its simplicity and profundity, is that we are time-filled, time-bound, time-centered. Consider how we might diagram ourselves in time. We can live in the past and past memories (anachronic time); we can live for the future (metachronic time); we can live above time (epichronic time) or below time (catachronic time); we can live in the present time (synchronic time). But in addition, we can *feel* about time (times past, present, future; time's time-lessness or crushingness) in sensitive or insensitive ways.[1]

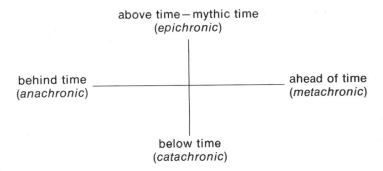

above time — mythic time
(*epichronic*)

behind time _____|_____ ahead of time
(*anachronic*)   (*metachronic*)

below time
(*catachronic*)

What is crucial for life and literature is **how time is felt,** its psychological effect. When we are young, the future seems remote, distanced, far away. When older, we sense future time differently — we know time is running out, life's processes are concluding. When we feel "above time," we discard interests in the daily and mundane; perhaps our interests become spiritual, religious, or philosophical. We feel about future time in terms of aspirations, hopes, plans. And when we think and feel about time past, we isolate the good times, the painful ones, the meaningful ones, the moments when something happened to us that we will long remember. When we live "below time," time itself seems weighted, we feel pulled down by events, almost stopped by time itself. We tend to feel less keenly about unknown future time, we are less sensitive to it; but because the past is known and can be made known to us, we can also be made to feel about it more trenchantly. It can bite and gnaw, reveal and talk to us. Time past is the sense of personal and social history. In one way or another, all literature exists within these domains of time.

The performance of literature exists in a present tense moment — it happens. The performer transforms the present tense moments of performance into the time of the literature. We feel that the literature becomes what it is at the same time it is being performed, that it springs into being, that it seizes and focuses all our sense of time upon the time contained in the literature. *In a performance of literature, time becomes only the time, or times, contained within the literature itself.*

The auxiliary interpretive artist, if he is to understand and capitalize upon the temporal dimensions of literature, must be aware of both *performing time* and *time in the literature* and must be able to blend them appropriately and sensitively. The highest achievement in the performance of time is a congruence between the performer and the experience contained in the literature.

1. I am indebted to Victor Gioscia's essay "On Social Time" for the terminology used here as well as for his diagrammatic approach to it. In *The Future of Time,* ed. Henri Yaker, Humphrey Osmund, and Frances Cheek (New York: Doubleday & Co., 1971), p. 88.

PERFORMING TIME

Essentially, there are three kinds of performing time: (1) event time, (2) set time, and (3) symbolic time.[2]

EVENT TIME

In event time the performer must accomplish his task in a certain manner or form, regardless of how much or how little time is required. Until the form has been completed, the performance is not ended. In the game of baseball, for instance, nine innings must be played to complete the game, regardless of the amount of time this takes; and in the case of a tie at the conclusion of nine innings, the game is continued indefinitely until the tie is broken. Rituals also exist in event time. A funeral service, a wedding ceremony, and similar rites and rituals have no predetermined duration. They end only when the ritual is complete. In a sense a performance of literature is event time when the literature is performed in its entirety, or when a play is presented, or when a program of literary selections is conceived as a presentation; that is, the program or play must be presented in its entirety before the event can be considered complete. In these instances the audience experiences event time and reacts to it.

PRESCRIBED TIME OR SET TIME

In set time a specific amount of durational or clock time is prescribed for the event. A game of football, for example, is played on this basis. A clock time of four quarters of fifteen minutes each is imposed upon the game; and when that time has elapsed, the game is ended arbitrarily. When "x" number of minutes or hours are prescribed for a performance, the presentation must be completed within those limits. Contests commonly are characterized by set time, and frequently those who exceed the limitation are penalized.

The parallel in literature is a set literary form or composition. For example, a sonnet is a set form, and the original artist must have "performed" (created) it within the limitations of fourteen lines, a rhyme scheme, and lines of specific length. However, when performed by the auxiliary artist, a sonnet does not take place in set time. The performer is free to use his time in whatever manner he feels is appropriate and necessary in terms of the material.

2. For a more detailed discussion of performing time, the student is urged to read Richard Schechner, *Public Domain* (Indianapolis: Bobbs-Merrill Co., 1969), pp. 43–119.

SYMBOLIC TIME

In symbolic time there is event time but no prescribed time. The performer is primarily concerned with what takes place within the time of the literature, however long or short that time may appear to be. Most performances of literature, while they may be influenced to a degree by event time, have symbolic time as their primary concern. In symbolic time our sense of familiar clock time fades, and we experience instead a sense of floatation in the other dimensions of time.

The importance of event time, set time, and symbolic time and their influences upon the lives of all of us are difficult to overemphasize. The impact of television, and specifically of commercial television, has been to impose set time as a cultural phenomenon. What takes place does so within thirteen, twenty-eight, or fifty-five minutes; and to accommodate these limitations, the dramatic and/or literary structure of the piece must be fashioned accordingly. Adaptations of existing dramatic literature, short stories, and even novels must be made in terms of specific set time. The aesthetic achievement of the adapter depends upon his ability to match the content of the literary experience with the time dictated by television and/or radio program scheduling. The longer the set time, of course, the greater the freedom for the adapter.

SPARSITY AND DENSITY FACTORS IN LITERARY TIME

In analyzing literature for performance, the interpretive artist will soon notice that the ideas or events in the material create a sense of *density* or of *sparsity*. A rapid succession of events or ideas produces a sense of density; a slow progression of ideas or events, with numerous interruptions of one kind or another, creates a feeling of sparsity. Two examples will serve to illustrate these contrasting terms. In an hour-long television adaptation intended to convey the sweep of a novel, the effect, generally, will be one of density, of a rapid succession of events necessitating close attention and skill in developing a logical story line. In contrast, consider the daytime television serials. The movement within these serialized dramas is slower. Indeed, the episodes are so dragged out and are so sparse in their structure and presentation that if the auditor/viewer happens to miss all of the programs for a week, the interruption does not destroy significantly his sense of the continuity of the drama itself. A writer who would choose to make a serial denser would thereby create a presentation which the viewer would have to see in its entirety every day in order to keep up with the progression of events. The implications in sparsity and density, of course, are far more important in literary time than these illustrations drawn from the medium of television.

Literary forms create a sense of density or sparsity. The density of a short story

is significantly different from that of a novel. *The effects of fast and slow happenings in performance are derivative of the literature and not of the performer.* When the time within the performance is focused on the interpreter rather than on the nature of the time within the literature he is performing, the interpreter can be criticized for creating a distorted experience for his audience. Generally speaking, then, the interpreter creates an event time and a symbolic time; and these times, or the sensed times of the performance, are closely intertwined with the density or sparsity of the succession of events or ideas within the literature.

THE TIME IN THE LITERATURE ITSELF

When we noted earlier that time in the performance of literature "becomes," it is only natural to ask, "Becomes *what?*"[3] This question can be answered both indirectly and directly. First, consider the forms created by plastic art. Architecture, painting, and sculpture create new space; landscape, wall, and space itself are altered and given over to new spaces, new creations, new perceptions. Second, consider music, poetry, and story. These forms, in contrast to the plastic forms, create new time.[4] In the silent or behavioral performance of literature, the perceiver or auditor enters the time given to him by the writer. This time is created by writers in certain ways; it is sustained; and it is shared. This sharing of time by writer and perceiver can be called *common time* or time that is mutually experienced by those speaking from the literature and those perceiving it within the literature. This common time is emotionally sustained, and only when there is release is the perceiver thrown back into himself and his own sense of personal/psychological time. During the performance an emotional time is created that makes the nature of personal/psychological time more real, more felt. Indeed, unless a performance of literature achieves this shared and common time, all that may be felt is the passing of clock time.

PSYCHOLOGICAL TIME

What kinds of time are revealed in literature? One, already suggested, is *psychological time.* In Chapter 2, psychological time was introduced indirectly into the discussion when the student was urged to think about behaviors in literature. Psychological time is the manner and way in which life is felt or, as we said, is "pressed." What is the psychological time in depression? in exuberant expression? How is the passing of

3. For their perceptive and penetrating discussions of time, the author is indebted to the following writers: Paul Weiss, *Nine Basic Arts* (Carbondale: Southern Illinois University Press, 1961), particularly Chapters 7, 8, and 9; Victor Zuckerkandl, *Sound and Symbol* (New York: Pantheon Books, 1956), Chapters 11, 12, and 13; and George Kubler, *The Shape of Time* (New Haven: Yale University Press, 1962).

4. Weiss, *Nine Basic Arts,* p. 8.

time felt when life's possibilities are suppressed? Psychological time is revealed by the rhythm of an individual's expression, language, life. While the relationship of rhythm to language will be treated later in this chapter, we should recognize here that it is *rhythm in the performance of ourselves* that yields key information as to who we are. It is no less true in literature, certainly.

Just as in the performing time of a presentation there is a sense of density and sparsity, so also does psychological time reveal itself in the same terms. Density of psychological time would be characterized by an unfolding profusion of language; sparsity is characterized by the absence of language, the presence of silences. Read Keats' "When I Have Fears That I May Cease to Be."

When I Have Fears That I May Cease to Be

John Keats

When I have fears that I may cease to be
Before my pen has gleaned my teeming brain,
Before high-piled books, in charactry,
Hold like rich garners the full-ripened grain;
When I behold, upon the night's starred face,
Huge cloudy symbols of a high romance,
And think that I may never live to trace
Their shadows, with the magic hand of chance;
And when I feel, fair creature of an hour!
That I shall never look upon thee more,
Never have relish in the faery power
Of unreflecting love!—then on the shore
Of the wide world I stand alone, and think
Till Love and Fame to nothingness do sink.

Study the rhythm and density of expression in the poem. Psychological time presses and, from the presses, erupts into expression. In what ways? In ways related to density of expression and sparsity of expression.

Psychological time is experienced as the quality of time's duration: how time is passed, and the conscious or subconscious reaction to that passing. Psychological time is sensed time, and it results from how our attention is spent. In literature it is the result of where the writer put his attention, of how his attention was arrested, of how he felt time. Unless the performance of Patrick Morgan's "Nocturne" suggests the totality of psychological time, there is literally no performance of the literature. Explain this statement after reading the poem.

Nocturne[5]

Patrick Morgan

It is one of those nights tonight,
when, face to darkness with the ungraspable,
neither to be, nor to be not, brings
any succour to the mind.

    It is one of those nights tonight,
when the trap that is life bites harder
than usual, and one hates the unimaginative,
obeisant earth, and its perennial orbitation
around this candle-affair, this tepid sun
that lights up the universal cage.

    It is one of those nights tonight
when to despise is stronger than to love,
when to fear is larger than to sleep,
and to despair, more painful than to sing.

    When life of a sudden is a vast abyss,
as usual, except that we realise,
more clearly, that it is long since
that we leapt off the cliff of birth,
and there is nothing left to us now
but the term downwards. No longer is death
a facile word; there is no sort of
consolation, no hope, no form of escape
for the logical and the brave.

    Man is a great boatsman, a great
builder of ships, a rusty sailor
who can weather the storm; a battled captain
who cannot turn back the wave.

    It is one of those nights tonight
when the focused brain peers
and sees not, when the attentive ear
listens and hears not, and one longs
for the rugged bestiality of the bear
or the natural elegance of the antelope;

5. "Nocturne" by Patrick Morgan from *Encounter,* (January 1966). Reprinted by permission of the author and *Encounter.*

the unworried power of the lion's paw,
the sleekness of the tiger, the hyena's
crude hunger, the quiet unintelligence
that blesses the jungle grass. Anything
but humanity!
    It is one of those nights tonight,
when life, turned loose, runs naked
crying in the inhuman wilderness, knowing,
full well, there is no solution in the blood.
When one sits, face to face with
The Other Man; the one who can wait
and is always waiting; the one who watches
in the sky, with the lightning, and whose grimace
is always gone, after the storm subsides;
whose teeth shine, and whose eyes,
though one glance often, are always hollow. . . .

    To understand psychological time we must comprehend its different qualities:
time as *slow time, fast time, unchanging psychological time, heavy time, joyous time,
changing time, traditional time, anxious time, fulfilling time.* To sense the quality of
psychological time in a selection of literature can challenge the depths of the performer's being and is essential to a performance of that literature. The performer's artistic responsibility is to evoke the psychological time of the material, not to project
his own psychological time onto or into a piece of literature. In Ecclesiastes the teacher, reflecting in old age, views life as a series of psychological events.

Ecclesiastes 3:1–8

To every thing there is a season, and a time to every purpose under the heaven:
A time to be born, and a time to die; a time to plant, and a time to pluck up that
        which is planted;
A time to kill, and a time to heal; a time to break down, and a time to build up;
A time to weep, and a time to laugh; a time to mourn, and a time to dance;
A time to cast away stones, and a time to gather stones together; a time to em-
        brace, and a time to refrain from embracing;
A time to get, and a time to lose; a time to keep, and a time to cast away;
A time to rend, and a time to sew; a time to keep silence, and a time to speak;
A time to love, and a time to hate; a time of war, and a time of peace.

The psychological time of these events is presented objectively, quite differently from the psychological time in Morgan's "Nocturne."

The performance of psychological time creates new time, freshly stating and revealing the inner being and the nature of its existence.

MYTHIC TIME

Mythic time is above time (epichronic time) and signals the presence of holiness, rite, and ritual. It is the evocation of mystery, of secrets, of the eternal present. It suggests a symbolic time and a recurring time: planting, harvest; spring, summer, autumn, winter; birth, death, rebirth; childhood, manhood. Mythic time can be simultaneous with psychological time, but not necessarily. Psychological states of mind can be portrayed in literature without being part of a larger plan. Characteristically, however, great literature moves from internal states of being into associational patterns of thinking that

Jerry N. Uelsmann

have universal meaning. By finding suitable language to express the psychological awareness of a particular moment, the writer somehow achieves a sense of hallowedness about the special observation of that moment. Note how Robert Bly in his "Driving to Town Late to Mail a Letter" takes an ordinary event in a moment of time and finds in it something unique.

Driving to Town Late to Mail a Letter[6]

Robert Bly

It is a cold and snowy night. The main street is deserted.
The only things moving are swirls of snow.
As I lift the mailbox door, I feel its cold iron.
There is a privacy I love in this snowy night.
Driving around, I will waste more time.

Some might call this a symbolic moment: the moment is suddenly representative of something very special. Others might suggest that the moment is sacral: a moment in which something very holy is achieved. In this latter sense the poem has dimensions of mythic time.

Another example of mythic time is Denise Levertov's "The Novices."

The Novices[7]

Denise Levertov

They enter the bare wood, drawn
by a clear-obscure summons they fear
and have no choice but to heed.

A rustling underfoot, a
long trail to go, the thornbushes grow
across the dwindling paths.

Until the small clearing, where they
anticipate violence knowing some rite
to be performed and compelled to it.

The man moves forward, the boy
sees what he means to do: from an oaktree
a chain runs at an angle into earth

6. Reprinted from *Silence in the Snowy Fields*, Wesleyan University Press, 1962, Copyright © 1962 by Robert Bly. Reprinted by permission of the author.
7. Denise Levertov. *O Taste and See.* Copyright © 1964 by Denise Levertov Goodman. Reprinted by permission of New Directions Publishing Corporation.

and they pit themselves to uproot it,
dogged and frightened, to pull the iron
out of the earth's heart.

But from the further depths of the wood
as they strain and weigh on the great chain
appears the spirit,

the wood-demon who summoned them.
And he is not bestial, not fierce
but an old woodsman,

gnarled, shabby, smelling of smoke and sweat,
of a bear's height and shambling like a bear.
Yet his presence is a spirit's presence

and awe takes their breath.
Gentle and rough, laughing a little,
he makes his will known:

not for an act of force he called them,
for no rite of obscure violence
but that they might look about them

and see intricate branch and bark,
stars of moss and old scars
left by dead men's saws,

and not ask what that chain was.
To leave the open fields
and enter the forest,

that was the rite.
Knowing there was mystery, they could go.
Go back now! And he receded

among the multitude of forms,
the twists and shadows they saw now, listening
to the hum of the world's wood.

The moment is one of initiation into mysteries. Called by the wood demon, two men —one young, the other old—are faced with an evocation of mystery and wonder and admonition. Unless the performance itself unfolds in harmony above time and with the mythic time evoked by the poem, the power of the poetic event is lost.

Mythic time is accepted effortlessly by children. The phrase "once upon a time" conveys a sense of something happening above time as well as in a past time. Time *upon* time is an automatic indication that time can be conjured and played with. Dylan Thomas in his poem "Fern Hill" achieves a dual sense of mythic time and catachronic time by suggesting the power inherent in mythic childhood (above time) while at the same time indicating from the perspective of adulthood the sense of being weighted down (below time). In changing the phrase "once upon a time" for "once below a time," Thomas has intensified that specialness of memory and feeling.

Fern Hill[8]

Dylan Thomas

Now as I was young and easy under the apple boughs
About the lilting house and happy as the grass was green,
    The night above the dingle starry,
      Time let me hail and climb
    Golden in the heydays of his eyes,
And honoured among wagons I was prince of the apple towns
And once below a time I lordly had the trees and leaves
      Trail with daisies and barley
    Down the rivers of the windfall light.

And as I was green and carefree, famous among the barns
About the happy yard and singing as the farm was home,
    In the sun that is young once only,
      Time let me play and be
    Golden in the mercy of his means,
And green and golden I was huntsman and herdsman, the calves
Sang to my horn, the foxes on the hills barked clear and cold,
      And the sabbath rang slowly
    In the pebbles of the holy streams.

All the sun long it was running, it was lovely, the hay-
Fields high as the house, the tunes from the chimneys, it was air
    And playing, lovely and watery
        And fire green as grass.
    And nightly under the simple stars
As I rode to sleep the owls were bearing the farm away,
All the moon long I heard, blessed among stables, the nightjars
    Flying with the ricks, and the horses
        Flashing into the dark.

And then to awake, and the farm, like a wanderer white
With the dew, come back, the cock on his shoulder: it was all
    Shining, it was Adam and maiden,
        The sky gathered again
    And the sun grew round that very day.
So it must have been after the birth of the simple light
In the first, spinning place, the spellbound horses walking warm
    Out of the whinnying green stable
        On to the fields of praise.

And honoured among foxes and pheasants by the gay house
Under the new made clouds and happy as the heart was long,
    In the sun born over and over,
        I ran my heedless ways,
    My wishes raced through the house-high hay
And nothing I cared, at my sky blue trades, that time allows
In all his tuneful turning so few and such morning songs
    Before the children green and golden
        Follow him out of grace,

Nothing I cared, in the lamb white days, that time would take me
Up to the swallow thronged loft by the shadow of my hand,
    In the moon that is always rising,
        Nor that riding to sleep
    I should hear him fly with the high fields
And wake to the farm forever fled from the childless land.
Oh as I was young and easy in the mercy of his means,
        Time held me green and dying
    Though I sang in my chains like the sea.

By substituting the tension-creating paraphrase for the tattered phrase of "Once upon a time . . . ," Thomas is noting that his memory of childhood was *below* a time. To be either *above* or *below* time—and, indeed, even *upon* a time—is to be freed of time. Only events and participation are important. A world without time is a fey one, a suspended one, a magical kingdom of "for ever and ever," the only phrase available to indicate eternity in the literature of childhood. As you have noted, if you read the poem carefully, "Fern Hill" is dense in its language, language which cascades with the memory of childhood and its psychological suspension of time, and which at the same time evokes that holy, sacred, and mystery-filled mythic memory of childhood.

Critics have frequently pointed out that the work of William Faulkner evokes a mythic past whose memory cripples the lives of those who must and do live in it. In Faulkner's writing the dream and myth of an agricultural society of landowner and those who till the land, of the privileged and the nonprivileged—all and each persist in a present moment in which these concepts are no longer appropriate. It is not the present clock time which enslaves Faulkner's characters: the slavery is the result of being unable to change and move with different, changing times. Any performance of a Faulkner work has to evoke this peculiar dimension of mythic time in order to give the characters the sense and the feeling of where psychologically they are existing and of how mythic time is eroding their lives.

One of the oldest concepts of mythic time is that which the Greeks called *kairos:* the propitious moment, that moment in history when an inevitable and momentous event occurs, and occurs at the *only* moment that it could occur. In our Western world an example of the propitious moment is the birth and life of Jesus. Important to an understanding of kairos is the recognition of the significance of the event. In the light of this concept, read T. S. Eliot's poem, "Journey of the Magi," a moving monologue of a wise man struggling to comprehend the implications of the birth: Is it merely another birth? Is it fulfillment? Is the timing of the event to affect the time of the magi's life? These and other questions related to kairos are raised by the speaker.

Journey of the Magi[9]

T. S. Eliot

"A cold coming we had of it,
Just the worst time of the year
For a journey, and such a long journey:
The ways deep and the weather sharp,

The very dead of winter."
And the camels galled, sore-footed, refractory,
Lying down in the melting snow.
There were times we regretted
The summer palaces on slopes, the terraces,
And the silken girls bringing sherbet.
Then the camel men cursing and grumbling
And running away, and wanting their liquor and women,
And the night-fires going out, and the lack of shelters,
And the cities hostile and the towns unfriendly
And the villages dirty and charging high prices:
A hard time we had of it.
At the end we preferred to travel all night,
Sleeping in snatches,
With the voices singing in our ears, saying
That this was all folly.

Then at dawn we came down to a temperate valley,
Wet, below the snow line, smelling of vegetation;
With a running stream and a water-mill beating the darkness,
And three trees on the low sky,
And an old white horse galloped away in the meadow.
Then we came to a tavern with vine-leaves over the lintel,
Six hands at an open door dicing for pieces of silver,
And feet kicking the empty wine-skins.
But there was no information, and so we continued
And arrived at evening, not a moment too soon
Finding the place; it was (you may say) satisfactory.

All this was a long time ago, I remember,
And I would do it again, but set down
This set down
This: were we led all that way for
Birth or Death? There was a Birth, certainly,
We had evidence and no doubt. I had seen birth and death,
But had thought they were different; this Birth was
Hard and bitter agony for us, like Death, our death.
We returned to our places, these Kingdoms,
But no longer at ease here, in the old dispensation,
With an alien people clutching their gods.
I should be glad of another death.

How is mythic time performed? Mythic time is revealed through performative behavior which clearly indicates that it has divorced itself from the present. In common, everyday conversation we hear such indicators as "While I was talking with him, he had a faraway look!" "It was as if he did not hear a word I said." "His face suddenly lit up, and he seemed to be completely lost in his thoughts." We might note, in passing, that individuals having serious mental disturbances oftentimes live in mythic time. To escape the traumas of life, they transport themselves mentally into a world of complete imagination, believing totally that they are living embodiments of times past. When Richard Schechner defined an act of interpretation as "tracing one's own madness," he was in a sense suggesting the line that may be drawn between interpretive acts, on the one hand, and "normal" or "sane" activities, on the other.

When we fail to sense that ritual has mythic pasts and a sacred present, rites and rituals become hollow and meaningless. When the ritualist himself suggests that he does not believe in the purpose or the credibility of the ritual, there is no sense of the mythic present. The power of mythic time is known by the imaginative power it communicates in performance.

The presence of the symbol, the highly structured language of metaphor, the tortuous paradoxes of life convey the coalescence of mythic time and psychological time. The power of this coalescence lies in the haunting extension of their meanings in us and the recognition that their meanings link us to the experiences of all mankind in all times. Of these matters more will be said in later chapters.

RHYTHMIC TIME

As we have said, time is the manner in which life is sensed; rhythm is the manner in which life is performed. There is a rhythm to the walk of a man: the manner in which he strides, shuffles, strolls, trudges, runs, paces himself. Literature lives also, and the rhythm of literature is the way it is felt in performance, whether that performance be the act of silent reading, an internal and mental reaction to it, or the manner in which it is perceived in an actual presentation. The perception of rhythm in literature is an act of responding to its organic nature: the manner in which it breathes, flows, beats.

Rhythm can be distinguished from meter by the simple observation that meter is a *regularized form* of beat, a repetition of similar units. Rhythm is flow, but it is an irregular flow. It is linked to psychological time by the sensed time of the characters or events. In attempting to define and identify rhythm in literature, the sensitive reader reacts to ways in which lives are spent: the rituals they employ, however small or innocuous. The rhythm which characterizes their ritual of tea time may be more important in understanding a set of characters than their awareness of and responsiveness to the quality of their psychological lives. For the performing artist rhythm is the pace of life as it is revealed in the literature.

Rhythm emerges *out* of the material and the experience. In James Applewhite's "My Grandfather's Funeral," we sense the movement of the funeral, the reaction of those in attendance, the rhythm of the event as it impinges not only upon those observed by the speaker in the poem, but also upon the speaker himself as he moves and is forced to participate in mythic time—a fact so very clearly indicated by the last line.

My Grandfather's Funeral[10]

James Applewhite

I knew the dignity of the words:
"As for man, his days are as grass,
As a flower of the field so he flourisheth;
For the wind passeth, and he is gone"—
But I was not prepared for the beauty
Of the old people coming from the church,
Nor for the suddenness with which our slow
Procession came again in sight of the awakening
Land, as passing white houses, Negroes
In clothes the colors of the earth they plowed,
We turned to see bushes and rusting roofs
Flicker past one way, the stretch of fields
Plowed gray or green with rye flow constant
On the other, away to unchanging pines
Hovering over parallel boles like
Dreams of clouds.

                At the cemetery the people
Surprised me again, walking across
The wave of winter-bleached grass and stones
Toward his grave; grotesques, yet perfect
In their pattern: Wainwright's round head,
His bad shoulder hunched and turning
That hand inward, Luby Paschal's scrubbed
Square face, lips ready to whistle to
A puppy, his wife's delicate ankles
Angling a foot out, Norwood Whitley
Unconsciously rubbing his blue jaw,

10. "My Grandfather's Funeral" by James Applewhite. Copyright © 1966 by *Shenandoah*, reprinted from *Shenandoah; The Washington and Lee University Review* with the permission of the editor and the author.

Locking his knees as if he were wearing boots—
The women's dark blue and brocaded black,
Brown stockings on decent legs supporting
Their infirm frames carefully over
The wintry grass that called them down,
Nell Overman moving against the horizon
With round hat and drawn-back shoulders—
Daring to come and show themselves
Above the land, to face the death
Of William Henry Applewhite,
Whose name was on the central store
He owned no more, who was venerated,
Generous, a tyrant to his family
With his ally, the God of Moses and lightning
(With threat of thunderclouds rising in summer
White and ominous over level fields);
Who kept bright jars of mineral water
On his screened, appled backporch, who prayed
With white hair wispy in the moving air,
Who kept the old way in changing times,
Who killed himself plowing in his garden.
I seemed to see him there, above
The bleached grass in the new spring light,
Bowed to his handplow, bent-kneed, impassive,
Toiling in the sacrament of seasons.

Here, rhythm is not the metrical form of the poem; rhythm is the psychological form of the experience. Rhythm is intuited, sensed, felt; and one of the abiding functions of literature has been to interpret the rhythms of life—rhythms which, like waves, flow over and upon the perceiver.

Now read Matthew Arnold's "Dover Beach," noting that the effect of this poem derives from the *conflict* in rhythms.

Dover Beach

Matthew Arnold

The sea is calm tonight,
The tide is full, the moon lies fair

Upon the straits;—on the French coast the light
Gleams and is gone; the cliffs of England stand,
Glimmering and vast, out in the tranquil bay.
Come to the window, sweet is the night-air!
Only, from the long line of spray
Where the sea meets the moon-blanched land,
Listen! you hear the grating roar
Of pebbles which the waves draw back, and fling,
At their return, up the high strand,
Begin, and cease, and then again begin,
With tremulous cadence slow, and bring
The eternal note of sadness in.

Sophocles long ago
Heard it on the Aegean, and it brought
Into his mind the turbid ebb and flow
Of human misery; we
Find also in the sound a thought,
Hearing it by this distant northern sea.

The Sea of Faith
Was once, too, at the full, and round earth's shore
Lay like the folds of a bright girdle furled.
But now I only hear
Its melancholy, long, withdrawing roar,
Retreating, to the breath
Of the night-wind, down the vast edges drear
And naked shingles of the world.

Ah, love, let us be true
To one another! for the world, which seems
To lie before us like a land of dreams,
So various, so beautiful, so new,
Hath really neither joy, nor love, nor light,
Nor certitude, nor peace, nor help for pain;
And we are here as on a darkling plain
Swept with confused alarms of struggle and flight,
Where ignorant armies clash by night.

We note first the rhythms of nature. Next, the present-tense experience of nature's rhythms is thrown back to mythic time, to another ocean — the Aegean — and the perpetual effect of these rhythms. Then there is a return to psychological time — how the present moment is being felt; and, finally, there is a sense of hastening, of an onrushing realization that time is hurtling the speaker, and perhaps all mankind, toward a certain doom. In sudden counterpoint the value of love is invoked as one saving rhythm against advancing chaos.

Thus, literature explores the sensed rhythms of life; and, as we noted in Chapter 2, observable behavior in the presses of living reveal with considerable immediacy and some transparency the quality of inner life, its felt rhythm, its current pulse. In George Gershwin's popular song "I've Got Rhythm," the lyric is not saying "I've Got Meter." Rather, the song expresses the spontaneous and joyous notion that rhythm is a *reaction* to life, a sense of how life is to be felt and put into motion. The experience of rhythm is most often described as a psychic state in which the individual has the very real feeling of being alive. This contrasts dramatically with the measured beat of the funeral march, in which much of its terror is generated by the absence of a changing beat. The steady and measured cadence is portentous of death.

Consider John L'Heureux's poem, "Three Awful Picnics," in which the widow describes the *effect* of her husband's death.

Three Awful Picnics[11]

John L'Heureux

(as told by his widow to *Time* magazine)

1
When his head split open like a rotten
cantaloupe and seven birds flew out,
we were surprised. We fell silent.
You don't expect a thing like that —
not even on a weekend in the country.

He muttered, bubbling from his split
left mouth: "Christ, I'm schizo now
for real." His sense of humor was appalling.
I recall we raised our eyes deliberately

---

11. "Three Awful Picnics" by John L'Heureux from *Young American Poets.* Reprinted by permission of the author.

and watched the seven birds describe
the circle of descending day, fly back
to consciousness again, again. We
memorized their flaming throats, their cries.
How long until we can forget this place?

His suit was ruined. So was our cookout.
We gathered up the picnic things
and left at once. Walking to the cars,
his friend remarked to me concerned:
"Well, he's never done *that* before."

2
He had been trying to imagine God. Still,
when his head split open like a cantaloupe
and three brown birds flew out, we were
surprised. One   two   three. Sure enough.
There they were: like a judgment.

"Only who are loved are capable of loving,"
he used to say, though he himself
never seemed the kind to die for love
let alone to split in two for it. We knew
about his thing with God only when he told us.
Counted   measured   prayed   watched: he had
done it all, scrubbed his patience to a gloss,
finally lost interest in God. Resented him.
Resented God's impervious omnipotence, love
computerized and lavished on the hateful,
impossible demands of law. He lived his death.

So when his head split open and birds spilled
to the sky, he would have thought it judgment.
Perhaps it was. Certainly there *were*
three birds. But he was not the kind for that;
never the religious type, really.

3
Nature ceased to war with grace in him.
Sometimes when that melon has released

its sparrow, appearances will shift and what is
will be revealed; decision will evoke response.
So when, after we had passed the wine, his head
split open and five green birds flew out,
we were less surprised. We half expected it.
He always seemed the kind to die in public.

He had spoken often of his name. "No one
knew it," he said, "no one ever would."
No hands tender on his secret body,
exploring hidden reaches of knowledge and desire.
No lips upon his eyelids blind from the light.
No total knowledge ever; his name unknown.
He talked like that, a little overwrought.

Still he made a good death. Undertakers
fixed his head so—except up close—you'd never
guess what happened. The birds return
sometimes in spring. Then we think of him
and his odd ways. He was wrong, however.
We all remember his name.

At precise moments within the poem—two, to be exact—there are measured and funereal intervals of the death beat. In the fourth line of the second picnic, we find:

> One   two   three

and in the eleventh line of the same section, we note:

> Counted   measured   prayed   watched.

While, overall, the poem describes the effect of a death, the effect is given subtle counterpoint and finality by these two memorable moments of measured beat. Note, too, that the widow's performing voice is life speaking of death. The widow's voice, speaking *out of* the experience, gives to the listener the rhythm of her being, of her husband's being at the moment of death, and of the incredible, ever-changing events being changingly perceived: "seven birds flew out," "three brown birds flew out," "five green birds flew out."

Ray Metzker

SILENTIAL TIME

Freya Stark has written, "A part of all art is to make silence speak. The things left out in a painting, the note withheld in music, the void in architecture — all are as necessary and as active as the utterance itself."[12] The importance of silence is not always sensi-

12. Freya Stark, *The Zodiac Arch* (New York: Harcourt, Brace & World, 1968), p. 194.

tively appraised in *silent* reading, but in the performance of literature it is the *sine qua non* of sensitive perception and evocation. In considering silence Harold Pinter, the contemporary British playwright, observes:

There are two silences. One when no word is spoken. The other when perhaps a torrent of language is employed. This speech is speaking a language locked beneath it. That is its continual reference. The speech we hear is an indication of what we don't hear. It is a necessary avoidance, a violent, sly, anguished, or mocking smoke-screen which keeps the other in its place. When true silence falls, we are still left with echo but are nearer nakedness. One way to look at speech is to say that it is a constant stratagem to cover nakedness.[13]

The interpreter of literature has to make a number of decisions about silence and "its language," and often these decisions are difficult. When we consider the psychological impact of silence upon conversation, of silence in worship, of silence in a love relationship, the fact is that the flow of silence in each case is emotionally and psychologically quite different. In literature we find silential time taking at least three forms: (1) characterological silence, (2) situational silence, and (3) structural silence (negative space).

Characterological silence.   A character within a piece of literature may or may not have the capacity to utter what he feels and thinks or to extend his being into language. Rather than use language, he may employ the simplicity of a gesture, the anguish of a look, the stunned silence of reaction. In these cases the author usually carefully suggests characterological qualities. Terseness, for example, and the inevitable silence which falls after it are explored in Robert Frost's "Mending Wall." The speaker of the poem is met by a neighbor who helps to replace the fallen stones in a fence. Read the poem and note the impact of the neighbor's terseness upon the speaker.

Mending Wall[14]

Robert Frost

Something there is that doesn't love a wall,
That sends the frozen-ground-swell under it
And spills the upper boulders in the sun,

13. Harold Pinter in a program note for his play *Silence.*
14. "Mending Wall" from *The Poetry of Robert Frost,* edited by Edward Connery Lathem. Copyright 1923, 1930, 1939, © 1969 by Holt, Rinehart and Winston, Inc. Copyright 1951, © 1958 by Robert Frost. Copyright © 1967 by Lesley Frost Ballantine. Reprinted by permission of Holt, Rinehart and Winston, Inc.

And makes gaps even two can pass abreast.
The work of hunters is another thing:
I have come after them and made repair
Where they have left not one stone on a stone,
But they would have the rabbit out of hiding,
To please the yelping dogs. The gaps I mean,
No one has seen them made or heard them made,
But at spring mending-time we find them there.
I let my neighbor know beyond the hill;
And on a day we meet to walk the line
And set the wall between us once again.
We keep the wall between us as we go.
To each the boulders that have fallen to each.
And some are loaves and some so nearly balls
We have to use a spell to make them balance:
"Stay where you are until our backs are turned!"
We wear our fingers rough with handling them.
Oh, just another kind of outdoor game,
One on a side. It comes to little more:
There where it is we do not need the wall:
He is all pine and I am apple orchard.
My apple trees will never get across
And eat the cones under his pines, I tell him.
He only says, "Good fences make good neighbors."
Spring is the mischief in me, and I wonder
If I could put a notion in his head:
"*Why* do they make good neighbors? Isn't it
Where there are cows? But here there are no cows.
Before I built a wall I'd ask to know
What I was walling in or walling out,
And to whom I was like to give offense.
Something there is that doesn't love a wall,
That wants it down." I could say "Elves" to him,
But it's not elves exactly, and I'd rather
He said it for himself. I see him there,
Bringing a stone grasped firmly by the top
In each hand, like an old-stone savage armed.
He moves in darkness as it seems to me,
Not of woods only and the shade of trees.
He will not go behind his father's saying,

And he likes having thought of it so well
He says again, "Good fences make good neighbors."

The neighbor's silence and succinctness clearly conjure up many thoughts within the speaker of the poem. In performance the neighbor should be as memorable as the speaker's ruminations about him and the implications of his terse comment, "Good fences make good neighbors." One can well imagine that it is the nature of this taciturn New Englander never to speak much at all; it is not his character to do so. And yet his character *affects*—deeply affects—the very articulate neighbor who has come to meet him.

Situational silence.   This is the silence which falls upon one individual, or between two people, because of an event. A particularly intriguing and involving study of the effects of silential time can be found in John Keats' "Ode on a Grecian Urn."

Ode on a Grecian Urn

John Keats

1
Thou still unravished bride of quietness,
    Thou foster-child of silence and slow time,
Sylvan historian, who canst thus express
    A flowery tale more sweetly than our rhyme:
What leaf-fringed legend haunts about thy shape
      Of deities or mortals, or of both,
         In Tempe or the dales of Arcady?
What men or gods are these? What maidens loth?
      What mad pursuit? What struggle to escape?
         What pipes and timbrels? What wild ecstasy?

2
Heard melodies are sweet, but those unheard
    Are sweeter; therefore, ye soft pipes, play on;
Not to the sensual ear, but, more endeared,
    Pipe to the spirit ditties of no tone:
Fair youth, beneath the trees, thou canst not leave
    Thy song, nor ever can those trees be bare;
      Bold Lover, never, never canst thou kiss,

Though winning near the goal—yet, do not grieve;
    She cannot fade, though thou hast not thy bliss,
        For ever wilt thou love, and she be fair!

3

Ah, happy, happy boughs! that cannot shed
    Your leaves, nor ever bid the Spring adieu;
And, happy melodist, unwearied,
    For ever piping songs for ever new;
More happy love! more happy, happy love!
    For ever warm and still to be enjoyed,
        For ever panting, and for ever young;
All breathing human passion far above,
    That leaves a heart high-sorrowful and cloyed,
        A burning forehead, and a parching tongue.

4

Who are these coming to the sacrifice?
    To what green altar, O mysterious priest,
Lead'st thou that heifer lowing at the skies,
    And all her silken flanks with garlands drest?
What little town by river or sea shore,
    Or mountain-built with peaceful citadel,
        Is emptied of this folk, this pious morn?
And, little town, thy streets for evermore
    Will silent be; and not a soul to tell
        Why thou art desolate, can e'er return.

5

O Attic shape! Fair attitude! with brede
    Of marble men and maidens overwrought,
With forest branches and the trodden weed;
    Thou, silent form, dost tease us out of thought
As doth eternity: Cold Pastoral!
    When old age shall this generation waste,
        Thou shalt remain, in midst of other woe
Than ours, a friend to man, to whom thou say'st,
    "Beauty is truth, truth beauty,"—that is all
        Ye know on earth, and all ye need to know.

Here we feel the presence of mythic time and of ritualistic time; here we experience the presence of a past time (the Greek culture out of which the urn came); and here we encounter also the paradox of the silently speaking urn. When an event is momentous or deeply moving or disturbing or stunning, how does an individual react? Curiously enough, he reacts through words. Charles H. Long has rightly called this phenomenon *the irony of silence:*

It is difficult to get at the meaning of silence, for, though a kind of power is signified through its quality, the power of silence is so unlike the power of words that we have no words to express it. Or, to put it another way, the power of silence can be expressed only through words, words which are able to move beyond and break through their own creative intent to the intentionality of silence. Silence is, thus, radically ironic.[15]

The irony of silence, we must conclude, is that it ultimately "speaks." In "Ode on a Grecian Urn," Keats is hearing what silence is speaking. The situational silence which is speaking *is* the performance of the "Ode." There exists on the urn the eternally frozen moment of unsullied love, the uncompleted rite, the totally informed silence of inexpressible beauty, the timeless time of a transfixed moment. While the "Ode" can be analyzed from many perspectives—structural, philosophical, thematic—the student preparing the poem for performance is helped considerably when he starts his appraisal and appreciation by contemplating, as Keats himself did, the impact of situational silence.

A less complex example of situational silence is William Wordsworth's "Composed upon Westminster Bridge, September 3, 1802." It, too, exemplifies the irony of poetry that speaks of silence, words becoming the appropriate response for the spellbinding silences of experience.

**Composed upon Westminster Bridge,
September 3, 1802**

William Wordsworth

Earth has not anything to show more fair:
Dull would he be of soul who could pass by
A sight so touching in its majesty:
This City now doth, like a garment, wear
The beauty of the morning; silent, bare,

15. Charles H. Long, "Silence and Signification," in *Myths and Symbols, Studies in Honor of Mircea Eiliade,* ed. J. M. Kitawaga and Charles H. Long (Chicago: University of Chicago Press, 1969), p. 148.

Ships, towers, domes, theaters, and temples lie
Open unto the fields, and to the sky;
All bright and glittering in the smokeless air.
Never did sun more beautifully steep
In his first splendor, valley, rock, or hill;
Ne'er saw I, never felt, a calm so deep!
The river glideth at his own sweet will:
Dear God! the very houses seem asleep;
And all that mighty heart is lying still!

Note that the impact of the poem, the distilled utterance of experience, is withheld until the last two lines. It is the silence that precedes the first line of the poem that makes it work: so moving, so calming, so touching is the sight of silent London that "Earth has not anything to show more fair." The experience is framed in silence as much as the silence is articulated in the fourteen lines of Wordsworth's sonnet.

Structural silence. There are two ways in which structural silence or negative space appears in literature: (1) through punctuation and (2) through the arrangement of the word units on the page. The degree to which performance of literature is congruent to these structural factors is of utmost importance; and the interpreter should consider particularly the care and precision with which writers set words apart by careful and, in some cases, crucial punctuation, as well as the manner in which they spatially arrange words and phrases. *Sound, silence, and behavior are the performing equivalents of punctuation and spacings.*

When an individual speaks and converses, he does not *think* punctuation, of course. The natural rhythm of his language, the effortless emphasis of his words, the regionalism of his intonation and inflection are learned behaviors, acquired so early that they become unconscious elements of everyday expression. The genius of a writer may lie in his capturing these elements, elements which are the true essence of style. However, a writer's care in punctuating his material, or in not punctuating it, must be given careful attention and analysis by the interpreter of the literature. As most of us are aware, the function of punctuation is the visual separation of material into meaningful parts. The function of the performer is to transform visual groupings into auditory groupings.

The relationships between punctuation and silence are determined by the marks themselves. The period, the question mark, and the exclamation point suggest the silences of longest duration. (In a poem in which no end mark appears, the reader/perceiver must decide whether the poem ends or is meant to continue in the silence of audible space.) Pauses denoted by the semicolon, the comma, and the dash are typically shorter than those following the end marks. The silence following the semicolon is less than that following the period, for instance; and so on in descending order: the comma is usually followed by less silential time than the semicolon, and the dash by less than the comma. In fact, the dash is usually employed to suggest a hastening to the material following it. The use of parentheses customarily suggests the interpolation of new material, and the degree of silence framing the parentheses can only be determined by the context of the sentence. The context also must determine the amount of silence following the colon, which is usually employed to denote a series of items to follow or an important isolation of thought.

An interesting poem for a careful study of punctuation is "How Do I Love Thee?" written by Elizabeth Barrett Browning to her husband, Robert Browning. First, read the sonnet aloud; second, analyze the poem's punctuation carefully; and third, read the lines aloud again in the light of your analysis.

How Do I Love Thee?

Elizabeth Barrett Browning

How do I love thee? Let me count the ways.
I love thee to the depth and breadth and height
My soul can reach, when feeling out of sight
For the end of Being and ideal Grace.
I love thee to the level of everyday's
Most quiet need, by sun and candle-light.
I love thee freely, as men strive for Right;
I love thee purely, as they turn from Praise.
I love thee with the passion put to use
In my old griefs, and with my childhood's faith.
I love thee with a love I seemed to lose
With my lost saints—I love thee with the breath,
Smiles, tears, of all my life!—and, if God choose,
I shall but love thee better after death.

If your analysis has been an accurate one, you will have noted that in the sonnet there are seven end marks, one semicolon, ten commas, one set of dashes, and one internal exclamation mark. From the standpoint of audible space—or phrasing, as it is usually called—the interpreter is dealing with seven discrete sentences, or units, which require frames of silence in some degree or another. He is involved, moreover, with one unit wherein two sentences are closely joined by a semicolon; and he will have to pay attention to ten smaller partitions of thought as set apart by commas. Because *it is not the interpreter's prerogative to repunctuate a writer's work,* he must focus his attention on the thought units as given, and determine the implications of the silence which is to frame those units.

More specifically, consider the following questions:

1. How many sentences are there in the first line? How much negative space exists between the end of the question and the beginning of the second sentence? Because the second sentence ends with a period rather than a colon, what are the implications? (If the second sentence ended with a colon, there would be no choice but to hasten the audible space to the third sentence. Because it does not, what are the implications of a silence of an undetermined duration preceding the third sentence?)

2. The third and fourth sentences end with periods. How is the content of sentence three different from that of sentence four? How does the silence that frames "Being and ideal Grace" balance the concrete image of "sun and candle-light"?

3. Why is the semicolon the logical mark to divide sentence five? How is parallel structure enhanced by Mrs. Browning's accurate punctuation?

4. Examine the sixth and seventh sentences carefully. The seventh is exactly twice the length of the sixth. How does the absence of silence and the urgent hastening of language, as indicated by the dashes, balance the first five sentences (and the first eight lines)?

A careless performance of this poem will destroy the *implied* silences, silences which can only be made structurally clear by a careful analysis of punctuation.

In the poem "Novel/" by the contemporary poet Robert Lax, the interpreter is faced with structural silences of two kinds: the first derives from the placement of punctuation in space and the second from the arrangement of language in space. Here again, reading aloud the three sentences is a helpful step toward understanding the profound impact of silence or negative audible space that should be generated in performance. If you utter the sentences with no regard for the unique arrangement of the parts, you will be ignoring silences of the most interesting and provocative kinds. Look carefully at the three parts: one statement made in the voice of "she," followed by a question asked by the same voice, and a concluding statement made in the voice of an observer.

Novel/[16]

Robert Lax

1.

oh
well

(she
con-
soled

her-
self)

some-
thing

good

is

bound
to
hap-
pen
(I'll
die)

&
go
to
heav-
en

which
has
al-
ways

sound-
ed

so
love-
ly

or
to
hell
which
sounds

even

worse

2.

why
does-
n't
any-
one

ever
die
&
go
to

(new-
port)

?

3.
sud-
den-
ly
she
real-
ized

that
there
was-
n't

a
resort

in
the
world

she
want-
ed

to
go
to

any-
way

so
that
was
that

16. "Novel/" by Robert Lax from *Thirty-One New American Poets*, edited by Ron Schreiber. Reprinted by permission of the author.

Again, some analytical questions may offer guidance to the interpreter:

1. How much negative space of silence precedes the first word of the first sentence? How are the phrases and words arranged for silences and for a sense of fragmentation?
2. The second statement, a question, is short and moves quickly. How does the isolation of the question mark influence the performance of this section?
3. What is the overall rhythm of the poem? How does it move? What is the effect of the "spaced fragments"?

In summary, then, silential time in literature may be classified in three ways: *characterologically, situationally,* and *structurally.* These three subdimensions have been isolated and considered separately, but this isolation has been merely for the purposes of explanation and analysis. The effect of silence is to give to literature the organic sense of life and rhythm. Silence, like all other rhythm, flows out of the material, out of the experiences of confrontation and reaction to it. Rhythm changes language significantly, and never more significantly than in performance. As we have stressed, the time it takes to read a selection is not the time it takes to perform it. Performance time may be compressed or expanded, lengthened or shortened, or—in one sense or another—distorted. In it, the performer attempts to create rhythms close to life's more obvious realities: the psychological sense of time.

Our sense of time has much to do with our sense of life itself. Literature is a *now* experience: the language flows densely, sparsely, and rambles back and forth in time. The effects of literature are psychological, creating inner states of being within the perceiver/auditor. The profundity of literature's impact comes from its seemingly effortless ability to link the perceiver to all of man's experiences in mythic time. The rhythmic time of literature, its nowness, its organic sense of flow and life, is framed by silential time. We shall now consider one remaining aspect of time in literature: its *metrical* dimensions.

METRICAL TIME

John Ciardi has described metrical time in poetry as "language in motion."[17] However, all language is in motion when it is spoken as well as when it is perceived and scanned in the act of silent reading. Langauge that is not in motion, language that is not filled with a sense of life and organic movement, is a language of dead symbology. There is, for instance, no sense of movement and life in an unknown foreign language when you see it on the printed page. Of course, by *listening* to an alien language one can gain a certain sense of animation and vitality from the speaker's gestures and the ranges of his intonation; that is, one may intuit a paralanguage merely by being in the

17. John Ciardi, *How Does a Poem Mean?* (Boston: Houghton Mifflin Co., 1959), p. 920.

speaker's presence. However, metrical time as language in motion is obviously a special concept, closely and inevitably identified with literature and, specifically, poetry.

Poetry and prose: some distinctions.   At this point, before considering metrical time further, let us digress to make some essential distinctions between prose and poetry. For clarification consult the accompanying chart "Generalized Characteristics of Time in Prose and Poetry."

The single most important characteristic of time in verse is meter. While both prose and verse reveal the presence of rhythm, only verse reveals measured units of words. An examination of the Latin origins of the words emphasizes the distinction between the two terms. Verse, originating from *versus,* means "to turn" and—more specifically in verse—"to return." Prose, on the other hand, is derived from the Latin word *proversus,* meaning literally "to move forward." Thus, we may describe prose as language seized and propelled forward interestingly and rhythmically, and poetry as language turning and returning upon itself in arresting patterns.

Generally, most people employ the words *prose* and *poetry* in such a way as to suggest that they are opposites. Obviously, however, they are not opposites because the use of language as an art form is common to both. Well-wrought prose can be

---

GENERALIZED CHARACTERISTICS OF TIME IN PROSE AND POETRY

Prose

Encompasses a *single* time
(may include generations, years, months, days, hours; may be a single sustained period of time or a number of distinct occurrences).

Often *atomic time*
(again may have characteristics like those above; the important element in atomic time is that it is the time spanned in the formation of character).

Generally a smooth movement of time.

Prose environs the time it creates.

No fixed meter or fixed beat in language.

Mythic.

Psychological.

Forward motion (*proversus*).

Poetry

Creates a time *against* time
(psychological and mythic time against the measured time of metrics).

Has the effect of creating a *new time*
(creates the effect that common time as experienced is substituted for new times, i.e., sense of eternity, floatation, *kairos*).

Translucent time
(a sense of revelation about self and the self's time of being).

Metrical units
(language is metered, spaced, divided in perceivable ways and patterns).

Mythic.

Psychological.

Sense of return (*versus*).

highly "poetic," and incompetent poetry can be extremely "prosaic" if it employs merely workaday and uninventive language and form. Some who take the position that the opposite of prose is verse argue that the *manner* in which the language is used in each case is the determining desideratum, and they reserve the word *poetry* to describe the artistry of either form.[18]

Nevertheless, for the student's convenience in using this book, the term *poetry* will be used generically to suggest the patterning of language while *prose* will be employed to suggest the "filled page" of narrative, description, and the like. The forms of poetry and prose will be elaborated upon in Chapter 5, "The Perception and Evocation of Form." The metrical patternings of verse or metrical time we will consider here as a part of this chapter's overall discussion of time in literature.

Meter in poetic form.   The function of meter in poetic forms is to create a time (a series of measured units) that works within or against all of the other dimensions of time. Metrical language, as opposed to nonmetrical language, has the following characteristics:
1. The meter is *in* the language, *of* the language.
2. There is a repetition of identical units.
3. The language and its measured units can be analyzed.
4. The language is separated by metered beats.
5. The beats draw boundaries.
6. The beats form their own sounding patterns.

Children's games provide some of the best and most familiar patterns of metered, measured time. In the game "Ring-around-the-rosy," the chanted beat predominates and is *always* given identical, repeatable form:

> RINg-aROUND-the-ROSy,
> POCKet FULL of POSEy,
> ASHes, ASHes,
> we ALL FALL DOWN.

The "time" of the game would be seriously distorted if each participant varied this singsong meter. Skip-rope games, hopscotch chants, and numerous other childhood games are handed down from generation to generation in identical metrical patternings to facilitate memorization. So, too, did the troubadours and balladeers pass on their literature, not only creating metrical patternings, but also establishing four-line units, or stanzas, for segmenting the ballad into easily remembered parts.

The interpretive artist, in the performance of literature, faces the challenge of establishing the metered values and their pleasurable, aesthetic effects either over

---

18. This argument has been presented most persuasively in Paul Campbell, *Oral Interpretation* (New York: Harcourt, Brace & World, 1966), pp. 19–35.

and against or in harmony with the other dimensions of time.[19] This challenge is made more difficult by the fact that metered motion in language is the most easily "heard" quality in a poem, particularly when the meter is a highly conventional one. Ask any untrained interpreter to read such a poem aloud, and he will demonstrate the dominance of the meter. In fact, how often is the strongly metered poem *not* cast into a singsong rhythm, usually sacrificing most of the other values within the selection?

How is metered language identified? It is characterized by the patterning of stressed syllables in definite relationships to unstressed syllables. The basic element of metrical structure is the metrical foot. Present in a metrical foot are: (1) *an accented syllable or syllables* in a certain patterned relationship to (2) *an unaccented syllable or syllables.* When combined in appropriate ways, these units of accented and unaccented syllables are said to be the principal metrical feet of English verse.[20]

Another form of metered speech is the use of beats or regularized stresses within a line or lines of poetry. Early Anglo-Saxon poetry used stressed patterning: four stressed words or syllables to a line, regardless of the number of words or syllables in the line. Many contemporary poets have abandoned metrical lines for stress

---

CHARACTERISTICS OF TIME IN THE PERFORMANCE OF LITERATURE

Language	Psychological Time	Mythic Time	Rhythm	Meter
Dense	Slow	Eternal present	Organic	*Of* the material, *in* the material
Sparse	Fast	Past and future as magic-filled	Flow	Repetition of the identical
Common	Unchanging		Silence	
Uncommon	Heavy	Holy	Pulsation	Analyzed
Reference to present	Joyous	Sacred	Irregular	Draws boundaries
Reference to past	Changing	Awesome	Out of the material, experience	Interrupts
	Transitional	Symbolic		Separates
Reference to self	Anxious	Reoccurring	Activity	Beats
	Fulfilling	Rite	Sensory "materials"	
Reference to all man's experience	Emotional	Ritual	Sympathetic responses	
	Dull	Legacy	Unbroken continuity of flux	
		Participation	Intuited	
		Kairos	Waves	

---

19. See the accompanying chart "Characteristics of Time in the Performance of Literature."
20. Refer to the chart "The Principal Metrical Feet of English Verse."

lines, employing a pattern of three or four stresses per line, for example, to create the pulse that evokes the psychological and mythic times within the poem. The implications of metered speech and speech with beat will be fully explored in Chapter 5 in terms of the specific forms in which they occur.

THE PRINCIPAL METRICAL FEET OF ENGLISH VERSE

Name	Description	Marking	Effect
THE FOUR PRINCIPAL FEET			
IAMB	Two syllables: one unstressed, one stressed	ă - bōut al - low	Rising meter; hastens movement; the common foot
ANAPEST	Three syllables: two unstressed, one stressed	ĭn - tĕr - rūpt cig - a - rette	Rising meter; hastens movement; gallops in a natural, three-beat gait
TROCHEE	Two syllables: one stressed, one unstressed	trō - chĕe sum - mer	Falling meter; slows movement
DACTYL	Three syllables: one stressed, two unstressed	mēt - rĭ - căl gen - er - al	Falling meter; slows movement
EXCEPTIONS*			
SPONDEE	Two syllables: both stressed	āll - rīght!	Arrests; creates sense of emphasis. Often used in place of iamb for special effect
PYRRHIC	Two syllables: both unstressed	˘ ˘	Occurs *only* in a line of poetry; has the effect of calling attention to other stressed elements
RARE			
AMPHIBRACH	Three syllables: one unstressed, one stressed, one unstressed	pĕr - cēp - tiŏn	If these feet are used at all *throughout* a poem, the poet is deliberately attempting to create an effect. Usually, a poem can be analyzed in such a way as to avoid them.
AMPHIMACER	Three syllables: one stressed, one unstressed, one stressed	ūp - sĭde - dōwn	

*The spondaic and pyrrhic feet are labeled *exceptions* because it is impossible to write metered language using these units exclusively. They appear only in lines of verse to balance a metered line or to indicate special emphasis or absence of emphasis.

Because metrical time in poetry is associated with form, we have called attention here solely to the effects obtained by "regulated speech." We emphasize that a misuse of metered speech in performance can significantly detract from or even destroy the more important dimensions of psychological and mythic time, making the performance time an endurance test of unrelenting boredom. Thus, when we state that metrical time works *against* time, we do not intend to imply that a struggle, battle, or conflict takes place. Metered speech is like the grain in wood or the tactile surface of cloth. The poet, if he is a good one, has made metered speech an inherent element in the poem, setting the meter *against* the psychological state of the speaker in the poem, *against* the rich and powerful sense of mythic time. Metered speech complements the psychological rhythms, the inner being that is expressing itself in language. The interpretive artist always attempts to seek a balance among all of the elements which comprise performance time.

In summary, in this chapter we have explored the implications of performing time, of the effects created by density and sparsity of language, not only within literary forms, but within psychological time as well. We have shown the importance of psychological time and mythic time as domains which the interpreter enters and shares with the auditor, and which are therefore important constituents of the literary experience. We have distinguished between rhythm and meter and have examined the role which silential time plays in the complex interrelationships to which the auxiliary artist must be sensitive. Only by his sensitivity does the performer sustain and aesthetically fulfill the performing time of the literature.

CHECKLIST FOR ANALYSIS

1. How would the metaworld of the literature be described? What is the "stage of being" in the selection? What is the principal presentational value of the selection? (See chart on page 22.)

2. In what mode is the selection written? What are the central behavioral problems in the selection? in the "presses"?

3. How is literary time conveyed in language? How does psychological time function? mythic time? How are silences used and where? What are the principal rhythms of the literature? What is the prevailing meter of the poetry?

EXERCISES AND ASSIGNMENTS

1. Discuss the ways in which your sense of performing time has been influenced by (1) event time, (2) set time, and (3) symbolic time.

2. Compare and contrast the density and sparsity of language in the two poems, "Driving to Town Late to Mail a Letter" by Robert Bly and "Composed upon Westminster Bridge, September 3, 1802" by William Wordsworth. How do they compare in the use of mythic time and psychological time? In performance how do they differ from each other in the uses of silence?

3. Reread Patrick Morgan's "Nocturne." What psychological associations does it hold about night? Compare the experience of listening to Morgan's nocturne with the experience of listening to a musical nocturne by Chopin. How is Morgan affected by mythic time? Study the punctuation and explain how it influences the uses of silence in a performance of the poem.

4. Discuss the breakdown of mythic time in T. S. Eliot's "The Hollow Men" (Chap. 2). Analyze the uses of silence (characterological, situational, structural) in the poem, experimenting with various emphases as you perform the material. In what ways are these three dimensions of silence unified within the poem?

5. Make a metrical analysis of one or more of the following: "When I Have Fears That I May Cease to Be" by John Keats, "Mending Wall" by Robert Frost, or "Ode on a Grecian Urn" by John Keats. How does meter "set the grain" for the rhythmic elements in the poem? When *only* the meter is emphasized, how does it work *against* the other dimensions of time within the poem?

6. Analyze the punctuation in one of the following poems: "The Novices" by Denise Levertov or "Fern Hill" by Dylan Thomas. Show how the performance of the poem is influenced by the punctuation used by the poet.

7. From Chapters 1, 2, or 3, select any poem you particularly like and write a thorough analysis of the various dimensions of time contained in the work. Perform the poem and attempt to participate in and project its temporal dimensions to the greatest extent possible.

8. Keep a week-long journal of your personal reactions to the kinds of time you experience. Describe your reactions, for example, to some of the following: the set time of a classroom lecture, the game time of the ritual of eating, the mythic time of a religious service, the psychological time of late evening when you are alone.

9. Analyze the rhythm in "Edward" (Chap. 2). What effect is achieved by the repeated "O"? How does it vary in performance when the word is used by the mother? by the son?

10. Reexamine Robert Lax's "Novel/" and mark the words you would stress in a normal reading of the poem. Is there a recurring pattern? If so, describe it.

11. What is the stress pattern in T. S. Eliot's "Journey of the Magi"?

Objectives for Performance Growth

1 Exciting   **2** Enjoyable   **3** Adequate   **4** Need for Development

To Evoke the Metaworlds
_____ a sense of inner resonance
_____ a sense of attaining a state of being
_____ a responsiveness to presentational values
_____ IMPRESSION

To Relate the Performing Body to Literary Experience
_____ behavior congruent to mode
_____ language of gesture natural to literary space
_____ sound of language natural to literary space
_____ appropriate behavioral presses
_____ appropriate use of total bodily energy
_____ IMPRESSION

To Share Awareness of Literary Time
_____ sense of performing time appropriate to literary time
_____ literary time understood and evocated
_____ silences understood and evocated
_____ metrical time understood and evocated
_____ IMPRESSION

To Evoke Figurative Thought and Language
_____ appropriate exemplification of language
_____ a sense of symbolic intent
_____ a sharing of paradox and irony—where appropriate
_____ IMPRESSION

To Evoke Form
_____ form of experience immediate and compelling
_____ form of literary structure appreciated and evocated
_____ IMPRESSION

To Present Style as New Information
_____ expectations in performance congruent to language
_____ performer and style linked / fused
_____ stylistic elements perceived and evocated
_____ narrator attachment or detachment appropriate
_____ IMPRESSION

To Evoke the Presence of Personae
_____ interactional and / or transactional dialogue evocated
_____ significant gesture of characters evocated
_____ structure of dialogue evocated
_____ IMPRESSION

4

Ralph Gibson

**TO PERCEIVE AND EVOKE THE
FIGURATIVE LANGUAGE**

—through spontaneity and freedom
  in language

—through behavioral distinction
  between explicit and implicit
  metaphors

—through a participation of the senses

—through a knowledge of symbolic
  intent

—through an enjoyment of the figures
  of thought

CHAPTER FOUR

The Perception and Evocation of Figurative Language

LANGUAGE AS SYMBOLISM

When the fifth-century Greek poet Simonides observed, "Painting is mute poetry, and poetry is a speaking picture," he was of course commenting from the context of Greek culture, wherein poetry—its creation and performance—was rooted in the oral tradition. The statement remains a provocative one because it emphasizes *effect;* and more, it weds *ef*fectiveness with *af*fectiveness as inseparable processes. The oneness or unity of these two processes has been noted earlier, but the importance of this blending is never so important as when we consider the performance of figurative language.

To live in an environment of language, and especially in the contemporary media-dominated environment, is to live with a subconscious awareness that all language is symbolic, that the world of things inside and outside of us has been merged with the symbols for those things: the language we use. Our realities are our languages. This is what was meant in Chapter 1 by "speaking the world." The writer believes in the metaworld language creates, and we willingly are led into believing in it either because it is true for us or because we grant the possibility that it could be true. We willingly suspend our disbelief. Literature is what Kenneth Koch has sensed as "wishes, lies, and dreams."[1]

THE PERFORMER AS ICON

"The trouble with metaphor," one acute critic has observed, "is that we are one." We speak in language that is a symbol; we clothe ourselves symbolically; we dream in

---

1. See Kenneth Koch, *Wishes, Lies, and Dreams* (New York: Chelsea House Publishers, 1970), a delightful and profound book on teaching children how to write poetry.

symbols. We define ourselves *as* something; we lacerate somebody *as* something else; and we are—by our skin, muscle tone, and bodily frame—something to everybody: "a brain," "a slouch," "a ball of fire," "weak-kneed and lily-livered," "a panther," "a pig," "a whitey," an endlessly, effortlessly something in language. As the schizophrenic little boy observed of himself: "My language is me."

SYMBOLIC PROCESSES INHERENT IN PRESENTATION

This simultaneous duality and unity of language and person has to be considered as the first truly metaphorical problem in the performance of literature. For, as we have emphasized, the performer serves as the *source* of the literary experience. It is through him that the auditor receives the literature. Removed is the two-way relationship of reader-literature, and in its place is the three-way relationship of literature-

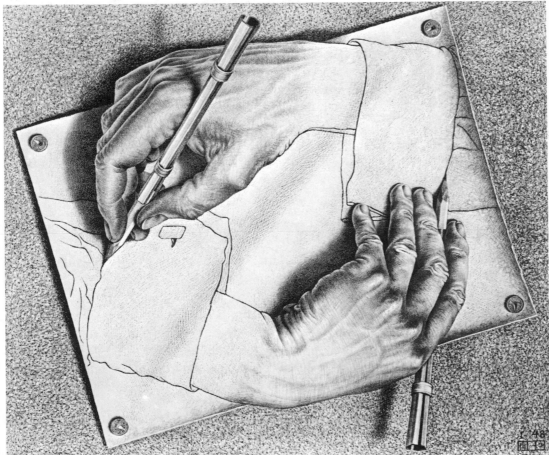

Maurits Escher: "Drawing Hands"

performer-perceiver. Those who have experienced a poet reading his own work have felt the poet, his poem, and the poetic experience become one, and they have a genuine sense of what the "source of poetic experience" means. To evoke this oneness among literature-performer-perceiver becomes one of the most serious challenges facing the auxiliary artist. How does he suggest the experience and at the same time remain the artist through whom the experience is emerging? He begins by becoming acutely aware that he is the one who is standing *for* the literature, that he is the one who is the visually present icon of the experience, and that he is the one who is becoming or indicating the metaphors and the symbolic language of the literature.

In silent reading the reader can grasp the impact of metaphorical language in some special ways not possible when hearing it presented to him. First, the silent reader may read at the rate most suited to his comprehension. Second, he may at the same time scan ahead, check backward, or stop the reading at any point. Third, his own cognitive-emotional processes are "originators" of translation. When the literature is performed, however, the interpretive artist is compelled to consider some important differences. For one thing the perceiver is tied to the performer's rate of performance; for another, the perceiver has no opportunity to stop, check, or recheck perceptions; and finally, he is presented with the performer's interpretation of an experience with which he may feel great congruence or indifference or even distaste. The auditor is, in short, never left alone with the literature, save in memory after the performance.

In perceiving and evoking figurative language, the performer must think carefully about his unique responsibility to *all* of the symbolic processes inherent in presentation; specifically:

His total behavior is iconic of the literature.
In performance the symbolic and the metaphorical are always presented in sound,
    sight, and time.
All symbolic processes and effects are tied to himself as the speaker of the literature.

Even though in Chapter 2 we have developed these ideas in some detail, we will consider them here briefly as they relate to this chapter's discussion of figurative language.

First, the performer has a responsibility to compensate for the shift from silent reading to oral performance. What in silent reading is linear and unfolding is in performance three-dimensional and dynamic. The sense of revelation is given a duplesensory impact: sight and sound are kaleidoscopic.

Second, the performer knows that it is not the printed page that is speaking, but that it is he, and he alone, through whom the language is originating. He knows, therefore, that the spontaneity of the language is important, that the source of the language is in *his* being. He becomes a sounding and visual representation of the literature, an icon, a being filled with sensuous form and structure, an iconic being that is *showing*.[2]

When a primitive pours water on the ground in a prayer for rain, he is utilizing a *process image:* water falling from a gourd is *like* the water which falls from the heavens. The primitive is enacting a process that is like another process. If the performer of literature can move to an understanding that he is a process image, he will realize that he is only *like* the literature, enacting in language and behavior all that he perceives in it. He is attempting to bring the literature to life, to give it form, to allow its language to work through him for its existence. All of his behavior is attuned to the language and what it is evoking, sensing, stating.[3]

FIGURATIVE LANGUAGE

SYMBOLS AND SENSORY PERCEPTION

To understand figurative language requires that the performer respond to what Elizabeth Sewell has called the "fertile and communicable energy" in it.[4] We have all seen sensitive children break down and cry when jeered at and called "'Fraidy cat, 'fraidy cat!" Adults, too, respond with tension and flushed faces when insulting figures of speech are hurled at them. Where does this "fertile and communicable energy" come from? And why does it so immediately affect our bodies? Do we believe those figures of speech? Can words increase blood pressure? The answer is, of course, "yes."

A person who feels insulted is apparently bothered by what he senses as the other person's intentional desire to affect. And to affect is the purpose behind all figurative language. To understand figurative language is to comprehend the nature of intent. In figurative language there is, consciously or subconsciously, an intent to use language in a more power-laden way than in literal usage. It is a seizure of language, and its seizure establishes a persuasive, non-factual truth or an equivalence or a combination of these two effects in what is called a *symbol*. Figurative language is a way of sensing—seeing, feeling, hearing; it is an encounter with a reality transformed into words.

To live a sensory life does not require will; the human condition senses automatically and effortlessly. To see, to hear, to taste, to feel, to touch, to smell, however sluggishly or alertly—these functions continue until accidental impairment or death.

---

2. See "The Poem as Icon," in *The Meaning of Poetic Metaphor* by Marcus B. Hester (New York: Humanities Press, 1967), p. 76.
3. Wayne Shumaker, *Literature and the Irrational* (New York: Washington Square Press, 1966), pp. 90 ff.
4. Elizabeth Sewell, *The Human Metaphor* (South Bend, Ind.: University of Notre Dame Press, 1964), p. 58.

But to see *as*—to transform sight into language and back again into another visual image—does require will. Consider, for instance, the transformation of "That man is coming toward me" into "That man is coming toward me like a wild beast!" Little is understood about this process, this willful, uniquely human use of language. There are many theories which attempt to explain why man has the ability to think in symbols and images and why particular men (artists) seem to have it in a larger measure than others. These theories, when they attempt to explain this use in literature, constitute the study of *poetics,* poetic theory, and the philosophy of literature. Literary critics often attempt to explain the *why* of a writer's use of certain symbols by examining closely the psychology of his family, his life, the books he read, and other minutiae of his background. Psychological theorists have examined man's use of symbology from the personal and unique "representations" and "symbologies" of an individual to the collective symbols societies hold in common.

ANIMISM

It is generally believed that the original meanings of all words are tied to man's sensory life, and that both what is said and what is heard are rooted in sensory impressions gained from touching, tasting, hearing, etc. The earliest uses of figurative language were extensions of man's consciousness onto and into the world surrounding him: the sun rises, the sun hides its face, the sky weeps tears, the earth moans. This *animism,* this giving of conscious life to nature, is still a basic factor in all figurative language. This hyper-verbal activity, this incredible use of verbal energy, is precisely what makes literature and poetry work; even a mere image is transformed in the performance of reading into a highly active, energized, hyper-verbal *meaning.*

FIGURATIVE MEANING VERSUS LITERAL MEANING

Tammi Thillins

Figurative language possesses a magical power that transcends literal meaning. The capacity to respond to the magical power of language is not something bestowed by nature upon certain individuals and denied to others. It is a capacity that can be cultivated and can give to the individual a greater sense of participation in the constantly intriguing flow of language.

The writer, as well as the performer of literature, *transfigures the concrete.* Language is entered into and experienced; and in the entering into it, the performer and his audience use their intuitive powers to try to understand it. The language becomes an experience in itself; and this is what Marcus Hester meant when he wrote, "Poetic language does not so much refer us *to* an experience as it presents us *with* an experience."[5]

5. Hester, *The Meaning of Poetic Metaphor,* p. 68.

THE PHYSIOLOGICAL FOUNDATIONS OF METAPHOR

Studies in perception reveal that "seeing" and symbol-making are far from passive processes. Perception is an active process within the human body in which "an external signal undergoes many transformations, transportations, interpretations, and recombinations before a person experiences seeing."[6] In literature the sensitivity of the writer allows us to see with an inner eye as he sees, to experience with him the transformations, transportations, and recombinations of his perceptual process.

THE METAPHOR THE EYE CREATES: METONYMY

The reader of literature who fails to sense the accuracy of metaphorical reality is failing to respond to an important fact: metaphor is truth transformed.

Consider the metaphorical device known as metonymy. Metonymy is the use of a part for a whole, *sail* for a ship, *steel* for a weapon, *feather* for a bird. This act of seeing a part for the whole of a thing appears to be related to the process of eye movements, those jerks of the eye that are observable in reading, scanning, looking around. These jerking movements, called *saccades,* tend to isolate the most important elements in the thing seen—elements most important to the seer and most strongly associated in his mind with the thing seen. Charlie Chaplin's Little Tramp is for some his oversized shoes, for others his derby hat, for others his moustache. Indeed, the presence of just one of these within a proper context will bring to mind *all* of the Little Tramp. The perceiver's isolation of a part may influence his attitude toward the whole.

Rather than an artificial poetic device, metonymy is fundamental in the act of perception. The poet uses the device almost automatically and for two reasons: (1) it is a natural act in perception and (2) it is richly suggestive. Those of us who think we are always seeing wholes, completes, entireties are deceiving ourselves.

Tensiveness in perception. Is the statement, "Whenever we blink we are blind, but we are not aware of it,"[7] any less true because it was written by a physiologist than by a poet? The assertion, "We spend much of our waking hours blind," is a true statement scientifically, and it is a true statement metaphorically. But the literal meaning and the metaphorical meaning are quite different, perhaps even mutually exclusive. The statement, if pondered, produces a kind of *tension,* a kind of swirl of meaning. The tension is not in the line; it is in us, our perception of it, our enjoyment of it. Tensiveness, therefore, while a factor in the perception of language, is a physiological

---

6. Mardi Jon Horowitz, *Image Formation and Cognition* (New York: Appleton-Century-Crofts, 1970), p. 201.
7. R. L. Gregory, *Eye and Brain* (New York: McGraw-Hill Book Co., 1966), p. 44.

fact within us. This seamless web of language and body is the persistent fact in the perception of literature, and of its presentation.[8]

COLOR IN PERCEPTION

In the eye are two sets of receptors for seeing in daylight and for seeing in darkness. For daylight the cones give color to vision; for low illumination the rods give vision only in shades of gray. Daylight vision is called *photopic vision;* the gray world of vision is called *scotopic.* But note: the depressed personality, who perceives life grayly and colorlessly, uses language that can only be called colorless, lifeless, gray. He is psychologically viewing life scotopically while literally, physiologically, seeing photopically. And contrariwise, the language of the poet filled with life is rich in color imagery.

THE PHYSIOLOGY OF GALVANIC PERCEPTION

The idea that words have an emotional power, as we have suggested, implies only psychological power. But they also have a purely physiological effect. It has been definitely established that there are measurable differences in the galvanic skin responses to the emotional impact of language. The skin responses are different depending on (1) the word itself, (2) whether the word is spoken or heard, (3) by whom it is spoken or heard, (4) whether the same concept is expressed in Latin, French, or in the English vernacular, (5) whether the word is said or heard privately or publicly, (6) the number of repetitions of the same word. If all elements are kept constant, no emotional response can be repeated a second time.[9] The important point to keep in mind is that this physiological response in skin changes is a mutual relationship between the one speaking and the one listening. The effect of language is physiological, as well as psychological; and it is this combination that is apparent in the behaviorial presentation of literature and in its effect upon the auditor. The fact of the matter is that "the normal person forgets the complicated system of verbal forms by which he transforms conceptual and emotional contents into the reality of speech."[10]

The foundations of language are physiological, and metaphorical language often transforms profound physiological facts. Images stem from our perceptual processes: *visual* (sight), *auditory* (hearing), *gustatory* (taste), *olfactory* (smell), *tactile* (touch), *thermal* (responsiveness to temperature changes), *equilibrium* (the organic sense of balance). Not all individuals respond with the same intensity to these stimuli, but writers often seem to have a highly developed sensory awareness of life: a keen

8. Students interested in pursuing this matter of tensiveness will find the books of Philip Wheelwright most instructive and illuminating, particularly *Metaphor and Reality* (Bloomington: Indiana University Press, 1962).
9. Theodore Thass-Thienemann, *Symbolic Behavior* (New York: Washington Square Press, 1968), p. 71.
10. Ibid., p. 119.

sense of visual image, of auditory environment, of reactions to textures and surfaces, of enjoyment of taste and smell. For some persons the thinking process itself, thinking abstractly, becomes the important, absorbing function. The philosopher and the critic "abstract" meaning from literature, and their insights may be revealing and profound. On the other hand, the artist and writer may be more sensory and intuitive, less abstract. What is important to remember is that one mode of thinking is not superior to the other. The choice for the performer is important, however; for in his presentation he is iconic, he is responding to language, and he is the source of experience.

THE PSYCHOLOGICAL FOUNDATIONS OF METAPHOR

There is, in a sense, one basic psychological foundation of metaphor: we willingly enter the poetic language of another. That his language may resonate and reverberate in us is crucial to us as perceivers and also to the performer in his behaviorial transformation of literature. Literature metaphorically traces and symbolically gives life to experience. We observed earlier that the problem of perceiving metaphor is not in seeing, but in seeing *as,* of seeing mystical, congruent, outrageous, witty, precise analogues, of laying one perception alongside another and letting it persuade, mean, or be. When Archibald MacLeish says "a poem must not mean/but be," he is stating his position as a poet. When a critic states that a poem means and is a being, he is stressing the analytical. When a philosopher states that poetic language is the difference between something living and working versus a ready-made thing or object, he is saying something about the process of language.[11] But it is, from whatever view, "an ever-repeated labor of the human mind to use articulated sounds to express thought."[12]

THE PRIMACY OF THE PERCEIVER

The psychological foundation of metaphor in the confrontation of literature rests with the perceiver. A metaphor appeals to the imagination; and if it should fail to take or to mean, it cannot function for the perceiver.

The moment any individual decides to participate consciously in a given symbol he commits himself to a determining tendency of his own subjective imagination which will "reveal" to him the significance . . . as it results from the workings of his own imagination. In accepting the challenge of a symbolic expression an individual is free to decide its significance for himself.[13]

11. Ernst Cassirer, *An Essay on Man* (New York: Bantam Books, 1970), p. 133. Original edition published by Yale University Press, 1944.
12. Ibid., p. 133.
13. Jaroslav Havelka, *The Nature of the Creative Process in Art, a Psychological Study* (The Hague: Martinus Nijhoff, 1968), p. 91.

The enjoyment of metaphor and its richness comes from a willingness to play with it, to let it find its own connections and meanings within us. Play is a process of imagination, and imagination is playful in that it knows no bounds: *it can connect anything with anything.* And that is the essence of metaphor. Old "connections" are dull and boring and no longer have play in them. They may fail to communicate at all. New connections are fresh and insight-filled; and even old connections compressed against new ones are suddenly filled with new life.

KINDS OF METAPHORS

There are basically two kinds of metaphors: an *explicit* metaphor and an *implicit* metaphor.[14]

Explicit metaphor.   An explicit metaphor says precisely that something is *like* something else, or functions *as* something. It is clearly and carefully grammatical:

> O, my luve's like a red, red rose . . .

My love *could be* like a lot of things: the morning dew, the summer flower, a pippin. Each of these transforms the loved one into a different thing with very different associations. The explicit metaphor, commonly called the *simile,* connects symbolically. Is it that the face of my lover is precisely like the image of the flower, the rose? Is it that my lover is precisely like a botanical specimen? No, Robert Burns was suggesting something very different when he wrote

A Red, Red Rose

Robert Burns

O, my luve's like a red, red rose,
    That's newly sprung in June:
O, my luve's like the melodie
    That's sweetly played in tune.

As fair art thou, my bonie lass,
    So deep in luve am I;
And I will luve thee still, my dear,
    Till a' the seas gang dry.

14. For a detailed and insightful discussion of explicit and implicit metaphors, see Hester, *The Meaning of Poetic Metaphor,* pp. 25 ff.

Till a' the seas gang dry, my dear,
    And the rocks melt wi' the sun:
I will luve thee still, my dear,
    While the sands o' life shall run.

And fare thee weel, my only luve!
    And fare thee weel a while!
And I will come again, my luve,
    Tho' it were ten thousand mile!

Once the simile is established by a connecting *as* or *like,* the objects of these prepositions become more than mere nouns. They function as evocative symbols, words having multiple associations within the perceiver. In the first stanza note that the similes do not stand alone; they are carefully intensified. The rose is a red, red rose newly sprung in June. The symbolic rose, alone rich in connotative meanings, is given deeper, more intense reverberations.

Paraphrasing, while sometimes helpful to clarify meaning, merely removes the tension of the simile. To say that "my love is very much like a red rose, a very red rose, a rose that in its rich color suggests to me life and coursing blood, a fresh bloom, a girl in her prime, robust, filled with life" is to remove all the intensity of Burns' condensation. A symbol produces reverberations which in their rightness reveal something that cannot be revealed without it. The impact of the symbol can be changed by tone, particularly in performance. To read the first stanza sarcastically is to change and negate the symbolic meaning. Under these circumstances the tone of voice is saying, "My love is old and haggard, past her prime, and the only 'melodie' suggestive of her is one so out of tune as to drive you to distraction. A crone, a very crone." Thus, behind the symbol is a psychological attitude derived from some feeling. A highly sensitive reading of even explicit metaphors, present as they are with the "likes" and "ases," is required to perform them congruently with the meaning.

Implicit metaphor.   Implicit metaphor, or what is usually designated simply metaphor, differs from the explicit metaphor in one important way: it is *literally* false. The explicit metaphor, while likening one thing to another—and in improbable ways, perhaps— makes very clear to the reader that it is *not* literally a true statement; it is only a parallel, a comparison. The implicit metaphor drops the *like* and the *as* and begins a tease with logic, truth, perception. An implicit metaphor is a self-contained metaworld of language. Though it may be non-sense, it is not necessarily nonsense; though it may be farfetched, it reverberates with a fetching truth.

The following poem was written by a fourth-grade student responding to the teaching of the American poet, Kenneth Koch.

The Pretzel Is a Mrs. Wiener[15]

Erin Harold

The pretzel is a Mrs. Wiener.
The rose is a ripe cherry.
The wasp is a scream from my big sister.
A bee is a jump underneath the bed by my sister.
A cloud is a kitten playing with a breeze.
A breeze is a string for a cloud to play with.
Is the sun a ball of string which the breeze was cut from?
Maybe, but the breeze is blue and the sun is orange.
Do cloud cats drink the rain?
Maybe, but do they like it?
No, because it isn't milk.

The poem, delightful in its ingenuousness, fulfills what we expect in implicit metaphor:
1. An implicit metaphor is literally false.
2. An implicit metaphor startles our literal language sense; it suggests an "odd" way of speaking.
3. An implicit metaphor establishes a "tension" in our body of knowledge.

These three aspects of implicit metaphor—and poetry is more often implicit in its metaphorical utterance than not—create problems in performance. Literal falseness is truth for the speaker; the oddness of the language is natural for the speaker; the resulting tension creates the power of the language.

     The following poem exemplifies these problems. Written when this sixteeth-century poet was twenty-seven or twenty-eight years old, it is useful not only in the study and understanding of the performing problems of implicit metaphor, but it is also rich in irony and paradox—figures of thought which are discussed later in this chapter.

On the Eve of His Execution

Chidiock Tichbourne

My prime of youth is but a frost of cares;
     My feast of joy is but a dish of pain;
My crop of corn is but a field of tares;
     And all my good is but vain hope of gain;
My life is fled, and yet I saw no sun;
And now I live, and now my life is done.

The spring is past, and yet it hath not sprung;
     The fruit is dead, and yet the leaves be green;
My youth is gone, and yet I am but young;
     I saw the world, and yet I was not seen;
My thread is cut, and yet it is not spun;
And now I live, and now my life is done.

I sought my death, and found it in my womb;
     I looked for life, and saw it was a shade,
I trod the earth, and knew it was my tomb,
     And now I die, and now I am but made:
The glass is full, and now my glass is run,
And now I live, and now my life is done.

The three criteria for implicit metaphor are all fulfilled in this poem:
1. The metaphors are not literally true.
2. The use of metaphor is unusual and startling.
3. A tension is created in the pull of opposites—youth-death, spin-cut, womb-tomb, and so on.

In performance the power of the implicit metaphor is given a new dimension with the coalescence of the following: the performer is iconic; non-rational truth is inherent in the implicit metaphors; the poet has a startling capacity to "speak to the condition" in a language congruent to the emotion. This coalescence of factors is what can be termed *exemplification of metaphor*.

    Exemplification, a showing, follows the path of *intimation and not imitation.* The iconic performer *intimates* in performance; in his understanding of explicit meta-phor, he points to outward similarities, while in his understanding of implicit metaphor, he points out and indicates inward conditions. That metaphors are not literally true is not important; that they are psychologically true is sufficient.

KINDS OF SYMBOLS

As we have seen, metaphor functions suggestively in literature; it involves a comparison. Symbols are also suggestive; however, they imply relationships approaching the nature of an equation. There are three kinds of symbols: (1) a symbol that is immediately *communicative,* (2) a symbol that is highly *creative* and original, and (3) one that becomes *contemplative.* How do these differ from each other? A communicative symbol has a universal, agreed upon value at a particular time and place. We agree that wings on a human suggest an angel, that a swastika from our most immediate historical past symbolizes a Nazi. A creative symbol is a discovery, and usually a fresh and arresting one, by a writer. He seizes upon an image that we recognize as holding the potential for a creative statement. It may suddenly become very popular and be used widely in a variety of meanings as happened when T. S. Eliot symbolized Western culture as a "wasteland." A contemplative symbol is the most difficult of the three to explain, but an example may clarify its meaning. A contemplative symbol is a creation so powerful, so unique that it stands alone. Although there have been many Hamlets, only one stands preeminent: Shakespeare's. There is only one Moby Dick; there is only one Faust. Contemplative symbols are the most challenging for the performer, and for obvious reasons. Each reader has developed his own image of what the contemplative symbol is, how it is to be interpreted, how it is to be experienced.

Writers naturally rely upon our cultural backgrounds for the immediate grasp of a communicative symbol; it "hits" instantaneously. The creative symbol arrests and refreshes by its impact. In recent time Holden Caulfield in *Catcher in the Rye* became a creative symbol for a whole generation of readers. The contemplative symbol is, in its simplest sense, the great, enduring art of a culture.

Allusions. For the performer and sensitive reader, the communicative, creative, and contemplative symbols have particular importance. These symbols become woven into language and literature; and when referred to, they are called *allusions.* For help in understanding them, we need (1) a background of literary knowledge which recognizes the allusion and (2) a probing mind and a questioning spirit to seek out allusive meanings. The three principal sources of allusion in the English-speaking world are Greek myths and fables, the Bible, and Shakespeare. Familiarity with these sources is essential for understanding the commonest clichés: "a Herculean task," "the patience of Job," "a Hamletic attitude." Allusions are seldom this obvious; but because they constitute a rich vein for poetic metaphor, any student of literature—including the performer of it—should enrich his reading background.

THE PERCEPTION AND EVOCATION OF FIGURES OF THOUGHT

Figurative language includes figures of thought as well as figures of speech. A figure of thought teases the imagination and is grasped only through an active participation in the language and situation of the literature. *Irony* and *paradox* are the two most commonly used figures of thought. An appreciation of irony and paradox is often cited as the most discriminating mental process in the enjoyment of literature, for it is in the ironies and paradoxes of life that character is revealed, tested, and stated. Appreciation is derived in part from tonality in that tone can change the direction of a writer's intent. The observation that ''it is a wonderful day'' when the weather is quite nasty can only be given its full intentional meaning by vocal tone and by the auditor's appreciation of that tone, its context on that day, and the speaker's intentional contradiction of fact.

IRONY

In irony apparent meaning and actual meaning are two different things. Irony is most often situational: intended outcome and actual outcome are different. The statement, ''The gold-thirsty Spaniards got what they wanted when the Incas poured molten gold down their throats,'' exemplifies irony in the sense of intent and outcome. The statement also plays upon language, ''gold-thirsty'' suggesting the greed of the Spaniards and the ironical way in which that thirst was quenched. The Cavalier poets made much of the ironies of love: its long-lasting intentions versus its fickleness and short-lived disappointment.

PARADOX

Paradox is an apparent contradiction in language. A paradoxical statement is one in which two ideas or concepts appear to be mutually exclusive of each other, but linked together they express a truth. In Peter Viereck's line, ''The day is no rounder than its angles are,'' the reader's or hearer's attention is held in attempting to reconcile *roundness* and *angularity.* Curiously, a paradoxical statement sets forth a truth, a perceived relationship that language coaxes into a comprehensible meaning. Do the angles and points of a day make a day round, complete, whole? Or, does the roundness of a day depend upon the elimination of the jabs, the points, the angles? And so on. Verbal paradox is a purposeful use of language to seize an intelligence willing to work with it, to play the language into a controlled ambiguity. In paradox, yes/no, good/bad, right/wrong, this/that—in short, *opposites*—do not function as being mutually exclusive of each other. The opposites, rather than negating each other, enhance each other, creating a new synthesis of meaning in which seeming contradictions can exist harmoniously.

Paradox can also be situational. When one reads the admonition, "Do not read this statement!" what is he to do? Having done it, he is trapped. If the reader smiles, the smile is a recognition of being trapped in a situation from which there is never an extrication. Consider, too, the statement, "The blind see and the seeing are blind." Here the statement is paradoxical as well as ironic. In the play *Oedipus Rex,* the statement is true; for Oedipus, failing to see his condition at a time when he has the physical capacity to use his eyes, is "blind." Conversely, old Teiresias, physically blind but a wise man, "sees" the direction that Oedipus' life will take.

While the perception of irony and paradox in literature can be cultivated and enhanced by an enjoyable exposure to situations and language, the evocation of irony and paradox in performance is in fact ironical and paradoxical. Because irony and paradox are perceived relationships, they rely for their existence upon the perceiver. And in the performance of literature, even though the literature itself may contain ample potential irony and paradox, unless the audience perceives them, they can be said not to exist. The performer can do little but prepare himself thoroughly in his own understandings of the paradoxes and ironies, and then hope that a sensitive listener will catch them. He should not lecture upon them, point them out, or in any other way destroy their self-energizing effectiveness. Irony and paradox are dependent upon many subtle factors: surprise, suddenness, tone, intelligence, slow revelation. It is an irony of performance that a naive listener may not perceive the irony of a naive speaker in a poem, yet this is the very essence of irony.

In summary, this chapter has explored the phenomenon of figurative language and thought. It has been pointed out that figurative language is so rooted in the perceptual processes of man that man's condition, his language, and his environment become one. The image-making process is tied to our sensory life of sight, touch, taste, smell, and the like, although our individual sensitivities may differ considerably. That we may choose to be explicit or implicit in our metaphors is our choice between keeping language linked to perception through *like* or *as,* or in allowing language to become an environment of perception through *is-ness.* The psychological foundations of metaphor are rooted in the meaning-filled language of each man's perception; and while each individual may symbolize his perceptions differently, the commonality of language and symbol makes for communication. The capacity to entertain relationships in the mind, to perceive what is ironic and paradoxical, is a mental act of perception linked to tone, situation, and language.

We Were Not Expecting the Prince To-day[16]

Muriel Spark

As stated above, we were not expecting . . .
All the same, you had better show him the sleeping
Beauty upstairs with her powder still intact,
While the whole court on sentry duty, believe it,
Propped in their wigs a century exact,
Deplore her blunder, or rather, misconceive it.

And you had better and better deliver
The bat from her tresses, dispose for a kiss
That bluff on her webby mouth, for suppose he should call it,
And give her a nudge, and she take the hint, and this
Beauty be a cloud of powder over her pallet?

beware: do not read this poem[17]

Ishmael Reed

> tonite , thriller was
> abt an ol woman , so vain she
> surrounded herself w/
>   many mirrors
>
> it got so bad that finally she
> locked herself indoors & her
> whole life became the
>   mirrors
>
> one day the villagers broke
> into her house , but she was too
> swift for them . she disappeared
>   into a mirror

16. "We Were Not Expecting the Prince To-day" by Muriel Spark from *Collected Poems I*. Reprinted by permission of Harold Ober Associates Incorporated. Copyright © 1968 by Muriel Spark.
17. "beware: do not read this poem" by Ishmael Reed from *Soulscript*, edited by June Jordan. Copyright © 1970. Reprinted by permission of the author.

Michael Snow: "Five Girl Panels"

The Perception and Evocation of Figurative Language

each tenant who bought the house
after that , lost a loved one to
     the ol woman in the mirror :
     first a little girl
     then a young woman
     then the young woman/s husband

the hunger of this poem is legendary
it has taken in many victims
back off from this poem
it has drawn in yr feet
back off from this poem
it has drawn in yr legs
back off from this poem
it is a greedy mirror
you are into this poem . from
    the waist down
nobody can hear you can they ?
this poem has had you up to here
     belch
this poem aint got no manners
you cant call out frm this poem
relax now & go w/ this poem
move & roll on to this poem
do not resist this poem
this poem has yr eyes
this poem has his head
this poem has his arms
this poem has his fingers
this poem has his fingertips

this poem is the reader & the
reader this poem

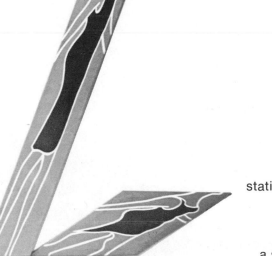

statistic : the us bureau of missing persons reports
    that in 1968 over 100,000 people disappeared
    leaving no solid clues
        nor trace   only
a space   in the lives of their friends

Alphabet for Joanna[18]

Horace Gregory

In a child's garden of drawings I came upon a book:
A for the serpent's Apple and wide-winged Albatross;
B was for Bull, Bible and Bell, and "to Be" spoken
In a voice out of a cloud. And there was C, the Cat, coiled in a Chair,
And three-headed Cerberus, the Dog, who stands for D,
Who ate his Dinner in the Dream's shadow
Where water flows behind an unopened Door;
E for the faceless Egg, Easter with dancing suns,
And E for Ermines worn by kings on cards,
By guilty, light-haired, pale-eyed player queens.
F for the Fish and Fox, the hooked and trapped,
Floundering and fleet in Flood and over Field,
And G for Grapes and Grass growing beyond a Gate
Where Hills are always H and Heaven and H's are
Horns blowing from Hell's Hearth and fiery Hedges
On Halloweens.

      Then I, thin "I,"
Myself walking in mirrors, wide-eyed, an Island
In green glass, speechless and half-asleep
Before J, the Judge in a white collar and a black nightgown
Where Jubal sings beneath a Judas tree.

          K for King in Kilts,
The gay Kinghorn who sits with a captured princess on his Knee;
L, the caged Lion from the age of gold
Stares at gray Lazarus risen from the dead
While M, the Man measures night's Mountains in the Moon,
And N glides near with a great spider's Net
That catches flies where numbed Napoleon stands
In a lead soldier's blackened uniform.
O is the Ocean and Ocarina, the sea and wind,
Orion in the sky and the Oriole's breast;
P is the Pole where weather turns to ice,

18. "Alphabet for Joanna" from *Selected Poems of Horace Gregory.* Copyright 1951 by Horace Gregory. Reprinted by permission of The Viking Press, Inc.

And P's are Palaces where Princes stalk at noon
To meet their Queens in Q's that stand in line
To answer Questions: "Is R the Rain?
Or is it Reindeer flying through snow, or Raphael,
Angel who spoke aloud to Adam?"

                    Swifter than S in the Snake,
And brighter than Snake's eyes is Saturn
Burning above the T-crossed earth where T is
The night-wandering Tapir and Targets pierced with darts,
Where Tambourines spin and dance under the bear,
Ursa, and U is Unicorn, the Visitor, V, at night
In snow-lit Visions.

              W is the Way, the hidden Walk
Beyond the Wall; X, the unknown, the blue-lighted
X-ray that shows the skeleton in a darkened glass,
And Y, the Year that runs long June to short December
While Z, the Zodiac, turns its wheel in heaven.

As the book closes, the difficult numerals begin
And multiply in twos and threes and fours,
Yet the alphabet remains where all things live—
The world through open windows and wide doors.

Lens[19]

Anne Wilkinson

1
The poet's daily chore
Is my long duty;
To keep and cherish my good lens
For love and war
And wasps about the lilies
And mutiny within.

My woman's eye is weak
And veiled with milk;

19. "Lens" from *The Collected Poems of Anne Wilkinson*, edited by A. J. M. Smith. Reprinted by permission of The Macmillan Company of Canada Limited.

My working eye is muscled
With a curious tension,
Stretched and open
As the eyes of children;
Trusting in its vision
Even should it see
The holy holy spirit gambol
Counterheadwise,
Lithe and warm as any animal.

My woman's iris circles
A blind pupil;
The poet's eye is crystal,
Polished to accept the negative,
The contradictions in a proof
And the accidental
Candour of the shadows;
The shutter, oiled and smooth
Clicks on the grace of heroes
Or on some bestial act
When lit with radiance
The afterwords the actors speak
Give depths to violence,

Or if the bull is great
And the matador
And the sword
Itself the metaphor.

2
In my dark room the years
Lie in solution,
Develop film by film.
Slow at first and dim
Their shadows bite
On the fine white pulp of paper.

An early snap of fire
Licking the arms of air
I hold against the light, compare

The details with a prehistoric view
Of land and sea
And cradles of mud that rocked
The wet and sloth of infancy.

A stripe of tiger, curled
And sleeping on the ribs of reason
Prints as clear
As Eve and Adam, pearled
With sweat, staring at an apple core;

And death, in black and white
Or politic in green and Easter film,
Lands on steely points, a dancer
Disciplined to the foolscap stage,
The property of poets
Who command his robes, expose
His moving likeness on the page.

To the Snake[20]

Denise Levertov

Green Snake, when I hung you round my neck
and stroked your cold, pulsing throat
        as you hissed to me, glinting
arrowy gold scales, and I felt
        the weight of you on my shoulders,
and the whispering silver of your dryness
        sounded close at my ears—

Green Snake—I swore to my companions that certainly
        you were harmless! But truly
I had no certainty, and no hope, only desiring
        to hold you, for that joy,
                which left
a long wake of pleasure, as the leaves moved
and you faded into the pattern

20. Denise Levertov, *With Eyes at the Back of Our Heads,* Copyright © 1958 by Denise Levertov Goodman. Reprinted
by permission of New Directions Publishing Corporation.

of grass and shadows, and I returned
smiling and haunted, to a dark morning.

Fairy Tale[21]

Miroslav Holub

He built himself a house,
       his foundations,
       his stones,
       his walls,
       his roof overhead,
       his chimney and smoke,
       his view from the window.

He made himself a garden,
        his fence,
        his thyme,
        his earthworm,
        his evening dew.

He cut out his bit of sky above.

And he wrapped the garden in the sky
and the house in the garden
and packed the lot in a handkerchief

and went off
lone as an arctic fox
through the cold
unending
rain
into the world.

21. "Fairy Tale" by Miroslav Holub from *Miroslav Holub: Selected Poems*, translated by Ian Milner and George Theiner. Copyright © 1967, Miroslav Holub. Translation copyright © 1967, Ian Milner and George Theiner. Reprinted by permission of Penguin Books Ltd.

CHECKLIST FOR ANALYSIS

1. How would the metaworld of the literature be described? What is the "state of being" in the selection? What is the principal presentational value of the selection? (See chart on page 22.)

2. In what mode is the selection written? What are the central behavioral problems in the selection? in the "presses"?

3. How is literary time conveyed in language? How does psychological time function? mythic time? How are silences used and where? What are the principal rhythms of the literature? What is the prevailing meter of the poetry?

4. How is figurative language employed? to what ends? How are paradox and irony employed?

EXERCISES AND ASSIGNMENTS

1. After analyzing the mythic and psychological time in Muriel Spark's "We Were Not Expecting the Prince To-day," what would a performer *do* with the symbolism of the prince? the sleeping beauty? What is the double meaning of the word *bluff*? What is implicit in the metaphor ". . . this/Beauty be a cloud of powder . . ."? How would you describe the energy of the poem? The poem begins in the title; discuss how the poem's title energizes the entire poem in time, in symbol. Is the poem photopic? scotopic? both? What is the central "sensory life" of the poem?

2. How does the impact of the poem "beware: do not read this poem" differ in a silent reading from a performing experience? How is paradox established in the poem? In performance is the paradox greater or less because of the word *read* in the title? What if the word were *hear*? How does the absence of capitalization affect your feeling about the words? If you were to capitalize the correct words, does any perceptual change occur in the poem? Analyze the poem "Novel/" in Chapter 3 using suggestions similar to those in this question. In what ways are the poems similar? dissimilar?

3. Analyze the poem "Alphabet for Joanna" for its varieties of metaphorical language. How is mythic time reinforced by images in the poem? What are the paradoxes of the poem? the ironies? What is the symbolic intent of the poem? How do you sense this? What elements in the poem make it a particularly effective poem for presentation?

4. Analyze how Anne Wilkinson's "Lens" develops the central metaphor of the lens. What turns and changes does it take? How do the metaphors accumulate in their meaning? How does mythic time pervade the poem?

5. "To the Snake" is obviously focused on the *symbolic* value of the snake. How does the associational process within the poem create the sensory awakenings of the speaker? Are

there paradoxes within the poem? How does the tense ("when I *hung* . . . ," etc.) affect the speaking performance of the poem? How does a performer dissociate himself from or associate himself with the conventional notions and feelings regarding snakes to amplify the symbolism of the poem?

6. Examine the figurative language in poems and selections in previous chapters along the lines suggested in this chapter and this chapter's questions.

Objectives for Performance Growth

1 Exciting   2 Enjoyable   3 Adequate   4 Need for Development

To Evoke the Metaworlds
- ____ a sense of inner resonance
- ____ a sense of attaining a state of being
- ____ a responsiveness to presentational values
- ____ IMPRESSION

To Relate the Performing Body to Literary Experience
- ____ behavior congruent to mode
- ____ language of gesture natural to literary space
- ____ sound of language natural to literary space
- ____ appropriate behavioral presses
- ____ appropriate use of total bodily energy
- ____ IMPRESSION

To Share Awareness of Literary Time
- ____ sense of performing time appropriate to literary time
- ____ literary time understood and evoked
- ____ silences understood and evoked
- ____ metrical time understood and evoked
- ____ IMPRESSION

To Evoke Figurative Thought and Language
- ____ appropriate exemplification of language
- ____ a sense of symbolic intent
- ____ a sharing of paradox and irony—where appropriate
- ____ IMPRESSION

To Evoke Form
- ____ form of experience immediate and compelling
- ____ form of literary structure appreciated and evoked
- ____ IMPRESSION

To Present Style as New Information
- ____ expectations in performance congruent to language
- ____ performer and style linked / fused
- ____ stylistic elements perceived and evoked
- ____ narrator attachment or detachment appropriate
- ____ IMPRESSION

To Evoke the Presence of Personae
- ____ interactional and / or transactional dialogue evoked
- ____ significant gesture of characters evoked
- ____ structure of dialogue evoked
- ____ IMPRESSION

TO EVOKE FORM

— through understanding the form of the experience

— through understanding form as structure

— through unifying the form of the experience and the form of the structure

— through understanding that performance is the transformation of form

5

André Kertész

CHAPTER FIVE

The Perception and Evocation of Form

Form, style, and character are probably the most elusive and yet most tangible elements of the literary experience. It would be a rare student of literature indeed who, when given the name of a well-known writer, could not recall the form in which that writer primarily expressed himself, could not recollect something of the style in which he cast his language, and could not people his imagination with some of the characters the writer created. Given a writer's name, the three elements—form, style, character—coalesce immediately: Mark Twain—prose/ native American speech/ Huckleberry Finn; T. S. Eliot—verse/ a flowing and highly imagistic language that startles and arrests in its sudden and unexpected shifts/ J. Alfred Prufrock; Tennessee Williams—dramatic mode/ a Southern lilt filled with the desperation of loneliness and despair/ Blanche DuBois. The interweavings of these elements constitute, ultimately, literature's very personality. To separate them is an unnatural act, yet to understand them, to perceive how they interrelate, requires just such individual attention. The problems of form discussed in this chapter develop from the question, "How is the nature of an experience related to the form in which it is cast?" Chapter 6, "The Perception and Evocation of Style," explores the elements of style, and the chapter asks, "How are the dynamics of linguistic style conveyed in performance?" Chapter 7, "The Perception and Evocation of Personae," poses the question, "How can the elements of dialogic characterization convey the significant aspects of personality?" Chapter 5 deals primarily with form *in poetry,* Chapter 6 with style *in prose,* and Chapter 7 with character *in drama;* however, the discussion in each chapter applies to all genres, and the student should be sensitive to the interrelation of the three chapters. For example, when characters in a narrative poem are given dialogue, the student would attend to the problems of characterization indicated in that dialogue. Or consider the problems inherent in a Shakespearean play where the form is largely poetic (iambic pentameter, blank verse) and where attention to form may be as important as attention to characterization. And finally, prose fiction's delicate matters of style are no less important than the dialogic evocation of the characters in the story. Discrete attention to the factors of form, style, and character will help the student to put the separate elements together as he progresses in the complexities of the performer's tasks.

FORM DEFINED IN POETRY AND PROSE

The study of literature with the purpose of giving it presentation stresses that *performance is the transformation of form*. The statement suggests that "the thorough completion" of a piece of literature is a "carrying across" of the elements perceived in the "shape, container, or mold" that the writer has created. Or, further, a performance, which is a total behaviorial act, carries over in space-time-sound those formal elements characteristic of the literature.

In either silent reading or performance, literature reveals two forms simultaneously: the form or the nature of the experience and the form in which the experience has been cast. More simply stated, these are "what happens" and "the form in which it happens." But they both happen at once. One can be designated as *form as experience* and the other as *form as structure.*

The terms *verse* and *prose* were discussed in an earlier chapter as return (or recurrent) patterns and forward movement, respectively. In both verse and prose, an experience takes shape and development. In verse, language may have fixed line length, metrical patterns, rhyme, and unit patterns (stanzas and other print configurations). In prose the form in which experience exists is more elusive. Prose is not easily "contained" on the page; it is expansive. Its structure develops out of the nature of the experience, how it happened, what caused it.

For the moment, then, consider poetic form as a pattern of definable dimensions imposed upon language and experience, the pattern exerting a variety of controls. Think of prose form as something looser, more open, less set in tight patterns, and moving more toward the shape of an experience. These distinctions can be best illustrated by two examples. The first (verse) suggests the sense of containment and return patterns; the second (prose) the sense of experience and forward movement.

I wandered lonely as a cloud
That floats on high o'er vales and hills,
When all at once I saw a crowd,
A host, of golden daffodils;
Beside the lake, beneath the trees,
Fluttering and dancing in the breeze.
           from *I Wandered Lonely As a Cloud*
           William Wordsworth

When David took leave of the Micawbers that evening they both pressed him to come and dine with them before they went away, and they urged him so that he could not refuse. They had a beautiful little dinner. Quite an elegant dish of fish; the kidney-end of a loin of veal, roasted; fried sausage meat; a partridge, and, a pudding. There was wine, and there was a strong ale; and after dinner Mrs. Micawber made them a bowl of hot punch with her own hands.

from *David Copperfield*
Charles Dickens

Leon D. Harmon and Kenneth C. Knowlton, Bell Telephone Laboratories

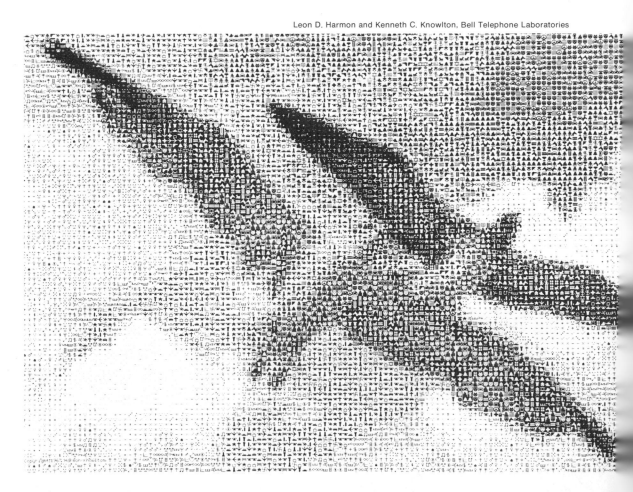

The Perception and Evocation of Form

In literature, form involves the building of fragments of information into structures which may vary from the tightly contained arrangements of poetry to the expansively organized patterns of prose. Robert Neale, in a long essay on play, has suggested that man has a conflicting dualistic nature and that this duality may be resolved ". . . into inner harmony. The two poles of the duality are *the need to discharge energy and the need to design experience.*"[1] This design in literature is form. Ernst Cassirer intimates the same idea when he observes that "the child plays with *things,* the artist plays with *forms,* with lines and designs, rhythms and melodies."[2] The auxiliary artist in the re-creation of literature will pay close attention to the form of the literary experience and will "play" with the elements in the literature for their rich and persuasive evocations.

In the study of literature as it is transformed into a performance, the form of the experience and the form of the structure are mutually complementary, just as is, for example, the shape of a container and what it may contain. In discussing the two kinds of form, to isolate one from the other is to alter both elements. Similarly, in the presence of artistic performances of literature, it is nearly impossible to discuss the effect of the experience apart from the manner in which it was cast.

FORM AS EXPERIENCE

It is time that permits the form of the literary experience to emerge, that allows us to determine what has happened.

If the genuine poem is made of words actually heard, no poem ever exists in its material totality; only one line of poetry at a time can exist and of this line only one word, and of this one word only one syllable or vocal emission, the whole being structured in the memory which absorbs its elements to the degree that the ear perceives them. What is true of the poem is first of all true of the elementary sonorous forms of which it is composed. It is therefore proper to classify poetry, along with music, the dance, and all the arts whose works depend for their actual existence on the existence of man himself, among the arts of movement and of time.[3]

Test this statement in two ways: first read the following poem quickly, silently, trying to perceive as much of it as you can at once visually; second, read the poem aloud.

1. Robert E. Neale, *In Praise of Play* (New York: Harper & Row, 1969), p. 22. (Italics his)
2. Ernst Cassirer, *An Essay on Man* (New York: Bantam Books, 1970), p. 182. Original edition published by Yale University Press, 1944.
3. Etienne Gilson, *Forms and Substances in the Arts,* trans. by Salvator Attanasio (New York: Charles Scribner's Sons, 1966), pp. 217–218.

The Sick Rose

William Blake

O rose, thou art sick!	Has found out thy bed
The invisible worm	Of crimson joy;
That flies at night	And his dark, secret love
In the howling storm	Does thy life destroy.

In a silent reading to perceive visually the two stanzas is to miss the reading and understanding of the lines; to perceive the rhyming words is to lose focus on the lines of which they are a part. There is, too, very little sense of passing time. When the poem is read aloud, all dimensions change and a sense of "what has happened" emerges. With the very first sound, there is a sense of experience, for the vocalized *O* sound portends a sense of inner happening. By the end of the first line, with the sounding of the word *sick,* the experience has reached a definitively articulated statement, and it is an exclamatory statement. There follows the paradox of a worm that flies at night and destroys life with a dark and secret love. But most importantly, the body has experienced the passing of time in a very different way.

Literature in performance automatically creates sonorous form (the acoustic space of the literature) and behavioral form (the visual languages of gesture and attitude with which the performer is surrounding sound), both existing in an absolute simultaneity of experience. The sonorous form of the Blake poem is two sentences. The utterance of these two sentences is the complete sonorous experience. How would the following questions be answered?

How does the visual experience of two stanzas differ from the auditory experience of two sentences?

How does the visual experience of the rhyming words (in this case, approximate rhyme) differ from the auditory experience?

Compare the saccades of the eye (the moving jerks of perception) with the sound of the words in time.

How is the metaphor of the rose given a behaviorial form that the mere visual presence of the word on the printed page does not necessarily suggest?

How do the fragments of information build into a structure of experience? How is this different from the structure of sight?

These questions are typical of those that should be asked in deciding what has happened, in looking at form as experience.

The language of literature is image-bearing; when the imagination receives the same images through sound and behavior, the result is image-amplifying. In silent reading the poem may be read and reread, contemplated and mulled over. In performance the poem is experienced syllable by syllable, word by word, phrase by phrase, and only once. Thus, the first overall effect becomes the form of the experience for the auditor, the "what happened" to the inner life of the writer. This experience and its visible effects were discussed at considerable length in Chapter 2 under the section "Presses in Literature." There, it will be recalled, the expressive, repressive, oppressive and other states of visible behavior were described. These can now be considered those behaviors which inform the form of the experience. They should with considerable accuracy indicate the shape of the experience and reveal, in the most literal sense of the word, the inner life of the literature. This is what Etienne Gilson was suggesting when he said of poetry that it demanded "the existence of man himself" to give the "actual existence" to the literature, and hence the importance of the auxiliary artist's coming to the truest understanding of the author's meaning and transforming it most effectively.

FORM AS STRUCTURE

Rudolph Arnheim, in his exploration of the importance of structure in art, observes that "form is the shape that makes content visible."[4] The two traditional forms in literature which have prevailed are the auditory form and the printed form.

THE AUDITORY FORM

The early rhapsodists relied upon patterns of language so that the experiences of such heroic figures as Achilles, Odysseus, and Beowulf, could not only be told, but be remembered as well. Scholars speak of these patterns as the *formula of epic verse.* This formula can be defined as the regular use of set groups of words employed under identical metrical conditions to express a given essential idea.[5] These regularly employed groups of words were not original figures of speech or inventions in language. They were formulated statements such as "Like the fated hour there is no escaping," "Rosey-fingered dawn," "Ox-eyed Hera." In learning the story and the stock figures of speech as well as matters of rhythm and form, the young rhapsodist developed his craft into ever increasingly complex patterns of language, meter and rhyme, assonance and consonance, melody and syntax. These conventions enabled the rhapsodist not only to learn the epic poem more easily, but also to create the epic freely and spontaneously anew in oral performance.

4. Rudolph Arnheim, *Toward a Psychology of Art* (Berkeley: University of California Press, 1966), p. 354.
5. For an examination of the aural/oral tradition in epic literature, see Albert B. Lord, *The Singer of Tales* (New York: Atheneum Publishers, 1965), particularly Chapter 3, "The Formula."

THE PRINTED FORM

These structural forms that came out of the oral tradition of epic verse seem far removed from the structural forms we recognize and look for in poetry. Today a new poet is usually published before he is heard. It is our custom to look at poetry, to read silently the poetry we look at, to establish an intimacy between paper and words. This is a circumstance of the print culture; it does not necessarily reveal where literature is "contained." In its first impact poetry in printed form appears to be arranged in stanzas, quatrains, and other spatially organized groups of words. Similar line lengths, recognizable visual rhyming patterns, repetitions of words beginning with the same consonants become visible.

The degree to which a performance of literature should imitate in audible space the way words are arranged in printed space, in an effort to suggest the nature of the visual, printed form, is subject to many judgments on the part of the performer. In the oral performance of literature, distinctions between auditory form and printed form are annihilated so that all aspects of the literature appear to be contained in acoustic and behaviorial spaces. The auditory form is the inheritance from an oral culture; the printed form is the heritage of our present print culture. The pervasive notion today is that literature is contained in print, that it belongs to and is in the print culture, not the oral culture. One of the goals of studying literature in performance is to bring together these two traditions.

To a student, struggling with form as structure, the following comments by John Ciardi may clarify its importance.

A poem exists in time. The first line comes first, the others follow in their order to the last line, and there is no other order in which the lines can be read.

And since a poem has duration, it also has pace. One poem may obviously urge the voice at a faster pace than does another. Within the same poem, moreover, one part may urge itself much more rapidly than another. Even within an individual line, one phrase may clearly be indicated as moving rapidly or more slowly than another. For just as music carries with it a notation that tells the musician at what rate and with what feeling to play a given passage, so every good piece of writing, and poetry in particular, carries within it a series of unmistakable notations that tell the good reader how any given passage should be read. One of the poet's chief delights is in the manipulation of his pace and its changes. He is deeply involved in the *feeling of his motion.* Since a poem is always about something felt, its motion is certainly a part of what it is about, part of what it feels, and therefore, part of what it "means." Even more importantly, the motion is fundamental to how the poem means.[6]

6. John Ciardi, *How a Poem Means* (Boston: Houghton Mifflin Co., 1959), pp. 920–921. Chapter 7, "The Poem in Motion," is an excellent, urbane, and concise examination of form and rhythm.

Michael Di Biase

The sense of form in motion has been discussed in Chapter 3, "Time in the Performance of Literature." There the basic English metric feet were explained, and the statement was made that "Metered speech becomes, in one sense, a container for movement; it complements the psychological rhythms, the inner being that is expressing itself in language." An examination of form as structure is a study of the containers in which the rhythmic force of the words are put. For John Ciardi's description of the unfolding of words and lines holds true for the arrangement of lines in a poem as well: the stanzaic structure.

SET PATTERNS AND FREE PATTERNS

Literature pulls between two extremes in its forms. On the one hand there are the familiar *set patterns,* and on the other, the *free patterns.* Form, and an awareness of it, suggests a certain expectation: the expectation that the container of the experience will be congruent to the experience, and further, upon reflection, that the container is a satisfactory means for expressing the writer's experience. Yet the word *expectation* in this case suggests a culturally acceptable norm, not necessarily a guide for the creative writer. The history of literature when it is paralleled with the history of criticism is often a story of writers who have defied the expectations of critics. At the time of their publication, there was reluctance to accept the work of such major writers as Walt Whitman, James Joyce, T. S. Eliot, and William Carlos Williams. Today, their free patterns are praised by critics as a significant contribution to literature. Yet, set patterns also intrigue poets, challenging them to transform the set patterns to their own needs and creative purposes. A Shakespearean sonnet, an example of a transformed set pattern, looks quite different from the open and free sonnet by E. E. Cummings, and yet a careful examination of the Cummings sonnet surprisingly will reveal a set pattern.

Set patterns are established by conventions, by early writers, by traditions now lost, or they may be new inventions by writers who seek to place controls upon their writing. They function in a disciplinary way: the writer is challenged to put the experience of the literature into a determined physical form—for example, a ballad, ode, sonnet, or blank verse.

Free patterns are those created by poets who are responding to what they feel as a changing sensibility. Writing in free patterns, writers consciously attempt to break with the past, to create a new tradition, a new form. Motivating the search for free patterns is an impulse for change, for putting the contemporary experience into a form congruent with it. This impulse is obvious in popular music. For many older people popular music has a set pattern (that it was once a new and free pattern is forgotten) and variances from that set pattern are not "music."

For the current generation the impulse for change takes precedence over interest in set forms, and composers and writers of this generation are quick to sense this. They often create new set patterns in substitution for the old, but the new provide a sense of liberation and release from the old. Sometimes new forms of expression are genuinely free and open, exploratory and ranging. What applies to music applies equally to today's literature. Like an extremely flexible musician, the performing artist of literature is responsive to all literature, and is capable of disciplining his awarenesses and sensitivities to the forms of expression as they have been used, continue to be used, and as they change.

FORM AS STRUCTURE: SOME CONVENTIONAL
SET PATTERNS IN POETRY

Set patterns demand that the form of the experience be contained within the limitations of the structure. Thus, the performer in the transforming of literature is challenged to fuse the values inherent in the form of the language to the experience described in the language. For the sensitive auditor the aesthetic experience is enhanced by the performer's success in this fusion.

A set pattern can be achieved in one of two ways: (1) by arranging lines into a stanzaic structure with repetitions or rhymes in certain patterns, or (2) by establishing criteria for qualities in a line. Examples of set patterns in the first category are the ballad quatrain, villanelle, triolet, terza rima, the ode, and the elegy. Examples of set patterns in lines are blank and Anglo-Saxon verse. While there are many set patterns in both categories that poets have used, those mentioned are among the most common and are valuable to identify for several reasons. First, they represent a sense of tradition in English language poetry, and particular achievements in form by English-speaking poets. Second, with the possible exception of the terza rima, these forms, in their purity and variation, continue to be most frequently used. And third, the challenge of containing the nature of an experience within the limitations of a given form necessarily exerts a compelling discipline upon the creative artist and therefore upon his interpreter.

THE BALLAD QUATRAIN

One of the oldest and most enduring set patterns in the English language is the ballad quatrain. It consists simply of four lines in any meter with a rhyme scheme that is consistent. The ballad quatrain imposes a sense of structure upon an experience that haunts the perceiver by its insistent repetition. The repetition may come through repeated structural patterns or by incremental repetitions of identical lines or words. Some common rhyme schemes of ballad quatrains are the following: *abab, abcb, aaaa, abba, aaab, aaba.* Frequently used forms of the ballad quatrain are: (1) the common measure of alternating lines of eight and six syllables (which can be indicated 8, 6, 8, 6) with a rhyme scheme of *abab* or *abcb.* (Many of the old ballads are in this form, including one of the masterpieces of English literature, Samuel Taylor Coleridge's "The Rime of the Ancient Mariner."); (2) the long measure consisting of eight syllables in every line, rhyming *abab, abcb,* or variations; (3) the short measure consisting of lines in the patterns of six, six, eight, and six syllables (6, 6, 8, 6) in rhyming patterns similar to those already listed. The enduring influence of these quatrains can be attested by any student who takes the time to examine the hymnals that have played such an important role in American social and religious life. The simplicity of these repeated patterns makes for easy memorization.

Several factors should be considered in the performance of the ballad quatrain. Questions which the performer must answer include these:

1. What effect is being produced by the measure?
    - Is the length creating an effect that is important to the form of the experience?
    - Is the shortness of the measure producing a quickening, a shortening, a truncating of the experience?
2. What effect does the rhyme scheme produce?
    - Are the rhyming words intensifying the experience by their locations at line endings?
    - Are the rhyming words adding a tonal setting to the experience that is complementary to the form of the experience in the poem?
    - In the case of the single unrhymed word (i.e., abcb), is it serving some purpose in isolating aspects of the experience?
3. What is the accumulative effect of the quatrains?
    - Is each quatrain a contained event?
    - What is the relationship of each quatrain to the other?
    - What quatrains need to be more or less isolated from the others in order for the experience to be contained logically in chronological, psychological, or mythic time?

One of the more curious and compelling qualities of the ballad, whether a part of the folk tradition or a modern composition, is that the power of the subject matter is contained in the simplest of forms. The ballads tell of murderous deeds, demon lovers, gigantic heroes, epochal events. In ballad country tortured personalities are given the purest language and form in which to live out their lives. It is precisely at this junction of form and content that the performer must make discreet decisions. Generally, the force of the narrative is subordinated to the flow of the balladic form; however, this does not suggest that the performer should eliminate the sense of dramatic event. The ballad stems directly from the oral tradition in literature and has, for most of its existence, been sung. The singing is usually simple, a haunting melody enhanced by repetitions, the events within the experience of the poem punctuated by musical bridges, silences, beats. Keeping these historical origins in mind, the performer must blend, in an aesthetically satisfactory manner, the elements of form and experience. One of the values of set form is that it allows for the visibility of form when it is appropriate to counterpoint the experience with the formality of the structure. Some problems to be studied and resolved are the following:

1. To what degree should the voices of the characters in the ballad be approximated and suggested?
    - Does the rhythmic flow of the ballad permit the sense of voice? of character?

—If the ballad is told through a narrator, what decisions must be made regarding his primacy as the "telling voice"?

—If the ballad is revealed in a dramatic mode, that is, solely through the characters in the ballad, what should be the relationship of the form of the ballad to the speaking characters?

2. To what degree are the events in the ballad distanced in mythic time? in psychological time?

—Does the repetition of the form create the distancing?

—Does the neutrality of attitude on the part of the performer create the distancing?

Sir Patrick Spens

Anonymous

The king sits in Dunfermline toune
    Drinking the blude-red wine:
"O whar will I get guid sailor,
    To sail this schip of mine?"

Up and spak an eldern knicht,
    Sat at the kings richt kne:
"Sir Patrick Spens is the best sailor
    That sails upon the se."

The king has written a braid letter,
    And signed it wi his hand,
And sent it to Sir Patrick Spens,
    Was walking on the sand.

The first line that Sir Patrick red,
    A loud lauch lauched he;
The next line that Sir Patrick red,
    The teir blinded his ee.

"O wha is this has don this deid,
    This ill deid don to me,
To send me out this time o' the yeir,
    To sail upon the se!

"Mak hast, mak haste, my mirry men all,
    Our guid schip sails the morne":
"O say na sae, my master deir,
    For I feir a deadlie storme.

"Late late yestreen I saw the new moone,
    Wi the auld moone in hir arme,
And I feir, I feir, my deir master,
    That we will cum to harme."

O our Scots nobles wer richt laith
    To weet their cork-heild schoone;
Bot lang owre a' the play wer playd,
    Thair hats they swam aboone.

O lang, lang may their ladies sit,
    Wi thair fans into their hand,
Or eir they se Sir Patrick Spens
    Cum sailing to the land.

O lang, lang may the ladies stand,
    Wi thair gold kems in their hair,
Waiting for thair ain deir lords,
    For they'll se thame na mair.

Haf owre, haf owre to Aberdour,
    It's fiftie fadom deip,
And thair lies guid Sir Patrick Spens,
    Wi the Scots lords at his feit.

The Demon Lover

Anonymous

"O where have you been, my long, long love,
    This long seven years and mair?"
"O I'm come to seek my former vows
    Ye granted me before."

"O hold your tongue of your former vows,
    For they will breed sad strife;
O hold your tongue of your former vows,
    For I am become a wife."

He turned him right and round about,
    And the tear blinded his ee:
"I wad never hae trodden on Irish ground,
    If it had not been for thee.

"I might hae had a king's daughter,
    Far, far beyond the sea;
I might have had a king's daughter,
    Had it not been for love o thee."

"If ye might have had a king's daughter,
    Yersel ye had to blame;
Ye might have had taken the king's daughter,
    For ye kend that I was nane.

"If I was to leave my husband dear,
    And my two babes also,
O what have you to take me to,
    If with you I should go?"

"I hae seven ships upon the sea—
    The eighth brought me to land—
With four-and-twenty bold mariners,
    And music on every hand."

She has taken up her two little babes,
    Kissd them baith cheek and chin:
"O fair ye weel, my ain two babes,
    For I'll never see you again."

She set her foot upon the ship,
    No mariners could she behold;
But the sails were o the taffetie,
    And the masts o the beaten gold.

She had not sailed a league, a league,
    A league but barely three,
When dismal grew his countenance,
    And drumlie grew his ee.

They had not sailed a league, a league,
    A league but barely three,
Until she espied his cloven foot,
    And she wept right bitterlie.

"O hold your tongue of your weeping," says he,
    "Of your weeping now let me be;
I will shew you how the lilies grow
    On the banks of Italy."

"O what hills are yon, yon pleasant hills,
    That the sun shines sweetly on?"
"O yon are the hills of heaven," he said,
    "Where you will never win."

"O whaten a mountain is yon," she said,
    "All so dreary wi frost and snow?"
"O yon is the mountain of hell," he cried,
    "Where you and I will go."

He strack the tap-mast wi his hand,
    The fore-mast wi his knee,
And he brake that gallant ship in twain,
    And sank her in the sea.

The Ballad of the Dark Ladié
A FRAGMENT

Samuel Taylor Coleridge

Beneath yon birch with silver bark,
And boughs so pendulous and fair,
The brook falls scatter'd down the rock:
    And all is mossy there!

And there upon the moss she sits,
The Dark Ladié in silent pain;
The heavy tear is in her eye,
 And drops and swells again.

Three times she sends her little page
Up the castled mountain's breast,
If he might find the Knight that wears
 The Griffin for his crest.

The sun was sloping down the sky,
And she had linger'd there all day,
Counting moments, dreaming fears—
 Oh wherefore can he stay?

She hears a rustling o'er the brook,
She sees far off a swinging bough!
"'Tis He! 'Tis my bethrothéd Knight!
 Lord Falkland, it is Thou!"

She springs, she clasps him round the neck,
She sobs a thousand hopes and fears,
Her kisses glowing on his cheeks
 She quenches with her tears.

  . . . . .

"My friends with rude ungentle words
They scoff and bid me fly to thee!
O give me shelter in thy breast!
 O shield and shelter me!

"My Henry, I have given thee much,
I gave what I can ne'er recall,
I gave my heart, I gave my peace,
 O Heaven! I gave thee all."

The Knight made answer to the Maid,
While to his heart he held her hand,
"Nine castles hath my noble sire,
 None statelier in the land.

"The fairest one shall be my love's,
The fairest castle of the nine!
Wait only till the stars peep out,
 The fairest shall be thine:

"Wait only till the hand of eve
Hath wholly closed yon western bars,
And through the dark we two will steal
 Beneath the twinkling stars!" —

"The dark? the dark? No! not the dark?
The twinkling stars? How, Henry? How?"
O God! 'twas in the eye of noon
 He pledged his sacred vow!

And in the eye of noon my love
Shall lead me from my mother's door,
Sweet boys and girls all clothed in white
 Strewing flowers before:

But first the nodding minstrels go
With music meet for lordly bowers,
The children next in snow-white vests,
 Strewing buds and flowers!

And then my love and I shall pace,
My jet black hair in pearly braids,
Between our comely bachelors
 And blushing bridal maids."

. . . . .

Frankie and Johnny

Anonymous

Frankie and Johnny were lovers, O, how that couple could love.
Swore to be true to each other, true as the stars above.
He was her man, but he done her wrong.

Frankie she was his woman, everybody knows.
She spent one hundred dollars for a suit of Johnny's clothes.
He was her man, but he done her wrong.

Frankie and Johnny went walking, Johnny in his bran' new suit,
"O good Lawd," says Frankie, "but don't my Johnny look cute?"
He was her man, but he done her wrong.

Frankie went down to Memphis; she went on the evening train.
She paid one hundred dollars for Johnny a watch and chain.
He was her man, but he done her wrong.

Frankie went down to the corner, to buy a glass of beer;
She says to the fat bartender, "Has my loving man been here?
He was my man, but he done me wrong."

"Ain't going to tell you no story, ain't going to tell you no lie,
I seen your man 'bout an hour ago with a girl named Alice Fry.
If he's your man, he's doing you wrong."

Frankie went back to the hotel, she didn't go there for fun,
Under her long red kimono she toted a forty-four gun.
He was her man, but he done her wrong.

Frankie went down to the hotel, looked in the window so high,
There was her lovin' Johnny a-lovin' up Alice Fry;
He was her man, but he done her wrong.

Frankie threw back her kimono, took out the old forty-four;
Roota-toot-toot, three times she shot, right through that hotel door.
She shot her man, 'cause he done her wrong.

Johnny grabbed off his Stetson. "O good Lawd, Frankie, don't shoot."
But Frankie put her finger on the trigger, and the gun went roota-toot-toot.
He was her man, but she shot him down.

"Roll me over easy, roll me over slow,
Roll me over easy, boys, 'cause my wounds are hurting me so,
I was her man, but I done her wrong."

With the first shot Johnny staggered; with the second shot he fell;
When the third bullet hit him, there was a new man's face in hell.
He was her man, but he done her wrong.

Frankie heard a rumbling away down under the ground.
Maybe it was Johnny where she had shot him down.
He was her man, and she done him wrong.

"Oh, bring on your rubber-tired hearses, bring on your rubber-tired hacks,
They're takin' my Johnny to the buryin' groun' but they'll never bring him back.
He was my man, but he done me wrong."

The judge he said to the jury, "It's plain as plain can be.
This woman shot her man, so it's murder in the second degree.
He was her man, though he done her wrong."

Now it wasn't murder in the second degree, it wasn't murder in the third.
Frankie simply dropped her man, like a hunter drops a bird.
He was her man, but he done her wrong.

"Oh, put me in that dungeon. Oh, put me in that cell.
Put me where the northeast wind blows from the southeast corner of hell.
I shot my man 'cause he done me wrong."

Frankie walked up to the scaffold, as calm as a girl could be,
She turned her eyes to heaven and said, "Good Lord, I'm coming to thee.
He was my man, and I done him wrong."

The Card Party[7]

Muriel Spark

Pacified, smooth as milk, by cakes and tea,
Four ladies took their chairs accordingly;
Each, picking up her cards in slow suspense,
Preened up her creamy neck to Providence.

7. "The Card Party" by Muriel Spark from *The New Yorker*, (December 29, 1963). Reprinted by permission of Harold Ober Associates Incorporated. Copyright © 1963 by Muriel Spark.

Somewhat apart from this important four,
Two sisters, knitting, settled near the door,
Cautioned each other, bending eye to eye,
Then watched the game together in rivalry.

Each player felt reluctantly compelled
To know what mystery the other held;
As one white neck rose taller with desire
The other three stretched likewise snakier.

And all the afternoon, discomfited,
Those four swans turned disdainful head from head;
Erect, they cast their cards throughout the night.
Each throat thinned upward like a stalagmite.

By dawn they bent and buried their flexible
Extending isthmuses beneath the table,
Upraising with apologetic pride
Those graceful members at the other side.

And what about the two beside the door?
They veered from cross to curious, hour by hour.
The knitting tangled, bound both necks askew,
And from this loggerhead a spiral grew

From which the sister-heads peered forth to pry—
What cards? All six got coiled there, finally.
Set in a formal knot and inextricable,
Two died beside the door, four at the table.

How brave these darlings, and how marvellous
That all their lovely necks should mingle thus.
Thus twined it was in death they coincided
Who always in their lives had been divided.

THE SONNET

Perhaps no set pattern of poetry is more associated with love and its dimensions, life
and its parameters, death and its toll than the sonnet. Its Italianate origins are steeped

in love — Dante to his Beatrice and Petrarch to his Laura. The most famous sonnet sequence in the English language is Shakespeare's memorable tribute of friendship and love to two of the most mysteriously obscure people in all literary history. A paradox is their high visibility in Shakespeare's confessions despite their anonymity, an historical question apparently never to be resolved.

What is a sonnet? An inductively interesting way of defining it is to examine carefully Richard Watson Gilder's "The Sonnet." And though certainly no brief is made for its appeal to our time and sensibility, it is something of a tour de force which controls and sustains itself.

The Sonnet

Richard Watson Gilder

What is a sonnet? 'Tis a pearly shell
    That murmurs of the far-off murmuring sea;
    A precious jewel carved out most curiously;
    It is a little picture painted well.
What is a sonnet? 'Tis the tear that fell
    From a great poet's hidden ecstasy;
    A two-edged sword, a star, a song — ah me!
    Sometimes a heavy-tolling funeral bell.
This was the flame that shook with Dante's breath;
    The solemn organ whereon Milton played,
    And the clear glass where Shakespeare's shadow falls:
    A sea this is — beware who ventureth!
    For like a fiord the narrow floor is laid
    Mid-ocean deep to their sheer mountain walls.

The observations that can be made are simple enough: (1) the sonnet consists of fourteen lines; (2) this sonnet appears to be arranged into three sections, i.e., "What is a sonnet? . . . What is a sonnet? . . . This was the flame . . ."; (3) the rhyme scheme appears to be *abba, abba, cde, cde;* (4) the rhythm is predominantly iambic. These observations would satisfy technical questions of form. But what of the arrangement of the fourteen lines? There is, upon inspection, a form to the thought and content within the poem. The first eight lines (the octave) attempt to define metaphorically what a sonnet is and what its content is: (1) it is a small, crafted, delicate object, and

(2) it speaks of life. The second half of the poem, the last six lines (the sestet), reflects upon the difficulty of mastering the form and notes that only the masterful have crafted it well. The form of the experience is linked to the form of the poem.

There are three widely recognized forms of the sonnet: (1) the Petrarchan, named after the fourteenth-century Italian poet, Francesco Petrarca, and the form in which Gilder wrote "The Sonnet"; (2) the Spenserian, named after the sixteenth-century English poet, Edmund Spenser, and characterized by three quatrains and a couplet, rhyming *abab, bcbc, cdcd, ee,* and predominantly iambic in rhythm; and (3) the Shakespearean, named for him not because he invented the particular style but rather because he perfected a form popular with Elizabethans, its structure consisting of three quatrains and a couplet in the rhyme scheme of *abab, cdcd, efef, gg.* Most sonnets in English consist of five metrical feet to the line.

In all sonnets the importance of the form is its condensation, its careful structuring of thought into sections, each section building upon and complementing the other to the eventual summation—the final couplet in the Spenserian and Shakespearean sonnet or the sestet in the Petrarchan. So carefully is the form of the experience linked to the formal structure of the poem, and, at the same time, so short and brief is the poem, that the performer must analyze carefully the relationships established in any sonnet between form and content. Problems important to the performer in the transformation of the sonnet are the following:

1. What is the form? (Petrarchan, Spenserian, Shakespearean, variation of one, original)
2. How is the form of the experience structured?
   - Is the problem stated in the octave?
   - Is the octave used to describe a condition, a state of mind?
   - How is the problem resolved in the sestet or final couplet?
   - In a Shakespearean sonnet how is the couplet used? How does it frame the preceding twelve lines?
3. What is the prevailing rhythm of the sonnet?
   - If it is prevailing iambic, are there significant variances? Where are they? Are they structurally important?
   - How is the rhythm of the poem tied to the form of the experience? congruent? non-congruent?
4. How do the line lengths function in the form of the poem?
   - Are all line endings uniform?
   - In the case of run-on lines, where do the pauses occur? in mid-lines? at end of sections?
5. Is the form of the experience linked inevitably to the sonnet form employed?

Whilst It Is Prime

Edmund Spenser

Fresh Spring, the herald of loves mighty king,
In whose cote-armour richly are displayd
All sorts of flowers, the which on earth do spring,
In goodly colours gloriously arrayd—
Goe to my love, where she is carelesse layd,
Yet in her winters bowre not well awake;
Tell her the joyous time wil not be staid,
Unlesse she doe him by the forelock take;
Bid her therefore her selfe soone ready make,
To wayt on Love amongst his lovely crew;
Where every one, that misseth then her make,
Shall be by him amearst with penance dew.
    Make hast, therefore, sweet love, whilst it is prime;
    For none can call againe the passèd time.

When most I wink, then do mine eyes best see

William Shakespeare

When most I wink, then do mine eyes best see,
For all the day they view things unrespected;
But when I sleep, in dreams they look on thee,
And darkly bright are bright in dark directed.
Then thou, whose shadow shadows doth make bright,
How would thy shadow's form form happy show
To the clear day with thy much clearer light,
When to unseeing eyes thy shade shines so!
How would, I say, mine eyes be blessed made
By looking on thee in the living day,
When in dead night thy fair imperfect shade
Through heavy sleep on sightless eyes doth stay!
    All days are nights to see till I see thee,
    And nights bright days when dreams do show thee me.

In faith, I do not love thee with mine eyes

William Shakespeare

In faith, I do not love thee with mine eyes,
For they in thee a thousand errors note;
But 'tis my heart that loves what they despise,
Who in despite of view is pleased to dote;
Nor are mine ears with thy tongue's tune delighted,
Nor tender feeling, to base touches prone,
Nor taste, nor smell, desire to be invited
To any sensual feast with thee alone:
But my five wits nor my five senses can
Dissuade one foolish heart from serving thee,
Who leaves unsway'd the likeness of a man,
Thy proud heart's slave and vassal wretch to be:
    Only my plague thus far I count my gain,
    That she that makes me sin awards me pain.

Since there's no help, come, let us kiss and part!

Michael Drayton

Since there's no help, come, let us kiss and part!
Nay, I have done; you get no more of me!
And I am glad, yea, glad with all my heart
That thus so cleanly I myself can free.
Shake hands for ever; cancel all our vows;
And when we meet at any time again,
Be it not seen in either of our brows
That we one jot of former love retain!
Now at the last gasp of Love's latest breath,
When, his pulse failing, Passion speechless lies,
When Faith is kneeling by his bed of death,
And Innocence is closing up his eyes—
    Now, if thou wouldst, when all have given him over,
    From death to life thou might'st him yet recover!

Death

John Donne

Death, be not proud, though some have called thee
Mighty and dreadful, for thou art not so,
For those whom thou think'st thou dost overthrow,
Die not, poor Death, nor yet canst thou kill me.
From rest and sleep, which but thy pictures be,
Much pleasure, then from thee, much more must flow,
And soonest our best men with thee do go,
Rest of their bones, and souls' delivery.
Thou art slave to fate, chance, kings, and desperate men,
And dost with poison, war, and sickness dwell,
And poppy, or charms can make us sleep as well,
And better than thy stroke; why swell'st thou then?
One short sleep past, we wake eternally,
And death shall be no more; Death, thou shalt die!

God's Grandeur[8]

Gerard Manley Hopkins

The world is charged with the grandeur of God.
    It will flame out, like shining from shook foil;
    It gathers to a greatness, like the ooze of oil
Crushed. Why do men then now not reck his rod?
Generations have trod, have trod, have trod;
    And all is seared with trade; bleared, smeared with toil;
    And wears man's smudge and shares man's smell: the soil
Is bare now, nor can foot feel, being shod.

And for all this, nature is never spent;
    There lives the dearest freshness deep down things;
And though the last lights off the black West went,
    Oh, morning, at the brown brink eastward, springs—
Because the Holy Ghost over the bent
    World broods with warm breast and with ah! bright wings.

8. "God's Grandeur" by Gerard Manley Hopkins from *Poems* by Gerard Manley Hopkins. Published by Oxford University Press.

Leda and the Swan[9]

William Butler Yeats

A sudden blow: the great wings beating still
Above the staggering girl, her thighs caressed
By the dark webs, her nape caught in his bill,
He holds her helpless breast upon his breast.

How can those terrified vague fingers push
The feathered glory from her loosening thighs?
And how can body, laid in that white rush,
But feel the strange heart beating where it lies?

A shudder in the loins engenders there
The broken wall, the burning roof and tower
And Agamemnon dead.
                              Being so caught up,
So mastered by the brute blood of the air,
Did she put on his knowledge with his power
Before the indifferent beak could let her drop?

Eben Sayles[10]
Arthur Davison Ficke

To Edwin Arlington Robinson

When Eben Sayles strolled down that April day
From his small fields, it was not, as some think,
That he had had more than his more of drink
Nor that his wits were vanished clean away.
Guess as the tongues of all the neighbors may,
Rolling their doubts to speculation's brink,
They are no wiser than the owls that blink

9. Reprinted with permission of The Macmillan Company, A. P. Watt & Son, The Macmillan Company of Canada Ltd. and M. B. Yeats from *Collected Poems of William Butler Yeats.* Copyright 1928 by The Macmillan Company, renewed © 1956 by Georgia Yeats.
    10. "Eben Sayles" from *Tumultuous Shore and Other Poems* by Arthur Davison Ficke. Reprinted by permission of Mrs. Arthur Davison Ficke.

In the confusion of an obvious ray.
Not one of them, for all their prying tales,
Knows why that day old Eben sauntered down
With his own mumbled words for company,
And paid the official crier of the town
To cry all afternoon:—"Old Eben Sayles
Last night saw angels in his apple-tree!"

a wind has blown the rain away[11]

e. e. cummings

a wind has blown the rain away and blown
the sky away and all the leaves away,
and the trees stand. I think i too have known
autumn too long

        (and what have you to say,
wind wind wind—did you love somebody
and have you the petal of somewhere in your heart
pinched from dumb summer?
               O crazy daddy
of death dance cruelly for us and start

the last leaf whirling in the final brain
of air!)Let us as we have seen see
doom's integration . . . . a wind has blown the rain

away and the leaves and the sky and the
trees stand:
         the trees stand. The trees,
suddenly wait against the moon's face.

You were born; must die[12]

Stephen Spender

You were born; must die; were loved; must love;
Born naked; were clothed; still naked walk
Under your clothes. Under your skin you move
Naked; naked under acts and talk.
    The miles and hours upon you feed.
They eat your eyes out with their distance
They eat your heart out with devouring need
They eat your death out with lost significance.
    There is one fate beneath those ignorances
Those flesh and bone parcels in which you're split
O thing of skin and words hanging on breath:
Harlequin skeleton, it
Strums on your gut such songs and merry dances
Of love, of loneliness, of life being death.

Sonnet 9[13]

May Sarton

What if a homing pigeon lost its home,
Were wrenched out of the orbit of sensation,
Its instinct killed, what would it then become?
A haunted traveller with no destination,
Circling the air above strange roosts to climb
Upward again, more fearful, more harassed,
The gentle voice repeating all the time
The phrases that had meaning in the past,
"Where is my true love, O where is my nest?
Where can I shut this terrible bright eye
And put my head under a wing to rest?"
That baffled wanderer, that lost one, I
Who for a whole month now have flown and flown,
And cannot land, and cannot find my own.

12. "You were born; must die" Copyright 1946 by Stephen Spender. Reprinted from *Poems of Dedication*, (British title: *Collected Poems 1928–1953*) by Stephen Spender, by permission of Random House, Inc. and Faber and Faber Ltd.
  13. "Sonnet 9" from *Cloud, Stone, Sun, Vine*, Poems, Selected and New by May Sarton. Copyright © 1961 by Sarton. Reprinted by permission of W. W. Norton & Company, Inc.

Some Conventional Set Patterns in Poetry   211

THE VILLANELLE AND THE TRIOLET

One of the most powerful poems written by a modern poet is, in its form, one of the most arbitrary and artificial. The poem is Dylan Thomas' "Do Not Go Gentle," and the form is an artificial French form, the villanelle. The form is simple enough: five three-line stanzas (tercets) followed by a sixth stanza of four lines; the rhyme scheme for the poem is a constant *aba* patterning save for the last stanza where the rhyme scheme becomes *abaa.* The artificial quality of the poem, its arbitrary rule, is in its total repetition of complete lines. That is, the first line is repeated three times: at the conclusion of the second and fourth stanzas and in the third line of the last stanza. The last line of the first stanza is repeated three times: at the conclusion of the third, fifth, and sixth stanzas. The individual poet may choose to vary the length of the lines, but the general rules of arrangement constitute the "game" of writing the villanelle.

The triolet, like the villanelle, is French in origin and plays the game of repetition. The triolet is only eight lines and, like the villanelle, uses just two rhymes. The rhyming pattern, *ab, aa, ab, ab,* is complicated in that the first line is repeated at the end of the second couplet and at the beginning of the fourth, while the second line is repeated once at the end.

The implications for the performer are clear: to make the repetitions function, and to make them function in such a way that the repetitions appear to be natural ones, counterpointing the changes in meaning, emphasis, and tone as the poem progresses. In both artificial forms it is the performer's responsibility through his total behavioral responses to the poem to shade and to structure the form of the experience, and to do both simultaneously and effortlessly. While there may not be many poets writing in these artificial forms, the forms provide excellent challenges to the performer of literature.

The House on the Hill[14]

Edwin Arlington Robinson

They are all gone away,
  The House is shut and still,
There is nothing more to say.

Through broken walls and gray
  The winds blow bleak and shrill;
They are all gone away.

14. "The House on the Hill" reprinted by permission of Charles Scribner's Sons from *The Children of the Night* by Edwin Arlington Robinson (1897).

Nor is there one today
  To speak them good or ill:
There is nothing more to say.

Why is it then we stray
  Around that sunken sill?
They are all gone away,

And our poor fancy-play
  For them is wasted skill:
There is nothing more to say.

There is ruin and decay
  In the House on the Hill:
They are all gone away,
There is nothing more to say.

Do Not Go Gentle into That Good Night[15]

Dylan Thomas

Do not go gentle into that good night,
Old age should burn and rave at close of day;
Rage, rage against the dying of the light.

Though wise men at their end know dark is right,
Because their words had forked no lightning they
Do not go gentle into that good night.

Good men, the last wave by, crying how bright
Their frail deeds might have danced in a green bay,
Rage, rage against the dying of the light.

Wild men who caught and sang the sun in flight,
And learn, too late, they grieved it on its way,
Do not go gentle into that good night.

15. *The Poems of Dylan Thomas.* Copyright 1939 by New Directions Publishing Corporation, 1952 by Dylan Thomas. Reprinted by permission of New Directions Publishing Corporation, J. M. Dent & Sons Ltd. Publishers and the Trustees for the Copyrights of the late Dylan Thomas.

Grave men, near death, who see with blinding sight
Blind eyes could blaze like meteors and be gay,
Rage, rage against the dying of the light.

And you, my father, there on the sad height,
Curse, bless, me now with your fierce tears, I pray.
Do not go gentle into that good night.
Rage, rage against the dying of the light.

If I Could Tell You[16]

W. H. Auden

Time will say nothing but I told you so,
Time only knows the price we have to pay;
If I could tell you I would let you know.

If we should weep when clowns put on their show,
If we should stumble when musicians play,
Time will say nothing but I told you so.

There are no fortunes to be told, although,
Because I love you more than I can say,
If I could tell you I would let you know.

The winds must come from somewhere when they blow,
There must be reasons why the leaves decay;
Time will say nothing but I told you so.

Perhaps the roses really want to grow,
The vision seriously intends to stay;
If I could tell you I would let you know.

Suppose the lions all get up and go,
And all the brooks and soldiers run away;
Will Time say nothing but I told you so?
If I could tell you I would let you know.

Jerry N. Uelsmann

If You Love the Body[17]

Richard Tillinghast

If you love the body you must know the bone
that ribs and peoples it; deeper than flesh you feel
the beauty. That will last, simply as stone

upheaves in season where the winter rain
rakes asters and drooping cornstalks from a hill.
If you love the body you must know the bone

17. Copyright © 1965 by Richard Tillinghast. Reprinted from *Sleep Watch*, by Richard Tillinghast, by permission of Wesleyan University Press.

of fingers that touch, of the high case where the brain
lurks, of the deep knock and door and sill.
The beauty that will last, simply as stone

remains, is what you love when the blossom is gone—
petals and sepals and stem, roots and soil—
if you love the body you must know. The bone

smiles behind our faces when we frown,
knowing while the sweet flesh will not hold
the beauty, that will. Last, simply as stone

lasts, my love. For saying what I can
I ask forgiveness—in time we'll know it well.
If you love the body you must know the bone,
the beauty that will last simply as stone.

The Waking[18]

Theodore Roethke

I wake to sleep, and take my waking slow.
I feel my fate in what I cannot fear.
I learn by going where I have to go.

We think by feeling. What is there to know?
I hear my being dance from ear to ear.
I wake to sleep, and take my waking slow.

Of those so close beside me, which are you?
God bless the Ground! I shall walk softly there,
And learn by going where I have to go.

Light takes the Tree; but who can tell us how?
The lowly worm climbs up a winding stair;
I wake to sleep, and take my waking slow.

18. "The Waking" from the book *Collected Poems of Theodore Roethke*. Copyright 1953 by Theodore Roethke. Reprinted by permission of Doubleday & Company, Inc.

Great Nature has another thing to do
To you and me; so take the lively air,
And, lovely, learn by going where to go.

This shaking keeps me steady. I should know.
What falls away is always. And is near.
I wake to sleep, and take my waking slow.
I learn by going where I have to go.

A Kiss

Austin Dobson

Rose kissed me today.
    Will she kiss me tomorrow?
Let it be as it may,
Rose kissed me today.
But the pleasure gives way
    To a savor of sorrow;—
Rose kissed me today—
    Will she kiss me tomorrow?

When First We Met[19]

Robert Bridges

When first we met we did not guess
That Love would prove so hard a master;
Of more than common friendliness
When first we met we did not guess.
Who could foretell this sore distress
This irretrievable disaster
When first we met?—We did not guess
That Love would prove so hard a master.

19. "When First We Met" from *The Poetical Works of Robert Bridges.* © Clarendon Press, Oxford. Reprinted by permission of The Clarendon Press, Oxford.

Some Conventional Set Patterns in Poetry   217

THE ODE AND THE ELEGY

The ode and the elegy originated as responses to particular experiences in life which compel a reaction. The ode, as it developed in ancient Greece, celebrated important occasions; it was also used in Greek drama to comment upon the action and events. It was, in both cases, a form of poetry whose origins were clearly in the oral tradition. The stanzaic structure of the ode is created by the poet, who usually attempts to achieve an intricate pattern of line and sound. The sense of movement is genuine, for the early choral odes were chanted and sung and, at the same time, danced. It is important to notice in the odes what the sense of movement is: is it a movement of rapid mental shifts? is it a movement of external events as they affect the poet? is it a movement of thought derivative of an encounter with a precise event or thing? In a performance of an ode, the auditor should sense what the movement, what the sense of the song is about. Odes which suggest the classical tradition will be highly irregular in line lengths and stanzaic structure. Stanzaic odes, like Shelley's "Ode to the West Wind"[20] and William Moebius' "Ode 10," represent an individual poet's attempt to establish his own creative form for the ode.

Generally speaking, an elegy is a poetic response to a loss, to an emptiness, to a void created either by death or by a change in life. Thomas Gray's "Elegy Written in a Country Churchyard" elegizes the life of those who "lived far from the madding crowd," and who, in death, achieved a reward as bountiful as those who strove for fame and glory. An elegy attempts to explain the intensity of the loss, its meaning and its personal pain. While the ode sings of man's condition, the elegy reflects on the significance of death; while an ode explores a condition of life, the elegy ruminates on the meaning of life from the event of death. Both the ode and eleogy are without traditional set form.

In the performance of the ode and elegy, the problems of transformation involve some of the following questions:

1. Is the form of the ode a complex and intricate pattern or a uniform stanzaic pattern?
   —What do the various stress patterns achieve in the intricate design?
   —What is the relationship of the spatial arrangements of language to the sense of the experience?
   —If the ode is in stanzaic pattern, what is the structure? What are its problems in regard to repetition of form? What is the relationship of the form to the experience?

20. Shelley's ode is written in terza rimas, that is, iambic pentameter lines rhyming *aba, bcb, cdc, ded,* continuing indefinitely. The terza rima structure is concluded with either a rhyming couplet or quatrain so that the poet can avoid leaving one word unrhymed. Dante's *Divine Comedy* is structured in terza rimas, a rhyme scheme better suited to Italian than English. The student should be aware, however, that in the performance of "Ode to the West Wind" his challenge is not only to evoke the sense of ode but also to master the stylistic and formal structure of the rhyme scheme.

—What sense of movement is achieved? How is it achieved? Is there a sense of paradox regarding the movement?

2. How is the elegy structured?

—What is the relationship of the form to the kind of loss described in the poem?

—Is there a sense of formality? informality? How are these effects achieved?

Ode 31[21]

Sappho   (trans. Robert George)

He appears like a god to me
that man who sits by
your side and hears you
gently talking

and laughing so sweetly.
That image has made the heart
in my breast beat fast, I can
not speak,

my tongue won't work, a thin
flame crawls under my skin,
sight evades my eyes,
my ears ring,

a cold sweat runs down me,
trembling takes my body,
my skin is the color of grass—
I might as well be dead.

Ode to the West Wind

Percy Bysshe Shelley

1

O wild West Wind, thou breath of Autumn's being,
Thou, from whose unseen presence the leaves dead
Are driven, like ghosts from an enchanter fleeing,

Yellow, and black, and pale, and hectic red,
Pestilence-stricken multitudes: O thou,
Who chariotest to their dark wintry bed

The wingèd seeds, where they lie cold and low,
Each like a corpse within its grave, until
Thine azure sister of the Spring shall blow

21. Reprinted with the permission of the translator.

Her clarion o'er the dreaming earth, and fill
(Driving sweet buds like flocks to feed in air)
With living hues and odours plain and hill:

Wild Spirit, which art moving everywhere;
Destroyer and preserver: hear, oh, hear!

2

Thou on whose stream, mid the steep sky's commotion,
Loose clouds like earth's decaying leaves are shed,
Shook from the tangled boughs of Heaven and Ocean,

Angels of rain and lightning: there are spread
On the blue surface of thine aëry surge,
Like the bright hair uplifted from the head

Of some fierce Maenad, even from the dim verge
Of the horizon to the zenith's height,
The locks of the approaching storm. Thou dirge

Of the dying year, to which this closing night
Will be the dome of a vast sepulchre,
Vaulted with all thy congregated might

Of vapours, from whose solid atmosphere
Black rain, and fire, and hail will burst: oh, hear!

3

Thou who didst waken from his summer dreams
The blue Mediterranean, where he lay,
Lulled by the coil of his crystalline streams,

Beside a pumice isle in Baiae's bay,
And saw in sleep old palaces and towers
Quivering within the wave's intenser day,

All overgrown with azure moss and flowers
So sweet, the sense faints picturing them! Thou
For whose path the Atlantic's level powers

Cleave themselves into chasms, while far below
The sea-blooms and the oozy woods which wear
The sapless foliage of the ocean, know

Thy voice, and suddenly grow gray with fear,
And tremble and despoil themselves: oh, hear!

4
If I were a dead leaf thou mightest bear,
If I were a swift cloud to fly with thee;
A wave to pant beneath thy power, and share

The impulse of thy strength, only less free
Than thou, O uncontrollable! If even
I were as in my boyhood, and could be

The comrade of thy wanderings over Heaven,
As then, when to outstrip thy skiey speed
Scarce seemed a vision; I would ne'er have striven

As thus with thee in prayer in my sore need.
Oh, lift me as a wave, a leaf, a cloud!
I fall upon the thorns of life! I bleed!

A heavy weight of hours has chained and bowed
One too like thee: tameless, and swift, and proud.

5
Make me thy lyre, even as the forest is:
What if my leaves are falling like its own!
The tumult of thy mighty harmonies

Will take from both a deep, autumnal tone,
Sweet though in sadness. Be thou, Spirit fierce,
My spirit! Be thou me, impetuous one!

Drive my dead thoughts over the universe
Like withered leaves to quicken a new birth!
And, by the incantation of this verse,

Scatter, as from an unextinguished hearth
Ashes and sparks, my words among mankind!
Be through my lips to unawakened earth

The trumpet of a prophecy! O, Wind,
If Winter comes, can Spring be far behind?

Ode[22]

Ruth Krauss

hot-maker   snow-melter   river-sweller
bud-buster   watermelon-ripener   pattern-maker-through-forest-trees-one
rooster-waker   people-browner   shadow-of-migrating-bird-maker
in-the-east-one   in-the-west-one   straight-up-one
neck-breaker   Moslem-bender   noodle-dryer
hypnotizer-of-morning-glories   bell-ringer   spitfire
made-small-shining-in-my-eye-one   parade-encourager   picnic-monger
democratic-one   undemocratic-one   silhouetter-of-tall-pines-in-the-air
candle-lighter   dragon-lighter   red-sky-at-evening-lighter
thunder-maker   groundhog-fooler   pot-boiler
who-threw-the-first-stone-one   Old-Sol   New-Sol
duck-sitting-on-own-self-in-lake-maker   Soleil   Eye-of-Mexico
uns snu nussy   shine-in-the-coal   moon-hider
sky-cleaner   and-makest-thou-the-wind-to-blow   makest-thou-the-balloon to-bust
the-streams-that-are-hot-in-the-cold-sea-maker   leaf-turner   century-turner
sky-ticker   what-would-happen-if-you-skipped-a-day-one
blood-light   vein-light   bone-light
phoenix-imitator   daisy-symbol   Indian-giver
apple-on-head-of-Sir-Isaac-hitter   on-the-topmost-tip-of-the-mast-gleam
old-dogtail-wagger   shady-side-of-the-street-maker   shine-on-shoe-maker
in-the-puddles-one   in-the-tide   lighting-the-mountain
right-at-my-own-doorstep-you-are-one   stoop-sitter   moth-maker
lunchtime-bringer   bogeyman-assistant   old-x-behind-the-x-ray
to-stud-nightfall-with-sparks-one   old-sunnyside-up-in-the-sky   pretty-day
bringer-of-bluebells   buttercup-yellower   strawberry-reddener
dark-horse-of-another-color   who-saw-the-Golden-Age-one
second-fiddle-to-Nero   glacier-giver   engine-driver
devil-driver   wingtip-lighter   old-hotstuff

22. "Ode" from *The Cantilever Rainbow* by Ruth Krauss, Pantheon Books.

Ode to the Hippies by Way of Gloss on the Text:
"He Was Born with the Gift of Laughter and a Sense That the World Is Mad"[23]

Paul Carroll

    Profile
of that chauffeur, rigid
inside pearl-grey limousine,
looks Florentine. The Medicis
own this world and the next,
almost — certainly New York City, brutal,
exquisite, nittygritty.

    Yet hide of old Missouri mule
color of the calm lagoon
      there where it mosies among Central Park sidewalks,
   nooks and rocks below
copse of elms in which confetti of pigeons
      sparkles in sunlight, Howells,

were you amused when you strolled across the street
from your new town house on 59th near 6th and saw,
    leaning from this concrete bridge
    or enjoying a Havana on a bench,
this bit of the Mississippi
      smack in the middle of Manhattan?

I wish you'd been with my wife and me today
when we explored the Different Drummer clothing store
    where a rosy race called hippies mill about
      amid skull-cracking music
and with joyous concentration try on costumes which recall
    your Midwest of 100 years ago:

    Stovepipe hats tall as Tom Thumb.
Muleskinner belts thick as New Year's virtues.
    Bowlers. Bonnets. Buckskin boots.
Granny spectacles for girls whose breasts are still about to bloom.

23. "Ode to the Hippies by Way of Gloss on the Text: He Was Born with the Gift of Laughter and a Sense That the World Is Mad" from *Odes* by Paul Carroll. Copyright © 1969 by Paul Carroll. Reprinted by permission of the author and Follett Publishing Company, division of Follett Corporation.

Some Conventional Set Patterns in Poetry   223

Ruffled shirts for riverboat gamblers.
Carpetbagger waistcoat brocade intricate as literary politics.
Bandanas for a stagecoach desperado.
Jeb Stewart capes and caps.
Denim. Gingham. Calico.
Even a Sioux headdress or two.

Hair cascades past shoulders of some boys.
Girls are sparrows among black cherries
in orchards outside Martins Ferry
where you wandered after work
as printers devil in your father's typeshop.
One lanky lad looked like an Ostrogoth.
A few handlebar moustaches too—
the kind your friend Sam Clemens grew,
"the Lincoln of our literature."

You two knew gaudy times together, sipping
Old Crow bourbon at the breakfast table,
swapping shaggy dog tales till afternoon,
talking about the health of American prose.

Emerson, Holmes, Lowell,
Longfellow, Margaret Fuller,
Whittier: all
good Medicis. Not one wanted
words to jump like a bullfrog about the page.
Or taste like cattail puffed in corncob pipe.
Or try to tickle the funnybone of God.
Or like the everyday insanity of the race
infect the marrowbone.

Twain did.

He might have walked among the hippies happy, sporting
silk top hat and spats, knowing
his river like the sweat and sweaty talk of Nigger Jim
waits here forever for him
at the tip of Central Park.
And while Mrs. Clemens

and the daughters order high tea in The Plaza
          he might have cocked that hat and spit
     and let 'er rip for all the hippies
ebullient with their babies and music on the grass:

Willie   Willie   Willie   WillieWillieWillie
    Whaooooooooooooooooo ooooooooooo   ooooooooooooooooo
         Whaoooooooooooooooo

Ode 10[24]

William Moebius

Put me in that revolving chair,
free me from the words I cannot use;
let my eyes close,
and turn me round and round.

I will get dizzy and protest
the giddy framework of the stool
I'm riding on
but turn me round and round.

Put your hand (you love me!)
on my neck, the other on my thigh,
and walk beside,
and turn me round and round.

I see no alternative, the gate
of my remembrance is ajar,
I open it,
you turn me round and round.

In that rotunda many people
stand around and smile
I've never met—
you turn me round and round.

24. "Ode 10" by William Moebius from *Elegies and Odes*. Copyright © 1969 by Swallow Press, Chicago. Reprinted by permission.

On us that they remembered
to turn back to, as we pitch forward
into darkness—
you turn me round and round—

they look ineffably, like princes,
men and women of a miracle
withheld so long—
you turn me round and round.

This is a sign of their protection,
our awe in their reflection,
our short transport,
you turn me round and round,

our amazement and the firmness
of your hand upon my neck,
upon my thigh,
you turn me round and round,

soothing me in memory
with people of one strength
and of one piece,
I see them gathered in a throng,

our ancestors, the recent deceased
no one knows about but us,
and we are here—
I see them gathered in a throng.

When Lilacs Last in the Dooryard Bloom'd

Walt Whitman

1
When lilacs last in the dooryard bloom'd,
And the great star early droop'd in the western sky in the night,
I mourn'd, and yet shall mourn with ever-returning spring.

Ever-returning spring, trinity sure to me you bring,
Lilac blooming perennial and drooping star in the west,
And thought of him I love.

2

O powerful western fallen star!
O shades of night—O moody, tearful night!
O great star disappear'd—O the black murk that hides the star!
O cruel hands that hold me powerless—O helpless soul of me!
O harsh surrounding cloud that will not free my soul.

3

In the dooryard fronting an old farm-house near the white-wash'd palings,
Stands the lilac-bush tall-growing with heart-shaped leaves of rich green,
With many a pointed blossom rising delicate, with the perfume strong I love,
With every leaf a miracle—and from this bush in the dooryard,
With delicate-color'd blossoms and heart-shaped leaves of rich green,
A sprig with its flower I break.

4

In the swamp in secluded recesses,
A shy and hidden bird is warbling a song.
Solitary the thrush,
The hermit withdrawn to himself, avoiding the settlements,
Sings by himself a song.

Song of the bleeding throat,
Death's outlet song of life, (for well dear brother I know,
If thou wast not granted to sing thou would'st surely die.)

5

Over the breast of the spring, the land, amid cities,
Amid lanes and through old woods, where lately the violets peep'd from the ground,
                spotting the gray debris,
Amid the grass in the fields each side of the lanes, passing the endless grass,
Passing the yellow-spear'd wheat, every grain from its shroud in the dark-brown
                fields uprisen,
Passing the apple-tree blows of white and pink in the orchards,
Carrying a corpse to where it shall rest in the grave,
Night and day journeys a coffin.

6

Coffin that passes through lanes and streets,
Through day and night with the great cloud darkening the land,
With the pomp of the inloop'd flags with the cities draped in black,
With the show of the States themselves as of crape-veil'd women standing,
With processions long and winding and the flambeaus of the night,
With the countless torches lit, with the silent sea of faces and the unbared heads,
With the waiting depot, the arriving coffin, and the sombre faces,
With dirges through the night, with the thousand voices rising strong and solemn,
With all the mournful voices of the dirges pour'd around the coffin,
The dim-lit churches and the shuddering organs—where amid these you journey,
With the tolling tolling bells' perpetual clang,
Here, coffin that slowly passes,
I give you my sprig of lilac.

7

(Nor for you, for one alone,
Blossoms and branches green to coffins all I bring,
For fresh as the morning, thus would I chant a song for you O sane and sacred
            death.

All over bouquets of roses,
O death, I cover you over with roses and early lilies,
But mostly and now the lilac that blooms the first,
Copious I break, I break the sprigs from the bushes,
With loaded arms I come, pouring for you,
For you and the coffins all of you O death.)

8

O western orb sailing the heaven,
Now I know what you must have meant as a month since I walk'd,
As I walk'd in silence the transparent shadowy night,
As I saw you had something to tell as you bent to me night after night,
As you droop'd from the sky low down as if to my side, (while the other stars all
            look'd on,)
As we wander'd together the solemn night, (for something I know not what kept me
            from sleep,)
As the night advanced, and I saw on the rim of the west how full you were of woe,
As I stood on the rising ground in the breeze in the cool transparent night,

As I watch'd where you pass'd and was lost in the netherward black of the night,
As my soul in its trouble dissatisfied sank, as where you sad orb,
Concluded, dropt in the night, and was gone.

9
Sing on there in the swamp,
O singer bashful and tender, I hear your notes, I hear your call,
I hear, I come presently, I understand you,
But a moment I linger, for the lustrous star has detain'd me,
The star my departing comrade holds and detains me.

10
O how shall I warble myself for the dead one there I loved?
And how shall I deck my song for the large sweet soul that has gone?
And what shall my perfume be for the grave of him I love?

Sea-winds blown from east and west,
Blown from the Eastern sea and blown from the Western sea, till there on the
         prairies meeting,
These and with these and the breath of my chant,
I'll perfume the grave of him I love.

11
O what shall I hang on the chamber walls?
And what shall the pictures be that I hang on the walls,
To adorn the burial-house of him I love?

Pictures of growing spring and farms and homes,
With the Fourth-month eve at sundown, and the gray smoke lucid and bright,
With floods of the yellow gold of the gorgeous, indolent, sinking sun, burning,
         expanding the air,
With the fresh sweet herbage under foot, and the pale green leaves of the trees
         prolific,
In the distance the flowing glaze, the breast of the river, with a wind-dapple here and
         there,
With ranging hills on the banks, with many a line against the sky, and shadows,
And the city at hand with dwellings so dense, and stacks of chimneys,
And all the scenes of life and the workshops, and the workmen homeward returning.

12

Lo, body and soul—this land,
My own Manhattan with spires, and the sparkling and hurrying tides, and the ships,
The varied and ample land, the South and the North in the light, Ohio's shores and
        flashing Missouri,
And ever the far-spreading prairies cover'd with grass and corn.
Lo, the most excellent sun so calm and haughty,
The violet and purple morn with just-felt breezes,
The gentle soft-born measureless light,
The miracle spreading bathing all, the fulfill'd noon,
The coming eve delicious, the welcome night and the stars,
Over my cities shining all, enveloping man and land.

13

Sing on, sing on you gray-brown bird,
Sing from the swamps, the recesses, pour your chant from the bushes,
Limitless out of the dusk, out of the cedars and pines.

Sing on dearest brother, warble your reedy song,
Loud human song, with voice of uttermost woe.

O liquid and free and tender!
O wild and loose to my soul—O wondrous singer!
You only I hear—yet the star holds me, (but will soon depart,)
Yet the lilac with mastering odor holds me.

14

Now while I sat in the day and look'd forth,
In the close of the day with its light and the fields of spring, and the farmers
        preparing their crops,
In the large unconscious scenery of my land with its lakes and forests,
In the heavenly aerial beauty, (after the perturb'd winds and the storms,)
Under the arching heavens of the afternoon swift passing, and the voices of children
        and women,
The many-moving sea-tides, and I saw the ships how they sail'd,
And the summer approaching with richness, and the fields all busy with labor,
And the infinite separate houses, how they all went on, each with its meals and
        minutia of daily usages,
And the streets how their throbbings throbb'd, and the cities pent—lo, then and
        there,

Falling upon them all and among them all, enveloping me with the rest,
Appear'd the cloud, appear'd the long black trail,
And I knew death, its thought, and the sacred knowledge of death.

Then with the knowledge of death as walking one side of me,
And the thought of death close-walking the other side of me,
And I in the middle as with companions, and as holding the hands of companions,
I fled forth to the hiding receiving night that talks not,
Down to the shores of the water, the path by the swamp in the dimness,
To the solemn shadowy cedars and ghostly pines so still.

And the singer so shy to the rest receiv'd me,
The gray-brown bird I know receiv'd us comrades three,
And he sang the carol of death, and a verse for him I love.

From deep secluded recesses,
From the fragrant cedars and the ghostly pines so still,
Came the carol of the bird.

And the charm of the carol rapt me,
As I held as if by their hands my comrades in the night,
And the voice of my spirit tallied the song of the bird.

Come lovely and soothing death,
Undulate round the world, serenely arriving, arriving,
In the day, in the night, to all, to each,
Sooner or later delicate death.

Prais'd be the fathomless universe,
For life and joy, and for objects and knowledge curious,
And for love, sweet love—but praise! praise! praise!
For the sure-enwinding arms of cool-enfolding death.

Dark mother always gliding near with soft feet,
Have none chanted for thee a chant of fullest welcome?
Then I chant it for thee, I glorify thee above all,
I bring thee a song that when thou must indeed come, come unfalteringly.

Approach strong deliveress,
When it is so, when thou hast taken them I joyously sing the dead,
Lost in the loving floating ocean of thee,
Laved in the flood of thy bliss O death.

From me to thee glad serenades,
Dances for thee I propose saluting thee, adornments and feastings for thee,
And the sights of the open landscape and the high-spread sky are fitting,
And life and the fields, and the huge and thoughtful night.

The night in silence under many a star,
The ocean shore and the husky whispering wave whose voice I know,
And the soul turning to thee O vast and well-veil'd death,
And the body gratefully nestling close to thee.

Over the tree-tops I flout thee a song,
Over the rising and sinking waves, over the myriad fields and the prairies wide,
Over the dense-pack'd cities all and the teeming wharves and ways,
I float this carol with joy, with joy to thee O death.

15
To the tally of my soul,
Loud and strong kept up the gray-brown bird,
With pure deliberate notes spreading filling the night.

Loud in the pines and cedars dim,
Clear in the freshness moist and the swamp-perfume,
And I with my comrades there in the night.

While my sight that was bound in my eyes unclosed,
As to long panoramas of visions.

And I saw askant the armies,
I saw as in noiseless dreams hundreds of battle-flags,
Borne through the smoke of the battles and pierc'd with missiles I saw them,
And carried hither and yon through the smoke, and torn and bloody,
And at last but a few shreds left on the staffs, (and all in silence,)
And the staffs all splinter'd and broken.

I saw battle-corpses, myriads of them,
And the white skeletons of young men, I saw them,
I saw the debris and debris of all the slain soldiers of the war,
But I saw they were not as was thought,
They themselves were fully at rest, they suffer'd not,
The living remain'd and suffer'd, the mother suffer'd.
And the wife and the child and the musing comrade suffer'd,
And the armies that remain'd suffer'd.

16
Passing the visions, passing the night,
Passing, unloosing the hold of my comrades' hands,
Passing the song of the hermit bird and the tallying song of my soul,
Victorious song, death's outlet song, yet varying ever-altering song,
As low and wailing, yet clear the notes, rising and falling, flooding the night,
Sadly sinking and fainting, as warning and warning, and yet again bursting with joy,
Covering the earth and filling the spread of the heaven,
As that powerful psalm in the night I heard from recesses,
Passing, I leave thee lilac with heart-shaped leaves,
I leave thee there in the door-yard, blooming, returning with spring.

I cease from my song for thee,
From my gaze on thee in the west, fronting the west, communing with thee,
O comrade lustrous with silver face in the night.

Yet each to keep and all, retrievements out of the night,
The song, the wondrous chant of the gray-brown bird,
And the tallying chant, the echo arous'd in my soul,
With the lustrous and drooping star with the countenance full of woe,
With the holders holding my hand nearing the call of the bird,
Comrades mine and I in the midst, and their memory ever to keep, for the dead I
        loved so well,
For the sweetest, wisest soul of all my days and lands—and this for his dear sake,
Lilac and star and bird twined with the chant of my soul,
There in the fragrant pines and the cedars dusk and dim.

In Memory of Dylan Thomas[25]

C. Day Lewis

"it was Adam and maiden"

Too soon, it is all too soon
Laments our childhood's horn
Husky and cool at the close
Of its dove-note afternoon.
Too soon, a red fox echoes
Old on the hunted hill
Where dewfall mirrors the dawn
And dawn rides out for a kill.
It is too soon, too soon
Wails the unripened barley
To flailing storms: *too soon*
Pipes the last frail leaf in the valley.

A poet can seem to show
Animal, child and leaf
In the light of eternity, though
It is but the afterglow
From his consuming love,
The spill of a fabulous dawn
Where animal, leaf and child,
Timelessly conceived,
With time are reconciled.

Now we lament one
Who danced on a plume of words,
Sang with a fountain's panache,
Dazzled like slate roofs in sun
After rain, was flighty as birds
And alone as a mountain ash.
The ribald, inspired urchin
Leaning over the lip
Of his world, as over a rock pool
Or a lucky dip,

Found everything brilliant and virgin,
Like Adam who went to school
Only with God, and like Adam
He gave that world a tongue.
Already he has outsung
Our elegies, who always
Drew from creation's fathomless
Grief a pure drop of praise.

Elegy for Jane[26]
MY STUDENT, THROWN BY A HORSE

Theodore Roethke

I remember the neckcurls, limp and damp as tendrils;
And her quick look, a sidelong pickerel smile;
And how, once startled into talk, the light syllables leaped for her,
And she balanced in the delight of her thought,
A wren, happy, tail into the wind,
Her song trembling the twigs and small branches.
The shade sang with her;
The leaves, their whispers turned to kissing;
And the mold sang in the bleached valleys under the rose.

Oh, when she was sad, she cast herself down into such a pure depth,
Even a father could not find her:
Scraping her cheek against straw;
Stirring the clearest water.

My sparrow, you are not here,
Waiting like a fern, making a spiny shadow.
The sides of wet stones cannot console me,
Nor the moss, wound with the last light.

If only I could nudge you from this sleep,
My maimed darling, my skittery pigeon.
Over this damp grave I speak the words of my love:
I, with no rights in this matter
Neither father nor lover.

BLANK VERSE AND OLD ENGLISH VERSE

In blank verse and Old English verse, the container, the form into which the experience is put, is the individual line, and not larger stanzaic or poetic forms such as we have been discussing. These two forms have been widely used by poets in the English-speaking world for the manner in which they approximate the everyday rhythm of spoken English. Blank verse, for instance, is unrhymed, allowing for a flowing sense of uncluttered language. The individual line consists of five metrical feet, with the iambic foot ($\cup$/) tending to predominate. Because the iambic foot itself tends to hasten language, lines move; because the lines are unrhymed, the flow of the experience, its form and development, is usually unimpeded. The discipline of the line is apparent; the freedom of the form is suitable to any style of language. The masters of blank verse—Shakespeare, Milton, Wordsworth, Frost—never exhausted its endless capacity for variation and its uncanny responsiveness to the language of a period.

Old English verse, like the ballad quatrain, is an inheritance from the earliest origins of Anglo-Saxon literature. Its form, even freer than blank verse, demands but four stressed words (or syllables), regardless of the number of words in the line. Early Anglo-Saxon verse was characterized, too, by alliteration in the line. Many contemporary poets, finding the freedom of the form most attractive, have tended to forsake the alliterative patterns while retaining the four-beat-stress line.

The performing effect of both blank verse and Old English verse is to submerge the form and to give over the primacy of the experience. Yet there is a paradox, for the effect of both is subtle and enriching, as the unconscious awareness of ordered speech always persists. The effect is rhythmic and pulsating, and the importance of this effect should not be overlooked. The form of the experience, freed from any arbitrary constraint of form or repetition of elements, becomes experience informed by beat, by stress. Thus, while it is true that blank verse, and to a lesser extent Old English verse, is that poetic form most like normal speech, it is also true, and perhaps more important, that *the form is organic.* Test these observations in the example that follows.

The Phoenix[27]

Cynewulf (?)

When the gem of the sky   in the summer season,
The burning sun,   shines over the shades
Scanning the world,   the Phoenix sits

27. "The Phoenix." From *Early English Christian Poetry* translated by Charles W. Kennedy. Oxford University Press, 1952. Reprinted by permission.

Fain of departure,   fulfilling his fate.
His house is kindled   by heat of the sun;
The herbs grow hot,   the pleasant hall steams
With sweetest odours;   in the surging flame,
In the fire-grip, burns   the bird with his next.
The pyre is kindled,   the fire enfolds
The home of the heart-sick.   The yellow flame
Fiercely rages;   the Phoenix burns,
Full of years,   as the fire consumes
The fleeting body.   The spirit fades,
The soul of the fated.   The bale-fire seizes
Both bone and flesh.
                    But his life is reborn
After a season,   when the ashes begin
After the fire-surge   fusing together
Compressed to a ball.   The brightest of nests,
The house of the stout-heart,   by force of the flame
Is clean consumed;   the corpse grows chill;
The bone-frame is broken;   the burning subsides.
From the flame of the fire   is found thereafter
In the ash of the pyre   an apple's likeness,
Of which grows a worm   most wondorous fair,
As it were a creature   come from an egg,
Shining from the shell.   In the shadow it grows
Fashioned first   as an eagle's young,
A comely fledgeling;   then flourishing fair
Is like in form   to a full-grown eagle
Adorned with feathers   as he was at first,
Brightly gleaming. . . .

                    Brightly the King,
Fair Gem of light,   from His lofty seat
Shall beam on the holy.   Blessed is he
In that fearful hour   who finds favour with God!
    Then go glad-hearted   the pure of sin;
Souls pass back again   into their bodies
While high to the heavens   the bale-fires burn.
Bitter for many   that fearful blaze
When blessed or sinful,   body and soul,
Each from the grave   goes to God's Judgment

Some Conventional Set Patterns in Poetry   237

Shaking with fear.   The fire rages
Consuming the sinful;   but blessed souls
After their exile   are garbed in good works,
The deeds they have done.   These are sweet spices,
The winsome herbs   wherewith the wild bird
Besets his nest   till it burns with fire,
And the Phoenix with it   flames in the sun;
Then after the burning   the bird is reborn!
So every soul   shall be swathed in flesh,
Shall be young and fair,   who fervently strives
By his deeds on earth   that on Judgment Day
The King of glory,   Almighty God,
Gracious and mild   may show him mercy.

Caesura and enjambment.   Two important technical terms are helpful in analyzing the way poets vary the structures of individual lines. They are the terms *caesura* and *enjambment*, and both have to do with breaks and pauses. A caesura is a pause in a line; an enjambment is the manner in which a sentence runs on from one line to another. A caesura establishes the structural sense of a sentence as the pauses occur in places other than a line ending. Enjambment is the manner in which a sentence is written in blank verse so that it does not end at the end of the line. These two elements can be illustrated in the opening lines of Robert Frost's "Home Burial."

He saw her from the bottom of the stairs
                    ENJAMBMENT
Before she saw him. She was starting down,
Looking back over her shoulder at some fear.
She took a doubtful step and then undid it
                    ENJAMBMENT
To raise herself and look again. He spoke
                CAESURA
Advancing toward her: "What is it you see
                CAESURA
From up there always?—for I want to know."
She turned and sank upon her skirts at that,
And her face changed from terrified to dull.
                CAESURA
He said to gain time: "What is it you see?"
Mounting until she cowered under him.

CAESURA
"I will find out now—you must tell me, dear."
CAESURA
She, in her place, refused him any help,
With the least stiffening of her neck and silence.
CAESURA
She let him look, sure that he wouldn't see,
CAESURA
Blind creature; and awhile he didn't see.[28]

For the transformation of form, the caesuras and enjambments are ways of describing rhythmical changes in the poem, are means by which the organic nature of blank verse becomes alive and vital.

In the presentation of blank verse and a four-beat cadenced verse, the performer is challenged by these aesthetic considerations:

1. How is the sense of naturalness achieved?
   —How closely is the rhythm of the meter linked to the rhythm of the experience?
   —How do the line structures vary to achieve effects and changes in rhythms? through caesuras? enjambments?
2. How does the overall form of the poem coalesce? Why is blank verse the most suitable form?
   —If there are divisions established, or breaks in the continuity of the printed lines, how do these parts (or chapters of the experience) function?[29]

FORM AS STRUCTURE: SOME FREE PATTERNS IN POETRY

Art is always in search of new forms of expression. The set patterns of a previous period often seem overused, no longer functional, dead to a new generation. This sense of changing structures is one of the more interesting aspects of literary history, for in this history is the struggle between freedom of form and the aesthetic constraints of form. Students are unquestionably attracted to the voices of their generation, those writers who sense and seize the language, rhythm, and form of expression that fuse with the psyches of that generation.

28. From "Home Burial" from *The Poetry of Robert Frost,* edited by Edward Connery Lathem. Copyright 1923, 1930, 1939, © 1969 by Holt, Rinehart and Winston, Inc. Copyright 1951, © 1958 by Robert Frost. Copyright © 1967 by Lesley Frost Ballantine. Reprinted by permission of Holt, Rinehart and Winston, Inc.
29. Because blank verse does not possess a stanzaic structure, the term *stichic* is employed to describe its appearance. The word is derived from the Greek for "line" or "row." Occasionally poets will break the stichic structure by creating sections in the poem. How these individual sections function is very important to note.

Twentieth-century poetry has been particularly marked by poets seeking fresh and freeing patterns. The first "modern" American poet, although he wrote in the latter half of the nineteenth century, broke completely with the set patterns of poetry that reflected what literature "should be" for an age. That poet was Walt Whitman, and his unrestraining influence can be felt a hundred years after his time. There are few poets of the nineteenth century about whom this can be said. The pattern that he gave us was free verse.

FREE VERSE

In a sense the set patterns that have been discussed in this chapter are easier to understand and define than the free pattern of experience and language known as free verse, identified occasionally by the French term, *vers libre*. Though it is seldom helpful to explain something by noting what it is not, the negative approach may clear the field for a discussion of what free verse is. It is, first of all, *not* an agreed upon set pattern like the sonnet or villanelle, or even the less stringent pattern in blank verse. Free verse is *not* tied to the old and traditional metrics (iamb, trochee, anapest, etc.). It is *not* tied to any convention or stabilizing element. Free verse can be defined anew by any poet who attempts to find for himself a fresh, disciplined freedom. For to understand free verse, as well as the other free patterns discussed in this section, is to understand that it is *a disciplined freedom.*

The student is justified in thinking the statement paradoxical that free verse is not a set pattern but is a disciplined freedom. The explanation is that in free verse the poet establishes his own ground rules, and once they have been established for a poem, he attempts to make them work consistently. What kinds of ground rules function in free verse? Three general approaches to form can be identified. The first is the form in which the primary communication is that of images that flow and weave and create tensions with each other, images that may move from visual to auditory to tactile, but always in a way that informs one sense with another, one image with another. In this case the form springs from language. A second form of free verse originates in the meditative impulse, the impulse for incantation, repetition, or profoundly meaningful observation. In this second approach there is an inner necessity to sing, within a free and open structure, the sense of one's being. This form originates in experience. Third, and finally, is a form of free verse that sets up some structural patterns that are arbitrary to the poet and the poem. A "freely disciplined structural pattern" would be an agreed syllable count for a poem, as in the Japanese haiku of seventeen syllables, or the cinquain of twenty-two syllables. Another structural pattern might be that of line length, or a beat pattern that cannot be explained by any of the older and more familiar metrical patterns of versification. It would be wise to think of these three forms not as discrete categories, but rather as approaches that may function in free verse separately and in combination. In the first category would be such poets as Amy Lowell, William Carlos Williams, the French *symbolistes* (Paul Verlaine, Charles Baudelaire), and Wallace Stevens. In the second and third categories would be such poets as Walt Whitman, Gerard Manley Hopkins, Allen Ginsberg, though each of these poets is very much identified with his own cadence patterns. An example of a poem in each category, however, will assist the student performer in understanding what the elements of form are, how they can be identified, and the implications of these for transformation.

Free verse as imagery is an intriguing experience of an "imaged" moment, of a perceived constellation of events communicated solely through the "things" in the event. In "The Great Figure" by William Carlos Williams, each line provides an image in its sensory effect.

The Great Figure[30]

William Carlos Williams

Among the rain
and lights
I saw the figure 5
in gold
on a red
firetruck
moving
tense
unheeded
to gong clangs
siren howls
and wheels rumbling
through the dark city.

A number of aspects of the images of the poem are intriguing. First, the title suggests the presence of a "something" either *in* a figure of speech or *about* a figure in the speech of the poem. Second, the images of the weather and the time of day, the thing perceived and how, all follow a simple pattern of how and when, what and how, concluding with where. But in the simple enumeration of the images, there is a coales-

30. William Carlos Williams, *Collected Earlier Poems*. Copyright 1938 by New Directions Publishing Corporation. Reprinted by permission of New Directions Publishing Corporation.

cence that transcends the mere images; there is a sudden sense of informing. An over-all feeling emerges from the perception of the images, a feeling that is almost a sense of foreboding, of doom. Though the power of the poem comes first through its images, the student should observe the uncanny relationship of the impact of the poem's images to the syllable count in each line. First, there are thirteen lines, a number unlucky and foreboding. In these thirteen lines the syllables are arranged as follows: 4, 2, 6, 2, 3, 2, 2, 1, 3, 3, 3, 4, 5. Because thirteen is an uneven number, the precise center of the poem is line seven, "moving." On either side of line seven are exactly nineteen syllables, establishing a perfectly symmetrical structure in the poem. All images in the first nineteen syllables hasten *toward* "moving," and the remaining nineteen syllables rumble *away from* "moving." The sensitive student, too, cannot help but be fascinated by the mystical connotation of the number "five." Here in a short, free verse poem, one finds unusual coincidences of structure: the images move in forty syllables through a careful patterning of 19-2-19, the thirteen lines establish a sense of a "great figure" on a particular thing on a particular night in particular weather and with a particular effect. Williams' poem represents a marvelous example of disciplined freedom.

Free verse as a form of invocation, of singing the sense of one's being, is well exemplified in D. H. Lawrence's "Song of a Man Who Has Come Through." Here the theme of the song is indicated by the title, and the sense of Lawrence's "Being being sung" is given intensified utterance through the structural repetitions, the almost impulsive, incantatory celebration of an event and a time in life.

Song of a Man Who Has Come Through[31]

D. H. Lawrence

Not I, not I, but the wind that blows through me!
A fine wind is blowing the new direction of Time.
If only I let it bear me, carry me, if only it carry me!
If only I am sensitive, subtle, oh, delicate, a winged gift!
If only, most lovely of all, I yield myself and am borrowed
By the fine, fine wind that takes its course through the chaos of the world
Like a fine, exquisite chisel, a wedge-blade inserted;
If only I am keen and hard like the sheer tip of a wedge
Driven by invisible blows,
The rock will split, we shall come at the wonder, we shall find the Hesperides.

Oh, for the wonder that bubbles into my soul,
I would be a good fountain, a good well-head,
Would blur no whisper, spoil no expression.

What is that knocking?
What is the knocking at the door in the night?
It is somebody wants to do us harm.

No, no, it is the three strange angels.
Admit them, admit them.

In looking at the poem, one can make several obvious observations: (1) the poem is divided into four units or sections; (2) the lines in each section are 10, 3, 3, 2; (3) the poem consists of eleven sentences; (4) nine of the eleven sentences are individual line lengths and thus are self contained on the line; (5) in the two sentences that carry over, the line lengths carry a line sense so that even though they constitute a part of a longer sentence, each line makes contained emotional sense in its phrasing. The structuring of the types of sentences is interesting to notice, too; the poem's construction is remarkably tight and powerful. In the first section there are three exclamatory sentences and three declarative (the last sentence in the first section is a two-part sentence separated by a semicolon; technically it is one sentence). The second section consists of one declarative sentence. The third section contains two interrogative and one declarative sentence. In the fourth are one declarative and one imperative (or a repeated imperative). The movement of the poem in sentence forms contains an exciting sense of experience:

exclamatory	*Section 1*
declarative	
exclamatory	
exclamatory	
declarative	
declarative	
declarative	*Section 2*
interrogatory	*Section 3*
interrogatory	
declarative	
declarative	*Section 4*
imperative / imperative	

The sense of invocation of self, the incantatory celebration of having come through and hoping to continue, is interrupted by two questions of fright and a response in a declarative sentence of fear. In the negative space between the third and fourth sections, a miraculous perception occurs, and the poem ends on the imperative commands to admit. By maintaining a self-contained meaning to every line, by artistically using sentence forms to create contained experience and suspense, Lawrence has achieved in a free form a disciplined sense of artistic experience.

Free verse that sets up a structural pattern is usually the easiest of the three forms to perceive and the one in which the elements for transformation are most obvious. A favored form of structuring among some poets is the discipline of syllable count. In much free verse that is dependent for its structure upon syllable count, the tension in the poem is created by the fusion of the images with the limitations of sounds in which the image can be conveyed. In a sense such a pattern is as rigorous as the set patterns in a sonnet or villanelle with the exception that nothing is required other than obedience to syllable count; there is no rhythm, and no rhyme scheme is demanded. One American poet, obviously influenced by the Oriental haiku, developed a free pattern which she called the *cinquain*, a five-line poem of twenty-two syllables.

Cinquain: The Warning[32]

Adelaide Crapsey

Just now,
Out of the strange
Still dusk . . . as strange, as still . . .
A white moth flew. Why am I grown
So cold?

The form is simple: five lines with a sequential syllable count of 2, 4, 6, 8, 2. The effect achieved within disciplined freedom is evident. Each group of syllables introduces information that remains incomplete until completed by the following group. The last two syllables give structure to the complete experience. This structure must be grasped to understand the manner in which the cinquain form works. By putting the poem in a linear arrangement, perhaps this point is more clearly made: "Just now—out of the strange—still dusk—as strange, as still—a white moth flew.—Why am I grown—so cold?" The effect of these spacings is quite different from the effect, say, of

32. "Cinquain: The Warning" by Adelaide Crapsey from *The New Poetry* by Harriet Monroe. Reprinted by permission of Marguerite F. Fetcher.

"Just now, out of the strange still dusk . . . as strange, as still . . . a white moth flew. Why am I grown so cold?" When perceived in their proper spacings, the words have the effect of fragmentary pieces of information in an energy field of "something happening." A premonition of death? A chilling sense of a mysterious participation that haunts? However the effect is described, it is achieved, in part, by the careful laying out of utterance, of syllables, of sound. And the relationship of the word/syllables to the negative spaces surrounding them creates the tension of the experience. The poem is not a simple matter of two sentences; it is a profound matter of a disciplined unfolding, an unfolding that withholds the chilling effect until the final two syllables. The blending of the form and the experience is complete.

Another kind of structural pattern or form in free verse is cadence, the effect achieved by the repetition of certain stressed words in a sentence. This kind of effect is achieved with great mastery and sophistication in the poetry of Walt Whitman. In the following poem, note only the words that you emphasize in reading aloud.

Yonnondio[33]

Walt Whitman

   /   /   /   /   /   /
A song, a poem for itself—the word itself a dirge,
   /   /   /   /   /   /
Amid the wilds, the rocks, the storm and wintry night,
   /   /   /   /   /   /   /
To me such misty, strange tableaux the syllables calling up;
   /   / /   /   /   /   /   /
Yonnondio—I see, far in the west or north, a limitless ravine, with plains and
                /   /
         mountains dark,
/ /   /   /   /   /   /   /
I see swarms of stalwart chieftains, medicine-men, and warriors,
    /   /   /   /   / /   /   /
As flitting by like clouds of ghosts, they pass and are gone in the twilight,
   /   /   /   /   /
(Race of the woods, the landscape free, and the falls!
/ /   /   /   /   /   /
No picture, poem, statement, passing them to the future:)
   /   /   /   /
Yonnondio! Yonnondio!—unlimn'd they disappear;

33. This is an Iroquois term, often used as a proper noun. Whitman uses it in this sense, but also in its literal meaning: "lament for the aborigines."

/   /   /   /   /   / /   /
To-day gives place, and fades—the cities, farms, factories fade;

/   /   /   /   /   /   /   /
A muffled sonorous sound, a wailing word is borne through the air for a moment,

/   /   /   /   /
Then blank and gone and still, and utterly lost.

Now by making a count of the number of *syllables* in the line as well as the number of *accented* words (or syllables), the count for the line can be tallied, as in the first line— 14^6. That is, in the first line there are fourteen syllables with six stresses. Note, however, that the first line is punctuated into three units of thought: "A song/a poem for itself/the word itself a dirge." In the first unit there are two syllables, in the second, six, and in the third, three. In the first unit there is one stress, in the second, two, and in the third, three. Thus, the completed analysis can be designated 14^6 $(2^1\text{-}6^2\text{-}6^3)$. In analyzing the entire poem in similar fashion, counting the syllables in each line and the stressed units, the poem appears as shown at left. By count, a most interesting pattern emerges. Rather than an uncontrolled covering of the page with language, Whitman achieves a surprising regularity of cadenced beat, and the beat is in the repetition of *small units*. In the poem are twelve sections that have one beat, eleven sections that have two beats, nine sections that have three beats. As counterpoint to this overwhelming predominance of one, two, and three beats, there are two sections with four beats, occurring at the approximate midpoint of the poem, and three sections of five beats. In Whitman's free verse there is a freedom, but there is a control as well. The performer must seek what that controlling element is, and in Whitman, as in much free verse, it is often in the smallest units, the units, by the way, which ultimately control the speech phrases and thus, in turn, the meaning.

As stated earlier, free verse is not a matter solely of arrangement of images, arrangement of evocative utterances, or patterns of cadences. Free verse can be made of complex patterns and combinations of two or three of these elements. The performer should not be deceived by appearances nor should he conclude that there is no structure or form, for the paradoxical wonder of art is that it always has shape, always has form.

14^6 $(2^1\text{-}6^2\text{-}6^3)$
12^6 $(4^2\text{-}2^1\text{-}6^3)$
15^7 $(5^2\text{-}10^5)$
24^{11} $(4^1\text{-}2^2\text{-}6^3\text{-}6^2\text{-}6^3)$
15^8 $(8^5\text{-}4^2\text{-}3^1)$
17^8 $(8^4\text{-}9^4)$
11^5 $(4^2\text{-}4^2\text{-}3^1)$
14^7 $(3^2\text{-}2^1\text{-}2^1\text{-}7^3)$
14^5 $(4^1\text{-}4^1\text{-}6^3)$
14^8 $(4^3\text{-}2^1\text{-}3^1\text{-}1^1\text{-}4^2)$
20^8 $(7^3\text{-}13^5)$
11^5 $(6^3\text{-}5^2)$

PROJECTIVE VERSE

The twentieth-century artist is committed to the notion of spontaneity, of freedom, of losing inhibiting restraints. Often he has felt that any sense of formal structure is an imprisoning limitation. Musicians, painters, sculptors, and writers have explored ways of preserving spontaneity in artistic creation. Action painting, scores of music indicating only improvisational possibilities, and sculptures created by assembling and arranging the "found objects" in an environment have been attempts to value the unfiltered and spontaneous sense of creation. In poetry, too, the twentieth-century artists have experimented in the total freedom and spontaneous creation of poetic utterance.

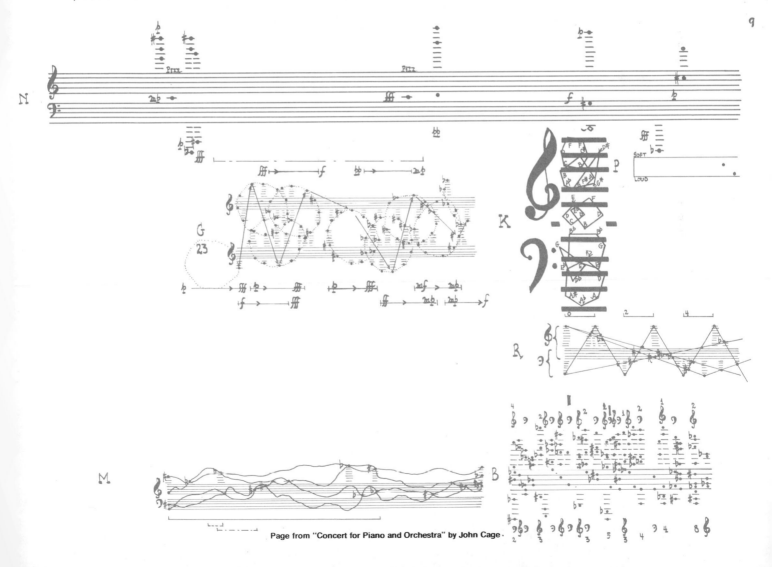

Page from "Concert for Piano and Orchestra" by John Cage

In Michael McClure's "Ode for Soft Voice," the words flow onto the page not from any pattern of free verse, but from the necessity of the experience. The words "become" on the page, the punctuation and use of capital letters is unusual, the lines expand and contract and even coalesce into what appears to be a prose section. But everything that happens in the poem happens in the expansiveness, pain, and love in the experience. The paragraph of language occurs at a precise moment in the poem after the intensity of a sexual experience, and suggests not only the poet's sense of exhaustion but also his awareness of his incapacity ever to be an emotional part of another's life. The sense of movement in the poem is mirrored by the form in which the experience takes place. The poem is projected onto the page with an intensity that leaves no doubt that this is the language of experience. The cues for the performance of projective verse come from the spatial arrangements of the material, from the typographical variances, but primarily from the emotionally infused sense of line. Charles Olson, writing of projective verse, states that it possesses two halves:

> the HEAD, by way of the EAR, to the SYLLABLE
> the HEART, by way of the BREATH, to the LINE

And the joker? that it is in the 1st half of the proposition that, in composing, one lets-it-rip; and that it is in the 2nd half, surprise, it is the LINE that's the baby that gets, as the poem is getting made, the attention, the control, that it is right here, in the line, that the shaping takes place, each moment of the going.[34]

There was for Charles Olson what he called "the law of the line" which projective verse creates. This law is the law of human energy that exists for that line and that line alone. A composed poem in projective verse is a spatial tension of energies, a spontaneous putting on the page of thoughts of the poet without conscious attention to a form.

Ode for Soft Voice[35]

Michael McClure

                                           for Jo Ann
And sometimes in the cool night I see you are an animal
LIKE NO OTHER AND HAVE AS STRANGE A SCENT AS
                   [ANY AND MY BREATH AND

---

34. Charles Olson, *Selected Writings* (New York: New Directions, 1966), p. 19.

energy go out to you.
And see love as an invention and play it extemporaneously.

And I who cannot love can love you.
OH THIS THIS THIS IS THE HURT   /   THAT WE DO
                                                                    [NOT KICK
down the walls and do not see them.
And I do not ache until I scent you. And I
do not scent you. Breathing moves us. Breath is . . .

And more than this that we are huge and clear
                    and open—locked inside
and moving out and we make outlines in the air the shapes
they are. And we shift so. We move and never keep our forms
                                                                    [but stare
at them address them as if they were there. This is my hand with
                5 fingers, my heart nerves lungs
                        are there and part of me
                            and I move.
I have no form but lies and drop them from me.

                I am a shape and meet you
                    at our skins edge.
We change and speak and make our histories. I am all I feel
                and what you see and what you touch.
                There are no walls but ones we make.
    I AM SICK CONFUSED AND DROP IT FROM ME
The nerves are dead that feel no hunger or pain theres no triumph but failure. This
is the last speech of seraphim or beast sick in need for change and chaos. The room
of banished love for beauty. The tooth in our breast. What we see is real and able to
our hand, what we feel is beauty (BEAUTY   ) what we strike is hatred, what we
scent is odorous. This about me is my bride if I kick aside the forms of it for woman
world and mineral for air for earth for fire and water for table chair and blood.

35. "Ode for Soft Voice" by Michael McClure from *The New American Poetry*, edited by Donald M. Allen. Copyright ©
1960 by Donald M. Allen. Reprinted by permission of Grove Press, Inc.

Anecdotes of the Late War[36]

Charles Olson

1.
the lethargic vs violence as alternatives of each other
                                        for los americanos

    & U S Grant (at Shiloh, as ex.) had the gall to stay
    inside a lethargy until it let him down into either
    vice (Galena, or, as president) or
    a virtue of such a movement as, example,
    Vicksburg

    say that he struck, going down, either
    morass or
    rock—and when it was rock, he was

—this wld seem to be the power in the principle—

able to comprehend the movement of mass of men, the

transposition of the

Mississippi   (Or

continents, example,

somebody else than:

grant

    better, that is, that a man stay lethargic than

blow somebody's face off—off,

the face of, blow

the earth

36. "Anecdotes of the Late War" from *The Distances* by Charles Olson. Copyright ©1950, 1951, 1953, 1960 by Charles Olson. Reprinted by permission of Grove Press, Inc.

2.
that (like the man sd) Booth
killing Lincoln is the melodrama right with
the drama: Mister Christ and
Broadway
          Or going out to Bull Run looking for
Waterloo. the
diorama. And having to get the fastidious hell home
that afternoon
as fast as the carriage horses
can't make it (Lee Highway
littered with broken
elegances

          Reverse of
sic transit gloria, the
Latin American whom the cab driver told me
he picked me up at Union Station had
one word of english—link-
cone. And drove him
straight to the monument, the man
went up the stairs and fell down on his knees
where he could see the statue and stayed there
in the attitude of prayer

3.
whoop,
went the bird
in the tree the day
the fellow
fell down
in the thicket

whoop, was the bird's
lay as the fellow lay

and I picked up a minie ball
(the way
it can be
again
of an afternoon,

or with the French girl Brandy Station
was
thick grass
and the gray house and back of it

yes   mam   the   movement

of horses, as

—I repeat—

the bird.

4.
West Point it wasn't. Nor New England. Nor
those cavalry
flauntlets
      As the Mexican War was
      filibusterers
      in the West,
      and cadets
      before Chapultepec: the elevator
      goink down

      from waterloo,

      the Civil War

was the basement. Only nobody

except butternut

and his fellow on the other side

wanted to believe it, they all wanted

what Jay Gould got

(and Joe Blow got swap
in the side of the head

5.

Now you take this Forrest, Nathan Bedford Forrest. He stalks the Western theater of
operations as something the English, to this day, think Lee wouldn't have surpassed
had anybody dared to give this Memphis slave-trader the width of men and field to
command which he only had as first Grand Wizard of the Ku Klux Klan. And didn't
use, Forrest could already avoid the temptation of the Filibusterer, he had applied
first principles in the War.

What I'd wanted to say was,
that he's a man so locked in the act of himself

    (right up to after Davis had been taken
    and no last movie scene to the way he was still
    cutting tracks behind U. S. Army units, a very

exact and busy man.

I also have to voice this impression of him to give, if it
does, the sense of how he was:

    he's like a man his tongue was cut out,
    before even Shiloh showed him
    an extraordinary executive
    of men horses and goods

6.

Two things still aren't brought in to give context to the War: (1), that you don't get
Grant except as you find what he was that Geo Washington also comes alive at only
if you realize he was to real estate—

    and I mean land
when land was as oil steel and what, now?

Managing men, wasn't it, when men suddenly what was Grant's

because of the industrial revolution

were what the guys who died then were

For the first time,
like that, the sprawled fellow Devil's Glen, natural
resource.

The other half of it — (2) — that each one of them,

Butternut,

and Yankee Doodle,

weren't as different as North and South, farmer and factory etc.

They were — for the first time — enough of them.

Plus railroad tracks
to be moved around as
utility

The leaders,   Grant Sherman Forrest not
Jeb Stuart
and themselves

the birth of

the recent   And Lincoln

likewise   (after Christ

Link-cone

7.
You take it
from there

8.
What he said was, in that instance
I got there first
with the most men

Grant didn't hurry.
He just had the most.

More of the latter died.

CONCRETE POETRY

Concrete poetry is free of all or any preconceived notions of poetry. While some concrete poems may appeal primarily to the ear, others may appeal to the eye, and others,
still, may appeal to a sense of motion. Developed shortly after World War II, this expansive and engaging form of poetry is the one truly international style to which poets
of all nations have been attracted.

In concrete poetry that appeals to the eye, the poet achieves something of a
constellation that is perceived rather than read. Like a picture or painting, the concrete poem is seen in a "field of vision," and it is not dependent upon perceptions
stemming from patterns of literacy, i.e., to read from left to right, syntax, etc. It is not
so much a linear creation as a "happening" which can be explored right to left, up and
down, down and up. Pedro Xisto's "Epithalamium II" is such a poem. It consists of a
total configuration that incorporates the word *she*. When studied, the poem vacillates
between the dominance of the "she" and the "he" entwined in the serpentine "S."
Either the "S" appears in the foreground or it recedes into the background. The longer the poem is studied, the more complex and compelling it becomes. But consider
for a moment the sounds in the poem: *S, sh, h, e, he, she*. A sensitive performer, playing with these elements, can produce an auditory transformation of the visual components. There are, too, a number of behavioral possibilities.[37]

The appeal of sound, of long historical importance in poetry, is given orchestration and musicality in concrete poetry. Reinhard Döhl's "Apfel" and Eugene Gomringer's "silencio" are exciting and diverting uses of sound. "Apfel" demands a controlled virtuosity of sound while "silencio" is dependent upon the paradox of the
poem's insisting upon silence while at the same time providing it at the poem's core.
"silencio" is a good example of a concrete poem that can be read in any direction
with the same resulting formalistic structure.

37. For a discussion of transformations of concrete poems, with an emphasis upon group performance, see Chapter 8,
"Multiforms: Experimental Approaches."

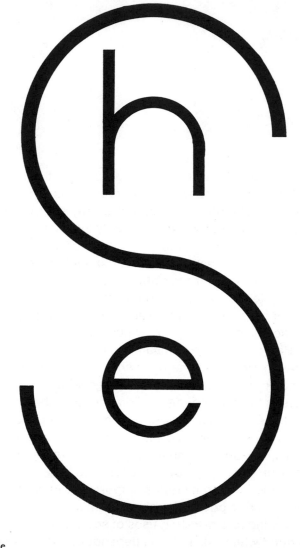

Epithalamium II[38]

Pedro Xisto

he=êle   S=serpens
&=e   h=homo
she=ela   e=eva

38. "Epithalamium II" from *Concrete Poetry* by Mary Ellen Solt. Copyright © 1968. Reprinted by permission of Indiana University Press.

Apfel[39]
PATTERN POEM WITH AN ELUSIVE INTRUDER

Reinhard Döhl

silencio[40]

Eugene Gomringer

```
silencio  silencio  silencio
silencio  silencio  silencio
silencio          silencio
silencio  silencio  silencio
silencio  silencio  silencio
```

40. "silencio" from *Concrete Poetry* by Mary Ellen Solt. Copyright © 1968. Reprinted by permission of Indiana University Press.

Forsythia[41]

Mary Ellen Solt

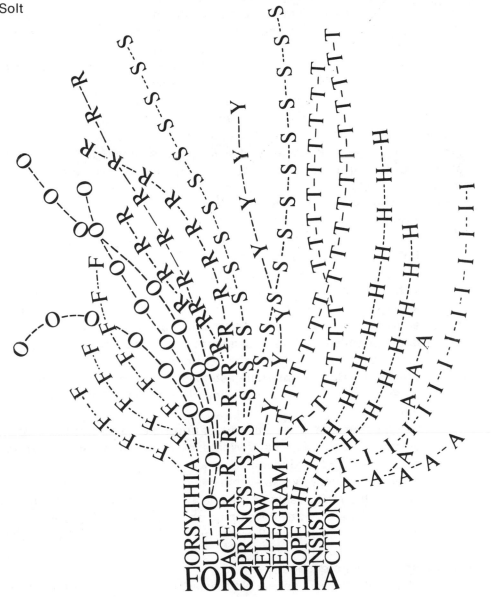

41. "Forsythia" from *Concrete Poetry* by Mary Ellen Solt. Copyright © 1968. Reprinted by permission of Indiana University Press.

Some Free Patterns in Poetry   259

Mary Ellen Solt's "Forsythia," a poem of stunning visual movement, is filled with marvelous tonalities springing from the arranged branches of forsythia, each branch a verbal message. The kinetic movement of the poem is as joyful as spring itself. In "Forsythia" the combination of sight, sound, and movement offers a concert of elements.

The form of concrete poetry must be discovered in the structure of each individual poem. The patterns of sound, sight, movement occur only in the order in which they are perceived, the possible perceptions almost as numerous as the audience, thus creating a freedom of perception that is as expansive as the medium itself.

Form in the free patterns has been shown to be a variety of freedoms, but always with that sense that the artist has imposed his own discipline to make the freedom work. The free patterns demand as much sensibility in their perception as the set patterns, for the form in the free pattern is more elusive, more merged with the form of the experience. Questions that the student performer may ask himself in his analysis of free and open structured poems are these:

1. If the poem is free verse—
   —Is the poem a coalescence of images? If so, what is the movement of the images? How do the images inform one another? What mood is achieved by the images? How does line length prepare and develop the sense of image?
   —Is the poem structured by syllable count? What is the arrangement of the syllable/word count to the sense of the line? the emotional sense? If it is a short poem, what is the transcendence achieved in the brevity of form?
   —Is the poem's structure dependent upon a cadenced beat? What is the predominant beat? How is the beat related to the sense of the experience in the poem? How do internal cadenced structures of a line relate to the overall experience or sense of the line? How do the lines build into an overall effect?
   —Is the poem's structure dependent upon the pattern of the sentences? How do the sentences function? What kind of movement in the experience is established by the kinds of sentences?

2. If the poem is projective verse—
   —What is the relationship of the spacings of the language to the experience?
   —What are the energies developing and working in the poem? memory? association? celebration? sex? emotion (anger, love, pity, etc.)? the need for self-expression?

3. If the poem is concrete poetry—
   —What is the primary appeal? to the ear? eye? sense of motion? fusion?
   —How many sensory explorations are inherent in the poem? sight? sound? behaviorial?
   —Is there a sequential development to the poem? Is it free of sequentiality and open?

FORM AS STRUCTURE: PATTERNS IN PROSE

It cannot be stressed enough that form in literature means two things: the form of the experience and the form in which the experience takes place. The concept of poetic form as explored in this chapter has been that of "shape" or "container." Obviously, there are no forms in prose the equivalent of the set and free poetic forms we have been discussing. However, the same congruent relationship should exist between the experience and its form in prose as we sought in poetry. Prose writers must find an appropriate form in which to present the experience. An example of prose form would be an epistolary story (a story consisting of what appears to be an exchange of letters). The first novel experimentations in English were epistolary ones, Richardson's *Pamela* being an important contribution in the attempt to make prose function in a form. Another form might be a diary or a carefully contrived fictional biography or autobiography. The search for new and innovative prose forms in which to present experience constitutes the provocative history of fiction itself. One contemporary novel, *Le Prix Nobel,* is based solely upon messages sent and received on a teletype machine, an example of an experimental attempt to find a form for the experience.

At the beginning of this chapter we said, "In prose the form in which experience exists is more elusive [than in poetry]. Prose is not easily 'contained' on the page; it is expansive. Its structure develops out of the nature of the experience, how it happened, what caused it." In prose it is often easier to hear the "style" of the experience first, the sounding experience of the words and the language page after page, than it is to identify its form. Thus, to speak of form in prose is to speak of style, the manner in which the sense of ongoing experience and ongoing story is achieved. That there is structure in prose is not denied, but it is the structuring of experience through sequence. And the sequence should seem new, fresh, inevitable. The interrelatedness of form and style in prose will be more apparent in the following chapter which has style as its subject.

CHECKLIST FOR ANALYSIS

1. How would the metaworld of the literature be described? What is the "state of being" in the selection? What is the principal presentational value of the selection? (See chart on page 22.)

2. In what mode is the selection written? What are the central behavioral problems in the selection? in the "presses"?

3. How is literary time conveyed in language? How does psychological time function? mythic time? How are silences used and where? What are the principal rhythms of the literature? What is the prevailing meter of the poetry?

4. How is figurative language employed? to what ends? How are paradox and irony employed?

5. What is the form of the experience in the selection? What is the form into which the experience has been put? What precise poetic form is used? (See questions at conclusion of discussion on each poetic form.)

EXERCISES AND ASSIGNMENTS

1. The text on "form as structure" includes a list of questions for each poetic form. Make a thorough analysis of one poem. What happens in the transformation of form from silent structural analysis to oral reading? from study to performance?

2. For additional study of form, analyze poems from the previous chapters. The following poems are of particular interest:

Chapter 2 Shelley, "Stanzas Written in Dejection, Near Naples"
Eliot, "The Hollow Men"
    "The Love Song of J. Alfred Prufrock"
Housman, "When I Was One-and-Twenty"
Anonymous, "Edward"
Plath, "Lady Lazarus"

Chapter 3 Keats, "When I Have Fears That I May Cease to Be"
Bly, "Driving to Town Late to Mail a Letter"
Levertov, "The Novices"
Thomas, "Fern Hill"
Keats, "Ode on a Grecian Urn"
Wordsworth, "Composed upon Westminister Bridge, September 3, 1802"
Lax, "Novel/"

Chapter 4 Reed, "beware: do not read this poem"
Wilkinson, "Lens"
Spark, "We Were Not Expecting the Prince To-day"
Levertov, "To the Snake"

3. Experiment with the performing possibilities of concrete poetry. What elements of transformation are difficult? simple? How does a careful study of the form of concrete poetry enhance the study of more conventional forms of poetry? Why is *discipline* of attitude in the performance of concrete poetry essential? What is the experience of *time* in concrete poetry? When is the performance of a concrete poem complete?

Objectives for Performance Growth

1 Exciting   **2** Enjoyable   **3** Adequate   **4** Need for Development

To Evoke the Metaworlds	____ a sense of inner resonance ____ a sense of attaining a state of being ____ a responsiveness to presentational values ____ IMPRESSION
To Relate the Performing Body to Literary Experience	____ behavior congruent to mode ____ language of gesture natural to literary space ____ sound of language natural to literary space ____ appropriate behavioral presses ____ appropriate use of total bodily energy ____ IMPRESSION
To Share Awareness of Literary Time	____ sense of performing time appropriate to literary time ____ literary time understood and evocated ____ silences understood and evocated ____ metrical time understood and evocated ____ IMPRESSION
To Evoke Figurative Thought and Language	____ appropriate exemplification of language ____ a sense of symbolic intent ____ a sharing of paradox and irony—where appropriate ____ IMPRESSION
To Evoke Form	____ form of experience immediate and compelling ____ form of literary structure appreciated and evocated ____ IMPRESSION
To Present Style as New Information	____ expectations in performance congruent to language ____ performer and style linked / fused ____ stylistic elements perceived and evocated ____ narrator attachment or detachment appropriate ____ IMPRESSION
To Evoke the Presence of Personae	____ interactional and / or transactional dialogue evocated ____ significant gesture of characters evocated ____ structure of dialogue evocated ____ IMPRESSION

6

Photos by Harry Callahan

TO EVOKE THE SENSE OF LITERARY STYLE

— by making the style of performance congruent to the style of literature
— by providing the information of the literature in the expectations that it develops
— by perceiving stylistic elements
  — in word symbolism
  — in sentence structurings
— in an understanding of how the units develop (paragraphs, chapters)
— by perceiving the role of the narrator
  — his attachment or detachment

CHAPTER SIX

The Perception and Evocation of Style

The sense of ease we may feel when discussing form is absent in a discussion of style. The sense of neatness and order, of perceivable limits in a discussion of the elements of poetic form, for example, vanishes when we turn to the question of a writer's style. Both the perception and evocation of style are matters of intuition, and the training of intuitive judgment is impossible. Taste is cultivated, not trained; intuition is nurtured, not learned.

The performer of literature must sooner or later confront the matter of style if he is to do no violence to the style of the writer he is transforming into the domain of sight and sound. It is not his prerogative to change the writer's style in performance; it is his obligation to assist in its transformation. Many performing arts are dedicated to the cultivation of individual performing styles, for the presence of technique without style is the mark of a second-rank artist. But the performer of music, of dance to a great extent, and of literature is an auxiliary artist, performing another man's artistry; he is a transformer of all the elements that cohere in a work of art, and he does not project his own idiosyncrasies onto it.

In this chapter all preceding discussions of literary elements come together and fuse, and while emphasis here will be largely upon style in prose, the implications extend to all types of literature. The step that the performer of literature is being asked to take is a great one and can be stated simply: *The style of the performing artist must be congruent to the style of the literature performed.* The key word is *congruent.* The implications of this idea will be the subject of this chapter.

STYLE AND EXPECTATION

To pair the words *style* and *expectation* may seem strange. A feeling of surprise is legitimate, for the concept of originality and freshness of style suggests the opposite of expectation. Yet, consider for a moment how they are linked.

Most of our concepts of style have developed out of our experiences. If a child's initial experience with poetry, for example, is in the style of the singsong, regularized rhyme and rhythm of oral nonsense verse and street games, he builds a rather logical expectation that poetry is conceived in this style, and more, that it takes certain forms: "Poetry is done in the style of the thing I have heard." Style is an environment of language, and at its least challenging, an environment of expected language. A style of total expectation is one of low information. Edmund Carpenter has called this the "numbing in the naming."

If we accept the idea that communication automatically excludes the familiar and predictable, then most so-called communication media are grossly mislabeled. Everything in *Reader's Digest* is either familiar or predictable to all its readers. That's why they subscribe. Last month's issue is identical with this month's issue. If you've seen them all, you've seen one. What you've seen is a particular format, and once having experienced it, you know it. Repeating it merely establishes it as a cliché.[1]

As readers and perceivers of literature, we often build expectations of language, believing that what is comfortable is understandable. Hence, the immense popularity of "pop" poets who speak the language of a generation: a James Whitcomb Riley, an Edgar A. Guest, a Don Blandings, a Rod McKuen. In Carpenter's words, "If you've seen them all, you've seen one."

CHANGING EXPECTATIONS

Radical stylistic changes alter the way we perceive the world, ourselves, and our language, and these changes often must wait a period of time for public acceptance. The American novelists of the nineteenth century who were widely read were not Hawthorne and Melville, just as the radical innovators in the twentieth-century novel are only gaining a sizable audience at the end of this century.

Radical stylistic changes in any medium provide new information, and this information creates new demands in reading. The student who is bewildered by this statement may study the phenomenon of multimedia presentations. Multimedia presentations obliterate the linear and sequential sense of development; they provide a

1. Edmund Carpenter, *They Became What They Beheld* (New York: Outerbridge & Dienstfrey, 1970), unpaged.

stylistic presentation of all-at-onceness everywhere. New information is thus created. And once the perceptual style is learned, once one knows how to read the environment, expectations change. There was a time when having seen one multimedia presentation you had not seen them all; consistent exposure reversed this. At this point the creative artist should change his language, his style of presentation, in order to create new informational patterns out of fresh and arresting multimedia material. Literature faces similar problems.

Great writers create new expectations in language or carry old expectations into fresh arrangements and startling relationships. Writers take the environment of language—essentially invisible to us as an environment because we use it constantly—and give it back in ways which suddenly define others or ourselves. This was the genius of Mark Twain. In *Huckleberry Finn* the soul and language of a significant sector of American nineteenth-century life is laid bare. Stylistically, the grammatical niceties are supplanted by the power of common speech. Through the eyes and language of Huck, the reality hidden behind the hypocrisies and false pieties is given high visibility. Twain's accomplishment is the deceptive ease by which expected language reveals the environment of false morality.

Leonard Meyer has observed that "the more certain we are that a particular consequence will be forthcoming, the greater the effect of uncertainty."[2] This is to say that a stylistic mode is developed in such a way that the reader's expectation of the completion of the event is generally unlike that of the artist. An example is the following statement from a lecture by E. E. Cummings at Harvard: ". . . although [my mother's] health eventually failed her, she kept her sense of humour to the beginning."[3] This short sentence illustrates well two points: (1) given the dynamics and high expectations of hearing E. E. Cummings lecture, we expect that he will use language arrestingly; (2) an anticipated cliché (keeping one's sense of humour to the *end*) is given a sudden twist that reveals new information. *Style, at its best, is*

2. Leonard Meyer, *Music, the Arts, and Ideas* (Chicago: University of Chicago Press, 1967), p. 9.
3. E. E. Cummings, *Six Non-lectures* (New York: Atheneum, 1971), p. 12.

new information, and style is, as well, an environment of language in which expectations are surprised or arrested. Any style that is utterly predictable is necessarily tedious.

STYLE AND THE MAN

CONGRUENCE OF STYLE AND WRITER

Every man affects a style in spoken language. We may forget that the oral style we have all learned in our families, our neighborhoods, our country, is man-made, but we seldom forget that it is man-controlled. The controls are exerted by those who surround us, by those groups to which we aspire, or by those individuals we admire. We have recently become extremely sensitive to white style and black style of spoken language. Blacks, concerned that primers in no way represented the lives or language of black children, argued that the expectations set up in the readers were white, middle-class, and ultimately irrelevant for black children, turning them away from reading. Their authentic sense of self, some argued, can and should be reflected by the language style familiar to them. Readers have been developed that do represent this sense that blacks have of themselves. A black style has evolved at all levels of writing that has resulted in a new black literature.

All serious writers search for this same kind of authenticity of style, the encapsulation of language that most reflects who they are and how they want to be perceived. The writer uses language in his own special way to create a reality communicated to us. The base of style is spoken language because it is "the completest form of communication, and every other form is embodied in it to a greater or less degree."[4] Indeed, so true is this statement that we dismiss any piece of literature in which we feel that the thoughts and speeches of the characters are not possible. A writer who seizes a language, making it work within the literature, makes it identifiable with himself.

The identity between a style and a writer becomes most visible in *parody.* The intent of the original author is lost in a parody, and all that is visible, all that remains is the carapace, the shell into which the experience was cast. The value of a parody is that it forces the parodist to master the style of the original writer, the flow, rhythm, beat, and construct of his language. Parodies can isolate for study the elements in a writer's style, and they can point out stylistic weaknesses. Often writers use parody as a way of satirizing, of stating indirectly their exasperation at stylistic excesses and aberrations.

4. J. L. Aranguren, *Human Communication,* trans. Frances Partridge (London: World Universal Library, 1967), p. 88.

Tension in style.   A *tension* always exists between a language shared by all and an individual's personal style of speech that is unique to him. It is this tension between the shared language and a personal style of language that a writer shapes into his work. Readers and interpreters often struggle with this tension when writers extend that mutually shared language into new domains of expression. James Joyce was incomprehensible to those with nineteenth-century expectations of what language should do. Great writers almost always extend language by carrying it into new possibilities of information, of symbolization, of impact. The inseparable link between a writer and his style is well expressed in Buffon's statement, "The style is the man himself."

CONGRUENCE OF STYLE AND PERIOD

A student of literature can, without too much difficulty, identify a style within a given century. He can do this because, as Aranguren points out, "It is very easy to tell what generation a person belongs to . . . before we have seen him or know his age, simply by the way he talks, the words he uses, the construction of his sentences, the slowness, periphrases, circumvolutions, padding or rapidity ('directness') with which he expresses himself."[5] It is not unusual, nor should it be, for a reading audience to enjoy its contemporary stylists, for they are articulating what it means to see, to feel, to be in their own time and place. Curiously, though, much literature produced during an age drops from sight and is forgotten, even though it might speak in its own generation with insistency and bravura.

What makes for lastingness? What contributes to a writer's continued popularity or to a sudden discovery of a forgotten writer? The answer is related to the nature of communication itself: *that which endures is a consistent source of information*, regardless of the "age" of the style. Has any century found Shakespeare exhaustible? or Dostoevski? or Melville? There may be those few students of literature for whom style and its study are enough and are satisfying. However, writers, in attempting to establish their own voice, use style as a means, not an end; and most students do not pursue the study of style alone, but rather seek the personal voice in a style *subordinated* to continual unfolding of information.

The difficulty in discussing anything so evanescent as style is well put in George Kubler's statement that "Style is like a rainbow. It is a phenomenon of perception governed by the coincidence of certain physical conditions. We can see it only briefly while we pause between the sun and rain, and it vanishes when we go to the place where we thought we saw it."[6]

5. Ibid., p. 98.
6. George A. Kubler, *The Shape of Time* (New Haven: Yale University Press, 1962), p. 129.

STYLE AND IDENTIFIABLE ELEMENTS

There may be problems in asking that a student pause "between the sun and rain" to examine identifiable elements in style. Yet, the performer of literature must understand stylistic elements if he is to realize fully what the literature can become in performance. While the emphasis in this chapter is upon prose, the discussion applies to verse as well.

Scholars disagree over how to study or analyze stylistic elements. While some argue for a quantitative approach, analyzing vocabulary usage, sentence structure, paragraphing, and the like, others denounce such approaches, arguing that style is essentially intuitive in a writer and intuitive in its perception, and that you either see it, sense it, feel it, or you do not. For the performer's purposes, perhaps both extremes can be avoided. The performer can benefit from an examination of technique, of the way a writer has put together his piece, and at the same time can recognize that an individual writer's genius makes the whole greater than the sum of the parts. The intent of this particular section is to generalize about what is present in prose, and how these presences inform the style of the writer. What a reader encounters are (1) words, (2) sentences, and (3) flowing units, all three of these united with (4) a narrator.

WORDS

It is easy to forget the primacy of the *word*. Words are not merely names of things. A single word is an extension of human perception. A single word organizes the way we think and feel about a thing, and it is akin to a note of music in that a word sets or fails to set the right tone. So keen is human perception in isolating out of a jumble of words a single responsive note that a single word in a sentence can obliterate the sense of the sentence. The eye, quickly scanning pages of words, picks out certain words that fairly leap from the page into consciousness, so sensitive and persuasive is the presence of these key words in us. Similarly, a reader can fail to read a word.

We see mostly what we have learned to look at. We look at what we think we *need* to look at. We ignore what seems unnecessary or, in some cases, what seems threatening. However, we are *sensitive* to far more stimuli than we may realize. . . . [An] experiment testing one's ability to recognize words flashed on the screen for a very short time indicated that individuals characteristically "see" words that are consistent with their personal values and misread words that are irrelevant or opposed to their value systems. For example, one subject who had ranked low in the "aesthetic" area of a standard value test misread the word *elegant* as *hypocrisy*.[7]

7. John C. Condon, *Semantics and Communication* (New York: Macmillan Co., 1966), p. 16.

Not only do the words one perceives shape the quality of his perception, the words one uses establish the manner in which one thinks.

The Greek word *logos* unites the essences of the term *word*. *Logos* may be defined as "word" or "idea" or "speech," and the writer strives to unite these three elements of *logos* in the most singular way he can, to share the unique nature of his observations.

A word has the power to evoke a world of its own. It is impossible to use the commonest words without the perceiver informing them with his own ideas of what they are and look like. Take, for example, the following short list: table, chair, lamp, telephone. Imagine how each of these "looks." What kind of table, chair, lamp, and telephone do you conceive? Now read the following sentence, "He went to the table, sat down on the chair, turned on the lamp, and looked at the telephone." How would the "world" of this sentence vary if you knew the scene of the sentence was England? Russia? India? Japan? a bedroom on the eastside of New York? In each case only the sense of the event is the same; the world of the event is considerably different.

Literature creates a specific world from specific "namings." There have been many rafts; the raft in *Huckleberry Finn* is a specific world. The reader learns to know it perhaps even to the extent that in the context of Twain's novel the word *raft* transcends its literal meaning and becomes for the reader a *symbol:* an idea-word-utterance of incredible power. Wolfgang Köehler uses the word *sponge* to describe this process:

Concepts and words are in one respect similar to sponges. If for generations an object has been highly valued, the corresponding concept and even its verbal symbol will eventually be thoroughly impregnated with dignity—precisely as a sponge absorbs a liquid by which it is surrounded. In a case of aversion both the concept and its name will soon be charged with negative qualities. While it is not easy to dry a wet sponge entirely and quickly, it sometimes seems almost impossible to remove from a concept those value-qualities which it has once absorbed.[8]

It is the reader's responsibility, and no less the interpreter's, to enter the world of the literature on the writer's own terms, to sense those terms, to try to understand them, and, in performance, to evoke them. Precise words in a precise order is what every reader and interpreter must accept; he may take no liberties with what is written. A precise word does three things: (1) it sets up a sound, (2) it condenses perception, and (3) it symbolizes experience.

---

8. Wolfgang Köehler, *The Place of Value in a World of Facts* (New York: Liveright Publishing Corp., 1938), p. 186.

Roy Lichtenstein: "Varoom"

Sound in verbal style. It is difficult to separate the sound of words from personal associations with the sound. F. L. Lucas recounts a story of a group of aestheticians debating what was the most beautiful word in the English language: "[They] had almost decided on 'swallow,' when some ill-intentioned person asked 'Bird or gulp?' After that, no more was heard of 'swallow.' "[9] Sound has a perceptual bias: which of the two meanings did you hear? Lucas argues that sound should be thought of as a conductor. "Think of the meanings (*and* associations) of a group of words as an electric current; of their sounds as the conductor."[10] A writer sounds in a particular way, and the words affect us in a particular way. Our responses to sounds in language are the results of our conditionings. When an actor or interpreter states that he cannot utter a particular word, his feelings usually stem from one of two conditions: (1) he feels that the sound is wrong and inappropriate, and/or (2) he feels that it is wrong and inappropriate for him to utter it. The unnaturalness with which some students handle expletives in their interpretations attests to this.

9. F. L. Lucas, *Style* (London: Cassell and Co., 1955), p. 249.
10. Ibid., p. 250.

Another aspect of sound that is rooted in language has been called "sound symbolism."

It is an empirical fact, felt by many speakers, that some sound patterns of their native language truly describe and represent meaning. For the English speaker, verbs such as *clash, tap, trap, crack, split, bang, hit, hitch, dump, boom, stop*, or words like *pin-prick* are felt to have some descriptive value; while to a German speaker the word *spitz*, "pointed," or *Blitz*, "lightning," are felt to be descriptive of an atmospheric explosion—more so than equivalent English terms. There is no denying that such empirical facts can be observed in all vocabularies of all languages.[11]

This idea of sound symbolism extends to the source of language: the human voice. The voice shapes the world of experience, not only in the manner in which it names an event, "that crack over there," but in the manner in which it speaks the style of the man. For example, think for a moment of a person named Percival Eggleston Wormsworth III. Meeting him in literature, one might conjecture what he would sound like, so effortless is it to link a name to sound. Or take the name Sam Spud. One would hardly anticipate that he would sound like the imagined Percival Eggleston Wormsworth III. Writers are very careful in naming their characters. An attempt is often made to give a sound symbolism to their names. This is what we mean by a writer's linking sound and sense.

Because the performance of literature exists in sound, the attention given to *sound as style* is crucial. Why? For the important reason that sound strikes below the level of consciousness, evoking responses that cannot be controlled or predicted. The sounds of sounds set up associations in the perceiver. Often, the association is a rhyming word, and the associated word creates tensions because it is in direct opposition to the word heard. For example, *womb* and *tomb* inevitably attract one another, for birth and death are the points of beginning and ending in life. Words are not merely presented in isolation; they are in a continual state of association. That the human continually integrates sound sensations is one of the most subtle and compelling aspects of the impact of style.

Condensation of experience.   A single word condenses experience, and its repetition reinforces the "force" of the word. Our language requires that entities be named one after the other sequentially so that what we experience in language, and prose particularly, is the sense of things in succession.

11. Theodore Thass-Thienemann, *Symbolic Behavior* (New York: Washington Square Press, 1968), pp. 335–336.

This linear, successive order which characterizes language is known as discursiveness. It limits our speech and writing to only those thoughts which can be disposed in this peculiar order. All other thoughts, ideas, and especially feelings which do not lend themselves to this order must be called in fact ineffable; they are largely incommunicable by means of words alone.[12]

Note how the repetition of a single word in the following opening passage of Charles Dickens' *Bleak House* illustrates this principle. One word emerges to condense the experience in a series of linear, successive sentences. Note, too, not only the effect of sound symbolism but the recurrent presence of particular vowel sounds. And note, finally, the effect of this discursive passage: the force of condensation, the power of a single word to symbolize the place and the scene of impending action.

London. Michelmas Term lately over, and the Lord Chancellor sitting in Lincoln's Inn Hall. Implacable November weather. As much mud in the streets, as if the waters had but newly retired from the face of the earth, and it would not be wonderful to meet a Megalosaurus, forty feet long or so, waddling like an elephantine lizard up Holborn Hill. Smoke lowering down from chimney-pots, making a soft black drizzle, with flakes of soot in it as big as full-grown snow-flakes—gone into mourning, one might imagine, for the death of the sun. Dogs, undistinguishable in mire. Horses, scarcely better; splashed to their very blinkers. Foot passengers, jostling one another's umbrellas, in a general infection of ill-temper, and losing their foothold at street-corners, where tens of thousands of other foot passengers have been slipping and sliding since the day broke (if the day ever broke), adding new deposits to the crust upon crust of mud, sticking those points tenaciously to the pavement, and accumulating at compound interest.

Fog everywhere. Fog up the river, where it flows among green aits and meadows; fog down the river, where it rolls defiled among the tiers of shipping, and the waterside pollutions of a great (and dirty) city. Fog on the Essex marshes, fog on the Kentish heights. Fog creeping into the cabooses of collier-brigs; fog lying out in the yards, and hovering in the rigging of great ships; fog drooping on the gunwales of barges and small boats. Fog in the eyes and throats of ancient Greenwich pensioners, wheezing by the firesides of their wards; fog in the stem and bowl of the afternoon pipe of the wrathful skipper, down in close cabin; fog cruelly pinching the toes and fingers of his shivering little 'prentice boy on the deck. Chance people on the bridges peeping over the parapets into a nether sky of fog, with fog all around them, as if they were up in a balloon, and hanging in the misty clouds.

Gas looming through the fog in divers places in the streets, much as the sun may, from the spongey fields, be seen to loom by husbandman and ploughboy. Most of the shops lighted two hours before their time—as the gas seems to know, for it has a haggard and unwilling look.

The raw afternoon is rawest, and the dense fog is densest, and the muddy streets are muddiest, near the leaden-headed old obstruction, appropriate ornament for the threshold of

12. Donald L. Weismann, *Language and Visual Form* (Austin: University of Texas Press, 1968), p. 42.

a leaden-headed old corporation: Temple Bar. And hard by Temple Bar, in Lincoln's Inn Hall, at the very heart of the fog, sits the Lord High Chancellor in his High Court of Chancery.

Never can there come fog too thick, never can there come mud and mire too deep, to assort with the groping and floundering condition which this High Court of Chancery, most pestilent of hoary sinners, holds, this day, in the sight of heaven and earth.

At what points in this passage do words create their impact by sound? What words reinforce the impact of the style by sound symbolism? And how does the word *fog* condense, truncate, foreshorten the impact of the scene?

Word symbolism.   The impact of word symbolism is illustrated in the passage from Dickens. The word *fog* will become something of the prevailing symbol of the book: the fog which surrounds justice and the understanding as well as administration of it. Symbolism affects us first through the associations buried in our consciousness. When we think about a word, the associations rise effortlessly from the values we have given to it. In literature symbols are richly evocative, summoning forth an active participation in the literature. The simplest words have become the most easily evoked symbols of association: a tree, a snake, an egg, a gate, a beast, the light, the water, the dust. Curiously, we often give little conscious value to these words due to their commonness and their overuse. Because of overuse they simply are not heard meaningfully.

In considering style the performer of literature must be aware that ". . . no word which has a meaning for a speaker or hearer is ever entirely isolated; its utterance arouses associations which are wholly personal, and if analyzed, may appear to be entirely irrational."[13] The interpreter knows this of himself, and he knows it of his auditors. But he knows at the same time ". . . for most writers words qua words are objects of love. Good writers are sensitive to the slightest gradations of meaning among words, to their emotional connotations, they way they accommodate themselves to their neighbors, even to the nuances of sound."[14] Thus, his attention to single words springs from his interest in a word's sound and sound symbolism and its condensation of meaning which leads to its potential symbolic value.

SENTENCES

A sentence is a happening or process, and for that reason one cannot hold out for a strict definition of it. From a purist's point of view, a sentence expresses a complete thought; it is conveniently structured with a subject and verb sustained and shaped by surrounding modifiers. From a realistic point of view, a sentence can also be a frag-

13. H. J. Chaytor, *From Script to Print* (New York: October House, 1967), p. 76.
14. Simon O. Lesser, *Fiction and the Unconscious* (New York: Vintage Books, 1962), p. 163.

ment of a thought, an incomplete utterance without a verb. Writers shape their own sense of a sentence, their sentience of what a sentence is. For these reasons a sentence might best be defined as an *informational patterning*. A writer may develop any informational patterning he wishes, and it is the cumulative effect of these patternings that defines his stylistic thrust.

Most who read literature in English have built into their perceptual processes some anticipations of what a sentence does. At its simplest a sentence is a group of words; it is a group of words in a particular order. This last sentence would not convey its sense if its words were arranged as follows:

Simplest group its it is particular at a sentence a is a group of order in words of a words.

This arrangement provides an English reader with practically no sense of experience. While there have been writers who have attempted to arrest readers' attention by non-order, most writers still work within the notion of a unit of predictable informational patterning.

Patterning. What are the predictabilities of patternings? In English there are basically three: (1) Given a subject of a sentence, we predict a verb that may be action (*Father Brown preached.*) (2) Given an action verb, we may predict an object (*Father Brown preached a sermon.*) (3) Given a subject, the verb may refer back to the subject descriptively with either an adjective or noun (*Father Brown is exhausted* or *Father Brown is a buffoon.*) What these sample sentences possess in clarity, they lack in style, with the possible exception of the last one. They are simple, too simple to maintain reader interest for any length of time. Yet the point to understand in the patternings of the basic English sentences is that each does something quite specific, regardless of its simplicity or complexity. The first keeps a subject in action; the second tells us what a subject does to something or someone; the third clarifies, expands, or describes the subject.

Note carefully how Jean Toomer uses the simplicity of these patternings in the following paragraph from his novel *Cane.*

Carma, in overalls, and strong as any man, stands behind the brown mule, driving the wagon home. It bumps, and groans, and shakes as it crosses the railroad track. She, riding it easy. I leave the men around the stove to follow her with my eyes down the red dust road. Nigger woman driving a Georgia chariot down an old dust road. Dixie Pike is what they call it. Maybe she feels my gaze, perhaps she expects it. Anyways, she turns. The sun, which has been slanting over her shoulder, shoots primitive rockets into her mangrove-gloomed, yellow flower face. Hi! Yip! God has left the Moses-people for the nigger. "Gedap." Using reins to slap the mule, she disappears in a cloudy rumble at some indefinite point along the road.[15]

15. Selection from "Carma" from *Cane* by Jean Toomer. Permission of Liveright, Publishers, N.Y. Copyright renewal 1951 by Jean Toomer. (Available in Perennial Classic Edition, Harper & Row, Publishers, 1969)

In this paragraph the being of Carma is stated simply and directly through a series of simple subjects and verbs: "Carma stands . . . feels gaze . . . expects it . . . turns . . . disappears. . . ." One senses an enigmatic quality about her through the simplicity of the patternings. The patternings establish the essential action of the prose, its sense of direction or reflection. When the performer can perceive how sentence patternings are operating and what the sentences are establishing, he is at the threshold of understanding how a writer's style is functioning. However, the patternings are not so much the style, per se, as they are indices of movement. A writer's style is indicated by the movement the sentence takes through its modifications and isolation of units. We know that if we are to speak in the "style of English," these basic patterns will be used.

Structure. A sentence is a structure as well as a patterning. While a pattern may establish movement, as in the movement from a subject to its verb and perhaps on to its object, a sentence structure is like the edifice in which these basic predictabilities and non-predictabilities live and breathe. Thus, a subject and its verb of a particular patterning exist within a structure that determines their effect.

The possibilities for sentence structure include:

1. *a simple sentence;*
2. *an elliptical sentence,* one that has an implied subject that can only be understood contextually;
3. *an idiomatic sentence,* sometimes called a phatic sentence, one that is filled with the personal and emotional language of the writer and speaker, and one that is idiomatic to the extent that the alteration of a single word creates a meaningless sentence;
4. *a complex or compound or compound-complex sentence;*
5. *an ungrammatical sentence.*

The way a writer structures his sentences is fundamental to his style. The power of the paragraph from Jean Toomer's *Cane* lies principally in its use of simple sentences, though important variations exist. Anthony Burgess' novel *A Clockwork Orange* is stylistically built around the notion of the idiomatic, or phatic, sense of communication. The following sentence from it demonstrates how idiomatic communication cannot be divorced from its context: "The chelloveck sitting next to me, there being this long plushy seat that ran around three walls, was well away with his glazzies glazed and sort of surbling solvos like 'Aristotle wishy washy works outing cyclamen get forficulate smartish.' "[16] The American-born Henry Janes cultivated a structural style that, among its many other qualities, exemplifies the compound-complex

16. Anthony Burgess, *A Clockwork Orange* (New York: W. W. Norton & Co., 1963); the above quoted from the paperback edition (New York: Ballantine Books, 1965), p. 11.

structure. The sentence below from the opening paragraphs of *The Ambassadors* is a typical example of his architectural constructions in language.

There were people on the ship with whom he had easily consorted—so far as ease could up to now be imputed to him—and who for the most part plunged straight into the current that set from the landing-stage to London; there were others who had invited him to a tryst at the inn and had even invoked his aid for a "look around" at the beauties of Liverpool; but he had stolen away from every one alike, had kept no appointment and renewed no acquaintance, had been indifferently aware of the number of persons who esteemed themselves fortunate in being, unlike himself, "met," and had even independently, unsociably, alone, without encounter or relapse and by mere quiet evasion, given his afternoon and evening to the immediate and the sensible.[17]

An ungrammatical sentence is not necessarily nonsense, though nonsense is often ungrammatical. In the Jean Toomer excerpt, two incomplete sentences are used effectively: "She, riding it easy" and "Nigger woman driving a Georgia chariot down an old dust road." The ungrammatical conveys feeling, intensity, and the essence of personality. The ungrammatical is the language of a people, the unconscious utterance of one's life. John Steptoe, a contemporary who writes of the children of the city and the ghetto, reaches his young readers because of his sensitivity to their ungrammatical "life in language."

We was in the park the other day. If you want to play some ball, you have to come early cause all the big guys, when they come, they chase all us little dudes off the court. Sometimes we be watchin' the old cats play, then after they get tired, they sit around and drink Colt 45 and they rap.[18]

A careful examination of the Henry James and John Steptoe excerpts will yield a surprising fact: they are both rooted in the oral tradition. For all of its intricacy of structure, the sentence of James has its orality; in the same sense the simple Steptoe sentences acquire their force by their congruence to the oral style of the boy speaking them. In the beginning pages of this chapter, we noted that in the oral performance of literature the style of the performer must be congruent to the style of the literature itself. Good writers seek this congruence, for they create the sense of the speaking narrator within the imagination of the silent reader, or in the case of performance, within the perceptions of the auditor. Style has a particular intention about it. As Merleau-Ponty observed, "For the speaking subject, to express is

17. Henry James. *The Ambassadors* (New York: W. W. Norton & Co., 1964), p. 18.
18. John Steptoe, *Uptown* (New York: Harper & Row, Publishers, 1970), unpaged.

to become aware of; he does not express just for others, but also to know himself what he intends."[19] Whatever the structure, the writer chose it as the best way of achieving his intent. The performer of literature can accept only what he finds in literature.

Thus far, style has been identified as an environment of language, as new information. We gain a sense of a writer's style through our awarenesses of predictable and non-predictable information, of the sound symbolism and power of words, of the patternings and structurings of the sentences. As our attention shifts from words to sentence patterns to paragraph structures, the obvious thing to note is that art in language is built upon simple (Jean Toomer's *Cane*) and complex (Henry James' *The Ambassadors*) systems of arrangement. Writers also create ingeniously their own sense of voice that is a personal amalgam of simple and complex systems (the novels of Charles Dickens). In the art of language, imitation is not the highest form of flattery. Each writer searches for his own voice, his own sense of how language speaks from him and from the world he creates.

In studying style and learning how to transform style into a performance, the performer becomes aware of its hierarchic nature. That is, he recognizes that style has elements that move from least to most complexity and impact. In the following list is a hierarchy:

> words
> phrases
> clauses
> sentences
> paragraphs
> chapters
> book-story

The book is held in memory as a total experience, a particular chapter stands out, a moment in the chapter is the most compelling in memory, a particular sentence is the crucial point of impact, and the memory of a word lingers. But similarly, given the single word, the whole process is reversed in memory. An excellent example of this phenomenon is the "story" that many people remember of the film *Citizen Kane*. The film develops in hierarchical order from a last word uttered by Kane on his deathbed, "Rosebud." To anyone who has seen the film, fragments of the film return, memory being controlled by the style of the photographic image, until the film is more or less contained by the memory process. All from a single word.

Prose fiction has only its separate units; a writer permits these units to cohere in such a way that from the smallest unit (the word) to the largest unit (the book), there is a sense of flow.

19. Maurice Merleau-Ponty, *Signs,* trans. Richard McCleary (Evanston, Ill.: Northwestern University Press, 1964), p. 90.

NARRATOR

All prose has a speaking voice, a controlling intelligence, a being who, through *his* language and *his* perception, is our guide—the seeing, hearing, touching, aware or unaware, involved or uninvolved, participating or non-participating, teller of the tale. The power of the narrator comes from his sense of what he knows and how he controls it. He is, ultimately, at the top of the hierarchic list. That list, reversed for purposes of emphasis, now appears as follows:

narrator	(the someone who knows)
story	(the "thing" the narrator knows)
units	(the "chapters" that his choice will dictate)
sentences words	(the system of predictables and non-predictables)

The narrator in literature (and we are speaking of the voice or intelligence within the literature, not the performing narrator) is a very complex subject.[20] As the intelligence controlling the unfolding of the event-in-language, the narrator may appear as: (1) *an all-knowing intelligence* that can shift from a physical "outside" world of phenomena to the physical "inner" world of sensation and feeling in people; (2) *an observing intelligence* that reports only what is perceived around him, limiting his powers of observation to the things he perceives, suggesting that he is concerned with a "them" that his camera eye and receiving ear capture in language; (3) *a character in the story,* a person in the event-in-language, one for whom memory is serving as a basis for recall. It is not enough to observe that a given story is written in either the first person or the third person (*I* am telling versus the detached sense of a *him,* a *her,* a *them,* or, even, an *it!*) To sense the closeness of the narrator to the story, his attachment or detachment is of equal importance.

Attachment / Detachment. Attachment or detachment is a matter of personal style, and every narrator has a style of his own. In literature the style may range from the emotional, intensely subjective to nearly total detachment. There is in the latter a devaluing of the personal and a valuing of the objective.[21] Especially interesting is the narrator who knows totally, or nearly totally, what is happening inside and outside the characters. Here his detachment or attachment is important. At one extreme is what may be called a "clinical sense," a profound understanding of human motivation and feeling. At the other extreme may be a strong necessity of perceiving the world in a particular way, a "personalist sense" in which subjectivity is all-important. Thus, in

20. Interested students will benefit from Wayne C. Booth's *The Rhetoric of Fiction* (Chicago: University of Chicago Press, 1961), particularly Chapter 6.

21. Compare the discussion of modes in Chapter 2 (the lyric mode, the epic mode, and the dramatic mode) with the problem of the narrator discussed here. The style of the narrator is obviously keyed to the mode in which he is experienced.

Ken Heyman

perceiving the narrator and his position, we can expand upon the earlier hierarchy.[22]

    narrator   (the someone who knows)
- all-knowing
- observing
- a character himself
- detached / attached
- interested / disinterested

    story   (the "thing" the narrator knows)
- detached / attached to the narrator
- narrator's style
- the style of others
- a combination

    units   (the "chapters" of his choice)
- carefully sequential, plotted
- random, non-sequential
- chronological / non-chronological

    sentences
    words   (the systems of predictables and non-predictables)
- attached to narrator
- detached from narrator
- rhythmic
- structures (simple, elliptical, etc.)
- patterned (subject / verb, subject / verb / object, etc.)
- familiar / non-familiar
- symbolic
- acoustically symbolic

    In the performance of literature, orality and behavior transform style. The performer through his sensitivity distinguishes the essential from the secondary aspects of the literary style, sorting and identifying those stylistic elements in terms of their priorities. What emerges is a co-expression of styles, a performance of literature that is

22. Compare now the narrator and his style with the presses that a writer may employ as discussed in Chapter 2 (expression, impression, etc.) The performer of literature should relate the artistic vision to the style in which it is encapsulated.

dependent upon two styles, two sensibilities — the narrator's and the performer's. In their coalescence we hope for a fresh kind of language, " . . . — demanding an interplay between words and image, and between word-image combination and the . . . viewer . . ."[23] The foundation of this co-expression remains *the word*, its sounding symbolic strategies in whatever patterning or structuring it is shaped, sounded by the voice of a narrator. And it is the performer who ultimately informs the vague shadows and changing features of the word with what Ted Hughes, the British poet, has called the unfathomable meaning of experience.

Words are tools, learned late and laboriously and easily forgotten, with which we try to give some part of our experience a more or less permanent shape outside ourselves. They are unnatural, in a way, and far from being ideal for their job. For one thing, a word has its own definite meanings. A word is its own little solar system of meanings. Yet we are wanting it to carry some part of our meaning, of the meaning of our experience, and the meaning of our experience is finally unfathomable, it reaches into our toes and back to before we were born and into the atom, with vague shadows and changing features, and elements that no expression of any kind can take hold of. And this is true of the simplest experiences.[24]

What is a strong sense of style? Merleau-Ponty has suggested that it involves a "warping" of the entire language system, what he calls "a new and very personal ordering of the words, forms, and elements of the narrative . . . style has the power to draw me out of my thoughts . . . to cut fissures in my private universe."[25] It is this cutting of fissures that allows literature to astound. The performance of literature should do no less.

23. Pierre Babin, *The Audio-Visual Man* (Dayton: Pflaum Publishers, 1970), p. 29.
24. Ted Hughes. *Poetry Is* (New York: Doubleday & Co., 1970), p. 2.
25. Merleau-Ponty, *Signs*, p. 235.

The Kool-Aid Wino[26]

Richard Brautigan

When I was a child I had a friend who became a Kool-Aid wino as the result of a rupture. He was a member of a very large and poor German family. All the older children in the family had to work in the fields during the summer, picking beans for two-and-one-half cents a pound to keep the family going. Everyone worked except my friend who couldn't because he was ruptured. There was no money for an operation. There wasn't even enough money to buy him a truss. So he stayed home and became a Kool-Aid wino.

One morning in August I went over to his house. He was still in bed. He looked up at me from underneath a tattered revolution of old blankets. He had never slept under a sheet in his life.

"Did you bring the nickel you promised?" he asked.

"Yeah," I said. "It's here in my pocket."

"Good."

He hopped out of bed and he was already dressed. He had told me once that he never took off his clothes when he went to bed.

"Why bother?" he had said. "You're only going to get up, anyway. Be prepared for it. You're not fooling anyone by taking your clothes off when you go to bed."

He went into the kitchen, stepping around the littlest children, whose wet diapers were in various stages of anarchy. He made his breakfast: a slice of homemade bread covered with Karo syrup and peanut butter.

"Let's go," he said.

We left the house with him still eating the sandwich. The store was three blocks away, on the other side of a field covered with heavy yellow grass. There were many pheasants in the field. Fat with summer they barely flew away when we came up to them.

"Hello," said the grocer. He was bald with a red birthmark on his head. The birthmark looked just like an old car parked on his head. He automatically reached for a package of grape Kool-Aid and put it on the counter.

"Five cents."

"He's got it," my friend said.

I reached into my pocket and gave the nickel to the grocer. He nodded and the old red car wobbled back and forth on the road as if the driver were having an epileptic seizure.

---

26. "The Kool-Aid Wino" from *Trout Fishing in America* by Richard Brautigan. Copyright © 1967 by Richard Brautigan. A Seymour Lawrence Book/Delacorte Press. Reprinted by permission of the publisher.

We left.

My friend led the way across the field. One of the pheasants didn't even bother to fly. He ran across the field in front of us like a feathered pig.

When we got back to my friend's house the ceremony began. To him the making of Kool-Aid was a romance and a ceremony. It had to be performed in an exact manner and with dignity.

First he got a gallon jar and we went around to the side of the house where the water spigot thrust itself out of the ground like the finger of a saint, surrounded by a mud puddle.

He opened the Kool-Aid and dumped it into the jar. Putting the jar under the spigot, he turned the water on. The water spit, splashed and guzzled out of the spigot.

He was careful to see that the jar did not overflow and the precious Kool-Aid spill out onto the ground. When the jar was full he turned the water off with a sudden but delicate motion like a famous brain surgeon removing a disordered portion of the imagination. Then he screwed the lid tightly onto the top of the jar and gave it a good shake.

The first part of the ceremony was over.

Like the inspired priest of an exotic cult, he had performed the first part of the ceremony well.

His mother came around the side of the house and said in a voice filled with sand and string, "When are you going to do the dishes? . . . Huh?"

"Soon," he said.

"Well, you better," she said.

When she left, it was as if she had never been there at all. The second part of the ceremony began with him carrying the jar very carefully to an abandoned chicken house in the back. "The dishes can wait," he said to me. Bertrand Russell could not have stated it better.

He opened the chicken house door and we went in. The place was littered with half-rotten comic books. They were like fruit under a tree. In the corner was an old mattress and beside the mattress were four quart jars. He took the gallon jar over to them, and filled them carefully not spilling a drop. He screwed their caps on tightly and was now ready for a day's drinking.

You're supposed to make only two quarts of Kool-Aid from a package, but he always made a gallon, so his Kool-Aid was a mere shadow of its desired potency. And you're supposed to add a cup of sugar to every package of Kool-Aid, but he never put any sugar in his Kool-Aid because there wasn't any sugar to put in it.

He created his own Kool-Aid reality and was able to illuminate himself by it.

from **To Kill a Mockingbird**[27]

Harper Lee

Thomas Robinson reached around, ran his fingers under his left arm and lifted it. He guided his arm to the Bible and his rubber-like left hand sought contact with the black binding. As he raised his right hand, the useless one slipped off the Bible and hit the clerk's table. He was trying again when Judge Taylor growled, "That'll do, Tom." Tom took the oath and stepped into the witness chair. Atticus very quickly induced him to tell us:

Tom was twenty-five years of age; he was married with three children; he had been in trouble with the law before: he once received thirty days for disorderly conduct.

"It must have been disorderly," said Atticus. "What did it consist of?"

"Got in a fight with another man, he tried to cut me."

"Did he succeed?"

"Yes suh, a little, not enough to hurt. You see, I—" Tom moved his left shoulder.

"Yes," said Atticus. "You were both convicted?"

"Yes suh, I had to serve 'cause I couldn't pay the fine. Other fellow paid his'n."

Dill leaned across me and asked Jem what Atticus was doing. Jem said Atticus was showing the jury that Tom had nothing to hide.

"Were you acquainted with Mayella Violet Ewell?" asked Atticus.

"Yes suh, I had to pass her place goin' to and from the field every day."

"Whose field?"

"I picks for Mr. Link Deas."

"Were you picking cotton in November?"

"No suh, I works in his yard fall an' wintertime. I works pretty steady for him all year round, he's got a lot of pecan trees'n things."

"You say you had to pass the Ewell place to get to and from work. Is there any other way to go?"

"No suh, none's I know of."

"Tom, did she ever speak to you?"

"Why, yes suh, I'd tip m'hat when I'd go by, and one day she asked me to come inside the fence and bust up a chiffarobe for her."

"When did she ask you to chop up the—the chiffarobe?"

"Mr. Finch, it was way last spring. I remember it because it was choppin' time and I had my hoe with me. I said I didn't have nothin' but this hoe, but she said she

27. From the book *To Kill a Mockingbird* by Harper Lee. Copyright, © 1960, by Harper Lee. Reprinted by permission of J. B. Lippincott Company.

had a hatchet. She give me the hatchet and I broke up the chiffarobe. She said, 'I reckon I'll hafta give you a nickel, won't I?' an' I said, 'No ma'am, there ain't no charge.' Then I went home. Mr. Finch, that was way last spring, way over a year ago."

"Did you ever go on the place again?"

"Yes suh."

"When?"

"Well, I went lots of times."

Judge Taylor instinctively reached for his gavel, but let his hand fall. The murmur below us died without his help.

"Under what circumstances?"

"Please, suh?"

"Why did you go inside the fence lots of times?"

Tom Robinson's forehead relaxed. "She'd call me in, suh. Seemed like every time I passed by yonder she'd have some little somethin' for me to do—choppin' kindlin', totin' water for her. She watered them red flowers every day—"

"Were you paid for your services?"

"No suh, not after she offered me a nickel the first time. I was glad to do it, Mr. Ewell didn't seem to help her none, and neither did the chillun, and I knowed she didn't have no nickels to spare."

"Where were the other children?"

"They was always around, all over the place. They'd watch me work, some of 'em, some of 'em'd set in the window."

"Would Miss Mayella talk to you?"

"Yes sir, she talked to me."

As Tom Robinson gave his testimony, it came to me that Mayella Ewell must have been the loneliest person in the world. She was even lonelier than Boo Radley, who had not been out of the house in twenty-five years. When Atticus asked had she any friends, she seemed not to know what he meant, then she thought he was making fun of her. She was as sad, I thought, as what Jem called a mixed child: white people wouldn't have anything to do with her because she lived among pigs; Negroes wouldn't have anything to do with her because she was white. She couldn't live like Mr. Dolphus Raymond, who preferred the company of Negroes, because she didn't own a riverbank and she wasn't from a fine old family. Nobody said, "That's just their way," about the Ewells. Maycomb gave them Christmas baskets, welfare money, and the back of its hand. Tom Robinson was probably the only person who was ever decent to her. But she said he took advantage of her, and when she stood up she looked at him as if he were dirt beneath her feet.

"Did you ever," Atticus interrupted my meditations, "at any time, go on the Ewell property—did you ever set foot on the Ewell property without an express invitation from one of them?"

"No suh, Mr. Finch, I never did. I wouldn't do that, suh."

Atticus sometimes said that one way to tell whether a witness was lying or telling the truth was to listen rather than watch: I applied his test—Tom denied it three times in one breath, but quietly, with no hint of whining in his voice, and I found myself believing him in spite of his protesting too much. He seemed to be a respectable Negro, and a respectable Negro would never go up into somebody's yard of his own volition.

"Tom, what happened to you on the evening of November twenty-first of last year?"

Below us, the spectators drew a collective breath and leaned forward. Behind us, the Negroes did the same.

Tom was a black-velvet Negro, not shiny, but soft black velvet. The whites of his eyes shone in his face, and when he spoke we saw flashes of his teeth. If he had been whole, he would have been a fine specimen of a man.

"Mr. Finch," he said, "I was goin' home as usual that evenin', an' when I passed the Ewell place Miss Mayella were on the porch, like she said she were. It seemed real quiet like, an' I didn't quite know why. I was studyin' why, just passin' by, when she says for me to come there and help her a minute. Well, I went inside the fence an' looked around for some kindlin' to work on, but I didn't see none, and she says, 'Naw, I got somethin' for you to do in the house. Th' old door's off its hinges an' fall's comin' on pretty fast.' I said you got a screwdriver, Miss Mayella? She said she sho' had. Well, I went up the steps an' she motioned me to come inside, and I went in the front room an' looked at the door. I said Miss Mayella, this door look all right. I pulled it back'n forth and those hinges was all right. Then she shet the door in my face. Mr. Finch, I was wonderin' why it was so quiet like, an' it come to me that there weren't a chile on the place, not a one of 'em, and I said Miss Mayella, where the chillun?"

Tom's black velvet skin had begun to shine, and he ran his hand over his face.

"I say where the chillun?" he continued, "an' she says—she was laughin', sort of—she says they all gone to town to get ice creams. She says, 'Took me a slap year to save seb'm nickels, but I done it. They all gone to town.'"

Tom's discomfort was not from the humidity. "What did you say then, Tom?" asked Atticus.

"I said somethin' like, why Miss Mayella, that's right smart o'you to treat 'em. An' she said, 'You think so?' I don't think she understood what I was thinkin'—I meant it was smart of her to save like that, an' nice of her to treat 'em."

"I understand you, Tom. Go on," said Atticus.

"Well, I said I best be goin', I couldn't do nothin' for her, an' she says oh yes I could, an' I ask her what, and she says to just step on that chair yonder an' git that box down from on top of the chiffarobe.''

"Not the same chiffarobe you busted up?" asked Atticus.

The witness smiled. "Naw suh, another one. Most as tall as the room. So I done what she told me, an' I was just reachin' when the next thing I knows she— she'd grabbed me round the legs, grabbed me round th' legs, Mr. Finch. She scared me so bad I hopped down an' turned the chair over—that was the only thing, only furniture, 'sturbed in that room, Mr. Finch, when I left it. I swear 'fore God.''

"What happened after you turned the chair over?"

Tom Robinson had come to a dead stop. He glanced at Atticus, then at the jury, then at Mr. Underwood sitting across the room.

"Tom, you're sworn to tell the whole truth. Will you tell it?"

Tom ran his hand nervously over his mouth.

"What happened after that?"

"Answer the question," said Judge Taylor. One-third of his cigar had vanished.

"Mr. Finch, I got down offa that chair an' turned around an' she sorta jumped on me."

"Jumped on you? Violently?"

"No suh, she—she hugged me. She hugged me round the waist."

This time Judge Taylor's gavel came down with a bang, and as it did the overhead lights went on in the courtroom. Darkness had not come, but the afternoon sun had left the windows. Judge Taylor quickly restored order.

"Then what did she do?"

The witness swallowed hard. "She reached up an' kissed me 'side of th' face. She says she never kissed a grown man before an' she might as well kiss a nigger. She says what her papa do to her don't count. She says, 'Kiss me back, nigger.' I say Miss Mayella lemme outa here an' tried to run but she got her back to the door an' I'da had to push her. I didn't wanta harm her, Mr. Finch, an' I say lemme pass, but just when I say it Mr. Ewell yonder hollered through th' window.''

"What did he say?"

Tom Robinson swallowed again, and his eyes widened. "Somethin' not fittin' to say—not fittin' for these folks'n chillun to hear—''

"What did he say, Tom? You *must* tell the jury what he said."

Tom Robinson shut his eyes tight. "He says you goddamn whore, I'll kill ya.''

"Then what happened?"

"Mr. Finch, I was runnin' so fast I didn't know what happened."

"Tom, did you rape Mayella Ewell?"

"I did not, suh."

"Did you harm her in any way?"

"I did not, suh."

"Did you resist her advances?"

"Mr. Finch, I tried. I tried to 'thout bein' ugly to her. I didn't wanta be ugly, I didn't wanta push her or nothin'."

It occurred to me that in their own way, Tom Robinson's manners were as good as Atticus's. Until my father explained it to me later, I did not understand the subtlety of Tom's predicament: he would not have dared strike a white woman under any circumstances and expect to live long, so he took the first opportunity to run—a sure sign of guilt.

"Tom, go back once more to Mr. Ewell," said Atticus. "Did he say anything to you?"

"Not anything, suh. He mighta said somethin', but I weren't there—"

"That'll do," Atticus cut in sharply. "What you did hear, who was he talking to?"

"Mr. Finch, he were talkin' and lookin' at Miss Mayella."

"Then you ran?"

"I sho' did, suh."

"Why did you run?"

"I was scared, suh."

"Why were you scared?"

"Mr. Finch, if you was a nigger like me, you'd be scared, too."

Atticus sat down. Mr. Gilmer was making his way to the witness stand, but before he got there Mr. Link Deas rose from the audience and announced:

"I just want the whole lot of you to know one thing right now. That boy's worked for me eight years an' I ain't had a speck o'trouble outa him. Not a speck."

"*Shut your mouth, sir!*" Judge Taylor was wide awake and roaring. He was also pink in the face. His speech was miraculously unimpaired by his cigar. "Link Deas," he yelled, "if you have anything you want to say you can say it under oath and at the proper time, but until then you get out of this room, you hear me? Get out of this room, sir, you hear me? I'll be damned if I'll listen to this case again!"

Judge Taylor looked daggers at Atticus, as if daring him to speak, but Atticus had ducked his head and was laughing into his lap. I remembered something he had said about Judge Taylor's ex cathedra remarks sometimes exceeding his duty, but that few lawyers ever did anything about them. I looked at Jem, but Jem shook his head. "It ain't like one of the jurymen got up and started talking," he said. "I think it'd be different then. Mr. Link was just disturbin' the peace or something."

Judge Taylor told the reporter to expunge anything he happened to have written down after Mr. Finch if you were a nigger like me you'd be scared too, and told the jury to disregard the interruption. He looked suspiciously down the middle aisle and waited, I suppose, for Mr. Link Deas to effect total departure. Then he said, "Go ahead, Mr. Gilmer."

"You were given thirty days once for disorderly conduct, Robinson?" asked

Mr. Gilmer.

"Yes suh."

"What'd the nigger look like when you got through with him?"

"He beat me, Mr. Gilmer."

"Yes, but you were convicted, weren't you?"

Atticus raised his head. "It was a misdemeanor and it's in the record, Judge." I thought he sounded tired.

"Witness'll answer, though," said Judge Taylor, just as wearily.

"Yes suh, I got thirty days."

I knew that Mr. Gilmer would sincerely tell the jury that anyone who was convicted of disorderly conduct could easily have had it in his heart to take advantage of Mayella Ewell, that was the only reason he cared. Reasons like that helped.

"Robinson, you're pretty good at busting up chiffarobes and kindling with one hand, aren't you?"

"Yes suh, I reckon so."

"Strong enough to choke the breath out of a woman and sling her to the floor?"

"I never done that, suh."

"But you are strong enough to?"

"I reckon so, suh."

"Had your eye on her a long time, hadn't you, boy?"

"No suh, I never looked at her."

"Then you were mighty polite to do all that chopping and hauling for her, weren't you, boy?"

"I was just tryin' to help her out, suh."

"That was mighty generous of you, you had chores at home after your regular work, didn't you?"

"Yes suh."

"Why didn't you do them instead of Miss Ewell's?"

"I done 'em both, suh."

"You must have been pretty busy. Why?"

"Why what, suh?"

"Why were you so anxious to do that woman's chores?"

Tom Robinson hesitated, searching for an answer. "Looked like she didn't have nobody to help her, like I says—"

"With Mr. Ewell and seven children on the place, boy?"

"Well, I says it looked like they never help her none—"

"You did all this chopping and work from sheer goodness, boy?"

"Tried to help her, I says."

Mr. Gilmer smiled grimly at the jury. "You're a mighty good fellow, it seems—

did all this for not one penny?''

"Yes suh. I felt right sorry for her, she seemed to try more'n the rest of 'em—"

"*You* felt sorry for *her,* you felt *sorry* for her?" Mr. Gilmer seemed ready to rise to the ceiling.

The witness realized his mistake and shifted uncomfortably in the chair. But the damage was done. Below us, nobody liked Tom Robinson's answer. Mr. Gilmer paused a long time to let it sink in.

"Now you went by the house as usual, last November twenty-first," he said, "and she asked you to come in and bust up a chiffarobe?"

"No suh."

"Do you deny that you went by the house?"

"No suh—she said she had somethin' for me to do inside the house—"

"She says she asked you to bust up a chiffarobe, is that right?"

"No suh, it ain't."

"Then you say she's lying, boy?"

Atticus was on his feet, but Tom Robinson didn't need him. "I don't say she's lyin', Mr. Gilmer, I say she's mistaken in her mind."

To the next ten questions, as Mr. Gilmer reviewed Mayella's version of events, the witness's steady answer was that she was mistaken in her mind.

"Didn't Mr. Ewell run you off the place, boy?"

"No suh, I don't think he did."

"Don't think, what do you mean?"

"I mean I didn't stay long enough for him to run me off."

"You're very candid about this, why did you run so fast?"

"I says I was scared, suh."

"If you had a clear conscience, why were you scared?"

"Like I says before, it weren't safe for any nigger to be in a—fix like that."

"But you weren't in a fix—you testified that you were resisting Miss Ewell. Were you so scared that she'd hurt you, you ran, a big buck like you?"

"No suh, I's scared I'd be in court, just like I am now."

"Scared of arrest, scared you'd have to face up to what you did?"

"No suh, scared I'd hafta face up to what I didn't do."

"Are you being impudent to me, boy?"

"No suh, I didn't go to be."

This was as much as I heard of Mr. Gilmer's cross-examination, because Jem made me take Dill out. For some reason Dill had started crying and couldn't stop; quietly at first, then his sobs were heard by several people in the balcony. Jem said if I didn't go with him he'd make me, and Reverend Sykes said I'd better go, so I went. Dill had seemed to be all right that day, nothing wrong with him, but I guessed he hadn't fully recovered from running away.

"Ain't you feeling good?" I asked, when we reached the bottom of the stairs.

Dill tried to pull himself together as we ran down the south steps. Mr. Link Deas was a lonely figure on the top step. "Anything happenin', Scout?" he asked as we went by. "No sir," I answered over my shoulder. "Dill here, he's sick."

"Come on out under the trees," I said. "Heat got you, I expect." We chose the fattest live oak and we sat under it.

"It was just him I couldn't stand," Dill said.

"Who, Tom?"

"That old Mr. Gilmer doin' him thataway, talking so hateful to him—"

"Dill, that's his job. Why, if we didn't have prosecutors—well, we couldn't have defense attorneys, I reckon."

Dill exhaled patiently. "I know all that, Scout. It was the way he said it made me sick, plain sick."

"He's supposed to act that way, Dill, he was cross—"

"He didn't act that way when—"

"Dill, those were his own witnesses."

"Well, Mr. Finch didn't act that way to Mayella and old man Ewell when he cross-examined them. The way that man called him 'boy' all the time and sneered at him, an' looked around at the jury every time he answered—"

"Well, Dill, after all he's just a Negro."

"I don't care one speck. It ain't right, somehow it ain't right to do 'em that way. Hasn't anybody got any business talkin' like that—it just makes me sick."

"That's just Mr. Gilmer's way, Dill, he does 'em all that way. You've never seen him get good'n down on one yet. Why, when—well, today Mr. Gilmer seemed to me like he wasn't half trying. They do 'em all that way, most lawyers, I mean."

"Mr. Finch doesn't."

"He's not an example, Dill, he's—" I was trying to grope in my memory for a sharp phrase of Miss Maudie Atkinson's. I had it: "He's the same in the courtroom as he is on the public streets."

"That's not what I mean," said Dill.

"I know what you mean, boy," said a voice behind us. We thought it came from the tree-trunk, but it belonged to Mr. Dolphus Raymond. He peered around the trunk at us. "You aren't thin-hided, it just makes you sick, doesn't it?"

from **Cane**[28]

Jean Toomer

Carma

Wind is in the cane. Come along.
Cane leaves swaying, rusty with talk,
Scratching choruses above the guinea's squawk.
Wind is in the cane. Come along.

Carma, in overalls, and strong as any man, stands behind the old brown mule,
driving the wagon home. It bumps, and groans, and shakes as it crosses the railroad
track. She, riding it easy. I leave the men around the stove to follow her with my eyes
down the red dust road. Nigger woman driving a Georgia chariot down an old dust
road. Dixie Pike is what they call it. Maybe she feels my gaze, perhaps she expects it.
Anyway, she turns. The sun, which has been slanting over her shoulder, shoots primitive rockets into her mangrove-gloomed, yellow flower face. Hi! Yip! God has left the
Moses-people for the nigger. "Gedap." Using reins to slap the mule, she disappears in
a cloudy rumble at some indefinite point along the road.
     (The sun is hammered to a band of gold. Pine-needles, like mazda, are brilliant-
ly aglow. No rain has come to take the rustle from the falling sweet-gum leaves. Over
in the forest, across the swamp, a sawmill blows its closing whistle. Smoke curls up.
Marvelous web spun by the spider sawdust pile. Curls up and spreads itself pine-high
above the branch, a single silver band along the eastern valley. A black boy . . . you
are the most sleepiest man I ever seed, Sleeping Beauty . . . cradled on a gray mule,
guided by the hollow sound of cowbells, heads for them through a rusty cotton field.
From down the railroad track, the chug-chug of a gas engine announces that the repair gang is coming home. A girl in the yard of a whitewashed shack not much larger
than the stack of worn ties piled before it, sings. Her voice is loud. Echoes, like rain,
sweep the valley. Dusk takes the polish from the rails. Lights twinkle in scattered
houses. From far away, a sad strong song. Pungent and composite, the smell of farm-
yards is the fragrance of the woman. She does not sing; her body is a song. She is in
the forest, dancing. Torches flare . . juju men, greegree, witch-doctors . . torches go
out. . . The Dixie Pike has grown from a goat path in Africa.

28. "Carma" from *Cane* by Jean Toomer. Permission of Liveright, Publishers, N.Y. Copyright renewal 1951 by Jean
Toomer.

Night

Foxie, the bitch, slicks back her ears and barks at the rising moon.)

Wind is in the corn. Come along.
Corn leaves swaying, rusty with talk,
Scratching choruses above the guinea's squawk,
Wind is in the corn. Come along.

Carma's tale is the crudest melodrama. Her husband's in the gang. And it's her fault he got there. Working with a contractor, he was away most of the time. She had others. No one blames her for that. He returned one day and hung around the town where he picked up week-old boasts and rumors. . . Bane accused her. She denied. He couldn't see that she was becoming hysterical. He would have liked to take his fists and beat her. Who was strong as a man. Stronger. Words, like corkscrews, wormed to her strength. It fizzled out. Grabbing a gun, she rushed from the house and plunged across the road into a cane-brake. . . There, in quarter heaven shone the crescent moon. . . Bane was afraid to follow till he heard the gun go off. Then he wasted half an hour gathering the neighbor men. They met in the road where lamp-light showed tracks dissolving in the loose earth about the cane. The search began. Moths flickered the lamps. They put them out. Really, because she still might be live enough to shoot. Time and space have no meaning in a canefield. No more than the interminable stalks. . . Some one stumbled over her. A cry went up. From the road, one would have thought that they were cornering a rabbit or a skunk. . . It is difficult carrying dead weight through cane. They placed her on the sofa. A curious, nosey somebody looked for the wound. This fussing with her clothes aroused her. Her eyes were weak and piti-able for so strong a woman. Slowly, then like a flash, Bane came to know that the shot she fired, with averted head, was aimed to whistle like a dying hornet through the cane. Twice deceived, and one deception proved the other. His head went off. Slashed one of the men who'd helped, the man who'd stumbled over her. Now he's in the gang. Who was her husband. Should she not take others, this Carma, strong as a man, whose tale as I have told it is the crudest melodrama?

Wind is in the cane. Come along.
Cane leaves swaying, rusty with talk,
Scratching choruses above the guinea's squawk,
Wind is in the cane. Come along.

CHECKLIST FOR ANALYSIS

1. How would the metaworld of the literature be described? What is the "state of being" in the selection? What is the principal presentational value of the selection? (See chart on page 22.)

2. In what mode is the selection written? What are the central behavioral problems in the selection? in the "presses"?

3. How is literary time conveyed in language? How does psychological time function? mythic time? How are silences used and where? In the case of poetry, what are the principal rhythms and what is the prevailing meter?

4. How is figurative language employed? to what ends? How are paradox and irony employed?

5. What is the form of the experience in the selection? What is the form into which the experience has been put? In the case of poetry, what precise poetic form is used? (See questions at conclusion of discussion on each poetic form.)

6. What elements of style are most attractive to the reader? What are the problems of style as you perceive them for performance? What kind of narrator appears in the selection? How attached or detached is he to the events in the literature? What are the implications for performance in the narrator's role?

EXERCISES AND ASSIGNMENTS

1. What elements of style contribute to the "expectations" and "new information" in Richard Brautigan's "Kool-Aid Wino"?

2. Analyze and discuss the function of the word symbolism in Thomas Wolfe's "Meadows of Sensation"(Chapter 1).

3. Discuss the role of the narrator in the excerpt from Harper Lee's *To Kill a Mockingbird*. (A dramatized version of the same chapter appears in Chapter 7.) What are the particular problems for the performer, considering that the narrator in the novel writes of childhood experiences from the perspective of adulthood? Discuss the role of the narrator in the performance of Thomas Wolfe's "Meadows of Sensation" and one other prose selection in earlier chapters.

4. How do the various stylistic elements inform themselves and coalesce in William Faulkner's "Wash" (Chapter 1)? In performance what problems of transformation emerge in an analysis of the detachment or attachment of the narrator? of the stylistic "expectations" and "new information"? of the word symbolism in the piece, including the title?

5. In what way does the structure of Franz Kafka's *Jackals and Arabs* (Chapter 1) create an impact? (Here Kafka is presented in *translation* from German to English, a kind of

transformation all its own. What similarities do you find between the art of translation and the art of performance? Why is this a particularly appropriate matter to discuss in a chapter on style?)

6. James Joyce's *Portrait of the Artist as a Young Man* (Chapter 1) is an autobiographical novel. To what degree must the performer inform himself on the personality of Joyce to effect a transformation faithful to Joyce's narrating self? Is there any suggestion of oral style (the spontaneously *speaking* self) in the selection of language in the piece? In what ways does an oral style in literature differ from a written one?

7. What is "oral" in Jean Toomer's *Cane?* The title when spoken aloud suggests a pun, or play, on a name. What is it? How does it inform the selection?

8. How does style inevitably lead an auditor or reader of a selection to conclude many things about the "tone" and "tone of voice" of a narrator? A discussion of this seemingly simple question can become most complex, but will enrich a student's attitudes and reactions to literature.

Objectives for Performance Growth

1 Exciting   **2** Enjoyable   **3** Adequate   **4** Need for Development

To Evoke the Metaworlds

_____ a sense of inner resonance
_____ a sense of attaining a state of being
_____ a responsiveness to presentational values
_____ IMPRESSION

To Relate the Performing Body to Literary Experience

_____ behavior congruent to mode
_____ language of gesture natural to literary space
_____ sound of language natural to literary space
_____ appropriate behavioral presses
_____ appropriate use of total bodily energy
_____ IMPRESSION

To Share Awareness of Literary Time

_____ sense of performing time appropriate to literary time
_____ literary time understood and evoked
_____ silences understood and evoked
_____ metrical time understood and evoked
_____ IMPRESSION

To Evoke Figurative Thought and Language

_____ appropriate exemplification of language
_____ a sense of symbolic intent
_____ a sharing of paradox and irony—where appropriate
_____ IMPRESSION

To Evoke Form

_____ form of experience immediate and compelling
_____ form of literary structure appreciated and evoked
_____ IMPRESSION

To Present Style as New Information

_____ expectations in performance congruent to language
_____ performer and style linked / fused
_____ stylistic elements perceived and evoked
_____ narrator attachment or detachment appropriate
_____ IMPRESSION

To Evoke the Presence of Personae

_____ interactional and / or transactional dialogue evoked
_____ significant gesture of characters evoked
_____ structure of dialogue evoked
_____ IMPRESSION

7

Jerry N. Uelsmann

TO EVOKE THE PERSONAE IN LITERATURE

— through an understanding of the
  nature of dialogue
  — as mythic enactment
  — as rhetorical presence
  — as psychological reality

— through a sensitivity to the
  processes of interactional and
  transactional dialogue

— through an awareness of
  functional and dysfunctional
  communication

— through an understanding and
  performance of the irreducible
  significant gestures of the
  personae

CHAPTER SEVEN

The Perception and Evocation of Personae

By custom a separate listing of the dramatis personae precedes the beginning of a play. So old is this custom, dating back to the beginnings of print when printers wished to offer something of a program, that it is seldom questioned. This list, sometimes in order of appearance, sometimes in order of importance, often describes briefly the characters in terms of their relationships to each other, or their physical attributes, or their social positions; it announces those who will appear in the "play" of human emotion, struggle, destiny. Interestingly, it is absent at the beginning of a novel, a short story, a narrative poem, and its absence is seldom noted. In these other literary forms, the reader assumes that it is the author's responsibility to introduce his characters and give them the language necessary to speak their worlds of experience and perception. Of course, this is the dramatist's responsibility as well. Yet, the presence of the list at the beginning of a play is more than a curiosity; it often creates in the reader a compulsion to master the list, to get the personae "straightened out" in his mind. The list, whatever its other uses, does underscore one insistent fact: drama is personae.

Our concern in this chapter is the perception and evocation of personae, specifically in dramatic literature. The centrality of character in drama is the reason for our concentrating upon that literary form. As in the preceding chapters in which form in poetry and style in fiction were discussed, many of the principles for perceiving and evoking personae in drama are applicable to the other literary genres. The discussion of dialogue later in this chapter, for example, applies to dialogue wherever it appears—fiction, drama, narrative poetry, epic poetry.

HISTORICAL BACKGROUND OF DRAMA

The word *drama* is derived from the Greek term suggesting a deed or action. In its earliest form the Greek *drainein* meant "to be ready to do." The word *persona,* virtually unchanged in meaning since its Latin origins, means "actor, role, character, or person." In the study of dramatic literature, the interpreter makes himself ready to *perform* a person, to allow *his* person to be the sounding voice and behavioral body of another.

While the personae have always been played within the theatrical conventions of their particular time, they have, nevertheless, been presented in one of two basic modes. Either the personae have been masked, literally, or they have been unmasked, and the perceiver has been asked to believe that the performer is the person portrayed. The masked player, with unchanging and static mask, frozen in its particular expression, depends on a plastic and changing body. For the unmasked player expression of the visible face is part of a totality of movement and expression. At various points in theatrical history, expressions have been conventionalized; in our present theater the expressive actor is defined largely in terms of naturalness, of an effortless deception that he who is on the stage is not unlike others who are off the stage. The mask has become makeup; the conventionalized expressions have become the extensions of man's own natural gestures.

CONTEMPORARY CHANGES

For most people today, however, an involvement with the dramatized person does not come through the theater of stage and set, lights and actors. Contemporary man experiences his sense of dramatized men largely through motion pictures and television. These two media have radically altered dramatic perception and in most important ways. First, motion pictures have *enlarged* what is perceived by sight. This enlargement has been in terms not only of the setting, but more significantly, of the size of the dramatized person. The motion picture close-up enlarges the very pores of a man's skin; the subtlety of breath itself is revealed. Second, amplification of sound has also changed what we hear and what we expect to hear. A wide-screen image counterpointed with multi-track amplification affects the human psyche in new ways that have barely been assessed. Third, the dominance of image or visual form has meant, most significantly, a radical change in the sense of *what is said*. A comparison between the text of a play and a script for a motion picture makes this clear.

While the enlargements of cinema occur in television as well, there are important differences. The television screen is significantly smaller than a motion picture screen. Admitting dramatized personae into one's home is of crucial importance. One notable effect has been that they do not go uncommented upon. The sense of being able to scan and to observe carefully the total physical presence in television is one of its results. In the theater or motion picture one sits in silence, but in one's home one is free to reject, to talk back to, to comment upon to another, to offer running criticism, to switch channels—all of these are facts of television behavior. Television has changed the sense of dramatized personae in yet another unprecedented way. The "dramatized" personae seen on television are those of our living world of politics, of catastrophes, of war, of sports, of "personalities" (a word related to *personae*). In the most uncanny sense, all the world is a stage, and the people merely players. The dramas of Presidents' families, the courtings of prime ministers, the court trials of soldiers, priests, blacks, politicians, radicals have become not merely news but the dramas of our everyday lives.

In summary, then, man's need to dramatize himself has evolved with his changing sensibilities, but wherever the changing sensibilities have led, there has been no shedding the past. One recent New York theatrical season saw productions of Greek tragedies, Shakespearean tragedies and comedies, nineteenth-century plays of Chekhov and Ibsen, revivals of early twentieth-century musicals and dramas, new plays in traditional form, traditional plays in new forms, plays based on court trials and public events, rock operas, traditional Noh plays of medieval Japan—to mention a few. The totality of man's past and present experience is the substance of theater, of television, and of motion pictures. The contents in all and each are the dramatis personae of ourselves, our collective history, our shared myths.

NON-THEATRICAL PRESENTATION OF DRAMATIC LITERATURE

What does the study of dramatic literature lead to when there is no intention of presenting it in the total theatrical sense? Can dramatic literature exist independent of the medium for which it is intended? Can a presentation of a play, or a scene from a play, be of theatrical value when one person becomes the dramatis personae? What are the aesthetics of a reading as compared with a production? Each of these questions is worthy of consideration.

What does the study of dramatic literature lead to when there is no intention of presenting it in the total theatrical sense? The study of dramatic literature, independent of theatrical production, emphasizes the psychology of human interaction and transaction. It is not a substitute for theatrical production; it is a complement to the understanding of dramatic form. When confronted solely with dialogue, the interpreter of drama functions in all the many ways a narrator does: he may be content to let the objective dialogue be its own "telling"; he may be omniscient and reach into the thoughts of the characters and attribute to them the motivations for their actions. His evoking of the drama is totally dependent upon what the playwright offers in the dialogue. The performance of dramatic literature by an interpreter is not a production; it is a "reading" of the play, in the punning sense of the word. From his understanding of human psychology, he delineates the natures of the characters; he reveals the quality of his insights about them. Unlike the actor whose concentration is upon one character, the interpreter shares his multiple perceptions of all the characters. The implications of this remain to be developed.

Can dramatic literature exist independent of the medium for which it is intended? This question has been answered in our earlier insistence on the value of the behavioral study of literature. A play can be transformed from the medium of print. All literature can be transformed from the medium of print. The totality of effect of the theatrical production is beyond question, but there are two theaters: the theater in the physical sense and the *inner* theater of the mind. The former is dependent upon the imagination of all those who create it; the latter is dependent upon the single imagination that transforms print into imaginative worlds. In writing of the latter, Thomas Sanders has said,

. . . be willing to imagine that what you read is not the creation of a playwright but a transcript of reality—a reality that has been pared of all but the necessary and basic ingredients for your understanding of the experience. Moving like a disembodied spirit, you are there, capable of seeing without being seen, hearing without being heard, examining without being examined. You can, at will, enter the minds of people and know the significance of their actions as even they do not. Because you have transcended the flesh, become free in time and in space, you can *be* a person in the play—or *all* of the characters.[1]

The proscenium arch of the human skull is the vastest arena of drama known. Allowing one's inner perceptions to be extended through the body is another form of knowledge which, when shared, is as rich and valuable as the most profound intellectual abstractions.

Can there be theatrical value when one person becomes the dramatis personae? The values of the theater need no defense, but neither do the values of the theatrical self, the self which transforms itself into a theatrical event. Peter Brook has written that "the one thing that distinguishes the theater from all the other arts is that it has no permanence."[2] By this he means that the produced play exists for only the time of its performance. The value of one person's *knowing* a play is that the play achieves a kind of permanence. And this, of course, is the aesthetic value of reading.

The study of dramatic literature is a continuation of a form of learning which stresses the awakening of man's inner potentialities. When one person becomes the

1. Thomas Sanders, *The Discovery of Drama* (Glenview, Ill.: Scott, Foresman and Co., 1968), p. 4.
2. Peter Brook, *The Empty Space* (New York: Atheneum Publishers, 1969), p. 129.

several persons in a drama, he learns something profound about himself. To permit the range of human conduct and emotion to become a part of himself, to allow quarrelling voices, paired opposites, the male and female parts of his most inner self to speak publicly, moves him toward himself; the drama is not objectified, it is subjectively perceived and experienced.

Richard Schechner has said, "The 'real events' of literature are grammar, rhetoric, verbal imagery, and so on. The 'real events' of theatre are performers performing."[3] Of course, Schechner is right; our experience with theater confirms this. And while he would probably not agree that the "theater of the mind" has the same value as the *performing* theater, he might agree that there are values inherent in the literary study of drama that move beyond literature as "grammar, rhetoric, verbal imagery, and so on." His principal concern is with the actor as persona; the interpreter's concern is with personae acting and interacting in the dialogic and situational matrix of life. The interpreter restores the primacy of the text, not because the text is superior to the total theatrical production, but because the text is a legitimate test of dramatic values.

DIALOGUE

We spoke at the start of this chapter of the centrality of personae in drama. The key to the successful performance of dramatic literature lies in the interpretive artist's grasp of the personality and psychology of his cast of characters. And his clues to this understanding are to be found in the dialogue.

THE PRESENCE/ABSENCE OF A NARRATOR

In the preceding chapter the role of the narrator in fiction was explored. The personae in fiction are viewed or shared with the person of the narrator. We experience these personae and their worlds and environments through the narrator's point of view. The dialogue is shaped by the narrator's recall or memory or knowledge.

In earlier chapters the lyric voice of the poet and his containment in time were explored. Here, too, is a "dramatic voice"—a voice seeking to express in language feeling, perception, commitment.

In this chapter the principal focus is upon dramatic literature of the theater and film. All characters in this genre speak only from and for themselves. The playwright forsakes his own intruding voice for those of the persons he wishes to dramatize. In early Greek drama the narrator was present in the form of the chorus which comment-

3. Richard Schechner, *Public Domain* (Indianapolis: Bobbs-Merrill Co., 1969), p. 51.

ed upon the action of the characters from one point of view or another—from what it meant to be an elder in Thebes, for example, or a citizen of a plagued city. Occasionally, playwrights return to this convention and put a narrator on the stage, as in Thornton Wilder's *Our Town*. Most dramatic literature, however, does not employ a narrator; a play is structured so that (1) the characters "present" themselves and speak for themselves; (2) they are perceived in some setting; and (3) they are perceived as existing at some time in their personal history or man's history or the collective mythic history of man's awareness. This information is conveyed largely through dialogue.

Because drama is presented without the presence of a narrator, some important information is missing. In any dramatic medium there is generally the sense of the "other" persona or personae listening. The matter of perceived listening is an important device in the theater which is absent in the interpreter's performance. The interpreter can only suggest the effect of listening as the dialogue weaves its web. In fiction the narrator can intrude upon the dialogue to comment, "While Edward talked to her, Lavinia looked absently out of the window." An actress does the action; the interpreter can only suggest by the use of a subtle eye movement the possibility that Lavinia might have been looking out of the window. The interpreter must concentrate only upon what is being said, and in so doing, the text of the play is foremost.

The interpreter is further challenged by another dynamic of "total theater." Total theater, even a group reading, with the presence of several actors, calls attention to the simultaneity of all physical behaviors in all of the characters on the stage. The individual interpreter is limited to the basic attitudinal posture or gesture of a respondent in dialogue.

And finally the absence of a narrator means that the environment in which the situational dialogue takes place is a matter of imagination—the physical setting is absent. The physical trappings of the stage setting, costumes, and lighting are eliminated in the interpretive performance. When one thinks of the degree to which these visual elements add to the aesthetics of the theatrical event, the interpreter can well pause and meditate upon what he is doing with the irreducible sense of text. Far from limiting his performance, the absence of the physical elements permits the interpreter to explore dynamics of his own media. His media of sight, sound, and time are the same media of theater; but the interpreter's use of them in dramatic literature frames the dialogue in an unusual purity, without distraction.

These problems arising from the absence of a narrator force the interpreter of dramatic literature to admit that many dramas simply do not lend themselves to his particular medium. Yet the number that do, give him ample challenges and give others rewarding pleasures. The behavioral performance of drama is not a substitute for theater, film, or television. Each medium has its own message, and each medium can do a number of things that another cannot do. The interpretive medium places its particular emphasis upon the language of the drama. The interpreter creates the illusion of dialogue, and if the illusion is suggestive enough and the dramatic dialogue compelling enough, the presumed necessities of settings, lights, costumes, makeup are forgotten in the perceiver's imagination. If the quality of the dramatic dialogue is compelling and structurally insistent, then there is ample basis for an aesthetic experience.

TRANSACTIONS AND INTERACTIONS

Dialogue is a process of giving and getting information from people.[4] In this process of giving and getting information, two forms of "action" occur: transactions and interactions. What are the differences between these? An interaction is a dialogue in which the necessity to disagree, to speak, to probe, to state one's views, and so on, is of greater priority than understanding the other person. An interaction need not be hostile, though it may be. And an interaction is not necessarily purposeful, though it may be. When Bif says to his father, Willy Loman, in Arthur Miller's *Death of a Salesman,* that there ". . . has never been an honest word spoken in this house," he is stating that there have been interactions. In this moment of reaching out to his father, however futilely or hostilely, he is attempting a transaction.

A transaction is a profound engagement with another person, one in which understanding and the intimacy of revelation take place. In Edward Albee's *Who's Afraid of Virginia Woolf*, George and Martha jockey and maneuver through one interaction after another, both with each other and their guests, Honey and Nick. The third act of the play is entitled "The Exorcism," and it suggests a freeing from the debilitating interactions that in the course of the previous two acts have led to the possibility of transaction at the play's conclusion.

Dialogue reveals the nature of interactions and transactions. In *Hamlet,* for example, the constellation of characters whirling about Hamlet's world are case studies in interactional and transactional capabilities. Polonius apparently never transacts with his two children Laertes and Ophelia; interacts, yes. Polonius' advice to Laertes illustrates well mere interaction. Laertes, who is about to return to university life, is counseled by his father.

Polonius: Yet here, Laertes? aboard, aboard, for shame!
    The wind sits in the shoulder of your sail,
    And you are stay'd for. There; my blessing with thee!
    And these few precepts in thy memory
    Look thou character. Give thy thoughts no tongue,

4. This discussion of dialogue is based in part upon the work and theoretical formulations of Virginia Satir, particularly as she has developed and postulated them in her important essay, "Communication: a Process of Giving and Getting Information," in *Cojoint Family Therapy,* rev. ed. (Palo Alto: Science and Behavior Books, 1964), p. 63. Of equal influence is the work of R. D. Laing, whose books *The Divided Self, The Politics of Experience,* and *Self and Others* explore the communicating self with great originality of thought. The importance of the phenomenon of "speaking" has been noted earlier in Georges Gusdorf's *Speaking.* Interested students are encouraged to explore these.

Nor any unproportion'd thought his act.
Be thou familiar, but by no means vulgar.
Those friends thou hast, and their adoption tried,
Grapple them to thy soul with hoops of steel;
But do not dull thy palm with entertainment
Of each new-hatch'd, unfledged comrade. Beware
Of entrance to a quarrel, but being in,
Bear 't that the opposed may beware of thee.
Give every man thy ear, but few thy voice;
Take each man's censure, but reserve thy judgment.
Costly thy habit as thy purse can buy,
But not express'd in fancy; rich, not gaudy;
For the apparel oft proclaims the man,
And they in France of the best rank and station
Are of a most select and generous chief in that.
Neither a borrower nor a lender be;
For loan oft loses both itself and friend,
And borrowing dulls the edge of husbandry.
This above all: to thine own self be true,
And it must follow, as the night the day,
Thou canst not then be false to any man.
Farewell: my blessing season this in thee!

Evaluate this speech in light of Virginia Satir's statement concerning words as tools:

Words are tools which people use to give and get information. If a person fails to realize that words are only abstractions he will tend to overgeneralize, and he will fall into the error of making the following assumptions:

a. He will assume that one instance is an example of all instances. He will be unclear, particularly in his use of who, what, where, and when. . . .

b. He will assume that other people share his feelings, thoughts, perceptions. . . .

c. He will assume that his perceptions or evaluations are complete. . . .

d. He will assume that what he perceives or evaluates won't change. . . .

e. He assumes that there are only two possible alternatives when assessing perceptions or evaluations; he dichotomizes or thinks in terms of black or white. . . .

f. He assumes that characteristics which he attributes to things or people are part of those things or people. . . .

g. He assumes that he can get inside the skin of another. He operates as if from a "crystal ball" and he acts as a spokesman for others. . . .

h. He also assumes that the other can get inside his skin. . . .[5]

5. Satir, *Cojoint Family Therapy*, p. 67.

Observe how Polonius uses language in his interaction with Laertes, for that is all his speech is. Of Satir's eight points, how many are present in Polonius' speech?

Consider, too, Ophelia's absolute trust in the presumed transaction that Hamlet has made with her. Her confusion over Hamlet's feigned madness, the move from transaction to aberrant interaction, tips the balance of her delicate hold on reality.

Any of the famous soliloquies of Hamlet are an intriguing study in this connection as interaction and transaction have moved within the human psyche. A soliloquy is an inner dialogue with self. A truly alienated person cannot transact with himself, he can only darkly interact with the forces pent up within him. A person in command of his personality, awake and alive to his own sense of self, transacts.

Linn Ehrlich

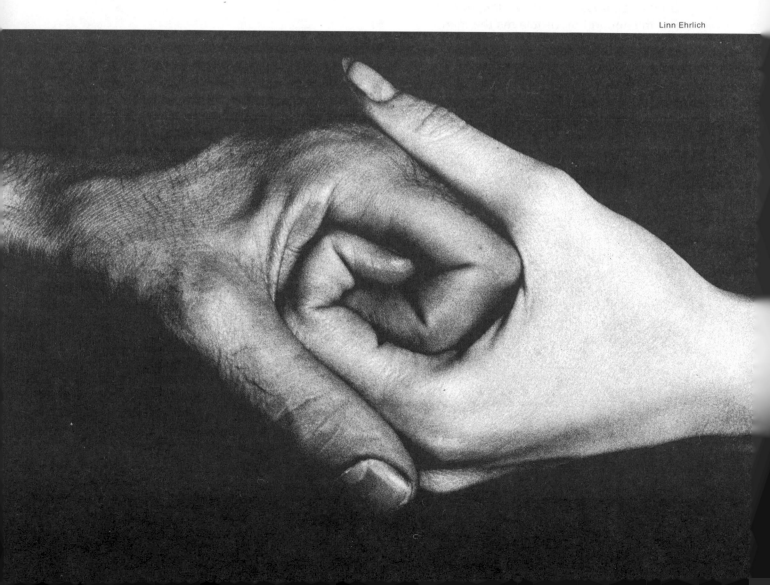

Functional and dysfunctional communication. Dramatic literature explores the nature of functional and dysfunctional communication, and in so doing reveals through dialogue the capacity of characters (1) to live without ever overcoming dysfunctional communication; (2) to struggle unsuccessfully to overcome it; (3) to succeed in overcoming it, but at great cost; (4) to live with a sense of functional communication in a world of dysfunctional communication, but capitulate; (5) to live with a sense of functional communication in a world of dysfunctional communication and succeed in authenticating existence. Dysfunctional communication is arrogant, unbending and unyielding, accusative or quarrelsome, and expresses a rigid view of oneself and the world. Functional communication seeks understanding, shares openly and freely the nature of inner life and feeling, moves toward greater transaction. Curiously, tragedy has a way of incorporating the functional and dysfunctional, particularly within the central characters. It is characteristic of tragedy that the central character be able to articulate, to state in a moment of unsullied personal or emotional transaction his knowledge of all that has been dysfunctional (foolish, arrogant, driven, hostile, murderous), that moment of shared honesty being a true example of functional communication.

Unlike tragedy, comedy is built on the humorous possibilities of dysfunctional communication—with two important qualifications: the odds are not great and the resolution is happy, congenial, pleasant. Comedies built upon necessary deceit and falsehood have created the most engaging and entertaining personae in all literature: Lysistrata, Falstaff, Mrs. Malaprop, Jack Worthing—to name a few.

THE PSYCHOLOGY OF THE PERSONAE

Personality is revealed in dialogue. How one articulates his being reveals the inner self as well as what he feels about himself and others. And so it is to dialogue that we turn in search of clues to the personalities of the personae.

Students today come to the study of personality with an arsenal of psychological terms. Some of these were suggested in Chapter 2, where we stated that one convenient way of describing behavior is to note what one senses or intuits in the presence of another. These intuitions, or presses as we called them, are germane to the study of personality; the terms *expression, repression, suppression, depression,* and *impression* are particularly relevant. Language expresses a personality; it gives an impression to another; it springs from the conditions within the personality. In assessing the personalities of the personae in literature, the interpreter must avoid the pitfalls of armchair psychologizing. Too often psychological terms are used before we know the depths and intricacies of their meanings. However, what is the interpreter to do, who must, after all, come to *some* conclusions about a personality in a drama before he can share this personality with others? In the suggested approach which follows, each step avoids over-intellectualization and emphasizes the quality most important in any discussion of personality: *caring.* Some might call it loving or respecting or cautiousness. Yet *caring* is probably the best word, for it suggests the capacity to listen. To perceive and evoke the personae of literature, one must listen to what is said.

The discussion that follows is based upon two important criteria:
1. No analysis of a character in drama is made until the play has been read carefully in its entirety, letting the play "happen" in its reading.
2. Any analysis is made only after prolonged reflection and the accumulation of a sizable amount of data taken directly from the dialogue of the play.

When these criteria are clearly understood, the student is ready to begin.

THE DANGER OF PROJECTION

The first step in assessing the personalities of the personae is the most crucial. We must not assume that the characters in literature are the projections in print of ourselves. When we project, we extend and give to others the characteristics of our own personalities. A generation of students seized upon the character of Holden Caulfield in *The Catcher in the Rye* as a projection of who they were, of what they represented, failing often to come to grips with who Holden is in the novel. This indulgence is certainly not proper for the evocator of literature. Hence, the interpreter must begin his study of the personae in literature with the knowledge that *the characters are not projections of his own persona.*

If not projection, then what? There may be points of identification, there may be moments of empathy, and there may be an intuition that somewhere in the life of the interpreter something like the personality in the literature has been experienced. Empathy, as already pointed out, is the capacity to feel with, to merge with the personality in literature because elements of one's experience are precisely like that of the fictional character. These moments of empathy are precise and rare. They are not to be confused with sympathy for a character, a response which occurs when we know that what is happening is a human possibility. Identification is not necessarily empathy; it may take place when a character fulfills one's wishes, desires, fantasies. An intuition is a non-rational knowing. However limited one's experience of life has been, one may feel intuitively that a character is right, that he rings true. Yet intuitions can lead the best interpreter astray if they are not tested against the literature itself. Empathy, sympathy, identification, intuition—these, and not projection, should guide the interpreter as he studies the personalities of his characters.

ANALYSIS OF DIALOGUE AND GESTURE

A close scrutiny of the dialogue—is it interaction? is it transaction?—is another guide in this study. From this accumulation of detail emerge the essential qualities of the personae. Kenneth Burke calls this accumulation of detail the establishment of the character's *gesture,* a word which, unfortunately, tends to mean "movement" in the minds of many (pointing, gesticulating, nodding, etc.). This is not Burke's meaning; he is suggesting that gesture can mean something much larger, as in the statement, "Tom made a gesture of friendship." (Tom's total behavior was of such a nature that he seemed in language and tone of voice and body to be saying I-am-going-to-be-friendly-with-you.) When an interpreter thinks about this larger concept of gesture, he is concerning himself with the thrust of the personality, with the manner in which it presents itself.

The following questions are opening probes for the interpreter, to be used after a careful reading of the play. The questions, you will notice, insist that what a person says can be a matter for close observation and detailed analysis. A short discussion of the four general questions will show the necessity for observation and analysis.

1. What is the general impression created by the character?
    —Is he complex?
    —Is he simple?
2. What are his basic attitudes toward life?
    —Does he appear trusting?
    —Does he view persons and things external to him as hostile? friendly? destructive?
    —Does he seem in conflict between his concept of what life should be and what it is?
    —Does he perceive life as something to be manipulated, used, seized?
    —Is he a fatalist?
    —Is life unimportant? important?
    —Is he locked in and rigid? free and open?
3. What are his important behaviors?
    —Is he bold and courageous?
    —Is he shy and withdrawn?
    —Is he cynical?
    —Is he loving?
    —Does he value thinking over feeling? or vice versa?
    —Does he seem intuitive? mystical?
    —Are his senses alive and alert? (touching, feeling, smelling, tasting, looking, etc.)

—Does he seem sensual? (seductive, sexual, conscious of his manhood, her womanhood)

—Is he compulsive? (must talk, must seduce, must manipulate, must move about, etc.)

—Is he impulsive? (acts without thinking)

—Is he a listener?

4. How does he use language?

—Does he talk in abstractions?

—Is he direct and simple in speech?

—Is his language colloquial?

—How does he use pronouns? (*I* and *you,* particularly)

—Does his language reveal his feelings?

—Is he more non-verbal than verbal?

—Does he tend to speak in fragments?

—Is his language allusive? indirect?

—Does his language ring true for what he says he is?

—Is his language an obstruction?

—Is his language affected?

—What kinds of questions does he ask? of whom? and why?

—Does he use language in the present tense? past tense? future tense?

—Is his language a part of a role?

—When does he "break through" in language?

—Does he speak in clichés?

—Is his language that of a particular group?

—Is his language inventive? original?

—Does he lie? distort the truth? hide the truth?

—How does he employ silence? Does he avoid silence?

—Is his language poetic?

—Does he ramble?

—Is his language truly "oral" (as opposed to literary)? literate?

1. *What is the general impression created by the character?* Our common language and our shared sensibilities acknowledge a range of human conduct along a continuum from simple to complex. In saying this we assume that all human beings are complex, but that some are more complex than others. What does an interpreter do with the phrases "a conniving king" or "a simple peasant girl"? Shakespeare's Richard III and Bernard Shaw's Joan of Arc can be described in these terms, but this is where the interpreter begins, not ends. A constant temptation in dramatic literature is to reduce all characters to simple terms in order to make them communicable. The fault is not with the dramatists so often as it is with the perceivers.

There is a dramatic and literary tradition of "stock characters," stereotypes of human behavior reduced to the simplest terms; the Western dramatic tradition has been richly influenced by these. Punch and Judy, lovers, faithful servants, misers, bores (these latter stemming from the commedia dell'arte tradition of Italian theater) are as alive and well today on television and in motion pictures as they were in Renaissance Europe. But this is not the kind of simplicity that is meant by "a simple approach to life."

Simplicity in a character may be seen in a strong and yet unsophisticated sense of purpose in life, an unquestioning acceptance of religious faith, a contentment with life as it is, a commitment and sense of purpose that comes in conflict with those who cannot even conceive of simplicity as a possibility. An interpreter who cannot accept simplicity as a viable life style without stereotyping it is woefully lacking in understanding of human conduct. That simplicity may be destructive, or destroyed or manipulated, or tragic in view of unperceived complexities of life is the basis for much dramatic action. One must not be so attuned to a psychologic view of man that he overlooks the fact of "simple lives."

Photos by Duane Michals

Complexity seems the more accepted view of man. And yet it is not sufficient to observe that a character is complex without being willing to state why this is so. What makes for a complex personality? Basically, *complexity is the degree of tension within the human psyche,* or, more accurately, tensions. In the simple personality there appears to be very little tension, very little sense that life perceived and life experienced are in conflict. In the play *Death of a Salesman,* Willy Loman appears from many perspectives to be "simple" — after all, his philosophy of salesmanship is reduced to a "shoeshine and a whistle," his sense of fatherhood is reduced to providing for his sons and wife, his very visual presence is a simple stereotype of a salesman. But soon after meeting this character, his inner tensions are felt, and the tensions amplify and grow. Willy Loman, the "low man," cannot be dismissed with a few clichés. The interpreter familiar with the character of Willy Loman should return to the list of questions on basic attitudes, behaviors, and language. In answering these questions the interpreter discovers tensions in his attitudes, behaviors, and language that create a very complex character.

Simplicity and complexity can, of course, be turned around and satirized. A simple person, for example, can become a buffoon with complex drives and motives. The interpreter accepts this possibility, but he begins his character analysis and un-

derstanding by sensing the general impression a character conveys, his stance toward life.

2. *What are the persona's basic attitudes toward life?* and 3. *What are his important behaviors?* While all four questions are bound together, these two must be considered together. An attitude is reflected in behavior. If an interpreter fails to suggest basic attitudes and important behaviors through verbal and non-verbal means, he has failed in the sense of dramatizing a person. An attitude is a bodily tone, a gestural thrust in space and time linked to the sounding voice and punctuating body in its total communicative impact. The interpreter must suggest "embodied persona."

The embodied person has a sense of being flesh and blood and bones, of being biologically alive and real: he knows himself to be substantial. To the extent that he is thoroughly "in" his body, he is likely to have a sense of personal continuity in time. He will experience himself as subject to the dangers that threaten his body, the dangers of attack, mutilation, disease, decay, and death. He is implicated in his bodily desire, and the gratifications and frustrations of the body. The individual thus has as his starting-point an experience of his body as a base from which he can be a person with other human beings.[6]

6. R. D. Laing, *The Divided Self* (Baltimore: Penquin Books, 1965), p. 67.

The interpreter starts with the embodied fact of his own being. He moves to accepting the embodied personae he perceives in print. He releases them from print to enter his own being. Their embodiment is then suggested by the interpreter. The interpreter seeks to know the sounding-body-voice of another human being. He cannot embody him totally, but *he knows what he feels like.*

This process of embodiment of personae challenges the interpreter's responsiveness and adaptability to the ongoing dialogue. Consider, as an illustration, Tennessee Williams' principal characters Blanche DuBois and Stanley Kowalski in *A Streetcar Named Desire.* In Blanche DuBois there has been in her recent life, as we experience her in the play, a drift away from a sense of embodiment. Her body is as languid as the moss which hangs and blows from the magnolias in the Louisiana setting of the play. Her very voice seems detached from the body which she has rejected as a suitable instrument of life. Stanley Kowalski, on the other hand, is all physical presence, animal and sensual. How does the interpreter embody these, in turn, two very opposing attitudes and behaviors? He does so by seeking the irreducible significant gesture (in Burke's sense) of each character.

What is the gesture of a person who does not accept his body as a sensual and sensuous, important part of his behaviorial stance? What does he *do* with his body?

He withdraws from it, and generally this withdrawal is suggested by a concave posture, a slouching forward of the shoulders, a sense of the personality moving away from the body. At the other extreme, animality is suggested by stalking, throwing the body into space, letting it "speak" before language itself speaks. Here are two rhythms that an interpreter can identify, two behaviors that can be reduced to some subtle physical bodily responses, small mannerisms, gestural responses.

The irreducible significant gesture is the important key to the interpreter's complex act of suggesting multiple personae in literature, and most noticeably dramatic literature. He must find those important behaviors and attitudes within a personality before he can even suggest who and what that personality is.

4. *How does the persona use language?* Language manifests persona, it manifests action, and it may, as well, point to a manifestation of potential action.[7] In dramatic literature a distance exists—sometimes great, sometimes small—between human action and the language. What a person says with words need not be congruent to what a person says with his physical self. The interpreter must ask, "What are people *doing* with language in this drama?"

Among the many uses of language, consider these possibilities: (1) an individual may use language to talk about doing something, but not do it, or wait to do it until it is too late (*Peer Gynt*); (2) a person may use language to talk about doing something and do it simultaneously with the talking (*Who's Afraid of Virginia Woolf?*); (3) he may talk about doing something to himself or others and do it eventually (*Death of a Salesman*); (4) he may talk about doing one thing but do another (*All My Sons*); (5) he may say very little or nothing and do or effect a great deal (*A Slight Ache*); (6) he may use language to talk about nothing and do nothing (*The Bald Soprano*).

The statement that language manifests action or points to a potential action makes the point that no language exists without some purpose, even if that purpose be purposelessness. The interpreter has to know why language/dialogue is being used in the manner it is—its orchestration, its rhythm, its inevitable purpose. The sense of a person and his relationship to his language is the sense of characterization.

CHARACTERIZATION

Dialogic characterization, from Greek drama to the contemporary theater, can be classified into three basic approaches: *characterization as mythic enactment, characterization as rhetorical presence*, and *characterization as psychological reality*. These categories are discrete and also interacting, as suggested in the diagram below.

---

7. "Language as manifest action" is developed by Albert Cook in *Prisms* (Bloomington: Indiana University Press, 1967), particularly in Chapters 5 and 6, "Action" and "Person."

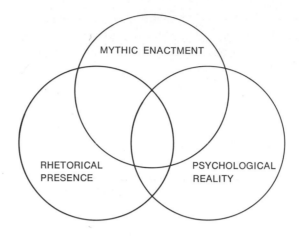

MYTHIC ENACTMENT

RHETORICAL
PRESENCE

PSYCHOLOGICAL
REALITY

CHARACTERIZATION AS MYTHIC ENACTMENT

Mythic enactment of a character depends upon (1) a cultural knowledge of the character and his story (mythologem), and/or (2) his embodiment as an archetypal character. The legend of Oedipus was well known to Greek audiences, as were the mythologic bases of all Greek tragedies. For Shakespeare and his contemporaries, the kings of England and the mythologems surrounding them, or the necessity of creating a "myth" pleasing to the reigning house, provided dramatic material. For American playwrights the Puritan and Pilgrim fathers, the political founding fathers such as George Washington and Benjamin Franklin, or even modern mythic personalities such as Abraham Lincoln and Woodrow Wilson constitute a mythologic base. An archetypal character is one that springs from the folk tales and myths of a culture. *The Devil and Daniel Webster* is a retelling of the archetypal *Faust,* who is, in turn, the symbol of the man who has sold his soul to dark and evil forces, the "man without a shadow" in the collective dreams of people in the Western world.

CHARACTERIZATION AS RHETORICAL PRESENCE

Characterization as rhetorical presence is a phenomenon that dates from Renaissance literature and the view of the purposes of language in that period. It means that a character's being and his language are synchronous, that language is thinking, thinking is language; language is emotion, emotion is language. The playwright does not motivate language; it exists, apparently self-motivated, within the characters. In a theatrical production in this tradition, language—a flowing, unimpeded sense of rhetorical presence, providing its own momentum—takes precedence over all other elements.

CHARACTERIZATION AS PSYCHOLOGICAL REALITY

Characterization as psychological reality can be said to have taken place when we feel that a character rings true, that he corresponds to one's knowledge of human nature. Of course, for any age the mode of theatrical characterization may have its own psychological reality. For Greek audiences the sense of an orchestrated, musical, rhythmic language of expression was "real"; for Elizabethans the sense of language first and language last was right, true, and expected; for contemporary audiences the acceptance of a character is overwhelmingly in terms of the possibility for his existence. His language and appearance must be right for who he is and where he comes from; he must be congruent with a contemporary awareness of man. The word which best sums up this expectation is *naturalness,* a quality that has been cultivated by television and motion pictures.

These three approaches to characterization are fused in many contemporary plays. Study the following examples: (1) In T. S. Eliot's *The Cocktail Party,* there is the contemporary "mythic" figure of the psychiatrist, Sir Harcourt-Reilly. The characters suffer from the contemporary identity crisis, and their condition rings true psychologically. The play itself is in poetic form, a four-stressed line that imposes a sense of rhetorical presence. How is the student to establish the proper priority of value and combine these elements in his interpretation? (2) In Eugene Ionesco's *The Bald Soprano,* a middle-class couple, a contemporary mythologem, literally waste their time with the language of cliché (a satirization of the rhetorical presence) only to discover at the end of their dialogue that they are man and wife, woman and husband, that their vacuity of language has been masking psychological truth. How does the interpreter combine these facts in working out the problems of characterization? (3) In John Osborne's *Luther,* the Reformation figure is analyzed psychologically. The play itself is almost a dramatization of Erik Erikson's *Young Man Luther,* in which Luther is analyzed from the point of view of identity crisis, its origins and its outcome. How is the mythical figure of Luther, counterpointed with his familiar rhetoric, related to his psychological reality? What does the emphasis upon psychological reality in interpretation do to the mythic and rhetorical elements?

In summary, what are the approaches of the interpreter in the preception and evocation of personae?

1. He analyzes the dialogue for its basic tensions and resolutions of interactions and transactions.
2. He analyzes the significant gesture of the characters—
   —the general impression of complexity or simplicity.
   —the basic attitude(s) expressed in the dialogue about life.
   —the important behaviors.
   —the manner in which language is used to express persona.

3. He analyzes the basic structure of the dialogic characterization—
    —characterization as mythic enactment.
    —characterization as rhetorical presence.
    —characterization as psychological reality.
    —combinations of the three.
Once the interpreter has applied these questions to his study of a piece of dramatic literature and has brought his characters into focus, he is ready to let them slip from the center of attention and concentrate on another factor. He is ready to put his emotions to work, to be "emotionally stimulated, emotionally guided, and emotionally satisfied."[8] He is ready to perceive the structure in which the drama takes place, its beginnings, its climax, its outcome.

DRAMATIC STRUCTURE

An interpreter seldom performs a play in its entirety; he is far more apt to present a scene, and more specifically, a confrontation of the personae. When the perception and evocation of dramatis personae is foremost, what are the useful elements of structure for him to identify? The play's *modulation*, its *development* and *spacings*, its where and when of *climax*, and its *tone* and *harmony*.[9]

Modulation is the manner in which characters in a drama fit together, the manner in which they fit into the transitions and movements of the play. A well-modulated play fits together in such a way that the flow of scenes and characters is logical within the context. Even abruptnesses and sudden shifts make sense. A lack of modulation stretches one's credulity and is ultimately unsatisfying. In Aeschylus' *Orestia* this sense of modulation can be found within the flow of the three plays, *The Agamemnon*, *The Eumenides*, and *The Libation Bearers*. The modulating element is the curse on the house of Atreus. Within each play the curse is given its own particular turn: in *Agamemnon* Orestes' mother, Clytemnestra, kills his father, Agamemnon, because the father sacrificed Orestes' sister, Iphegenia (though the origin of the curse lay with Agamemnon's father and constitutes the true mythic origin of the play); in *The Eumenides* Orestes kills his mother, Clytemnestra, and her lover, avenging his father's murder, but is doomed to be pursued by the *eumenides,* or furies, as retribution; and finally in *The Libation Bearers*, the curse is lifted when the god Apollo intervenes and purifies Orestes. Thus, there is a modulation within the trio of plays, and within each play there is another internal modulation of scenes and events which shapes the characters and their development.

8. Paul Weiss, *The World of Art* (Carbondale: Southern Illinois University Press, 1961), p. 83.
9. Adapted from "Common Features of the Arts" (Chapter 7) in Weiss, *The World of Art*.

Development is the structure in which modulation takes place.

A good structure is achieved when a theme is developed throughout a work. The theme must vary not only in emphasis, extent, luminosity, but must be stressed, qualified, contracted, expanded, dimmed, and intensified in various ways throughout.[10]

Spacing in drama is the method of achieving silence, rest. Sound is framed by silence, silence by sound. Edward Albee orchestrates spacing or silence particularly effectively in the last act of *Who's Afraid of Virginia Woolf.* For the two preceding acts, the dialogue has been at points furiously paced and at other points counterpointed by shifts and changes. But by the time the "fun and games" sequence is over, by the time the deceits and secrets have been laid bare, there is for George and Martha only the silence of the dawn. The final effect of the personae is framed by silence. Albee's play is also a superb study of development in which stress, contraction, expansion, intensification are employed with unusual dramatic skill.

Climax is ". . . the highest point of the work, the place at which all the problems are clustered and resolved. . . . [The] term 'climax' is to be understood to refer to an unusually stressed turning point. . . ."[11] The climax of *Who's Afraid of Virginia Woolf?* is that point in Act 3 in which George forces Martha to purge the make-believe son from her life. The play, a complex study in psychological, rhetorical, and mythic characterization, has for its climactic scene the sudden and abrupt shift to dialogue as mythic presentation, George's recitation of a section from the Holy Order of Requiem Mass. The climax is that point in the drama toward which all development has been progressing, and from which the new sense of happening proceeds.

Tone and harmony, musical terms, indicate the "note" the play is written in, the sound which the dialogue produces. Shakespeare's genius was, among other things, the capacity to give the right tone in language, word choice, and "harmonics" (the sense that all coheres) to his characters. When unrhymed iambic pentameter is appropriate, it is used, but when a character's total personality is such that a poetic form is inappropriate, he is given prose to speak. In *Love's Labor's Lost* dialogue is carried to the poetic extreme when a character speaks in sonnet form, a device artificial in its structure but right for the tone and harmony of the characters. The problem of tone and harmony is a difficult one for the interpreter, for the playwright attempts to choose the words and speech most suitable not only for his characters but for his concept of the play's complete structure. The intense "color" harmony of Christopher Fry's dialogue in such plays as *The Lady's Not for Burning* and *Venus Observed* means that the auditor will experience a rhetorical presence before a psychological one. That "nobody talks that way" is not the interpreter's concern. That

10. Ibid., p. 110.
11. Ibid., pp. 110–111.

they do, and that they do stunningly, is the play's most insistent fact. Tone and its resultant harmony, or disharmony, is the interpreter's challenge—to discover what it is that makes the unknown in the dialogue so compelling.

The actor's art of total illusion is not the interpreter's concern, but the suggestion of possibility is, through his behavioral presentation of dialogue. To perceive personae, to evoke and share that sense of all men's possibility within you, is to enrich not only your own emotional life, but also your awareness that the world speaks through you. He who hesitates at dialogue is turning his ear from man's ideas and inner being.

from **The Screenplay of "To Kill a Mockingbird"**[12]

Horton Foote

Courtroom — Later
The solicitor, Mr. Gilmer, *is examining the* Sheriff, Heck Tate.

Tate: On the night of August twenty-first, I was just leavin' my office to go home when Bob . . . Mr. Ewell . . . come in, very excited, he was. And he said get to his house quick as I could . . . that his girl had been raped. I got in my car and went out there as fast as I could. She was pretty well beat up. I asked her if Tom Robinson beat her like that. She said, "Yes, he did." I asked if he'd taken advantage of her and she said, "Yes, he did." That's all there was to it.
Gilmer: Thank you.

Atticus *is sitting behind his table, his chair skewed to one side, his legs crossed, and one arm is resting on the back of the chair.*

Judge: Any questions, Atticus?
Atticus: Yes, sir. Did anybody call a doctor, Sheriff?
Tate: No, sir.
Atticus: Why not?
Tate: Well, I didn't think it was necessary. She was pretty well beat up. Something sho' happened. It was obvious.
Atticus: Now, Sheriff, you say that she was mighty beat up. In what way?
Tate: Well, she was beaten around the head. There were bruises already comin' on her arms. She had a black eye startin' an' . . .
Atticus: Which eye?
Tate: Let's see . . . *(Heck Tate blinks and runs his hand through his hair. He points to an invisible person five inches in front of him.)* It was her left.
Atticus: Well, now, was that . . . er . . . that was her left facing you . . . or lookin' the way that you were?
Tate: Oh, yes . . . that . . . er . . . would make it her right eye. It was her right eye, Mr. Finch. Now I remember. She was beaten up on that side of her face.

Heck Tate *blinks again and then turns and looks at* Tom Robinson *as if something had been made clear to him at the same time.* Tom Robinson *raises his head. Something has been made clear to* Atticus, *too, and he gets to his feet. He walks toward* Heck Tate.

---

12. From *The Screenplay of "To Kill a Mockingbird"* by Horton Foote, based on the novel by Harper Lee, © 1964 by Boardwalk Productions and Brentwood Productions, Inc. Reprinted by permission of Harcourt Brace Jovanovich, Inc.

Atticus: Which side, again, Heck?

Tate: The right side. She had bruises on her arms and she showed me her neck. There were definite finger marks on her gullet.

Atticus: Uh . . . all around her neck? At the back of her throat?

Tate: I'd say they were all around.

Atticus *nods to* Mr. Gilmer *as he sits down.* Mr. Gilmer *shakes his head at the* Judge. *The* Judge *nods to* Heck, *who rises stiffly and steps down from the witness stand.*

Judge: Witness may be excused.

The Clerk *booms out:*

Clerk: Robert E. Lee Ewell. . . . *(Bob Ewell rises and struts to the stand. He raises his right hand, puts his left on the Bible, and is sworn in as a witness.)* Place your hand on the Bible, please. Do you promise to tell the truth, the whole truth, and nothin' but the truth, so help you God?

Ewell: I do.

Clerk: Sit down.

Mr. Gilmer *addresses* Ewell.

Gilmer: Now, Mr. Ewell . . . will you tell us, just in your own words, what happened on August twenty-first.

Ewell: Well, that night I was comin' in from the woods with a load of kindlin', and I heard Mayella screamin' as I got to the fence. So I dropped my kindlin', and I run just as fast as I could, but I run into the fence. But when I got loose, I run up to the window and I seen him with my Mayella!

The rest of the testimony is drowned out by the people in the courtroom, who begin to murmur with excitement. Judge Taylor begins to bang his desk with his gavel. Heck Tate goes to the aisle, trying to quiet the crowd. Atticus is on his feet, whispering to the Judge. The spectators finally quiet down, and Mr. Gilmer continues.

Gilmer: What did you do after you saw the defendant?

Ewell: I ran around the house tryin' to get in, but he done run through the front door just ahead o' me. But I seen who it was, all right. I seen him. And I run in the house and po' Mayella was layin' on the floor squallin'. Then I run for Mr. Tate just as quick as I could.

Gilmer: Uh huh. Thank you, Mr. Ewell.

Mr. Gilmer *sits down.* Atticus *rises and goes to the stand and faces* Ewell.

Atticus: Would you mind if I just ask you a few questions, Mr. Ewell?

Ewell: No, sir, Mr. Finch, I sho' wouldn't.

Atticus: Folks were doin' a lot of runnin' that night. Let's see, now, you say that you ran to the window, you ran inside, you ran to Mayella, and you ran to the Sheriff. Now, did you, during all the runnin', run for a doctor?

Ewell: There weren't no need to. I seen who done it.

Atticus: Now, Mr. Ewell . . . you've heard the Sheriff's testimony. Do you agree with his description of Mayella's injuries?

Ewell: I agree with everything Mr. Tate said. Her eye was blacked. She was mighty beat up . . . mighty.

Atticus: Now, Mr. Ewell, can you . . . er . . . can you read and write?

Ewell: Yes, Mr. Finch. I can read and I can write.

Atticus: Good . . . then will you write your name, please. Write there, and show us?

Atticus *takes paper and pen out of his coat. He hands them to* Ewell. Ewell *looks up and sees their attention.*

Ewell: Well, what's so interestin'?

Judge: You're left-handed, Mr. Ewell.

Ewell *turns angrily to the* Judge.

Ewell: Well, what's that got to do with it, Judge? I'm a God-fearin' man. That Atticus Finch is tryin' to take advantage of me. You got to watch lawyers like Atticus Finch.

Judge Taylor *bangs his gavel.*

Judge: Quiet! Quiet, sir! Now the witness may take his seat.

Ewell *sullenly leaves the witness stand.*

Clerk: Mayella Violet Ewell. . . . *(A silence comes over the court as* Mayella Ewell, *a young girl, walks to the witness stand. She is a thick-bodied girl, accustomed to strenuous labor.)* Put your hand on the Bible, please. Do you swear to tell the truth, the whole truth, and nothing but the truth, so help you God? *(*Mayella *nods.* Mr. Gilmer *rises and begins to question her.)*

Gilmer: Now, Mayella, suppose you tell us just what happened, huh?

Mayella *clears her throat.*

Mayella: Well, um . . . sir . . . I was sittin' on the porch, and . . . and he comes along. Uh, there's this old chiffarobe in the yard . . . and I . . . I said, "You come up here, boy, and bust up this chiffarobe, and I'll give you a nickel." So he . . . he come on in the yard and I go into the house to get him the nickel and I turn around, and 'fore I know it, he's on me . . . and I fought and hollered . . . but he had me around the neck, and he hit me again and again, and the next thing I knew, Papa was in the room, a-standin' over me, hollerin', "Who done it, who done it?"

Gilmer: Thank you, Mayella. Your witness, Atticus.

Gilmer *walks away.* Atticus *gets up smiling. He opens his coat, hooks his thumbs in his vest, walks slowly across the room to the windows.*

Atticus: Miss Mayella, is your father good to you? I mean, is he easy to get along with?

Mayella: He does tol'able. . . .

Atticus: Except when he's drinking? *(A pause. She glares at* Atticus.*)* When he's riled, has he ever beaten you? *(Mayella looks in* Ewell's *direction.)*

Mayella: My Pa's never touched a hair o' my head in my life.

Atticus' *glasses slip a little and he pushes them back on his head.*

Atticus: Now, you say that you asked Tom to come in and chop up a . . . what was it?

Mayella: A chiffarobe.

Atticus: Was this the first time that you ever asked him to come inside the fence?

Mayella *acts confused and shrugs.*

Mayella: Yes.

Atticus: Didn't you ever ask him to come inside the fence before?

Mayella *flinches.*

Mayella: *(evasively)* I mighta.

Atticus: But can you remember any other occasion?

Mayella *shakes her head.*

Mayella: No!

Atticus: You say, "He caught me and he choked me and he took advantage of me," is that right? *(Mayella nods her head.)* Do you remember his beating you about the face? *(Mayella hesitates.)*

Mayella: No, I don't recollect if he hit me. I . . . er . . . mean . . . yes! He hit me . . . he hit me!

Atticus *turns.*

Atticus: Thank you! Now will you identify the man who beat you?

Mayella *points to* Tom.

Mayella: I most certainly will . . . sittin' right yonder.

Atticus: Tom, will you stand up, please? Let's let Mayella have a good long look at you. (Tom Robinson *rises to his feet. It is our first good look at him. He is thirty. Atticus goes to the table and picks up a water glass.)* Tom, will you please catch this? (Atticus *throws the glass.* Tom *is standing at the defense table. He catches the glass with his right hand.)* Thank you. (Atticus *walks to* Tom *and takes the glass.)* Now then, this time will you please catch it with your left hand?

Tom: I can't, sir.

Atticus: Why can't you?

Tom: I can't use my left hand at all. I got it caught in a cotton gin when I was twelve years old. All my muscles were tore loose.

There are murmurs from the crowd in the courtroom. The Judge *pounds his gavel.*

Atticus: Is this the man who raped you?

Mayella: He most certainly is.

Atticus: How?

Mayella: I don't know how. He done . . . it . . . *(She starts to sob.)* He just done it.

Atticus: You have testified that he choked you and he beat you. You didn't say that he sneaked up behind you and knocked you out cold, but that you turned and there he was. Do you want to tell us what really happened?

Mayella: I got somethin' to say. And then I ain't gonna say no more. (Mayella *reacts in a frightened and hysterical way. She looks in* Tom's *direction.)* He took advantage of me. (Atticus *glances in* Mayella's *direction with a grim expression. She shouts and gestures with her hands as she speaks.)* An' if you fine, fancy gentlemen ain't gonna do nothin' about it, then you're just a bunch of lousy, yellow, stinkin' cowards, the . . . the whole bunch of you, and your fancy airs don't come to nothin'. Your Ma'am-in' and your Miss Mayellarin'—it don't come to nothin', Mr. Finch. Not . . . no . . . *(She bursts into real tears. Her shoulders shake with angry heaving sobs. Atticus* has hit her in a way that is not clear to him, but he has had no pleasure in doing it. He sits with his head down. Mayella *runs as* Ewell *and a man grab her.)*

Ewell: You sit down there!

Man: Come on, girl.

Ewell *holds* Mayella's *arms and starts for his seat.* Ewell *helps* Mayella *to be seated. She hides her head in the seat as* Ewell *sits down.*

The Judge *looks in the direction of* Atticus.

Judge: Atticus? Mr. Gilmer?

Gilmer rises.

Gilmer: The State rests, Judge.

Clerk: Tom Robinson, take the stand. *(Tom stands up and goes to the witness chair.)* Put your hand on the Bible. *(Tom puts his hand on the Bible.)* Do you solemnly swear to tell the truth, the whole truth, and nothing but the truth, so help you God?

Tom: I do.

Clerk: Sit down!

The clerk turns away as Tom *starts to sit.* Atticus *starts toward the* Judge *and* Tom. Atticus *starts to question* Tom.

Atticus: Tom, were you acquainted with Mayella Violet Ewell?

Tom: Yes, sir. I had to pass her place goin' to and from the field every day.

Atticus: Is there any other way to go?

Tom *shakes his head.*

Tom: No, suh. None's I know of.

Atticus: Did she ever speak to you?

Tom: Why, yes, suh. I'd tip m' hat when I'd go by, and one day she ask me to come inside the fence and bust up a chiffarobe for her. She give me the hatchet and I broke it up and then she said, "I reckon I'll hafta give you a nickel, won't I?" And I said, "No, ma'am, there ain't no charge." Then I went home. Mr. Finch, that was way last spring, way over a year ago.

Atticus: And did you ever go on the place again?

Tom: Yes, suh.

Atticus: When?

Tom: Well, I went lots of times. Seemed like every time I passed by yonder, she'd have some little somethin' for me to do . . . choppin' kindlin', totin' water for her.

Atticus: What happened to you on the evening of August twenty-first of last year?

Tom: Mr. Finch, I was goin' home as usual that evenin' and I passed the Ewell place. Miss Mayella were on the porch like she said she were. *(The spectators, white and colored, all lean forward. It is very quiet in the room.)* An' she said for me to come there and help her a minute. Well, I went inside the fence and I looked aroun' for some kindlin' to work on, but I didn't see none. An' then she said to come in the house, she . . . she has a door needs fixin' . . . so I follows her inside an' looked at the door an' it looked all right, an' she shut the door. All the time I was wonderin' why it was so quiet like . . . an' it come to me, there was not a child on the place, an' I said to Miss Mayella, where are the children? An' she said, they all gone to get ice cream. She said it took her a slap year to save seb'm nickels, but she done it, an' they all gone to town.

(Tom's black skin has begun to shine. He runs his hands over his face. He is obviously very uncomfortable.)

Atticus: What did you say then?

Tom: Oh, I . . . I said somethin' like, "Why Miss Mayella, that's right nice o' you to treat 'em." An' she said, "You think so?" Well, I said I best be goin', I couldn't do nothin' for her, an' she said, oh, yes I could. An' I ask her what, an' she said to jus' step on the chair yonder an' git that box down from on top of the chiffarobe. So I done what she told me, and I was reachin' when the next thing I knew she . . . grabbed me aroun' the legs. She scared me so bad I hopped down an' turned the chair over. That was the only thing, only furniture 'sturbed in that room, Mr. Finch, I swear, when I left it.

Atticus: And what happened after you turned the chair over?

Tom *comes to a dead stop. He glances at* Atticus, *then at the jury.*

Atticus: Tom? You've sworn to tell the whole truth. Will you do it? What happened after that?

Tom *runs his hand nervously over his mouth.*

Tom: Mr. Finch, I got down off the chair, and I turned around an' she sorta jumped on me. She hugged me aroun' the waist. She reached up an' kissed me on the face. She said she never kissed a grown man before an' she might as well kiss me. She says for me to kiss her back. *(Tom shakes his head with his eyes closed, as he reacts to this ordeal.)* And I said, Miss Mayella, let me outta here, an' I tried to run, when Mr. Ewell cussed at me from the window an' says he's gonna kill her.

Atticus: And what happened after that?

Tom: I was runnin' so fast, I don' know what happened.

Atticus: Tom, did you rape Mayella Ewell?

Tom: I did not, sir.

Atticus: Did you harm her in any way?

Tom: I . . . I did not, sir.

Atticus *turns and walks to his desk.* Gilmer *rises and goes to the witness chair.*

Gilmer: Robinson, you're pretty good at bustin' up chiffarobes and kindlin' with one hand, aren't you? Strong enough to choke the breath out of a woman and sling her to the floor?

Tom: *(meekly)* I never done that, sir.

Gilmer: But you're strong enough to.

Tom: I reckon so, sir.

Gilmer: Uh huh. How come you're so all-fired anxious to do that woman's chores?

Tom *hesitates. He searches for an answer.*

Tom: Looks like she didn't have nobody to help her. Like I said . . .

Gilmer: With Mr. Ewell and seven children on the place? You did all this choppin' and work out of sheer goodness, boy? Ha, ha, you're a mighty good fella, it seems. Did all that for not one penny.

Tom: Yes, sir. I felt right sorry for her. She seemed . . .

Gilmer: *(indignantly)* You felt sorry for her? A white woman? You felt sorry for her?

Tom *realizes his mistake. He shifts uncomfortably in his chair.*

Courtroom

Atticus *rises and walks toward the jury. They watch with no show of emotion. As Atticus talks, he looks into the eyes of the men of the jury as if to find one to encourage him.*

Atticus: To begin with, this case should never have come to trial. The State has not produced one iota of medical evidence that the crime Tom Robinson is charged with ever took place. It has relied instead on the testimony of two witnesses . . . whose evidence has not only been called into serious question on cross-examination, but has been flatly contradicted by the defendant. There is circumstantial evidence to indicate that Mayella Ewell was beaten savagely by someone who led almost exclusively with his left. And Tom Robinson now sits before you having taken the oath with his right hand, the only good hand he possesses. I have nothing but pity in my heart for the chief witness for the State. She is a victim of cruel poverty and ignorance. But my pity does not extend so far as to her putting a man's life at stake, which she has done in an effort to get rid of her own guilt. Now, I say guilt, gentlemen, because it was guilt that motivated her. She has committed no crime, she has merely broken a rigid and time-honored code of our society. A code so severe that whoever breaks it is hounded from our midst as unfit to live with. She must destroy the evidence of her offense. But what was the evidence of her offense? Tom Robinson, a human being. She must put Tom Robinson away from her. Tom Robinson was for her a daily reminder of what she did. And what did she do? She tempted a Negro. She was white, and she tempted a Negro. She did something that in our society is unspeakable. She kissed a black man. Not an old uncle, but a strong, young Negro man. No code mattered to her before she broke it, but it came crashing down on her afterwards. The witnesses for the State, with the exception of the Sheriff of Maycomb County, have presented themselves to you gentlemen, to this Court, in the cynical confidence that their testimony would not be doubted. Confident that you gentlemen would go along with them on the assumption, the evil assumption, that all Negroes lie, that all Negroes are basically immoral beings, all Negro men are not to be trusted around our women. An assumption one associates with minds of their caliber, and which is in itself, gentlemen, a lie, which I do not need to point out to you. And so, a quiet, humble, respectable Negro, who has had the unmitigated temerity to feel sorry for a white woman, has had to put his word against two white people. The defendant is not guilty, but somebody in this courtroom is. Now, gentlemen, in this country our courts are the great levelers, and in our courts all men are created equal. *(The faces of the men of the jury haven't changed expression.* Atticus' *face begins to perspire. He wipes it with a handkerchief.)* I'm no idealist to believe firmly in the integrity of our courts and in the jury system. That is no ideal to me. It is a living, working reality. Now I am confident that you gentlemen will review without passion the evidence that you have heard, come to a decision, and restore this man to his family. In the name of God, do your duty. In the name of God, believe Tom Robinson. *(*Atticus *turns away from the jury. He walks and sits down next to* Tom *at the defense table.)*

The Lady of Larkspur Lotion[13]

Tennessee Williams

Characters
Mrs. Hardwicke-Moore.
Mrs. Wire.
The Writer.

Scene: A wretchedly furnished room in the French Quarter of New Orleans. There are no windows, the room being a cubicle partitioned off from several others by imitation walls. A small slanting skylight admits the late and unencouraging day. There is a tall, black armoire, whose doors contain cracked mirrors, a swinging electric bulb, a black and graceless dresser, an awful picture of a Roman Saint and over the

13. *Larkspur Lotion is a common treatment for body vermin.* — Author's note.

Tennessee Williams, *27 Wagons Full of Cotton.* Copyright 1945 by Tennessee Williams. Reprinted by permission of New Directions Publishing Corporation.

Caution: Professionals and amateurs are hereby warned that this play, being fully protected under the copyright laws of the United States of America, the British Empire including the Dominion of Canada, and all other countries of the Copyright Union, is subject to royalty. All rights, including professional, amateur, motion picture, recitation, lecturing, public reading, radio and television broadcasting, and the rights of translation into foreign languages, are strictly reserved. Particular emphasis is laid on the question of readings, permission for which must be secured from the author's agent, Audrey Wood, c/o International Famous Agency, 1301 Avenue of the Americas, New York, New York 10019.

bed a coat-of-arms in a frame.

    Mrs. Hardwicke-Moore, *a dyed-blonde woman of forty, is seated passively on the edge of the bed as though she could think of nothing better to do.*

    There is a rap at the door.

Mrs. Hardwicke-Moore: *(in a sharp, affected tone)* Who is at the door, please?

Mrs. Wire: *(from outside, bluntly)* Me! *(Her face expressing a momentary panic,* Mrs. Hardwicke-Moore *rises stiffly.)*

Mrs. Hardwicke-Moore: Oh. . . . Mrs. Wire. Come in. *(The landlady enters, a heavy, slovenly woman of fifty.)* I was just going to drop in your room to speak to you about something.

Mrs. Wire: Yeah? What about?

Mrs. Hardwicke-Moore: *(humorously, but rather painfully smiling)* Mrs. Wire, I'm sorry to say that I just don't consider these cockroaches to be the most desirable kind of room-mates—do you?

Mrs. Wire: Cockroaches, huh?

Mrs. Hardwicke-Moore: Yes. Precisely. Now I have had very little experience with cockroaches in my life but the few that I've seen before have been the pedestrian kind, the kind that *walk.* These, Mrs. Wire, appear to be *flying* cockroaches! I was shocked, in fact I was literally stunned, when one of them took off the floor and started to whiz through the air, around and around in a circle, just missing my face by barely a couple of inches. Mrs. Wire, I sat down on the edge of this bed and *wept,* I was just so shocked and disgusted! Imagine! Flying cockroaches, something I never dreamed to be in existence, whizzing around and around and around in front of my face! Why, Mrs. Wire, I want you to know—

Mrs. Wire: *(interrupting)* Flying cockroaches are nothing to be surprised at. They have them all over, even uptown they have them. But that ain't what I wanted to—

Mrs. Hardwicke-Moore: *(interrupting)* That may be true, Mrs. Wire, but I may as well tell you that I have a horror of roaches, even the plain old-fashioned, pedestrian kind, and as for this type that flies—! If I'm going to stay on here these flying cockroaches have got to be gotten rid of and gotten rid of at *once!*

Mrs. Wire: Now how'm I going to stop them flying cockroaches from coming in through the windows? But that, however, is not what I—

Mrs. Hardwicke-Moore: *(interrupting)* I don't know *how,* Mrs. Wire, but there certainly must be a method. All I know is they must be gotten rid of before I will sleep here one more night, Mrs. Wire. Why, if I woke up in the night and found one on my bed, I'd have a convulsion, I swear to goodness I'd simply *die* of convulsions!

Mrs. Wire: If you'll excuse me for sayin' so, Mrs. Hardshell-Moore, you're much more likely to die from over-drinkin' than cockroach convulsions! *(She seizes a bottle from the dresser.)* What's this here? Larkspur Lotion! *Well!*

Mrs. Hardwicke-Moore: *(flushing)* I use it to take the old polish off my nails.

Mrs. Wire: Very fastidious, yes!

Mrs. Hardwicke-Moore: What do you mean?

Mrs. Wire: There ain't an old house in the Quarter that don't have roaches.

Mrs. Hardwicke-Moore: But not in such enormous quantities, do they? I tell you this place is actually crawling with them!

Mrs. Wire: It ain't as bad as all that. And by the way, you ain't yet paid me the rest of this week's rent. I don't want to get you off the subjeck of roaches, but, nevertheless, I want to colleck that money.

Mrs. Hardwicke-Moore: I'll pay you the rest of the rent as soon as you've exterminated these roaches!

Mrs. Wire: You'll have to pay me the rent right away or get out.

Mrs. Hardwicke-Moore: I intend to get out unless these *roaches* get out!

Mrs. Wire: Then get out then and quit just talking about it!

Mrs. Hardwicke-Moore: You must be out of your mind, I can't get out right now!

Mrs. Wire: Then what did you mean about roaches?

Mrs. Hardwicke-Moore: I meant what I said about roaches, they are not, in my opinion, the most desirable room-mates!

Mrs. Wire: Okay! Don't room with them! Pack your stuff and move where they don't have roaches!

Mrs. Hardwicke-Moore: You mean that you *insist* upon having the roaches?

Mrs. Wire: No, I mean I insist upon having the rent you owe me.

Mrs. Hardwicke-Moore: Right at the moment that is out of the question.

Mrs. Wire: Out of the question, is it?

Mrs. Hardwicke-Moore: Yes, and I'll tell you why! The quarterly payments I receive from the man who is taking care of the rubber plantation have not been forwarded yet. I've been expecting them to come in for several weeks now but in the letter that I received this morning it seems there has been some little misunderstanding about the last year's taxes and—

Mrs. Wire: Oh, now stop it, I've heard enough of that goddam rubber plantation! The Brazilian rubber plantation! You think I've been in this business seventeen years without learning nothing about your kind of women?

Mrs. Hardwicke-Moore: *(stiffly)* What is the implication in that remark?

Mrs. Wire: I suppose the men that you have in here nights come in to discuss the Brazilian rubber plantation?

Mrs. Hardwicke-Moore: You must be crazy to say such a thing as that!

Mrs. Wire: I hear what I hear an' I know what's going on!

Mrs. Hardwicke-Moore: I know you spy, I know you listen at doors!

Mrs. Wire: I never spy and I never listen at doors! The first thing a landlandy in the French Quarter learns is not to *see* and not to *hear* but only collect your *money!* As long as that comes in—okay, I'm blind, I'm deaf, I'm dumb! But soon as it stops, I recover my hearing and also my sight and also the use of my voice. If necessary I go to the phone and call up the chief of police who happens to be an in-law of my sister's! I heard last night that argument over money.

Mrs. Hardwicke-Moore: What argument? What money?

Mrs. Wire: He shouted so loud I had to shut the front window to keep the noise from carrying out on the streets! I heard no mention of any Brazilian plantation! But plenty of other things were plainly referred to in that little midnight conversation you had! Larkspur Lotion—to take the polish off nails! Am I in my infancy, am I? That's on a par with the wonderful *rubber* plantation! *(The door is thrown open.* The Writer, *wearing an ancient purple bathrobe, enters.)*

Writer: Stop!

Mrs. Wire: *Oh!* It's *you!*

Writer: Stop persecuting this woman!

Mrs. Wire: The second Mr. Shakespeare enters the scene!

Writer: I heard your demon howling in my sleep!

Mrs. Wire: *Sleep? Ho-ho!* I think that what you *mean* is your *drunken stupor!*

Writer: I rest because of my illness! Have I no right—

Mrs. Wire: *(interrupting)* Illness—*alcoholic!* Don't try to pull that beautiful wool over my eyes. I'm glad you come in now. Now I repeat for your benefit what I just said to this woman. I'm *done* with *dead beats!* Now is that plain to yuh? Completely fed-up with all you Quarter rats, half-breeds, drunkards, degenerates, who try to get by on promises, lies, delusions!

Mrs. Hardwicke-Moore: *(covering her ears)* Oh, please, please, please stop shrieking! It's not necessary!

Mrs. Wire: *(turning on* Mrs. Hardwicke-Moore*)* You with your Brazilian rubber plantation. That coat-of-arms on the wall that you got from the junk-shop—the woman who sold it *told* me! One of the Hapsburgs! Yes! A titled lady! *The Lady of Larkspur Lotion! There's your title!* (Mrs. Hardwicke-Moore *cries out wildly and flings herself face down on the sagging bed.)*

Writer: *(with a pitying gesture)* Stop badgering this unfortunate little woman! Is there no mercy left in the world anymore? What has become of compassion and understanding? Where have they all gone to? Where's God? Where's Christ? *(He leans trembling against the armoire.)* What if there *is* no Brazilian rubber plantation?

Mrs. Hardwicke-Moore: *(sitting passionately erect)* I tell you there is, there *is!* *(Her throat is taut with conviction, her head thrown back.)*

Writer: What if there *is* no rubber king in her life! There *ought* to be rubber kings in her life! Is she to be blamed because it is necessary for her to compensate for the cruel deficiencies of reality by the exercise of a little—what shall I say? —God-given—imagination?

Mrs. Hardwicke-Moore: *(throwing herself face down on the bed once more)* No, no, no, no, it *isn't*—imagination!

Mrs. Wire: I'll ask you to please stop spitting me in the face those high-flown speeches! You with your 780-page masterpiece—right on a par with the Lady of Larkspur Lotion as far as the use of imagination's concerned!

Writer: *(in a tired voice)* Ah, well, now, what if I am? Suppose there *is* no 780-page masterpiece in existence. *(He closes his eyes and touches his forehead.)* Supposing there is in existence no masterpiece whatsoever! What of that, Mrs. Wire? But only a few, a very few—vain scribblings—in my old trunk-bottom. . . . Suppose I wanted to be a great artist but lacked the force and the power! Suppose my books fell short of the final chapter, even my verses languished uncompleted! Suppose the curtains of my exalted fancy rose on magnificent dramas—but the house-lights darkened before the curtain fell! Suppose all of these unfortunate things are true! And suppose that I—stumbling from bar to bar, from drink to drink, till I sprawl at last on the lice-infested mattress of this brothel—suppose that I, to make this nightmare bearable for as long as I must continue to be the helpless protagonist of it—suppose that I ornament, illuminate—glorify it! With dreams and fictions and fancies! Such as the existence of a 780-page masterpiece—impending Broadway productions— marvelous volumes of verse in the hands of publishers only waiting for signatures to release them! Suppose that I live in this world of pitiful fiction! What satisfaction can it give you, good woman, to tear it to pieces, to crush it—call it a *lie?* I tell you this—now listen! There are no lies but the lies that are stuffed in the mouth by the hard-knuckled hand of need, the cold iron fist of necessity, Mrs. Wire! So I am a liar, yes! But your world is built on a lie, your world is a hideous fabrication of lies! Lies! Lies! . . . Now I'm tired and I've said my say and I have no money to give you so get away and leave this woman in peace! Leave her alone. Go on, get out, get away! *(He shoves her firmly out the door.)*

Mrs. Wire: *(shouting from the other side)* Tomorrow morning! Money or out you go! Both of you. Both together! 780-page masterpiece and Brazilian rubber plantation! *BALONEY! (Slowly the derelict* Writer *and the derelict woman turn to face each other. The daylight is waning grayly through the skylight. The Writer slowly and stiffly extends his arms in a gesture of helplessness.)*

Mrs. Hardwicke-Moore: *(turning to avoid his look)* Roaches! Everywhere! Walls, ceiling, floor! The place is infested with them.

Writer: *(gently)* I know. I suppose there weren't any roaches on the Brazilian rubber plantation.

Mrs. Hardwicke-Moore: *(warming)* No, of course there weren't. Everything was immaculate always—always. *Immaculate!* The floors were so bright and clean they used to shine like—mirrors!

Writer: I know. And the windows—I suppose they commanded a very lovely view!

Mrs. Hardwicke-Moore: Indescribably lovely!

Writer: How far was it from the Mediterranean?

Mrs. Hardwicke-Moore: *(dimly)* The Mediterranean? Only a mile or two!

Writer: On a very clear morning I daresay it was possible to distinguish the white chalk cliffs of Dover? . . . Across the channel?

Mrs. Hardwicke-Moore: Yes—in very clear weather it *was.* (The Writer *silently passes her a pint bottle of whisky.)* Thank you, Mr.—?

Writer: Chekhov! Anton Pavlovitch Chekhov!

Mrs. Hardwicke-Moore: *(smiling with the remnants of coquetry)* Thank you, Mr.— Chekhov.

Curtain

CHECKLIST FOR ANALYSIS

1. How would the metaworld of the literature be described? What is the "state of being" in the selection? What is the principal presentational value of the selection? (See chart on page 22.)

2. In what mode is the selection written? What are the central behavioral problems in the selection? in the "presses"?

3. How is literary time conveyed in language? How does psychological time function? mythic time? How are silences used and where? What are the principal rhythms of the literature? In the case of poetry, what is the prevailing meter?

4. How is figurative language employed? to what ends? How are paradox and irony employed?

5. In the case of poetry, what is the form of the experience? What is the form into which the experience has been put? What precise poetic form is used? (See questions at conclusion of discussion on each poetic form, Chap. 5.)

6. What elements of style are most attractive to the reader? What are the problems of style as you perceive them for performance? What kind of narrator appears in the selection?

How attached or detached is he to the events in the literature? What are the implications for the performance in the narrator's role?

7. What does an analysis of dialogue reveal? How do the interactional patterns develop? Is there a movement toward transaction? What are the significant gestures of the character? How would you characterize the structure of the dialogue — mythic enactment? rhetorical presence? psychological reality?

EXERCISES AND ASSIGNMENTS

1. A comparison of Horton Foote's screenplay of *To Kill a Mockingbird* to the novel is a provocative study of the transformation of one genre into another (the novel into drama) and of one mode into another (the epic into the dramatic). In the courtroom scene provided in this book, the interpreter is confronted with two distinct problems. In the novel he is faced with the presence of the narrating persona and her selection of descriptive and narrative details as well as the presence and dialogue of the personae within the novel. In the screenplay the interpreter must condense the event solely in terms of the dramatis personae. Though the intent of each scene is the same, the effect is significantly different. What are these differences in effect? How does dialogue as rhetorical presence differ? dialogue as psychological reality? An interesting classroom experience might be to hear selections from both presented at the same time. (A careful review of the problems of delivery as discussed in Chapter 2, along with a review of the chart of the differences in the presentation of modes, would be helpful.)

2. What are the significant gestures in the characters of *The Lady of Larkspur Lotion?* Trace the interactional and transactional elements of dialogue. How has Williams achieved his effects? Why is dialogue as mythic enactment a vital and pervasive element of the play?

3. The following list of plays is suggested for study. In these plays the elements discussed in this chapter are clearly presented.
> Anton Chekhov, *The Sea Gull*
> Henrik Ibsen, *A Doll's House*
> John Osborne, *Luther*
> Bertolt Brecht, *Galileo*
> Edward Albee, *Who's Afraid of Virginia Woolf?*
> Eugene Ionesco, *The Bald Soprano*
> Harold Pinter, *The Homecoming*

4. The principles discussed in this chapter apply to dialogue in any genre. Analyze the dialogue in any narrative poem and in any short story or selection from a novel.

PERFORMANCE EVALUATION FORM

bjectives for Performance Growth

1 Exciting   **2** Enjoyable   **3** Adequate   **4** Need for Development

To Evoke the Metaworlds

_____ a sense of inner resonance
_____ a sense of attaining a state of being
_____ a responsiveness to presentational values
_____ IMPRESSION

To Relate the orming Body to ary Experience

_____ behavior congruent to mode
_____ language of gesture natural to literary space
_____ sound of language natural to literary space
_____ appropriate behavioral presses
_____ appropriate use of total bodily energy
_____ IMPRESSION

are Awareness f Literary Time

_____ sense of performing time appropriate to literary time
_____ literary time understood and evoked
_____ silences understood and evoked
_____ metrical time understood and evoked
_____ IMPRESSION

To Evoke rative Thought and Language

_____ appropriate exemplification of language
_____ a sense of symbolic intent
_____ a sharing of paradox and irony—where appropriate
_____ IMPRESSION

o Evoke Form

_____ form of experience immediate and compelling
_____ form of literary structure appreciated and evoked
_____ IMPRESSION

Present Style w Information

_____ expectations in performance congruent to language
_____ performer and style linked / fused
_____ stylistic elements perceived and evoked
_____ narrator attachment or detachment appropriate
_____ IMPRESSION

To Evoke the Presence of Personae

_____ interactional and / or transactional dialogue evoked
_____ significant gesture of characters evoked
_____ structure of dialogue evoked
_____ IMPRESSION

8

André Kertész

CHAPTER EIGHT

Multiforms: Experimental Approaches

The preceding chapters have attempted to stimulate and to nurture the evocation of literature through the sensibility of the single performer. When an individual is secure in his performing abilities, when his awarenesses are attuned to the compelling and complex layers of the literary experience, and when he feels free to transform literature using all the knowledge that his body gives him, he should then be encouraged to explore the multiforms of literary performance. The influence of media and the generative excitement of performing arts, in all the engaging forms they take, make the step from the single performing voice and body to many performing voices and bodies a natural extension of the principles discussed in this book.

The evocation of literature in multiforms can be explored from four perspectives: (1) the use of *multiperformers,* (2) the employment of *mixed-media*, (3) the utilization of *multimedia*, and (4) the exploration of *creative syntheses*. The first includes all forms of group performance; the second, performers and media in combination; the third, media alone; and the fourth is a creative fusion of innovations in performing modes. Each is a direct challenge to creative energies and exploratory freedom.

MULTIPERFORMANCES

A number of terms have come into use to describe group performances: readers theater, chamber theater, choric speaking, multimedia. These terms define precise modes of performance for those who use them. They are, in all cases, probes into performance possibilities, and as such, represent what every group production is: *a search for presentational form.* A rigid classification system will be avoided in the following discussion of what can be done in multiperformance, in the hope of turning creativity loose in whatever ways seem most congenial to the creator. The points to be stressed are that any production fulfill its own expectations, and that it be as rich an evocation of the literature as possible. Multiperformances may be discussed in three transformations: (1) a *dramatistic-dialogic transformation,* (2) a *narrative transformation,* and (3) a *scored transformation.* An understanding of each leads, naturally, to the possibility that all three can be combined in one production.

DRAMATISTIC-DIALOGIC TRANSFORMATION

This form creates drama from an adaptation of literature. The transformation emphasizes the dialogue and the personae in the literature; it is the form most associated with theater, motion pictures, and television. *The Forsyte Saga, Gone with the Wind, Alice in Wonderland, Portnoy's Complaint, Tristram Shandy*—in short, the world's narrative prose is adapted to dialogic form. The challenge with narrative prose is to transform the expansiveness of a novel into a one- or two-hour dramatic experience. Though the camera's eye and its point of view may capture the narrative essence of the novel or short story in a television production or motion picture, the adaptation in dialogic form for the stage is a particular challenge, for the dialogue must reveal all those elements of personae discussed in Chapter 7.

Obviously, the reading of plays is not a transformation of the form of the work, and the interpretative approach to drama is not different in kind from a theatrical approach. A group of performers may choose to read a play without the accoutrements of production, allowing suggestion and imaginative participation to fill out settings, props, and even costumes. But the addition of any of these does not alter the interpretative problems of personae.

A dramatistic-dialogic approach can be taken to an epic poem. Milton's *Paradise Lost* contains dramatic confrontations and characterizations of intricate complexity and lamination. One valid approach to the poem is to transform it into a drama of conflicting wills. In such a treatment the inherent drama is given primacy, and the characters are given increased profile. While such an adaptation admittedly does not convey the structure of the poem, it remains, nevertheless, Milton's in every line and in the concept of character. In adapting material into the dramatistic-dialogic transformation, the performer must ask himself, however, what the elimination of the narrative voice does to the sense of event. Does the dialogue itself carry the intent of the literature? With the elimination of the narrative voice are the shifts in locale and setting clear? Can the elements in the production compensate for the loss of narrative detail and commentary? A satisfactory aesthetic experience can be effected through dialogue alone; this hardly needs saying. But if the presence of the narrator as narrator-character is so inextricably woven into the literature that his elimination in the dramatistic-dialogic form destroys the intent of the work, or distorts irreconcilably its aesthetic, the narrative transformation should then be employed.

NARRATIVE TRANSFORMATION

Aesthetically, this is the purest transformation of literature for multiperformance. As such, it is the transformation most in harmony with the principles of presentation discussed in this book. In this transformation the structure of the language is retained in toto. A performing narrator is present as well as performing characters. While the material may be cut and edited for suitable performing time, the language within the sequences to be used is untouched, even to the retention of "he saids" and "she saids." When, however, a short story is of performing length, within two hours or less, then the need for cutting and editing is eliminated. The performance itself establishes the relationship of the narrator to the events he is describing and narrating.

The difference between dialogic transformation and narrative transformation lies in the fact that the dialogic is an adaptation and the narrative is an editing or foreshortening of material. A creative combination of dialogic and narrative transformations is possible and should be encouraged when it is appropriate. For example, a production of Aesop's fables can be created in which the characters themselves pick up narrative threads, or offstage voices propel the action, or an onstage narrator provides the continuity. However, before an attempt is made at this form of creative combination, it would be wise to discover the stylistic problems that exist within each of the two.[1]

SCORED TRANSFORMATION

In scored transformations the emphasis is upon transforming material for multiple voices. This approach, suited to all forms of literature, means that the arranger aims for the fullest exploitation of the literature for vocal interest, vocal complexity, and vocal range.

A scored transformation achieves its impact through rhythms, orchestration of vocal color, and the unlimited variations and possibilities to which these can lead. A creatively scored transformation does not merely break up lines for light, medium, and dark voices, or alternate sections of poems or literature between two or more sets of voices. These steps may contribute to the overall effect, but they represent only a beginning understanding of where aesthetic possibilities lie.

1. Two handbooks that the student might consult for detailed discussions of the problems in narrative transformations are Leslie Irene Coger and Melvin R. White, *Readers Theatre Handbook* (Glenview, Ill.: Scott, Foresman and Company, 1967) and Joanna Hawkins Maclay, *Readers Theatre: Toward a Grammar of Practice* (New York: Random House, 1970).

Scored transformations should be considered music. They begin with a sense of rhythm, of how language may be worked into different patterns. First a beat is established (4/4, 3/4, 6/8, 7/8, etc.). The second step is to discover how a sequence of language fits into the beat, where accents are placed, what values lie in the language. Alterations of pitch and timbre are other factors to be considered.

Groups of voices can be scored for as simple a transformation as a round. The scored transformation can be employed with great interest in many poems, as well as in "scored moments" in both dialogic-dramatistic and narrative transformations. A student working with a tape recorder soon discovers that a tape, played at different rates from the one at which voices were recorded, offers intriguing possibilities for orchestration of vocal color. To attempt a scored transformation without creative zeal and without exploitation of all available means is to fall short of excitement and possible delight.

In each of the three types of multiperformances, the use of scripts by the performers is a matter of individual taste and judgment. Problems of staging and some elementary approaches are discussed at the conclusion of this chapter.

MIXED-MEDIA AND MULTIMEDIA

These two terms, much misused and misunderstood, mean the utilization of electronic devices that amplify, enlarge, surround, and impinge upon the sensorium of human perception, principally through sight and sound.

A mixed-media production is an evocation in which performers and media share in the transformation of literature. A piece of literature may be recorded and presented to the audience with amplification while simultaneously it is interpreted through dance or a choreography of some kind. Or visuals such as motion pictures, slides, transparencies, may be added to a multiperformance. Or lines of a poem may appear on multiple screens while the literature is heard through amplification and performers perform the literature and execute a choreography. All of these are examples of mixed-media—the presence of humans and media. The overwhelming number of productions employing media are mixed-media productions.

A multimedia production is one in which all elements are transposed to projected film, slides, and visuals, and sound is transcribed and presented through amplification systems. In both mixed-media and multimedia transformations, the emphasis is not upon a message delivered to a passive audience, but rather upon messages in which *the audience participates in order to complete the sense of "event."* While for some of the older generation this represents a new way of seeing, it is for the contemporary generation *the* manner which most media act upon them. But whether the production is mixed or multi, the problems of visual stimulation are the same.

The word *stimulation* brings up a problem in the evocation of literature in multi-forms. That problem is the possible emphasis in a production upon stimuli at the expense of content. Losing sight of the original literature can perhaps be permitted in early experiments in the use of media, while one is learning effects and exploring possibilities, but one must take a stern, uncompromising attitude in judging any finished performance. Has the use of media enhanced or detracted from the original artist's purpose?

THE EFFECT OF MEDIA

The effect of media is to "enable one to discover the frontiers of one's senses and perhaps push them so as to produce new dimensions for seeing, hearing, feeling, creating."[2] Each medium makes a distinct "imprint" upon the individual who has grown up with it. In the simplest terms books can *mean* something to the person who has experienced them since childhood, as can television, motion pictures, recorded music. The individual has learned how to read the medium, to perceive it, understand it, even though this understanding may not be conscious. He feels that it is something necessary to his life. Gattegno describes how this comes about.

Adults who functioned early in their childhood as "visual" have been distorted by a verbal education and no longer know what it is to be a "visual."
Television, as they see it, is an extension of the radio. But it is not. Television forces us to receive an infinite number of items at once all the time we are viewing. We need only to remove the verbal side of the programs to force viewers to use their gifts of vision. We must seek to develop a complete visual code that feeds information without words and forces viewers to drop the habit of verbalization they currently need in order to feel that they understand a message.
Adults in the space age, the nuclear age, the computer age, are still functioning as their ancestors did in the Middle Ages. Verbalization is really valid only for the areas where words can trigger images that become the carriers of meaning. People who feel the necessity to verbalize can be confounded if they are requested to express verbally what is inexpressable, or even extremely complicated.[3]

If one's frontiers of expression are the printed word, and the printed word alone, then he will insist upon the values that the printed word imposes. Anyone over thirty years of age can forget that he once lived in a totally "visual" world. Those under thirty know that a visual world is the preeminent fact of their lives. Because mixed-media and multimedia generally provide visual and auditory stimuli in far greater density

2. Caleb Gattegno, *Towards a Visual Culture* (New York: Discus Books, 1969), p. 37.
3. Ibid., p. 161.

than anything achievable in print, it is important to understand how these media affect an audience's visual and auditory perception.

The interpreter has already learned that he is for literature a kind of multimedia production as he translates verbal messages into behavioral domains. The word on the printed page is transformed by his being into the new message. This is what is meant by the transformation of form. Any kind of multiperformer production increases the number of media or performers through whom a literary experience is being shared. Add a scored transformation to the event, and the presence of simultaneous multiple sounds, and the two-dimensionality of the printed page has been far transcended.

Literature in the oral tradition is *invariably* accompanied by another sound. Whether that sound is a stringed instrument or drums or clapping hands, the literature is incomplete without it. In a sense, the simultaneous presence of media with literature is but a restoration of the sound in oral culture. The important question to ask is not "Are media necessary?" but rather, "What do media do to literature?"

Media increase the base of audience participation. Sound and sight, complementing the literature, enlarge the sense experience, and do so below the level of consciousness. But complements of sound and sight are not alike. Sound penetrates many obstacles; light rays cannot. Vision is in space while sound is in time. It takes far more energy to convey a message in sound than it does to convey the same message to the eye.

When we listen to speech, we need to wait until the end of each sentence to understand what is meant, while the act of looking at a landscape provides immediate and simultaneous information from an infinite number of sources. In other words, vision is essentially synthetic and hearing analytic.[4]

Marshall McLuhan has described this difference between sight and sound with the terms *hot* and *cool*.[5] These terms, as applied to media, describe the kind of responsive activity that goes on within the individual in the presence of the media. "Hot" media require more human activity and work (like the act of listening) than "cool" media (which like visual media allow for immediate scanning). Because so much can be perceived at once in a visual image, it *tends* to be "cooler" than "hotter." A visual image in order to remain "cool" must bear repeated scannings, yielding, as discussed in the chapter on style, more and more information.

Applying these terms to literature, we would classify T. S. Eliot's *The Waste Land* as "cool," for repeated scannings of the poem yield more and more information. Longfellow's "The Ride of Paul Revere" is "hot"; once heard or read, its linear, se-

4. Ibid., p. 34.
5. See Marshall McLuhan, *Understanding Media: The Extensions of Man* (New York: McGraw-Hill Book Co., 1964), pp. 22 ff.

quential development and logicality of parts fill the listener's or reader's ear/eye with a totality of information so that repeated scannings are not necessary. *Cool* and *hot* are not judgmental terms; they describe the nature of a response to an event.

When an individual chooses to use media in the performance of literature, his first task is to analyze very carefully the materials he proposes to use. If they are "hot" in structure and design, then his approach will be fundamentally different than if the materials are "cool." The accompanying lists give some useful guidelines for evaluating the literature and the accompanying media.

"Hot"	"Cool"
linear	non–linear
sequential	non–sequential
developmental plotting	parts intermingled
clear, chronological development	time cutting back and forth
transitions	abrupt changes
clear orientations to time, place, person	orientation is left to perceiver
logical	logic not immediately apparent (*not* necessarily illogical)

It is important to remember that in multiperformances (without the addition of media) the problem of literary "hotness" or "coolness" is solved by how *people* perform. When people and media interact, the complications in the style of the production have been compounded.

Because visual information is immediately perceived, it must move quickly and syncopatedly. It must not overexpose itself, extend itself in duration, or, as a rule, repeat itself (except for emphasis). When paced rapidly, visual information plays upon retinal perception, and the intent is not that it be "seen" and "understood" clearly, but rather that it be perceived below the threshold of total awareness. When prolonged images are used, they are used for a specific purpose—setting, counterpoint, counterdevelopment, mood, etc. Any production can have a combination of retinal and prolonged images, but the director should know clearly the purposes of each.

Visual images may accomplish two effects in production: they may offer iconic reinforcement or illustrative development. An iconic image is a piece of visual information that acts as "pattern recognition"; it offers additional views of the material being presented. It differs from illustration in that illustration completes, fills in, provides a backdrop of information that coincides with the information being presented by the performer or other aspects of the production. For example, a series of rapid retinal images of anguished faces, bombed-out cities, brutalized human beings accompanying a performance of "The Hollow Men" is the use of the iconic; providing a setting through prolonged concentrated images of deserts, wasted cities, etc., is illustrative. Television commercials are often "iconic" because they portray in a rapid series of flashing images the kind of people who *use* the product, and the perceiver may imagine himself as a member of that group if he will use the product.

Auditory images, sounds, and counterpoint function in much the same way as iconic and illustrative visual images. Illustratively, they may be the same sounds as in the text; iconically, they can punctuate the text, underscore it. Sound may be created live or be recorded. Use of the body or any physical material, alteration of the human voice by electrical or natural means, all create auditory images.

THE MESSAGE OF THE MEDIUM

Media are transmitters; they have no content; it is people who put content into them. But media have a "language," what Marshall McLuhan has called the message of the medium. The nature of a medium and the content that is put into that medium should be in harmony, not in conflict. There are, for example, expectations in the reader of this book that this chapter will explain the use of "multiforms," and will, even further, at this point clarify and expand upon the print that has led to this precise point on the page. If suddenly this print should change into a thiew ansket ajs guise ansdi hfdisg — that is, should change into a meaningless jumble or sequence of words, a person's notion of orderly, sequential *thought in print* would be challenged.

[Man] learns and communicates through the medium of print, and therefore becomes conditioned to sequential thought. One word follows another on the printed page, and linked together, they constitute a chain of thought. The literate man has a tendency to consider only one thing at a time, in a sequential fashion, and then to link these elements together into a meaningful whole. Anything which doesn't follow this sequential pattern, or which departs from the Western tradition of causality, he rejects as "meaningless" or "random chance."[6]

The factor most difficult to understand for those who initially experiment with media is this fact that the presence of any medium, human or electrical, is the presence of another message: the message of the medium itself. This means that the full and total language of that medium must be taken into account when it is used. This can be illustrated by examining all of the languages of a slide projector. A slide projector can project a filmed picture or it can project white light. Something between the projected white light and the screen casts its shadow upon the screen. The white

6. Peter Vanadia, "A New Way of Seeing," *Bolex Reporter* 17, no. 1, p. 10.

light of the projector is perceived as a "mistake" by those who assume that a light is only to be used to fill the screen with images. But how could the white light be used creatively? A slide projector can be equipped with a dissolve unit, special lenses, and be in focus or out of focus. The button for switching slides can be silent or noisy. If noisy, it can create an auditory rhythm, a click of sound that can be used to augment auditory images in a production. When the messages in a medium are fully explored, whole new realms of use begin to emerge.

What messages are inherent in the following: tape recorders, motion picture projectors, television monitors, overhead projectors, ring modulators, film strips, electrical display signs, billboards, radios? One can run a tape fast or slow; project a film forward or backward, in speed or slow motion, with sound synchronization or without, or with sound or without; television monitors can lose vertical hold, horizontal hold, be too bright, too dark, high grain, low grain; overhead projectors can go on and off, create light or reflect images, can introduce material from any direction, can reveal animate or inanimate forms (i.e., the hand, fingers, arm; picture, print, color); ring modulators can distort pitch and timbre, throb or pulse, be loud or soft.

Ultimately, the inquisitive and creative user of media will become more and more intrigued with what media can do within the range of their own messages as well as how they can be filled with content. Another word of caution should be inserted here. If your focus is primarily upon the media and their effects, then you are free to do anything that works and is interesting. However, that approach is the approach of another course and another book. In this book our central focus has been the literature itself. Experiment and innovation are essential in work with media, but for a finished performance, you must be able to say that your use of media has enhanced, not distorted, the original literature.

CREATIVE SYNTHESIS

The performing arts do not remain static. Innovators are constantly challenging audiences with new modes of perception, new experiences in media, new environments for creative events. One creative synthesis worthy of attention is the "happening." As developed by Allan Kaprow and Michael Kirby, the happening is as multiform in its format as the person planning it desires. There are some basic requirements, however, that contribute to the success of this form when it is used for literary evocation: (1) there is a script, a plan, a series of goals; (2) the audience is small and the audience participates; (3) it need not have any set durational period; (4) it is open and flexible.

The following description of a "production" or "evocation" of Albert Camus' *The Stranger* is offered only as a point of departure for discussion and evaluation. It was at the time of its happening a most successful and totally satisfying aesthetic event, fulfilled in unexpected ways, a total engagement with the thematic problems of the novel as those in the audience confronted it.

An invitation was extended to be at a particular address at ten o'clock one Sunday morning. As the small invited audience arrived, they were greeted at the door by a silent director. He handed to each entering person a piece of paper on which appeared a rather long section from the novel. The director instructed each person that he could read aloud his piece of paper any time he wished to do so. Each member of the audience was ushered into the living room, the windows of which were heavily draped. The audience sat in silence, rather uncomfortably (a discomfort which was to prove of extreme importance before the morning was out). At a seemingly undetermined moment, a tape recorder was turned on, then another, then another, then yet another, each recorder playing a scene from the novel. The director suddenly asked that the audience go to the bedroom where they saw a man and a woman, fully clothed, lying on the bed. They arose, and the man, who wore a tape recorder hung around his neck, turned it on. The opening lines to the novel were heard. The man put on his shoes, yawned, and went to the bathroom. (All the while the recorder played the opening scene of the novel.) A member of the audience looked at his piece of script and read it aloud. Others did the same. The mirror in the bathroom was covered with foil, but the man shaved, peering into an unreflecting mirror. The woman by this time had gone to the kitchen. Some members of the audience followed her there; others remained with the man. Members of the audience continued to read their selections, the tape machines continued to play, and the tape recorder hanging from the man's neck continued to narrate Chapter 1. The man, finished with his shaving, went into the kitchen to eat the breakfast the woman had been preparing. The audience waited for the coffee to boil, the eggs to cook, and the bread to be toasted. By this time anxiety within the audience was becoming acute; their reactions to where they were, what they were doing, and the events surrounding them ranged from "meaningless" to "involving"—but no one left. After breakfast, the couple went into the living room. There was a total freezing of action; the only thing heard were all the tape recorders playing at once. One of them, louder than the rest, narrated the "murder of the Arab on the beach outside Algiers." Unexpectedly, the woman moved to the windows and flung open the curtains. Sunlight flooded the room. There was a sound of pistol shots. A pause. The man got his top coat and prepared to leave. A member of the audience found he had the trial scene in his hand and began to read it. A tape machine synchronously played the final scene in the novel, and the audience heard the famous last line. The happening was over.

The event confronted the audience with the totality, more or less, of the events in the novel, with the totality of existential loneliness at ten o'clock on a Sunday morning, with the sense that all had been "directed," "planned," and "executed," and with a profound awareness that if the morning were to make sense, it had to make sense within the perceiver. The audience wanted to talk about what they had experienced, and they asked the director and the two members of the cast to participate. The group remained in that "theater" until well after two o'clock in the afternoon probing the novel, relating their awareness of the moment and the meaning or meaninglessness of that moment to the same elements in the novel. Those who had not read the novel felt it imperative to do so; those who had, felt the novel took on new dimensions.

While the production was not a *pure* happening, it relied on many of the elements of a happening to make it work: the chance readings of the parts handed to the audience members, the chance synchronizing of audience readings to taped readings, the juxtapositioning of "life events" to "fictive events," and the omnipresent "director" into whose hands the audience had by chance committed itself. There are not many audiences that remain three hours after a production, discussing it, and there are not many productions that live in the memory as continuing sources of information and delight.[7]

In order to make creative syntheses exciting and exploratory, preconceptions about the nature of a theatrical event have to be reconsidered. The risk in new forms and new styles, as we pointed out in earlier chapters, is in not finding immediate approval or understanding. And the risk of failure is a real one. For the audience, new approaches offer an education and allow all who will to be "humbled by our perceptual illiteracy," as Richard Kostelanetz has accurately described the effects of the new and unusual.[8] The creative artist is risk-oriented, and he is willing to experiment. There was a time in the not too distant past when multiperforming modes, to say nothing of mixed-media or multimedia presentations, were thought inappropriate to the interpretative study of literature. The intent of any transformation is to make literature a part of the total sensorium of the perceiver, to create a love and enjoyment of it that transcends previous notions of how it *ought* to be enjoyed and evoked. Creative syntheses are the freedoms emerging from a disciplined study of literature, a discipline which has demanded a perceptual commitment to the content and form of poesis.

NOTES ON SIMPLE STAGING PROCEDURES

The following questions are offered as beginning probes in determining staging procedures. They imply a setting in which sophisticated lighting is not a possibility, and one in which all stage equipment is minimal. The questions assume that even a stage, stage platforms, or risers are unavailable. In short, beginning with naked space, the individual is challenged to provide a compelling sense of event. Think through each

7. For discussions and ideas regarding happenings, see Allan Kaprow, *Assemblage, Environments and Happenings* (New York: Harry N. Abrams, 1966), Michael Kirby, *Happenings* (New York: E. P. Dutton & Co., 1966), and Richard Kostelanetz, *Theatre of Mixed Means* (New York: Dial Press, 1968).
8. Kostelanetz, *Theatre of Mixed Means,* p. 288.

question carefully and answer it in terms of the literature that is being evoked in multi-form.

1. How is the audience to arrange itself?
    —in a traditional pattern of facing the event?
    —in a two-sided pattern in which all that happens does so in the "corridor" separating both halves of the audience?
    —in a three-sided arrangement in which a central area as well as a back area are employed?
    —in a circular, or four-sided, pattern in which the audience surrounds the event?
    —in a reverse circular pattern in which the audience is clustered in a center area and events occur in the large perimeter surrounding the audience? (In this arrangement, no one audience member sees or experiences all of the action and this is deliberate.)
    —Is the audience to be seated in chairs? seated on the floor? standing?
    —Is the audience to move at any point? change positions?
2. How are the performers to be used?
    —Are they to remain static? seated on stools? standing?
    —Are the performers to "enter" the production by a sudden action? by moving into it? by turning into action?
    —Are the performers to be a part of the audience? detached from the audience?
    —How does audience arrangement change and alter the performers' sense of placement?
    —Are the performers to use scripts? have materials memorized?
    —Are the performers to interact with each other? *not* interact physically, but maintain a detached focus?
    —Are the performers maintaining the behaviorial modes of the literature? (See Chapter 2)
    —If the material is a scored transformation, are the performers grouped together? randomly scattered?
    —If the material is a narrative transformation, where is the narrator placed? Is he static? Is he moving about setting scenes, commenting on action, etc.? If he enters the action, how does he accomplish this? Has he maintained audience focus while the characters have maintained a stage focus?
3. How are the visual media to be used and where?
    —Is the visual medium to be shown in one place? How many screening areas are being used? How are the screening areas placed in relationship to audience placement?

Duane Michals

Multiforms: Experimental Approaches

—Are visuals being shown over one another, creating a sense of collage?

—Are visuals being shown separately? If so, in what arrangement? side by side? one on top of the other?

—Are the messages of the media accounted for? Do clicks of slide projectors, sounds of the motion picture rachets, etc., function as messages in the presentation?

—Are the color tones appropriate for the literature? full color? pastel? black and white? gray? overexposed? underexposed? etc.

—Has the rhythm of the visual projections been thought through carefully? Are the visuals predictable or non-predictable in their rhythmic presentation? Is there an even and deliberate beat? syncopated? Are they iconic? illustrative? Have rhythms been established in these terms?

4. How are the auditory media to be used and why?

—Is all sound to emanate from one source? multiple sources? on stage area? off stage area?

—Are the performers to use sounds? If so, how? imitative sounds? suggestive sounds? symbolic sounds?

—Are recorded sounds to be modulated? above the level of the performers? below? Is the audience to experience the sound below the level of awareness?

—Are sound collages to be used? If multiple sounds are used, is one to have a priority? Are all to be of the same intensity? Do they come from the same sense of source? Do they surround the audience?

—Are sounds to be carefully cued? continuous? arranged by chance?

—Are sounds to be synchronized with visual materials? non-synchronized?

5. What is the central aesthetic of the production?

—a sense of central focus?

—a sense of diffused focus? (a conscious use of separations and surroundings)

—a deliberate and conscious sense of rhythm?

—a mixed and variable rhythm?

—a sense of real time? symbolic time? mythic time? (A production is game time; it exists as long as it takes to fulfill the expectations of the material. Note: a careless production, particularly with visual materials, "ends" very quickly for an audience because of the synthesized information in visual materials.)

—Is the production to have a clean sense of beginning and ending?

—Is the audience to think that it has not arrived on time, for it arrives with the production already in progress?

—Is the audience to experience a diffused sense of ending? (Many modern songs that are recorded have a sense of "fading" rather than "ending.")

These probes, admittedly brief, have the value of forcing you to think carefully about your total intent. Because there are no rules, only conventions, the creative and intuitive student is prepared to commit himself and his being through the presentational form of literature into increasingly complex patterns of transformations. His guides are his intelligence, his taste, his sensibility. He will learn from excesses and understatements, audience bewilderments and approvals, but his fundamental commitment to the perception and evocation of literature is unswerving.

PROLOGUE from Paradise Lost

John Milton
TRANSFORMED FOR MULTI—VOICES

CHORUS: (whisper)		VOICE: (strong)	
what			
in			
me			
is			
	dark,	OF MAN'S FIRST	
illumine;		DISOBEDIENCE	
		AND THE FRUIT OF THAT	
what			
in			
me		FORBIDDEN TREE	
is			
dark,		WHOSE	
	illumine;	MORTAL	
what		TASTE	
in			
	me	BROUGHT	
is		DEATH	
dark,			
illumine.		INTO THE WORLD	
		AND ALL OUR WOE WITH LOSS OF EDEN.	

CHORUS: With loss

CHORUS²: (what in me is dark)

CHORUS: of Eden

CHORUS²: (illumine)

TILL ONE

GREATER

MAN

RESTORE US

AND REGAIN

THE BLISSFUL

SEAT

CHORUS:
(repeat
with singing
tones under
Chorus² in
free dissonance)

Sing,

heavenly muse

CHORUS²: THAT ON THE SECRET

TOP OF OREB

OR OF SINAI

DIDST INSPIRE

THAT SHEPHERD

WHO FIRST TAUGHT THE CHOSEN SEED

IN THE BEGINNING

HOW THE HEAVENS AND EARTH

ROSE OUT OF CHAOS

CHORUS: HIDEOUS RUIN AND

COMBUSTION

HIDEOUS RUIN

AND COMBUSTION

HIDEOUS

RUIN. . .

OR IF SION HILL

DELIGHT THEE MORE

I THENCE INVOKE THY

AID TO MY ADVENTUROUS

SONG

THAT WITH NO MIDDLE FLIGHT

RAISED IMPIOUS

WAR

IN HEAVEN

THAT WITH NO MIDDLE

FLIGHT

INTENDS TO SOAR

ABOVE THE AONIAN MOUNT,

WHILE IT PURSUES

BOTH CHORUSES:

(with great and
open freedom in
exploring in singing
and speaking tones
as many variations
as possible)

t h i n g s   u n a t t e m p t e d

y e t   i n   p r o s e

o r   r h y m e

CHORUS:

(in a sharp
and angular
rhythm
punctuating
various
syllables
and words
with varying
tonal values)

Nine times the space

that measures day and night

to mortal men

he

with his horrid

crew lay

vanquished —

rolling in the fiery

gulf

confounded

though immortal.

A dungeon horrible

on all sides round

as one great furnace

flamed

yet from those

flames

no light

but rather

darkness

visible

VOICE:
(as Satan)

WHAT THOUGH THE

FIELD BE LOST?

served only to discover

sights of woe

ALL IS NOT LOST.

regions of sorrow

THE UNCONQUERABLE

WILL

AND STUDY

doleful shades

OF REVENGE

where peace

and rest

can never dwell.

IMMORTAL HATE,

Hope never comes

that comes to all.

AND COURAGE

BUT TORTURE WITHOUT END

NEVER TO SUBMIT

(AMEN)

OR YIELD

TORTURE WITHOUT END

AND WHAT IS ELSE,

(AMEN)

NOT

STILL URGES

TO BE OVERCOME:

AND A FIERY DELUGE, FED

WITH EVER-BURNING SULPHUR

UNCONSUMED

THAT GLORY NEVER SHALL

HIS WRATH OR MIGHT

EXTORT FROM ME.

CHORUS:
(as devilish
counterpoint)

buh—buh—buh

    gruh—gruh—gruh

power

TO BOW AND SUE FOR GRACE

WITH SUPPLIANT KNEE,

AND DEIFY HIS POWER,

ter—r—or

WHO FROM THE TERROR

OF THIS ARM

SO LATE DOUBTED

HIS EMPIRE:

THAT WERE LOW INDEED,

THAT WERE AN IGNOMINY,

sh—sh—sh—ame
sh—sh—sh—ame

AND SHAME BENEATH THIS

DOWNFALL:

SINCE

BY FATE

THE STRENGTH OF GODS

strength of gods

AND THIS

EMPYREAL SUBSTANCE

CANNOT FAIL;

strength of gods

WE MAY WITH MORE SUCCESSFUL

HOPE RESOLVE TO WAGE

BY FORCE OR GUILE,

eternal war
eternal war
ETERNAL WAR

eternal war
IRRECONCILABLE TO OUR GRAND

eternal war
eternal war
FOE,

eternal war
WHO NOW TRIUMPHS, AND, IN

eternal war
eternal war
THE EXCESS OF JOY

eternal war
SOLE REIGNING, HOLDS THE

eternal war
eternal war
TYRANNY OF HEAVEN.

eternal war
eternal war

EXERCISES AND ASSIGNMENTS

1. Develop a mixed-media program in which you explore through sound the poetry of Emily Dickinson and Walt Whitman. Assume that all visual materials will be employed iconically.

   (a) Obtain fifteen to twenty portraits and pictures of Emily Dickinson and Walt Whitman at various ages. How would they be employed?

   (b) Develop Dickinson's world of perception from visuals which show a microscopic world—flies, flowers, grass, pebbles, curtains, grave headstones, angel wings, etc. Develop Whitman's world from the macroscopic view—landscapes, crowds of people, ocean, sky, cities, civil war scenes, etc. How would these materials develop the poetry iconically? Is there a difference in the visual rhythm of each poet?

   (c) Could the same materials be used illustratively? How would the program significantly change?

2. Develop a multimedia program on a poet whom you particularly like and appreciate, but who, you feel, is unknown or misjudged or needs to be reevaluated.

   (a) How is each poem to be presented? visually? auditorily?

   (b) What important sound do you find in the poetry? Is the presentation to use these sounds iconically? illustratively? What sounds are going to be used simultaneously? sequentially?

(c) What images are particularly impressive in the poet's work? Is it appropriate to expand them visually? Are the visuals to be used for counterpoint? for illustrative values? for what?

(d) How many media are you going to employ? Are you confident that you have enough material to use without repetition?

3. Examine Robert Frost's "The Death of the Hired Man" carefully for its imagery.

(a) Select the one important non-human image that establishes the time/hour of the poem. How could it be most effectively used? once? twice? often?

(b) How can the presence of the hired man be expanded and amplified? Shall he be given visual presence in some way? auditory presence? Would media presentation of him detract from the narrative dialogue? Can a visual or auditory metaphor stand for him? Is it to be an explicit or implicit metaphor? (What would a chair in a kitchen be visually? the sound of a rocking chair?)

(c) Using three persons for the presentation, how would you score the script? How does the narrator function in the poem? Is he attached to the scene? detached? How would you establish Warren's arrival? Mary's meeting him? Warren's leaving for the kitchen? Mary's waiting?

(d) What sounds and sights *not* described in the poem can be introduced with validity?

4. Create a scored transformation for "Sir Patrick Spens" or any folk ballad.

(a) Are there lines or rhythms you can use throughout as counterpoint?

(b) What elements are you going to repeat?

(c) What is the rhythmic time you are establishing and scoring for the poem? a natural speech rhythm? a rigidly scored pattern? Is the rigid scoring related to the meter of the poem? Are you changing the rhythm of the poem for another rhythmic element? If so, why?

(d) Experiment with making a round of each stanza (two-part, three-part, four-part, etc.) What does a round do to the sound and rhythm of the poem?

5. Create a behaviorial happening for the concrete poem "Epithalamium II" by Pedro Xisto (p. 256). Retain the *form* of the poem as it appears on the printed page in your transformation.

Index

References to selections reprinted in the text are in **bold face** type.